ILLIBERAL JUSTICE

ILLIBERAL JUSTICE

JOHN RAWLS VS. THE AMERICAN POLITICAL TRADITION

David Lewis Schaefer

University of Missouri Press
Columbia and London

Library of Congress Cataloging-in-Publication Data

Schaefer, David Lewis, 1943-
  Illiberal justice : John Rawls vs. the American political tradition / David Lewis
Schaefer.
      p. cm.
  Summary: "Schaefer challenges John Rawls's practically sacrosanct status among
scholars of political theory, law, and ethics by demonstrating how Rawls's teachings
deviate from the core tradition of American constitutional liberalism toward
libertarianism"—Provided by publisher.
  Includes bibliographical references and index.
  ISBN-13: 978-0-8262-1684-7 (hard cover : alk. paper)
  ISBN-10: 0-8262-1684-6 (hard cover : alk. paper)
  ISBN-13: 978-0-8262-1699-1 (pbk. : alk. paper)
  ISBN-10: 0-8262-1699-4 (pbk. : alk. paper)
  1. Liberalism.   2. Liberalism—United States.   3. Libertarianism   4. Justice.
5. Rawls, John, 1921–2002.   I. Title.
  JC574.S32 2006
  320.510973—dc22   2006032377

Designer: Jennifer Cropp
Typesetter: BookComp, Inc.
Printer and binder: The Maple-Vail Book Manufacturing Group
Typefaces: Palatino and Eplica

For permissions, see p. 367.

For Naomi and Jason, Rebecca and Josh,
and for Benjamin Mordechai Cypess, first of his generation

Contents

———— Preface

Besides having taught political philosophy at colleges in Massachusetts for the better part of our careers (and both having studied with Norman Malcolm), John Rawls and I had at least one other thing in common. Each of us published a book during the 1970s that he almost immediately wanted to revise. In Rawls's case, the book was *A Theory of Justice* (1971), which won instant acclaim as one of the twentieth century's preeminent works of political theory. Even though *Theory* was the product of roughly two decades of work, much of it previously published in scholarly journals, it was in circulation for only a couple of years before Rawls began responding to critics by modifying some details in his doctrine as well as his mode of presenting it. (The most important revisions were included in his 1993 book *Political Liberalism* and a volume based on his class lectures from the 1980s, *Justice as Fairness: A Restatement,* published in 2001.)

As for me, the book I soon wished I had written differently was *Justice or Tyranny? A Critique of John Rawls's "A Theory of Justice,"* which appeared in 1979. Like Rawls's first book, my much shorter tome was the offshoot of several previously published articles. But, as I realized in retrospect, its tone was sometimes inappropriate for making my points effectively.

In subsequent decades I have had the opportunity to set forth more moderately phrased, and therefore I hope more persuasive, assessments of Rawls's writings in other articles and reviews. But more than a year before Rawls's death in November 2002, I decided that the time had come to offer the comprehensive treatment of Rawls's oeuvre that is contained in the present volume. Besides issuing Rawls's last treatise, *The Law of Peoples,* and the revised edition of *Theory*, Harvard University Press had recently published Rawls's *Collected Papers* along with two volumes based on his class lectures, including *Justice as Fairness*. Thus we now have available the material to assess Rawls's theory in its completed form, as well as to trace its evolution.

The focus of this book differs from that of most published studies of Rawls's work, in that I am mainly concerned with considering its relation to the American political tradition and to the substantive tradition of political philosophy that arose with Plato. I will make relatively little reference to the voluminous literature on Rawls generated by practitioners of contemporary analytic philosophy, who share many of Rawls's theoretical and methodological assumptions. Aiming at a general audience that is chiefly concerned with questions of political justice and constitutionalism, I judge it more fruitful to focus on Rawls's texts and their relation to the two traditions I have mentioned rather than fill the book with discussion of other scholars' interpretations and criticisms on secondary issues. Additionally, writing as a political scientist, I have used the space saved to cite a sampling of the substantive literature, including news stories as well as scholarly analyses, on issues ranging from economic policy to campaign finance to military affairs that challenges Rawls's typically a priori pronouncements. These notes form an integral part of my argument, as I am trying to show how a genuinely philosophical approach to issues of justice requires a more thorough grounding in empirical and historical understanding than Rawls and his admirers have recognized. While hundreds of scholars have found in Rawls's writings a challenge to their own inventiveness in devising visions of the ideal society, few have endeavored to work out the political implications of his work and its underlying factual assumptions in an adequately serious and critical way. This is part of the contribution that I hope the present book makes.

I wish to emphasize that although Rawls identified himself (and was identified by others) as a political liberal, the following critique of his work is not animated by any hostility to liberalism, as originally understood. Rather, I undertake to defend the constitutional liberalism of the American founders, and the institutions and way of life they bequeathed us, against Rawls's attempt to reinterpret liberalism in what I believe is an ill-conceived way. I uphold the American people's right to govern themselves through representative, constitutional institutions against Rawls's invitation to judges to circumvent the democratic process so as to actualize his supposed "intuitions" about justice. I defend the founders' belief that there is an inextricable connection between political and economic freedom, in contrast to Rawls's depreciation of the latter. I stress the complexity of the policy problems, such as the most effective means of assisting the poor, about which Rawls moralizes with abandon, so as to challenge his claim that a "moral theory" severed from empirical knowledge or practical judgment can properly dictate the principles that statesmen should follow. And I seek to help restore appreciation of the wisdom of America's greatest statesmen, as well as of the liberal philosophers who guided them, in contrast to the abstract and dogmatic theorizing that Rawls purveys under the name of political philosophy. Finally, while Lockean liberalism is not without its theoretical deficiencies, I maintain that those deficiencies are best supplied by drawing from the wellsprings of classical political philosophy and from moderate liberal thinkers such as Tocqueville, rather than pushing the libertarian and egalitarian tendencies of Locke's thought to a doctrinaire extreme as Rawls would have us do.

My book is organized as follows. The introduction will situate Rawls's work in the context of American political thought during the first seventy years or so of the twentieth century. The next nine chapters offer critical commentary on *A Theory of Justice,* which remains Rawls's magnum opus, with each chapter being devoted to one of Rawls's chapters. For readers not already familiar with Rawls's work, I trust the following "road map" of *Theory* will suffice as an introduction. Part 1, comprising the first three chapters, explains Rawls's two principles of justice and argues that they would be chosen over rival theories by hypothetical parties in an "original position" of equality. Part 2 (chapters 4–6) outlines a scheme of just political and economic institutions that conform to the two principles. Part 3 (the last three chapters) aims to show that the principles harmonize with the human good.

Chapters 10 through 12 of my book address Rawls's updating of his theory in *Political Liberalism* and a later essay, "The Idea of Public Reason Revisited." The key move Rawls makes in these writings is to represent his theory as a purely "political" doctrine that does not embody any particular comprehensive view of the truth, but can be supported by an "overlapping consensus" among various comprehensive doctrines that people may hold. Chapter 13 considers Rawls's application of his theory to international justice in *The Law of Peoples.* (What I hope justifies the relative brevity of my analysis of Rawls's later books is not only that they are shorter than *Theory,* but that *Political Liberalism* is essentially parasitic on the original volume.) In my conclusion I address the implications of Rawls's work for the future of American political thought and for American politics itself.

Throughout my treatment of *Theory* I shall allude in notes to the most important modifications and elaborations Rawls made to his argument in *Justice as Fairness.* I will also refer to some of the essays in his *Collected*

Papers. But since my primary concern is with assessing Rawls's completed argument, rather than its development, and since the themes of most of his essays are given their final form in his published monographs, I have focused chiefly on those books.[1]

I have devoted the major part of my book to a chapter-by-chapter commentary on *Theory* so as to do my best to state Rawls's argument fairly, rather than run the risk through greater selectivity of seeming to misstate it. Recognizing that many moderate and serious scholars who acknowledge particular flaws in Rawls's claims nonetheless regard his work as an enormous contribution to our understanding of justice, I have sought to take his key theses seriously and to bring out their implications in such a way as to encourage even some of his partisans to rethink their position and, more important, to reconsider how philosophy can properly contribute to an understanding of justice.

The introduction, the conclusion, and first nine chapters of this book, as well as chapter 12, consist mostly of new material, though they draw on my previous book on Rawls, my review of *Justice as Fairness in Society* (September/October 2002), and two other essays: "John Rawls's 'Democratic' Theory of Justice," in *History of American Political Thought,* edited by Bryan-Paul Frost and Jeffrey Sikkenga (Lanham, MD: Lexington Books, 2003); and "Procedural Versus Substantive Justice: Rawls and Nozick," *Social Philosophy and Policy* 24, no. 1 (Winter 2007). Chapters 10 and 11 are an extensively revised and expanded version of "Rawls Redux," published in *Political Science Reviewer* 25 (1996). Chapter 13 is a much-expanded version of the last part of my article in the Frost-Sikkenga volume.

In closing, I want to thank my wife for her unwavering moral support and Holy Cross College and the Earhart Foundation for generous financial assistance that made this book possible. I am also grateful to Michael Zuckert for his meticulous and challenging commentary on my original manuscript and to Daniel Mahoney and the late Wilson Carey McWilliams for their encouragement and helpful suggestions. They are not responsible for the opinions I express herein or for any errors I may have made.

---

1. The editor of the *Collected Papers,* Samuel Freeman, cites Rawls's description of the papers as experimental works used to "try out ideas" that are later "developed, revised, or abandoned in his books" (editor's preface to *CP,* ix). Aside from one reference I also omit from consideration Rawls's *Lectures on the History of Moral Philosophy,* as it has no direct bearing on his account of justice.

—— Abbreviations

In citing Rawls's works I have adopted the abbreviations listed below.

"Comments" = "Comments on the 1973 APSA Panel," typescript in the author's possession.

CP = *Collected Papers.* Edited by Samuel Freeman. Cambridge: Harvard University Press, 1999.

FTR = "For the Record." In *Philosophers in Conversation,* edited by S. Phineas Upham. London: Routledge, 2002.

IPRR = "The Idea of Public Reason Revisited." In *The Law of Peoples with "The Idea of Public Reason Revisited."* Cambridge: Harvard University Press, 1999.

JF = *Justice as Fairness: A Restatement.* Cambridge: Harvard University Press, 2001.

LHMP = *Lectures on the History of Moral Philosophy.* Cambridge: Harvard University Press, 2000.

LP = *The Law of Peoples with "The Idea of Public Reason Revisited."* Cambridge: Harvard University Press, 1999.

PL = *Political Liberalism.* Revised paperback edition, New York: Columbia University Press, 1996.

Theory = *A Theory of Justice.* Revised edition, Cambridge: Harvard University Press, 1999.

Theory 1st ed. = *A Theory of Justice.* Cambridge: Harvard University Press, 1971.

ILLIBERAL JUSTICE

Above our modern socialism, and out of the worship of the mass, must persist that higher individualism which the centres of culture protect; there must come a loftier respect for the sovereign human soul that seeks to know itself and the world about it. . . . From out of the caves of evening that swing between the strong-limbed earth and the tracery of the stars, I summon Aristotle and Aurelius and what soul I will, and they come all graciously with no scorn nor condescension. So, wed with Truth, I dwell above the Veil.

W. E. B. Du Bois, *The Souls of Black Folk*

John Rawls and the Crisis
of American Liberalism

The United States occupies a unique position in the world's history. It was the first and remains essentially the only nation to have explicitly been founded, as Abraham Lincoln observed, on the proposition—originally held by the American people, according to the Declaration of Independence, as a "self-evident truth"—that all human beings are by nature equal. The recognition of that claim and its corollaries—that we are equally endowed by nature with certain inalienable rights that government is obliged to secure, and that just governments therefore derive their powers from the consent of the governed—has been the source of unparalleled blessings to many millions of Americans (ultimately including even the descendants of those unjustly enslaved in violation of our founding principles). They have also made this country, as Thomas Jefferson forecast and Lincoln stressed, a beacon of light and hope to other, oppressed peoples throughout the world.[1]

Yet for a nation to be founded on a theoretical proposition, rather than chiefly on ties of blood, language, or tradition, carries its own specific problems and difficulties. Among these are the need to transmit a proper understanding and appreciation of the nation's first principles to each new generation, both of children and of immigrants. As well, these principles

---

1. See Jefferson to Roger C. Weightman, June 24, 1824, in *Life and Selected Writings of Thomas Jefferson*, 729. For a defense of the doctrine of natural rights conjoined with the right of popular government, as Lincoln understood them, against the objections of twentieth-century revisionist scholarship, see Harry V. Jaffa, *A New Birth of Freedom*, chap. 2.

must continually be reinterpreted in applying them to the nation's and the world's changing circumstances. Finally, there is a difficulty characteristic of free government as such, described in Lincoln's 1838 address to the Young Men's Lyceum of Springfield, Illinois. That problem is the tension between the preservation of constitutional government and the passions both of the multitude and of the most ambitious individuals. Precisely the teaching that all human beings are naturally free, and that they have a right to be governed only with their consent, threatens to engender self-indulgence, self-interested "individualism," or (at worst) outright anarchy.[2] And the fact that the prosperity of a free nation redounds ultimately to the glory of its founders constitutes an implicit challenge to the most ambitious members of later generations, those who belong to "the family of the lion and the tribe of the eagle."[3]

Fortunately, this country's survival as a free regime has never been seriously threatened by any violent demagogue or would-be conqueror on the order of Caesar or Napoleon. Nor has it been endangered by widespread popular anarchy. (The only regime-threatening instance of civil strife, the Civil War, was not an instance literally of anarchy. It was the consequence of a glaring blot in the country's original institutions that conflicted with our fundamental principles, the practice of chattel slavery.) The immunity of the United States (thus far, and in the foreseeable future) to such threats must be attributed not only to the soundness of its founding principles and the abundance of the North American continent but, above all, to the genius of the authors of our Constitution, who employed what *The Federalist* calls "the inventions of modern political science," including the separation of powers, checks and balances, a powerful chief executive, and an independent judiciary, to provide the world with an unprecedented example of how the principles of republicanism could be combined with those of good government and individual liberty.[4]

Over time, however, the perpetuation of America's founding principles and institutions has been seriously affected by another sort of threat that reflects one of Lincoln's concerns. Barely two decades after the Civil War, and less than a half century after Lincoln's warning in his Lyceum address

---

2. The great account of the dangers of individualism and its remedies is Tocqueville's *Democracy in America*. See esp. vol. 2. pt. 1, chaps. 2–4.

3. Address before the Young Men's Lyceum of Springfield, Illinois, January 27, 1838, in *Collected Works of Abraham Lincoln*, 1:113–14. For a fine analysis of the address, see Harry V. Jaffa, *Crisis of the House Divided*, chap. 9.

4. See Alexander Hamilton, James Madison, and John Jay, *The Federalist*, No. 9 (1st par.) and No. 1, regarding the world-historic significance of the American experiment in free government.

of the need to promote a civil religion of constitutional reverence as a check on Caesarean ambition, Woodrow Wilson, later to become one of the twentieth century's most influential presidents, urged a liberation from constitutional piety in favor of thoroughgoing critical assessment of the Constitution.[5] In Wilson's account the American constitutional system with its elaborate system of checks and balances rested on a now-outdated "Newtonian" world view, which Darwinian evolutionary science had supplanted. Darwinism, according to Wilson, demonstrated the need to conceive the political community as a unitary organism directed toward growth, hence requiring a more unified leadership than the founders had provided for.[6] While Wilson discarded his original call for amending the Constitution to establish a system of cabinet government and instead advocated an informal reinterpretation of the constitutional system on the basis of a broadened understanding of the president's responsibility for political leadership (rather than as chief executive), his underlying aim remained the same: to institutionalize a system of government based on popular opinion leadership.[7] This reinterpretation was combined with a broadened and essentially open-ended conception of the purpose of government, which was no longer limited to securing the equal natural rights of individuals, but was aimed rather at equalizing the conditions of individual "self-development"—a goal that almost by definition could never be fully achieved. Precisely because of its open-ended character, the goal would serve as a continuing occasion for new enterprises of leadership.[8] Wilson's reinterpretation of American constitutionalism was elaborated by his professed heir Franklin Roosevelt, who successfully redefined the term "liberal" to entail progressivism rather than a commitment to preserving constitutional limitations on government.[9]

Wilson himself cannot be held solely accountable for the loss of belief in the principles of natural right that undergird our institutions. Rather, animated in great measure by his ambition to achieve a status of political leadership rivaling that of the founders by leading "a great movement of opinion," he was simply the most prominent statesman, and one of the

---

5. Wilson, *Congressional Government*, 27–30.

6. Wilson, *Constitutional Government in the United States*, 54–60.

7. On the difference between Wilson's plebiscitary conception of presidential leadership and the founders' vision of executive leadership, see Robert Eden, "The Rhetorical Presidency and the Eclipse of Executive Power."

8. Wilson, *The State*, 62, 65. On Wilson's project of facilitating popular opinion leadership, see Robert Eden, *Political Leadership and Nihilism*, chap. 1.

9. See Ronald Rotunda, "The 'Liberal Label.'" On John Dewey's role in this redefinition of liberalism, see Robert B. Westbrook, *John Dewey and American Democracy*, 430–39, and Paul Edward Gottfried, *After Liberalism*, 13–14.

most influential thinkers, to bring to bear on our politics the movement of "progressive," historicist thought that succeeded the liberalism of Locke and Montesquieu on the European continent.[10] In its immediate impact on the United States, that movement did not directly challenge the liberal doctrine of limited government and individual rights. Rather, it seems to have been assumed by Wilson and other leaders of the American Progressive movement, as well as by Roosevelt and advocates of his New Deal, that the principles of liberty and self-government bequeathed by the founders could easily survive without the archaic theoretical "baggage" of natural rights (now sometimes seen as an obstacle to needed political reforms, including an expansion of the federal government's responsibilities to meet the demands of a complex industrial society). The one indigenously American philosophical movement that arose late in the nineteenth century, pragmatism, explicitly rejected such "metaphysical" doctrines as natural rights, as if liberalism required no specific theoretical foundation.[11]

This conception of a foundationless liberalism underlay the development of American social science in the early decades of the twentieth century.[12] Whether on Darwinian grounds (as in the cases of Wilson and

10. The quotation is from Wilson's letter to his fiancée Ellen Axson, February 24, 1885, reprinted in E. David Cronon, ed., *The Political Thought of Woodrow Wilson*, 10. See also Wilson's unpublished manuscript on leadership from the 1890s, ibid., 20–27. Dewey's role in introducing "Hegelian and organicist concepts" into liberalism, paralleling the endeavor of such English Hegelians as Bernard Bosanquet and T. H. Green, is noted by Gottfried, *After Liberalism*, 13–14. On the more general transformation of the American academy in the nineteenth century under the influence of Hegel's historicism and Auguste Comte's positivism and the resultant disaffection with the doctrine of natural rights, see John Marini, "Theology, Metaphysics, and Positivism."

Progressivism was not the only form of European historicism to challenge natural-rights thinking in nineteenth-century America. As early as the 1830s, ideas borrowed from the conservative German historical school were used by apologists for slavery in the American South to discredit the principle of natural rights, as noted by Carl Becker in *The Declaration of Independence*, 247–56. See, on the influence of historicism in various forms on American political thought in the nineteenth century, James W. Ceaser, *Nature and History in American Political Development*; also, regarding its influence on American political science, Dennis J. Mahoney, *Politics and Progress*, chaps. 1, 5.

11. See Louis Menand, *The Metaphysical Club*; and the progressive historian Charles Beard's 1908 remark on the "decreasing reference to the doctrine of natural rights as a basis for political practice" over the preceding twenty-five years, owing to the judgment "that it really furnishes no guide to the problems of our time" as well as to the influence of Darwin ("Politics," 125). On the misleading character of the Progressives' labeling of the original natural-rights doctrine as a "metaphysical" view, rather than an empirical, quasi-scientific doctrine founded on the observation of human nature and the operation of political life, see Ceaser, *Nature and History*, 23–25.

12. See Edward Purcell, *The Crisis of Democratic Theory*. The most influential contemporary advocate of a "liberalism without foundations" is Richard Rorty. See, e.g., his "The Priority of Democracy to Philosophy."

Oliver Wendell Holmes Jr.), on "pragmatic" ones (as with John Dewey), or later on the ground of the ostensible distinction between facts and values, the leading schools of American social science and jurisprudence were united in their rejection of "absolutes"—that is, fixed moral norms.[13] Yet, far from thinking that this rejection weakened liberalism, its partisans typically maintained that moral skepticism was the bulwark of democratic tolerance: awareness that all "values" are ultimately subjective, it was believed, logically entailed a toleration of all perspectives, since none would be held with the certitude that would justify exclusivity, let alone tyranny. Hence when the pragmatic liberal historian Carl Becker published his classic study *The Declaration of Independence* in 1922, he dismissed the question of the truth of the Declaration's natural-rights doctrine as "meaningless"; at best it could be regarded as a "humane and engaging" but "naïve faith," which "could not survive the harsh realities of the modern world." Becker concluded his book by citing the French ultraconservative Joseph de Maistre, to the effect that the very concept of a human species ("man") in which inalienable rights inhere is a delusion.[14]

When Becker wrote a new introduction to his book in 1942, he sang a different tune, maintaining—in light of the endangerment of political freedom by the Nazi threat—that the phrase "the inalienable rights of man," and what he represented as its French counterpart, "liberty, equality, and fraternity," constituted "realities—the fundamental realities that men will always fight for rather than surrender."[15] But Becker did not acknowledge, let alone address, the inconsistency between this claim and his assertion within the main text that the very question of the truth of these phrases was meaningless. Yet surely—in view of his denunciation of Nazi aggression—Becker did not mean, as Holmes had once asserted, that the only meaning of the rights of man is "what the crowd will fight for."[16]

The tension in Becker's thought between a wish to attribute objective validity to individual rights and a denial that nature could provide a ground for those rights was not addressed any more seriously in American political thought during the decades immediately following World War II. If anything, the doctrine of rights became cloudier as its scope was expanded, from Franklin Roosevelt's Four Freedoms, which extended the

---

13. For valuable critical discussions of pragmatist jurisprudence, see Gary Jacobsohn, *Pragmatism, Statesmanship, and the Supreme Court,* and Paul Carrese, *The Cloaking of Power,* chap. 10.

14. Becker, *Declaration of Independence,* 277–79.

15. Ibid., xvi. Becker's inconsistency is noted by Jaffa in *New Birth of Freedom,* 99–102.

16. Holmes to Harold Laski, July 28, 1916, in Howe, ed., *Holmes-Laski Letters,* vol. 1, 8; similarly, "Natural Law," 314.

list of "essential human freedoms" that Americans were fighting to secure so as to encompass freedom from want and fear, to the United Nations Declaration of Human Rights, which offered such unenforceable "rights" as a paid vacation. As the Nazi threat to freedom was succeeded by the Communist one, the foundations of our way of life were defined chiefly, for most Americans, by what we were not—the subjects of a totalitarian state—rather than by any coherent positive doctrine. Meanwhile, the field of political science came increasingly to be dominated by social science positivism, which taught the equal validity of all "values." That this doctrine had an inherently corrosive effect on the principles of liberal constitutionalism was not seen as problematic by its advocates. Hence the outrage that greeted the charge by one profound critic who compared "behavioral" political scientists to Nero fiddling while Rome burned—albeit without Nero's awareness of what he was doing or the condition of his community.[17]

The insufficiency of positivism was soon manifested by political developments in the historic 1960s. Early in that decade, the "Port Huron Statement," issued by Students for a Democratic Society on behalf of the so-called New Left, denounced the failure of the contemporary academy to address values and urged the transformation of the American polity into a "participatory democracy" that would realize people's "potential for self-cultivation, self-direction, self-understanding, and creativity."[18] (The gap between SDS's aspirations and those of progressive liberalism can be seen in the statement's opening acknowledgment that its authors had been "bred in at least modest comfort," seemingly reflecting the achievement of FDR's promised "right to a comfortable living," yet nonetheless found themselves "looking uncomfortably" at the world they had inherited.)[19] By the end of the decade, the president of the American Political Science Association, David Easton, effectively announced the surrender of his profession to the demand that it directly serve the cause of justice.[20] But neither SDS nor Easton were aiming at renewed philosophic consideration of the nature of justice. Rather, Easton no less than SDS was calling for academic studies, particularly the social sciences, to be marshaled as instruments of social change in the direction of an ostensibly more democratic, egalitarian, and liberating political order. Yet the rapid evolution of SDS during the 1960s toward antidemocratic lawlessness, as well as its contempt for the

17. Leo Strauss, "An Epilogue," 327.
18. Students for a Democratic Society, "The Port Huron Statement," 359–62.
19. See Roosevelt, Commonwealth Club Address, *Public Papers and Addresses*, vol. 1, 754, with the "Port Huron Statement," 358.
20. Easton, "The New Revolution in Political Science."

very notion of academic objectivity or freedom of inquiry, had to give pause to anyone who still believed in the original liberal project.

It is against the foregoing background that the remarkable success of John Rawls's *A Theory of Justice*, first published in 1971, must be understood. Little in Rawls's previous work, or in the Anglo-American "analytic" school of philosophy out of which it emerged, would have generated the expectation that a book such as his would have a major political impact. (Although Rawls maintains that "the notions of meaning and analyticity play no role" in his theory, which relies instead on the approach adopted in his 1951 "Decision Procedure" article that I discuss in chapter 1 [*Theory*, xx–xxi], his work falls broadly within the analytic movement, since, as I shall observe, it aims to articulate the dictates of "our" moral outlook without consideration of serious alternative, substantive views.)[21] Following an early essay on moral decision making and another on the formulation of utilitarianism, Rawls had begun in the late 1950s to develop a "theory" of justice that would improve on utilitarianism.

Analytic philosophy at the time of Rawls's earlier work was hardly thought to have a political import at all. One of the few analytic works of the 1950s to address political subjects, T. D. Weldon's *The Vocabulary of Politics*, still reflecting the positivistic outlook, dismissed the theoretical foundations of liberal democracy, such as the idea of natural rights, as "worthless." (Weldon proceeded to suggest the substitution of an "empirical" test of legitimate government that only a liberal democracy could pass, though he acknowledged that this was merely "a personal view, or prejudice" that had "nothing philosophical about it.")[22] Commenting on the state of analytic writing on ethics at the time, another scholar lamented the failure of recent generations of English moral philosophers "to commit themselves to any moral opinions" at all, as opposed to merely analyzing the logic of moral discourse.[23] As two later commentators, Chandran Kukathas and Philip Pettit, thinking chiefly of the analytic approach observed, "the annals of early twentieth-century philosophy are long on rival analyses of utility and liberty and equality but extremely short on arguments in favour of these or other ideals." They attributed this "retreat from advocacy to commentary"

---

21. Rawls was introduced to philosophy as an undergraduate by Norman Malcolm, a leading American disciple of Ludwig Wittgenstein, whose later thought was the prime inspiration for the analytic movement in America (Ben Rogers, "Portrait: John Rawls," 53; Thomas Pogge, "A Brief Sketch of Rawls's Life," 5–6). As Peter Berkowitz puts it, Rawls's work is written "in the idiom of analytic moral philosophy" ("The Ambiguities of Rawls's Influence," 123.)
22. Weldon, *The Vocabulary of Politics*, 14, 87–101, 176.
23. Mary Warnock, *Ethics since 1900*, 144–45.

to the reluctance of philosophers, "given the widespread presumption that science deals with facts only . . . to present themselves as defenders of any particular values." Consequently, they remarked, at midcentury "there was no figure or text or even discipline which could have claimed continuity" with the great philosophers of the past.[24]

Theory thus appeared at a time when teachers of politics and ethics faced two intersecting demands: the call for a more politically relevant and morally substantive form of Anglo-American philosophizing and the quest to supply a more inspiring (and politically transformative) ground for liberalism than the pragmatic tradition (as well as an alternative to the now-discarded doctrine of natural rights). While the 1950s, as Brian Anderson observes, had been far from barren of major works of political theory, including Leo Strauss's *Natural Right and History* and Hannah Arendt's *The Origins of Totalitarianism*, neither book fit into the mainstream of academic political philosophy. It is in this context that Rawls's book inspired teachers of that discipline with a new sense of possibility.[25] In the words of Kukathas and Pettit, "*A Theory of Justice* breaks cleanly with the preference of philosophers in the previous half-century for the analysis of ethical ideals and principles rather than an exploration of which ideals and principles to advocate," making it "the big book" that marked the "resurgence" of political theory.[26]

Theory and Rawls's subsequent writings have generated a veritable industry of scholarly interpretation and criticism. What has thus far been lacking in Rawls scholarship, however, is a comprehensive consideration of the relation of his work to the American constitutional tradition exemplified at its peak by the *Federalist Papers* and the thought of Lincoln and to the broad tradition of Western political philosophy that originated with Plato. Does Rawls offer a more solid foundation for constitutional liberalism than his pragmatist predecessors or hasten its decay? Did he rejuvenate the enterprise of political philosophy or distort it? These are the central questions I shall address.

24. Chandran Kukathas and Philip Pettit, *Rawls: "A Theory of Justice" and Its Critics*, 3–5.

25. See Anderson, "The Antipolitical Philosophy of John Rawls," 42. On the perceived death of political philosophy in the English-speaking world during the 1950s, see Peter Laslett, ed., *Philosophy, Politics, and Society*, vii; Brian Barry, *Political Argument*, xxxi–xxxviii.

26. Kukathas and Pettit, *Rawls*, 5–6. In the fifth volume of the series *Philosophy, Politics, and Society*, in which the death of political philosophy had originally been proclaimed, the editors, Peter Laslett and James Fishkin, described *Theory* as the "Olympian work" that invalidated that judgment (1).

CHAPTER I

Justice as Fairness

I.

No academic writer on political philosophy in American history has achieved the renown or influence of John Rawls, who taught for three decades at Harvard University following stints at Princeton, Cornell, and MIT. A 1999 recipient of the National Humanities Medal, Rawls was frequently described in such terms as the "outstanding" or "most important" American political philosopher of the twentieth century.[1] Not long before Rawls's death a leading classicist called him "the most distinguished moral and political philosopher of our age"; to another prominent scholar, he was simply "America's greatest political philosopher."[2] Rawls's first and most comprehensive book, *A Theory of Justice,* has sold more than three hundred thousand copies in the U.S. alone and had been translated into twenty-seven languages, including Russian and Chinese, as of 2003.

1. Susan Okin, review of *PL,* 1010; J. B. Schneewind, review of *JF,* 21. In conferring the humanities medal on Rawls, President Bill Clinton hailed him for having "placed our rights to liberty and justice upon a strong and brilliant new foundation of reason," thereby helping "a whole generation of learned Americans revive their faith in democracy itself" ("Remarks").
2. Martha Craven Nussbaum, "The Enduring Significance of John Rawls," B7; Joshua Cohen, "The Pursuit of Fairness," *Boston Globe,* December 1, 2002, D1.

One early reviewer praised the book for providing "the principle of justice which social democrats have always groped for"; a second called it
"magisterial" and "peerless"; and a third commentator remarked that
"reading Mr. Rawls helps us in the endless task of maintaining those
taboos that guard both individual dignity and social solidarity." Even a
prominent Harvard colleague who found "deep-lying inadequacies in
Rawls's theory" and rejected the foundations of Rawls's vision of distributive justice nonetheless praised *Theory* as "deep and elegant," "a fountain
of illuminating ideas, integrated together into a lovely whole," and "a new
and inspiring vision" of "how *beautiful* a whole [moral] theory can be."[3]
Another scholar who devoted an entire book and parts of others to examining *Theory* compared Rawls's contribution to political philosophy to
what Beethoven had done for the symphony. A distinguished political theorist prefaced his trenchant criticisms by calling the book "the noblest in its
line of moral and political philosophy since Kant." And a more recent
writer, not uncritical of Rawls's work, termed it (probably accurately) "the
most discussed political theory written in English since the days of John
Stuart Mill."[4] Perhaps the apex of the scholarly reverence Rawls inspired
was expressed in a memorial tribute by a colleague comparing a call from
him to one from God.[5]

Despite Rawls's professed liberalism, admiration for his work was not
limited to the political Left. The Nobel Prize-winning economist and political theorist Friedrich Hayek, a classical liberal (and hence, in contemporary American political parlance, a "conservative") treated Rawls's work
with high regard.[6] Other erudite, avowedly conservative writers, while
taking issue with Rawls's political program, addressed his work as if it

3. Stuart Hampshire, "A New Philosophy of the Just Society," 37; Marshall Cohen,
review of *Theory*, 1, 18; Garry Wills, "Ethical Problems," 13; Robert Nozick, *Anarchy,
State, and Utopia*, 183, 230 (emphasis in original).

4. Barry, *Political Argument*, lxx. In the world of political philosophy, Barry remarks,
"*A Theory of Justice* is the watershed that divides the past from the present" (lxix). John
Schaar, "Reflections on Rawls' *A Theory of Justice*," 145; James P. Young, *Reconsidering
American Liberalism*, 270.

5. Michael Sandel, "A Just Man." Another associate, Isaiah Berlin, reportedly enjoyed
"likening [Rawls], mischievously, to Christ" (Ben Rogers, "John Rawls," *The Guardian*,
November 27, 2002 [obituary]). Doubtless, part of the reverence Rawls inspired among
his admirers stemmed from his character: he was esteemed for his benevolence and
humility. In this book, I am exclusively concerned with assessing Rawls's thought; having met him only once, I have no reason to doubt the personal testimonials of those
who knew him.

6. See Hayek, *Law, Legislation, and Liberty*, vol. 1, 170n; vol. 2, xii–xiii, 100, 183. Rawls's
"greatness" as "a genuine leader in philosophical and political thought" was similarly
praised by the classical liberal Richard A. Epstein in "Rawls Remembered."

were a worthy heir to that of such great modern thinkers as Locke and Rousseau.[7]

So widespread was Rawls's influence as a teacher, it is reported, that "most good philosophy departments in the US now have at least one prominent Rawls student" on their faculty, while his impact on students in such other disciplines as political science, law, and economics has promoted a sympathetic reception of his work in those specialties.[8] Indeed, Rawls's impact has extended as well into such academic fields as public administration, sociology, education, and religion, and there is growing evidence, as I shall note, of Rawlsian influence on American jurisprudence, possibly including decisions of the U.S. Supreme Court.

Yet any nonspecialist who delves into Rawls's often dense prose is likely to be surprised, perhaps even startled, by much of what he finds. He will discover, for instance, that this honored scholar teaches that no government is just if it allows people to earn rewards from the honest use of their own skills and talents, unless they somehow compensate the "least advantaged" members of society for their gains; that government has no authority to ban sexual practices that the large majority of its citizens deem degrading or shameful; that we are morally obliged to give the same public esteem to someone who devotes his life to counting blades of grass as we are to the greatest statesmen, heroes, or thinkers; that the very existence of the family is morally problematic and would probably be unacceptable without programs of economic redistribution designed to mitigate its "arbitrary" effects; and that the principles of justice are themselves historically relative, subject to unspecified alterations or corrections in the future. The reader may also be concerned to learn that Rawls speculates about the possibility of adopting eugenic policies to remake the human race so as to achieve greater equality, regards the contemporary United States as only an "allegedly" constitutional democratic regime that may not be any more democratic than Germany was between 1870 and 1945, and suggests that Marx may have been right in holding that no regime that allows private ownership of the means of production can be just. He may be puzzled to find that Rawls, a professed philosopher (literally, "lover of wisdom"), refuses to attribute greater value (from the standpoint of justice) to holding true rather than to false beliefs, and contends that

7. See Robert Nisbet, "The Pursuit of Equality," identifying Rawls's approach with that of Rousseau and the eighteenth-century *philosophes*. A later conservative critic, Ernest Van den Haag, judged "Rawls's attempt to justify equality, however unconvincing," to be "the best I know of," making "*A Theory of Justice* justly famous" ("Is Liberalism Just?" 126–27).

8. Pogge, "Brief Sketch," 13.

political philosophy should dispense with the very concept of truth. Finally, Rawls even wonders in print whether it is worthwhile for human beings to live at all unless they actualize his vision of justice.

To list some of Rawls's more bizarre claims is not of course to refute his theory. To participate in the enterprise of political philosophy requires entertaining the possibility that our own most cherished moral and political beliefs are fundamentally defective or at least stand in need of substantial modification and correction. I have highlighted these observations at the outset only to indicate what is at stake in the acceptance of Rawls's doctrine and its potential influence on American political thought and practice.

In this book, in contrast to the legions of academics who have lauded Rawls's work, I shall challenge the claims that it is a proper model of philosophic inquiry and that its effects on the American constitutional order promise to be salutary. I shall suggest that the very appeal and influence of Rawls's work within academia are due largely to his endeavor to accommodate, while elevating to "philosophical" status, his colleagues' frequently unreflective assumptions and prejudices. Indeed, I maintain, even the praise that Rawls's writings have won from some conservative critics should give pause to liberals, since those critics typically (and misleadingly) went on to argue that the flaws they uncovered in Rawls's reasoning exemplified defects in liberal thought as such. By contrast, I shall point out, such great liberal thinkers as Locke, Montesquieu, and Mill provide far more solid grounds for liberty than does Rawls, who hedges his ostensible prioritization of it in numerous ways.

Regardless of one's partisan position, I contend, Rawls's *mode* of philosophizing is politically harmful because it encourages a tendency to oversimplify complex issues and to assume that those who disagree with Rawls's partisan prescriptions do so because they are insufficiently committed to justice, rather than because of legitimate practical or theoretical objections. To reduce substantive political debates in a constitutional republic to a division between supporters of the just and the unjust is not only misleading but also detrimental to the liberal consensus that Rawls professes to refine and fortify. If the term *liberalism* is taken in its root sense, a partisanship for liberty, I shall maintain, Rawls's orientation is profoundly antiliberal. Indeed, despite the conventionally left-liberal, welfare-statist economic policies Rawls typically advocates, the deeper foundations of his position, derived from an incoherent blend of Kant, Marx, and (secondhand) Nietzsche, along with the apocalyptic rhetoric he sometimes resorts to, are potential constitutional dynamite.

Rawls's work, I shall observe, is exemplary of a new sort of enterprise that calls itself "political philosophy" or "moral theory," but which differs most starkly from the writings of the classic political philosophers both ancient and modern, as well as the greatest American political thinkers, in that it is not founded on any particular knowledge of political, economic, or historical facts. Whereas philosophers as diverse as Aristotle and Cicero, Locke and Montesquieu, and Rousseau and Hegel grounded their teachings about political justice on a thorough study of politics and history (sometimes acquired in part from firsthand involvement in political life, but always based on detailed empirical study), the new Anglo-American form of political philosophy begins by presupposing particular "intuitive" notions about social justice, typically derived from the theorists' academic environment, then demands that these notions be applied dogmatically to existing political regimes if they are to earn the label "just."

Perhaps the oddest aspect of Rawls's version of "political" philosophy, I shall observe, is that it is essentially hostile to both politics and philosophy. Curiously, Rawls represents the sort of open, though typically nonviolent and moderate, debate about issues of both principle and practice that most citizens and political analysts would regard as a sign of republican health as if it were a malady that needed to be remedied by inducing everyone to agree on a particular theory.[9] If, as Aristotle held, there is a fundamental link between the activities of politics and philosophy, inasmuch as both depend on the distinctively human faculty of rational speech and argument, then the elevation of Rawlsian "consensus" is detrimental not only to the perpetuation of a free political order but to the philosophic enterprise itself.

The foregoing charges will sound harsh and on their face, in view of the almost universal acclaim for Rawls's work, implausible. To readers who initially experience these reactions, I ask only for a fair hearing. And if I seem presumptuous in challenging a widespread scholarly consensus of our time, I answer that I am endeavoring to speak on behalf of a more significant consensus, that of the great tradition of political philosophy from Plato to Nietzsche, and that of the greatest American statesmen and political and jurisprudential thinkers from the time of the founding to at least that of Lincoln. Without minimizing the considerable differences that separate the great political philosophers, I believe that their writings embody a reasoned engagement with the most fundamental human issues to which there is no counterpart in Rawls's work or in that of his followers. And even in comparison with the narrower domain of British philosophical writing of the nineteenth and early twentieth centuries within which Rawls often situates his enterprise, I shall contend that his approach represents an enormous falling away in terms of substantive richness, moral sensitivity, and openness to diverse, serious points of view from what one finds in the writings of such predecessors as W. D. Ross, John Stuart

9. Cf. Benjamin Barber, *The Conquest of Politics,* chap. 4.

Mill, and Henry Sidgwick. Finally, I shall point out the contrast between Rawls's abstract approach to political issues and the reasoned and empirical, but far from morally neutral, way in which America's greatest statesmen addressed them, an approach that is not only more practically salutary but is the true propaedeutic to political philosophy. Even though not many Americans outside the academy have ever heard of Rawls, his influence, and that of the growing number of his imitators, should be of concern to all who care about the preservation of republican, constitutional government.

In this chapter I survey Rawls's introductory account of his project in the first chapter of *Theory*, "Justice as Fairness."

II.

As noted in the preface, *Theory* was the culmination of some two decades of reflection that had borne fruit in nine or ten previously published articles. It is helpful to take brief note at the outset of a few of Rawls's earliest essays, beginning with his first article, "Outline of a Decision Procedure for Ethics" (1951), for the way they exhibit the continuity of Rawls's approach to justice from the beginning to the end of his career, and what sets that approach apart from the concerns that animated the great political philosophers of the past as well as leading American statesmen and political thinkers.

The problem Rawls addressed in "Outline" was to formulate a method for assessing moral rules so as to resolve the issue of the "objectivity" of "moral knowledge." His proposed strategy was to identify "a class of competent moral judges" (i.e., "normally intelligent" human beings); then to define "a class of considered moral judgments" for them to make by specifying the conditions in which those judgments are to be made; and finally to "formulate a satisfactory explication" of the judgments, an explication being defined as a set of principles that would lead anyone to make the identical judgments in the same cases as the competent moral judges would have made on an intuitive basis (*CP*, 1–10). Rawls's procedure was a purely formal one: "objectivity" was interpreted as (near) unanimity, without reference to the substantive content of justice. Rawls hoped that the principles that met his tests would generate "a gradual convergence" of people's moral opinions (*CP*, 11).[10]

10. I offered a brief critical analysis of "Decision Procedure" in *Justice or Tyranny?* 16–17. See also Anthony Mardiros, "A Circular Procedure in Ethics."

Rawls's account of the relation between ethical principles and moral judgments seems to be modeled on the process of legal reasoning. Common-law rules as well as principles of statutory or constitutional interpretation ordinarily evolve as the consequence of judicial decisions in particular cases. Faced with the need to decide a case that does not precisely fit any previously established rule, the judge seeks to settle it in an equitable way that is faithful to the law, but he must ordinarily demonstrate how his decision is consistent with previous precedents on the basis of a principle that he shows they embody. His judgment or textual interpretation (unless overruled by a higher court) will in turn serve as a precedent for future judicial rulings.[11]

The requirement that judges justify their decisions in the light of settled precedents as well as statutes is obviously necessary as a constraint on what would otherwise be an unfettered and potentially arbitrary discretion. What remains unclear regarding Rawls's enterprise, however, is how far this pursuit of explicatory principles is necessary or possible regarding the broader realm of *moral* judgments, since in making such judgments citizens do not ipso facto have the authority to enforce them on other individuals—and hence have less need to formulate them in terms of universally shared principles.

The essays Rawls published over the following years embody a continuing attempt to develop a set of principles to explicate people's moral judgments, with particular reference to judgments of institutional justice. After initially attempting to develop such a theory through a reinterpretation of utilitarianism—broadly, a doctrine that identifies justice or morality with the greatest good or "utility" of society's members—Rawls abandoned that course in favor of a new doctrine he called "justice as fairness," according to which the utility principle must be constrained by the priority of justice, understood as the set of moral principles that persons in a hypothetical position of equality can be imagined to have agreed on.[12]

What is noteworthy about Rawls's initial approach to the problem of justice is the abstract or theoretical character of the motive and interest that animated it. At the outset, Rawls displayed little concern with the substantive content of justice or its relation to the human good as addressed, for instance, in Plato's *Republic*, Aristotle's *Politics* and *Ethics*, Hobbes's *Leviathan*, or Locke's *Two Treatises of Government*. Nor was he motivated in his early writings by any explicit concern with the advancement of justice

---

11. See Edward Levi, *An Introduction to Legal Reasoning*.
12. *CP*, 47–72. The genesis of this conception in Rawls's early writings is finely articulated by Michael Zuckert, "Big Government and Rights," in *Launching Liberalism*, 317–23.

in the world or the choice of institutions that would best promote it, unlike such philosophers as Aristotle, Locke, Montesquieu, and Rousseau, and American statesmen from the founders to Lincoln to Martin Luther King Jr. Rather, the concern that originally interested Rawls was a "technical" one: the pursuit of a formula that (for reasons that were hardly explained) would promote consensus among people's judgments of justice.

This same technical or academic concern is manifest at the beginning of *Theory,* where Rawls explains his aim as the development of a new theory of justice to improve on the "classical utilitarian and intuitionist conceptions" that "have long dominated our philosophical tradition." (He will define those terms, derived from the British philosophic tradition of the previous two centuries, later on.) He then offers a sweeping statement of "our intuitive conviction of the primacy of justice": "Justice is the first virtue of social institutions"; "laws and institutions no matter how efficient and well-arranged must be reformed or abolished if they are unjust." In a faint echo of the rights-language of the Declaration of Independence, Rawls holds that "each person possesses an inviolability founded on justice that even the welfare of society as a whole cannot override." Hence justice, like truth, is "uncompromising" (*Theory,* 3–4).

There is little in these claims (with the possible exception of the last) to which most Americans, living under a political regime expressly dedicated to securing the equal rights of all individuals, and characterized by a tradition of progressive reform movements aimed at actualizing or broadening those rights, would be likely to object.[13] But Rawls makes no reference to the Declaration or any other constitutional document before pronouncing the need for a new theory to "account for" these assertions. A "well-ordered" society in his view must be "effectively regulated by a public conception of justice" that "everyone accepts" and to which the society's "basic institutions" conform (*Theory,* 4).

A theory of justice, Rawls explains, must specify the "division of advantages" among society's members, or their "distributive shares." "Existing societies are . . . seldom well-ordered," he maintains, since they suffer from disagreement about what is just. Even though people formally agree that justice requires eliminating arbitrary distinctions among individuals and achieving "a proper balance" among competing claims to societal advantages, they disagree in practice about the meaning of those goals. In addition, Rawls observes, a shared view of justice is needed to enable people's

---

13. Cf. Hamilton, Madison, and Jay, *The Federalist,* No. 51, 292: "justice is the end of government . . . It ever has been and ever will be pursued until it be obtained, or until liberty be lost in the pursuit."

individual "plans" to be "fitted together . . . without anyone's legitimate expectations being severely disappointed" (*Theory*, 5–6).

The abstractness of the way Rawls frames the problem of justice is apparent in the following respects. First, in starting with "society," he implicitly sets aside the sphere of politics—the locus wherein enforceable rules governing human conduct are normally established.[14] Rawls does not identify the origin or sanction of the rules that are to specify the distribution of societal goods. Second, we wonder what it would mean for every member of a society to accept the same principles of justice and whether such a society has ever existed. Although documents like the Declaration of Independence set forth a certain general understanding of justice, it is doubtful that any public charter has specified in a meaningful way the manner of allocating people's societal "advantages" or "distributive shares" on the basis of a particular set of principles.[15] Third, it is hard to imagine how any agreement on justice could guarantee that people's "legitimate expectations," however defined, will never be disappointed.

The theme of government enters *Theory* in section 2, "The Subject of Justice," but only as part of a larger whole called "the basic structure of society," which is "the primary subject of justice." The basic structure includes not only a country's political constitution but also its "principal economic and social arrangements," such as "legal protection of freedom of thought . . . competitive markets . . . and the monogamous family." Rawls's "intuitive notion" is that people born into different social positions "have different expectations of life" that are "determined, in part, by the political system as well as by economic and social circumstances," yet these inequalities in people's life prospects are not grounded in any difference in their "merit or desert." While such inequalities are "presumably inevitable," they must be subordinated to "principles of social justice" (*Theory*, 6–7).

14. The implied priority Rawls gives to society over government links his approach to the historicist thought of Woodrow Wilson, who in his textbook *The State* (30–31) represents forms of government as derivative from the epoch of social evolution that they embody. Similarly, John Stuart Mill in *On Liberty* describes society rather than government as the chief obstacle to effectual liberty in the modern world. What connects Wilson and Mill (along with John Dewey) is not only their confidence in the inevitability of social progress but their implicit renunciation of the doctrine of natural rights as a limit to the scope or purpose of government. See Wilson, *The State*, 50–52; Dewey, *The Public and Its Problems*, 51, 65, 72–73; Mahoney, *Politics and Progress*, 78–80. Rawls, I shall observe, tenders barely a nod to the notion of natural rights.

15. On the historical novelty of the notion of "social justice," understood as the distribution of social and economic goods among the members of an entire society according to a given formula, see Samuel Fleischacker, *A Short History of Distributive Justice*, Introduction et passim.

Here, then, is Rawls's sweeping claim and aspiration. If the pragmatists threatened to leave us rudderless by dispensing with the principles of natural right embodied in the Declaration of Independence, Rawls, by contrast, seems to aim at an agreement on justice that is far more specific in its demands and broader in its scope than anything contained in the Declaration. By developing an appropriate set of principles he aims to mitigate if not eliminate the controversies over justice that have hitherto characterized political life. As a result, not only will arbitrary political inequalities be abolished (as the Declaration ordains), but all social institutions will be justly structured, and people's "legitimate expectations" guaranteed of achievement. As we shall observe, however, Rawls agrees with the pragmatists in dispensing with nature as the ground of justice.

III.

In the third section of chapter 1, Rawls identifies the "main idea" of his theory. He will raise "to a higher level of abstraction" the social-contract doctrine developed by such philosophers as Locke, Rousseau, and Kant. Unlike his predecessors Rawls will not represent the original contract "as one to enter a particular society or to set up a particular form of government." Instead, the object of the original agreement is "the principles of justice" for society's "basic structure," principles that "free and rational persons concerned to further their own interests would accept in an initial position of equality." This is what Rawls means by "justice as fairness" (*Theory*, 10).

Rawls's citation of the teachings of Locke, Rousseau, and Kant as a precedent for his own enterprise understates the differences between his approach and theirs, which start to emerge in the summary he provides of his project. Most obviously, whereas the philosophers just named used the social-contract idea to explain how naturally free individuals could be imagined to have agreed to surrender or limit their freedom for the sake of the goods provided by government of a certain kind, Rawls replaces their account of the state of nature with an "original position of equality" that "is not . . . thought of as an actual historical state of affairs" (*Theory*, 10–11).

In fact, it is unlikely that Locke or Rousseau intended their descriptions of the state of nature to be literally historical either; Kant certainly did not attribute historicity to his social contract.[16] But their accounts were

16. See Kant, "Theory and Practice," in *Political Writings*, 79. Thomas Hobbes, the originator of the state-of-nature doctrine, also denies that it was ever "generally" the human condition, but he cites the relation among nations to partly exhibit its character (*Leviathan*, chap. 13, pars. 11–12).

intended to articulate the essential elements of the human condition that make it necessary for human beings to limit their natural or inherent freedom by establishing government—and therefore determine the character that government must have to be legitimate. By contrast, Rawls is emphatic, later in *Theory*, that the original position from which he derives the principles of justice is not based on an empirical account of actual human motives (*Theory*, 104, 128). Rather, the original position is designed to generate "intuitively appealing" principles to which people's actual "propensities and inclinations" must be subordinated (*Theory*, 27).[17] At the same time, it incorporates "conditions that are widely thought reasonable to impose on the choice of principles" (*Theory*, 105). Most important, the parties in the original position will make their choice behind a "veil of ignorance" about their own capacities, so that nobody gains or loses from "natural chance" or social contingency (*Theory*, 11–12). In other words, the strong or the smart cannot favor their own interests by choosing principles that particularly benefit themselves, since they are unaware of their physical or mental superiority.

At this point Rawls offers a brief summary of the two principles that he argues would be chosen therein: one mandating "equality in the assignment of basic rights and duties," and the other holding "that social and economic inequalities . . . are just only if they result in compensating benefits for everyone, and in particular for the least advantaged members of society." Rawls maintains that since everyone's well-being "depends on a scheme of social cooperation," the benefits of such cooperation should be allocated in a way that elicits everyone's voluntary participation (*Theory*, 13). He then reveals another novel aspect of the original position: not only must the veil of ignorance prevent the choosing parties from knowing their particular natural talents or social status, it must also keep them ignorant of their "particular inclinations and aspirations" or "conceptions of the good," since these facts too are "irrelevant" to justice. To represent human beings as equal "moral persons," "systems of ends" are "not ranked in value." In ways to be spelled out, the parties to the original position are to seek to advance their interests without knowing what they specifically hold to be good (*Theory*, 16–17).

The description of the original position in Rawls's account has a two-sided character. Besides designing that situation to be fair, we can test the

---

17. In Rawls's bluntest formulation, in *JF* (55), his theory specifies the dictates of justice "apart from all historical conditions. What counts is the workings of social institutions now, and a benchmark of the state of nature . . . plays no role. It is a historical surd, unknowable, but even if it could be known, of no significance." Rawls further stresses the artificiality of the original position in *JF*, 81, 87.

account by assessing whether the principles it generates "match our considered convictions of justice or extend them in an acceptable way" (as outlined in "Decision Procedure"): "We can note whether applying these principles would lead us to make the same judgments about the basic structure of society which we now make intuitively and in which we have the greatest confidence; or whether, in cases where our present judgments are in doubt and given with hesitation, these principles offer a resolution which we can affirm on reflection" (*Theory*, 17).

As instances of the former sort of judgment, Rawls cites our confidence that religious and racial discrimination are unjust, having achieved "what we believe is an impartial judgment" of the issue. Whereas such beliefs are "provisional fixed points" that "any conception of justice must fit," we are less certain, Rawls maintains, about the just distribution of "wealth and authority." In the latter case, a proper account of the original position may "remove our doubts." Alternatively, if we don't wish to revise our existing judgments to accord with the principles initially derived from the original position, we can modify the account of that situation to produce more satisfactory principles. The goal of the process of "mutual adjustment of principles and considered judgments" is to reach a state of "reflective equilibrium." Although "this equilibrium is not necessarily stable," at least "for the time being" we will have "done what we can to render coherent and to justify our convictions of social justice" (*Theory*, 18).[18]

Rawls elaborates the methodology of the pursuit of reflective equilibrium in the concluding section of chapter 1. Here, still following the approach of his "Decision Procedure" essay (*Theory*, 40n), he represents the goal of "moral theory" as the description of people's "moral capacity"; correspondingly, a theory of justice is intended to describe our "sense of justice." Just as every competent human being in learning his native language acquires a "sense of grammaticalness" that exceeds his explicit grammatical knowledge, Rawls presumes that each person "beyond a certain age and possessed of a certain intellectual capacity" normally develops a sense of justice, encompassing "a skill in judging things to be just and unjust, and in supporting these judgments by reasons" as well as "some desire to act in accord with these pronouncements." "Considered" moral judgments, more specifically, are those "in which our moral capacities are most likely to be displayed without distortion," excluding, for instance, those we make hesitantly or under the influence of passion or self-interest. But since even judgments "rendered under favorable circum-

18. In chapter 9 (*Theory*, 480) Rawls acknowledges the historically contingent character of any particular set of principles of justice.

stances" are subject to "irregularities and distortions," a satisfactory set of principles should present the reader with an "intuitively appealing account" of his sense of justice that may persuade him to alter his previously deviating judgments to fit them (*Theory*, 41–43).

The foregoing account raises a number of issues that Rawls seems surprisingly disinclined to pursue. For instance, he will "not even ask" whether the principles underlying all people's considered judgments are the same but will "take for granted" that they are either approximately the same or "divide along a few main lines represented by the family of traditional doctrines" that he will take up. Lacking an adequate account of the "structure" of people's conceptions of justice, Rawls chooses to "suppose that everyone has in himself the whole form of a moral conception," so that "for the purposes of this book, the views of the reader and the author are the only ones that count. The opinions of others are used only to clear our own heads" (*Theory*, 44).

Let us engage here in a bit of head-clearing of our own. To begin with, we ought to weigh Rawls's analogy between moral and grammatical learning. It is undeniable that most native speakers of a language have a sense of its grammar that far outstrips their capacity to articulate it, but which grammarians aim to systematize, while scholars of linguistics contemplate the interplay between the two. But any particular language is essentially conventional. That is, no one maintains that the French article *le* is somehow more natural than the English "the" or vice-versa, or that it is more natural for nouns to be given inflected endings or not. Even in trying to wean young students from the use of dialect or slang, we are seeking to enable them to be better understood by educated speakers or to make a better impression, not (ordinarily) to correct their thought.

There is an obvious contrast in the case of moral learning. In training small children not to lie, cheat, or steal, are we not supposing that such actions are objectively wrong—not mere violations of local convention (such as saying "ain't")? Do we not assume, in other words, that our moral language somehow refers to an objective, if not always perfectly grasped, reality? The very fact that we need to explain why exceptions to the rules that forbid dishonesty or theft are sometimes allowable—say, in wartime —evinces our recognition that those rules would otherwise be universally valid, so in this sense the exceptions prove the rule.

We may readily grant Rawls's premise that most human beings, thanks to the combination of their upbringing and their developing rational capacity, acquire what is called a moral sense. But precisely what gives us confidence in that sense, or "conscience," is that in most of our everyday life, its dictates are unambiguous. Everyone "knows" that it is wrong to gratuitously injure or kill another human being, rob a bank, or cheat on an exam. (I put the word "knows" in quotation marks because in private life, at least, the intellectual component of justice is ordinarily less significant than having the correct moral disposition, or the desire to act rightly.)[19]

In appealing to people's intuitive sense of justice to develop principles to regularize or systematize people's judgments of institutional justice, Rawls has moved into a different terrain from everyday morality. While it is inconceivable that a human society could exist without legal and/or customary rules prohibiting crimes such as murder, theft, and fraud (whatever the local variation in the definition of these crimes), there has been no such universal agreement among societies, as Rawls seems to recognize, on such principles as the wrongness of religious intolerance and racial discrimination. Who, then, are the "we" in whose name Rawls pronounces "our" confidence that these things are unjust? The answer, pretty obviously, is modern partisans of what can broadly be termed, borrowing the title of Rawls's second book, "political liberalism."[20] If Rawls aims to uphold liberalism, however, will he not have to elucidate the evidence that shows the truth of that doctrine? How can he so easily set aside, in other words, the likelihood that different people's considered judgments of political justice vary considerably? Granted the variation among different societies' views of justice as well, in what sense can it be maintained that each person already possesses "the whole form" of an adequate account of it? To understand justice, don't we need to attend seriously to alternative views (besides those of the reader and author) for purposes that go well beyond clearing our heads? And is it not likely that some people's conceptions of justice will prove, upon analysis, to have been more fully thought out than those of others?

It is noteworthy in this connection that Rawls omits in the revised edition of *Theory* his original description of moral philosophy as a "Socratic" enterprise (*Theory* 1st ed., 49). It is characteristic of the Socratic approach, in contrast with Rawls's, to confront the widest variety of alternative, sub-

---

19. Cf. Aristotle *Nicomachean Ethics* (hereafter cited as *NE*) 1105b2–3. Herein is the kernel of truth in Kant's contention that in moral matters, "ordinary human understanding . . . may have as much hope as any philosopher of hitting the mark" (*Foundations of the Metaphysics of Morals*, pt. 1, 20 [Akad. ed. 404]). But consider *NE* 1.3, 1095a1–12, arguing that the *study* of ethics and politics presupposes a certain maturity and degree of experience.

20. In later writings, Rawls will be explicit that his theory is intended not as a statement of universal principles of justice, but only as an account of beliefs he thinks are "latent" in the "public culture" of a modern democratic society ("Kantian Constructivism in Moral Theory," *CP*, 305–6).

stantive views about the subject being investigated. Additionally, we note the contrast between the motive that animates Socrates' inquiries—the love of knowledge—and Rawls's description of his aim: "to render coherent *and to justify* our convictions of social justice" (*Theory*, 18 [emphasis added]). Rather than question "our" initial convictions, Rawls seems more interested in defending them against potential critics.[21]

Before addressing further problems inherent in Rawls's account of the pursuit of reflective equilibrium, let us try to understand what led him to this approach to justice. After comparing his enterprise to the endeavor of eighteenth-century British writers to provide "a theory of the moral sentiments," Rawls professes to be following the conception of moral philosophy that was adopted by "most classical British writers through [Henry] Sidgwick," a British ethical theorist of the late nineteenth century (*Theory*, 44–45). While also claiming that his approach reflects that of Aristotle's *Ethics*, Rawls cites Sidgwick's account of the history of moral philosophy as a series of attempts to state "in full breadth and clearness those elementary intuitions of Reason, by the scientific application of which the common moral thought of mankind may be at once systematized and corrected" (*Theory*, 45n).

An examination of Aristotle's *Nicomachean Ethics* and Sidgwick's *Methods of Ethics* confirms that both authors are indeed engaged in articulating, while endeavoring to refine, the moral judgments of a broad audience of their educated peers. But there are important differences from Rawls's procedure. Aristotle does not typically lay down a set of rules or principles for guiding people's judgments. In treating moral virtues such as courage, moderation, and liberality, he identifies the criteria by which we distinguish a particular virtue from its corresponding vices, but leaves it to the reader to determine whether any given action or character tends more to the former or the latter. In fact, Aristotle expressly warns against seeking a quasi-geometric precision in studying ethics.[22]

Turning to justice, we find that in book 5 of the *Ethics* Aristotle does lay out a set of principles to define the subject and even offers some quasi-mathematical rules for applying them. But he describes two different

21. Cf. Schaar, "Reflections on Rawls' *Theory*," 151–52. On Rawls's renunciation of "Socratism," see Rorty, "Priority of Democracy," 188. (Implausibly, in the same volume Rorty describes "liberal Rawlsian searchers for consensus" rather than truth as Socrates' "heirs," *Objectivity, Relativism, and Truth*, 29). Rawls's confidence that the meaning of justice is already sufficiently grasped by him and his interlocutors mirrors the complacency of Socrates' accusers: see Patrick Deneen, *Democratic Faith*, 207.

22. Aristotle *NE* 1.3, 1094b13 ff.

kinds of "particular" justice—rectificatory and distributive—and observes that to determine the latter in particular cases depends on judgments that are inherently disputable, and then discusses a quality (reciprocity) that looks like justice but isn't, yet has a more evident ground in human nature than the two ostensibly true kinds do. Finally, Aristotle depreciates justice as such by comparison with equity, which embodies prudential judgments rather than being bound by rules. In sum, Aristotle does not maintain that the dictates of justice can be settled on the basis of a formula that is present in everyone's moral consciousness, or which they can be persuaded to modify their judgments to fit. His approach is more a restatement and sharpening of the *problem* of justice than a resolution of it.[23]

Sidgwick also exhibits important contrasts to Rawls. While aspiring to discover significant "self-evident moral principles," in *Methods of Ethics* Sidgwick remarks that "the more we extend our knowledge of man and his environment, the more we realise the vast variety of human natures and circumstances that have existed in different ages and countries, the less disposed we are to believe that there is any definite code of absolute rules, applicable to all human beings without exception."[24] Sidgwick thus emphasizes the need for just that acquaintance with the diversity of human moral beliefs across the variety of cultures, as well as the diversity of philosophic teachings about morality, that Rawls seems to have set aside by assuring his readers that their views and his own are all that matter. And when he turns to justice, Sidgwick finds the definition of this virtue to be "obviously incomplete" for "practical guidance," and he adds, regarding the quest for "principles of distribution," that the "common notion of Justice" includes "distinct and divergent elements" that do not lend themselves to any simple resolution.[25] While aiming at a greater systematization of ethical thinking, Sidgwick does not profess any expectation that philosophy can settle fundamental issues of distributive justice merely by looking to some universal core contained in people's considered judgments.

23. Cf. Delba Winthrop, "Aristotle and Theories of Justice"; Bernard Yack, *The Problems of a Political Animal*, chap. 5. Consider also the dialectical treatment of justice in Aristotle *Politics* 3.9–13.

24. Sidgwick, *The Methods of Ethics*, 379. Sidgwick's emphasis on the diversity of moral beliefs among different societies and over time is not intended to justify a simple relativism, but issues rather in an account (reminiscent of Montesquieu) of how differing conditions have necessitated the adoption of different specific moral rules for the sake of the ultimate goal of morality as Sidgwick conceives it, the general happiness (454–55). See, for the same point, Jefferson to Thomas Law, June 13, 1814, in *Life and Selected Writings*, 639–40.

25. Sidgwick, *Methods of Ethics*, 293–94.

IV.

Returning to Rawls, he announces his intent to test his account of justice against two rival theories: "classical utilitarianism" and "intuitionism." (A third alternative, "perfectionism," is less fully developed.) But in neither case do the theories embody alternative substantive views of justice. Rather, the theories are to be tested by how well (in comparison with Rawls's theory) they conform to "our" considered judgments as Rawls conceives them.

Utilitarianism is the chief theoretical account of justice that Rawls confronts. He defines the central idea of classical utilitarianism, represented by Sidgwick, as the principle that society's institutions should "achieve the greatest net balance of satisfaction" among its members (*Theory*, 20). Utilitarianism in Rawls's account is part of a class of "teleological" theories (the others including perfectionism and hedonism) that define "the right . . . as that which maximizes the good."[26] The "striking feature of the utilitarian view of justice," Rawls observes, "is that it does not matter, except indirectly," how the "sum of satisfactions" it aims to maximize "is distributed among individuals."[27] Thus utilitarianism might in principle authorize imposing losses on some individuals so that others can enjoy greater gains, even to the point of sacrificing some people's liberty for the sake of "the greater good shared by many." The root problem of utilitarianism is that it "does not take seriously the distinction between persons": only the sum of pleasure in a society, not its distribution, matters (*Theory*, 21–24).

I shall consider Rawls's anti-utilitarian argument at length in the next two chapters. Here, however, it bears emphasis that Rawls's account of "classical" utilitarianism seems rather strained. Rawls acknowledges that the utilitarianism espoused by the eighteenth-century Scottish philosopher David Hume, who brought the term "utility" into currency as the ground of morality, would not serve his purpose, since "all Hume seems to mean by utility is the general interests and necessities of society" (*Theory*, 28–29).[28] Similarly, Mill, while describing utility as "the ultimate appeal on

26. For the origin of the distinction between teleological and deontological theories, see C. D. Broad, *Five Types of Ethical Theory*, 206–7. "Perfectionism" is apparently Rawls's own coinage, though it has subsequently come into widespread use among Anglo-American scholars of ethics.

27. See *Methods of Ethics*, 416–17, where Sidgwick himself observes that the utilitarian formula of maximizing the sum of happiness needs to be "supplement[ed] . . . by some principle of Just or Right distribution of this happiness."

28. See Hume, *An Enquiry Concerning the Principles of Morals*, bk. 3, chap. 1, 182 on "public utility" as "the *sole* origin of justice" and "the *sole* foundation of its merit" (Hume's emphasis); and bk. 3, chap. 2, 197n, describing "the ideas of natural justice" as

all ethical questions," emphasizes that he means "utility in the largest sense, grounded on the permanent interests of a man as a progressive being," not as a mere sum of individuals' pleasures and pains.[29] Later, Rawls acknowledges that "among the classical [utilitarian] writers the conflation of all [individuals'] desires into one system" so as to justify sacrificing the welfare of some for the greater pleasure of others "is not . . . clearly asserted." Even a more recent (non-"classical") statement of the view is cited only as "an empirical account of social value," not a utilitarian account of what is right. And Rawls finds "only hints" of his ostensibly classical doctrine in Sidgwick; none of his quotations from Sidgwick suggests that violating some people's rights is justified if it provides greater satisfaction to others (*Theory*, 164n).[30] More generally, Rawls acknowledges that historically "the utilitarians were strong defenders of liberty and freedom of thought, and they held that the good of society is constituted by the advantages enjoyed by individuals" (*Theory*, 26).

In sum, we have reason to doubt whether utilitarianism as Rawls has represented it is much more than a straw man. In practice, calculations of the "net balance of satisfaction" are typically only a tool employed by welfare economists, such as A. C. Pigou (*Theory*, 20n), to solve theoretical problems pertaining to limited aspects of public policy. (Rawls himself acknowledges elsewhere that the calculations of utility employed in welfare economics are not intended as statements regarding justice [*CP*, 66n].) Rawls supplies no

---

"conformable to" "the interests of society." Hume is identified by his contemporary Adam Smith as the author "who first explained why utility pleases" and hence explained our "approbation of virtue" as the consequence of our perception of "the appearance of utility" (*The Theory of Moral Sentiments*, bk. 4, chap. 2, sec. 3, 188). It was Frances Hutcheson, however, who coined the utilitarian formula "the greatest happiness for the greatest numbers," rooting it in a moral sense he believed to be innate in all human beings (*Inquiry Concerning the Original of Our Ideas of Virtue or Moral Good*, in L. A. Selby-Bigge, ed., *British Moralists*, bk. 3, chap. 8, sec. 121, 107; Gertrude Himmelfarb, *The Roads to Modernity*, 32). Like J. S. Mill but unlike Bentham, Hutcheson distinguished qualitatively among pleasures. Although he elsewhere argued that the greatest good is that which provides the greatest "aggregate of happiness" (*Essay on the Nature and Conduct of the Affections and Passions*, bk. 1, chap. 2, 17), Hutcheson did not infer that the rights of some individuals should be sacrificed to increase others' pleasure, but endeavored to show that the long-range good of society requires the observance of fundamental moral precepts.

29. Mill, *On Liberty*, in *"Utilitarianism," "Liberty," and "Representative Government,"* "Introductory," 97. In *Utilitarianism*, chap. 2, Mill emphasizes that the utility principle must distinguish qualitatively among pleasures and remarks, "It is better to be a human being dissatisfied than a pig satisfied; better to be Socrates dissatisfied than a fool satisfied" (10–12).

30. Even though Sidgwick suggests in *Methods of Ethics* (417n) that the maximization of collective happiness should override the principle of distributional equality, he does not call for abrogating some people's *rights or liberties* to benefit others.

evidence that persons in authority ever used such calculations to determine how to "allocate" citizens' fundamental rights—an unlikely possibility.

Be this as it may, Rawls contrasts justice as fairness with utilitarianism by describing the former as an attempt to account for our "common sense convictions concerning the priority of justice" over the collective good or "aggregate social welfare." The priority of "claims of liberty and right" reflects the individual's "inviolability," which is "founded on justice or, as some say, on natural right." (Rawls's casualness about the concept of natural right—"as some say"—as if it were merely an optional rhetorical trope without substantive implications, anticipates his endeavor to dispense with the doctrine outright in *PL*, as I will note in chapter 10.)[31] Justice as fairness will support those convictions "by showing that they are the consequence of principles which would be chosen in the original position" (*Theory*, 24–25).

In this initial overview Rawls acknowledges not yet having shown that his principles would in fact be preferred over utilitarianism in the original position. But this concession seems coy, since he will design that situation to support those principles. If the original position didn't generate a choice of the principles he attributes to common sense, the remedy would be to alter its description. Thus Rawls doesn't seem to be risking a great deal when he supposes "for the present" that the persons in the original position would adopt the two principles he has outlined (*Theory*, 25–26).

One other aspect of Rawls's comparison of justice as fairness to utilitarianism merits attention. Whereas utilitarianism, as already noted, is categorized as a teleological theory, justice as fairness is a "deontological" one, meaning that it "either does not specify the good independently from the right, or does not interpret the right as maximizing the good." The meaning of this formulation will be worked out in later chapters; but what is of interest here is the resultant contrast Rawls draws: whereas "in utilitarianism the satisfaction of any desire has some value . . . which must be taken into account in deciding what is right," in justice as fairness people "agree . . . to conform their conceptions of their good to what the principles of justice require." Thus it "does not take men's propensities and inclinations as given" and aim to satisfy them; instead, people's "desires and aspirations are restricted from the outset by the principles of justice." In other words, "certain initial bounds are placed upon what is good and what forms of character are morally worthy, and so upon what kinds of persons men should be" (*Theory*, 27–28). I cite this passage to indicate what a tall order

31. Ronald Dworkin's reconstruction of Rawls's theory is no more serious about the issue of natural rights, since he simply labels the rights that he thinks Rawls's doctrine presupposes as "natural," without offering any justification for that usage (*Taking Rights Seriously*, 177, 182; cf. Thomas Pangle, "Rediscovering Rights").

Rawls has set by making the priority of the right over the good central to his theory.[32] Granted, there is no reason to adopt the supposed utilitarian premise that any desire, however perverse, has some intrinsic claim to satisfaction. But is it possible, at the other extreme, for actual human beings to agree in advance to limit their views of the good in the way Rawls proposes? Can one reasonably expect to constrain people's very "desires and aspirations" (as distinguished from their conduct) to what one has determined justice to require?

V.

Postponing further consideration of this issue, it remains to examine the other theory with which Rawls contrasts his own in chapter 1: intuitionism. Giving the term what he acknowledges is an unusual sense, Rawls defines it as "the doctrine that there is an irreducible family of first principles which have to be weighed against one another by asking ourselves which balance . . . is the most just" (*Theory*, 30–31). Rawls recognizes that at a commonsense level, we normally decide public policy issues such as the allocation of taxes by balancing relevant factors like need and merit. But he observes that such "everyday ideas of justice" are "influenced by our own situation" and "colored by custom and current expectations," the justice of which in turn might be questioned (*Theory*, 31). More broadly "philosophical" conceptions of justice attempt to prescribe the proper balance of social ends but still are left indefinite without a "priority rule" to determine the balance. Whereas intuitionism denies that there is any identifiable formula to specify the weights that different principles should have in particular circumstances, holding that in the end we must simply be guided by our considered judgments, Rawls aims "to reduce the direct appeal" to such judgments, since if we cannot specify the weight to be given to alternative principles "the means of rational discussion have come to an end" (*Theory*, 34, 36–37).

This, then, is the problem Rawls confronts. Of the two moral theories he finds available, one—utilitarianism—provides a relatively clear principle

32. Although I shall take issue with Rawls's claim that the ground or content of his theory are Kantian (*Theory*, xviii), his uncompromising account of the primacy of morality over politics has roots in Kant's teaching. See, e.g., "Perpetual Peace," in *Political Writings*, app., sec. 1, 125 (last par.), on the need for politics to "bend the knee before right," along with the famous or notorious utterance, "*fiat iustitia, pereat mundus*" (123); also "Theory and Practice," ibid., 62–63, and 86 (asserting that the concept of political right "has an objective, practical reality irrespective of the good or evil it may produce"). As will be noted later, in his last writings (*LP* and the 1996 introduction to *PL*) Rawls echoes the apocalyptic millenarianism of these remarks.

of decision but leads to potentially unacceptable results; the other avoids those results but leaves us without coherent guidance beyond the need to balance various intuitions. Rawls's critique of intuitionism does echo Mill's advertisement for the utilitarian principle as providing a "common umpire" to assess the priority of alternative moral principles, in contrast to systems that embody a variety of "moral laws all claiming independent authority," leaving "free scope for the actions of personal desires and partialities" in resolving them.[33] Nonetheless, we must wonder whether Rawls's focus on purely theoretical issues has not obscured what—from most people's point of view—would seem to be the primary question: what *is* justice? In arguing the potential superiority of justice as fairness over intuitionism on the ground that it may promote the "convergence" of our judgments of justice (*Theory*, 40), Rawls oddly distances himself from that issue, just as he had done in his earlier articles.[34]

But it is not self-evident that our moral beliefs stand in need of, or are susceptible of, such systematization as Rawls seeks. (Nor is there any reason to think that most people's moral judgments are based on the "family of traditional doctrines" against which Rawls proposed to test his theory: it is unlikely that many people outside or even inside the academy derive their judgments in particular circumstances from academic theories about morality.) Indeed, people's tendency to apply competing principles to public policy disputes may reflect a truth about the human situation that is better captured by intuitionism (understood as a sort of moral pluralism) than by an endeavor to make them agree on one particular set of principles. That is, I suggest, every political society is confronted with the need to promote various goods, such as freedom, virtue, wealth, and security, for which there is never any single precise balance, and choices among which inevitably vary with circumstances—including, in a democratic regime, the wishes of popular majorities. In this connection, we might consider W. D. Ross's sensible observation: "It is more important that our theory fit the facts than that it be simple."[35]

33. Mill, *Utilitarianism*, chap. 2, 31.
34. In a later essay titled "The Independence of Moral Theory" (1975), Rawls is even more forthright in distinguishing his enterprise of "moral theory" from the substantive consideration of justice, describing it as "*the study of* substantive moral conceptions, that is, . . . of how the basic notions of the right, the good, and moral worth may be arranged to form different moral structures" so as "to determine the conditions they must satisfy if they are to play their expected role in human life" (*CP*, 286 [emphasis added]).
35. Ross, *The Right and the Good*, 19; cf. 23. For a plausible recent account of justice as requiring the balancing of various goods, without entailing moral relativism, see William Galston, *Liberal Pluralism*.

In defense of Ross's approach, moreover, it is somewhat misleading for Rawls to represent him as simply leaving it to the individual to decide how to rank various goods on the basis of "intuitive capacities unguided by constructive and recognizable ethical criteria" (*Theory*, 35–36): although Ross finds that no general rules can be laid down for estimating the comparative stringency of *"prima facie* obligations," he does offer a clear ranking of the preeminent goods of virtue, knowledge, and pleasure.[36] Ross's commonsensical point is that even though we can rank different goals or the weight of differing obligations in the abstract, no universal principle can dictate "our actual duty in particular circumstances" where differing goods and obligations may be mixed together in unpredictable ways and varying degrees of urgency. Hence "our judgements about our actual duty in concrete situations have none of the certainty that attaches to our recognition of the general principles of duty."[37]

As we prepare to examine the specifics of Rawls's theory, we must at least regard it as an open question whether it is truly more rational to agree to be bound in advance by a set of principles arranged in a particular order, rather than to reflect on the specifics of each case as they arise.[38] Why not regard debate among citizens who differ over "the weight to be given to alternative principles" in a given situation as the essence of "rational discussion," rather than, as Rawls maintains, its termination? Why should a moral theorist wish to foreclose such debate?

Beyond these issues, I note the oddity of the notion of "choosing" principles of justice, as Rawls proposes. We often speak of someone's choosing to *be* just or to "do the right thing," but is it intelligible to speak of choosing a conception of justice? Doesn't our everyday discourse presuppose rather that justice has an objective meaning or content, which it is our duty to try to discover in particular circumstances and then apply? Ross, whom Rawls cites as the most sophisticated exponent of a deontological version of intuitionism (*Theory*, 35), represents the "moral order" reflected in "our apprehension of the *prima facie* rightness of certain types of act" as "part of the fundamental nature of the universe" in the same manner as "the

---

36. Ross, *Right and the Good*, 41, 149–54.
37. Ibid., 23, 30; cf. 19.
38. The ultimate root of Rawls's quest for simple principles for assessing the legitimacy of governmental policies may be found in John Locke's assertion of a right of resistance against governments that are tyrannical, or threaten to become so, because they undermine the security of people's rights to life, liberty, and property. But Locke never claims that these broad criteria provide a detailed standard for assessing particular policies, so long as they do not violate the rule of law to the detriment of the people's perceived interests or otherwise exhibit a manifestly tyrannical pattern.

axioms of geometry or arithmetic."[39] By contrast, if justice is something we are free to define as we choose, how can we be bound to obey its mandates when they conflict with something else we wish to do?[40] On what ground can a *self-defined* conception of justice take priority over the pursuit of our own good as we conceive it?

With respect to the issues just raised, I suggest that Ross offers an account of moral reflection that on its face seems more plausible than Rawls's conception of reflective equilibrium. In his treatise *The Right and the Good*, Ross, a distinguished classicist as well as philosophical scholar, holds that "the moral convictions of thoughtful and well-educated people are the data of ethics just as sense-perceptions are the data of a natural science":

> Just as some of the latter [sense data] have to be rejected as illusory, so have some of the former; but as the latter are rejected only when they are in conflict with other more accurate sense-perceptions, the former are rejected only when they are in conflict with other convictions which stand better the test of reflection. The existing body of moral convictions of the best people is the cumulative product of the moral reflection of many generations, which has developed an extremely delicate power of appreciation of moral distinctions; and this the theorist cannot afford to treat with anything other than the greatest respect. The verdicts of the moral consciousness of the best people are the foundation on which he must build; though he must first compare them with one another and eliminate any contradictions they may contain.[41]

39. Ross, *Right and the Good*, 29–30. In his 1980 Dewey Lectures, Rawls explains that the "ideals" his principles embody are not simply chosen but are derived from the "culture" of a well-ordered society, i.e., one based on the two principles. But this argument is circular: since the culture of Rawls's well-ordered society is shaped to support his principles, it cannot offer independent support for them. Nor does Rawls overcome the difficulty by saying that the principles reflect the preference of parties in the original position for primary goods that enable them to exercise their "moral powers," since the original position is itself a construct ungrounded in nature (see "Kantian Constructivism in Moral Theory," *CP,* 354–55).

40. In the American constitutional tradition that stems from Locke, the people's duty to obey government is derivative from their consent. But the measure of legitimate government is ultimately its conduciveness to securing our equal and inalienable rights, which derive from "nature and nature's God" rather than from human choice.

41. Ross, *Right and the Good,* 40–41. The same respect for inherited moral understanding underlies Edmund Burke's warning against the conceit of "literary" politicians, ambitious to destroy inherited customs and institutions without adequate reflection on the consequences (*Reflections on the Revolution in France,* 10, 96–7), as well as the common law itself (see Stoner, *Common Law Liberty,* chap. 1). And cf. Aristotle's account of ethical inquiry as starting from commonly held opinions but aiming to refine out the contradictions among them (much as Socrates does) (*NE* 7.1, 1145b1ff).

Doubtless Ross's reference (published in 1930) to "the moral convictions of the best people" will strike contemporary readers as archaic on account of its "elitist" ring. But Ross is not being a snob. Rather, his contention, which follows from Aristotle's observation in the *Ethics* that accurate moral judgment presupposes a sound education and good character, is simply that the greatest contribution that philosophy can make to the understanding and practice of ethical behavior is to assist us in reflecting on the variety of circumstances that bear on those judgments and to help us pursue a greater degree of consistency or principle on the basis of such reflection.[42]

While aiming at a principled morality, Ross, unlike Rawls, refuses to sacrifice our primary perception of what seems right in particular circumstances to the demands of theory or the pursuit of consensus: "To ask us to give up at the bidding of a theory our actual apprehension of what is right and what is wrong seems like asking people to repudiate their actual experience of beauty, at the bidding of a theory which says 'only that which satisfied such and such conditions can be beautiful.'" Recognizing that in hard cases we are sometimes confronted with conflicting prima facie obligations (am I obliged to fulfill a promise I made to a dying friend when the promise seems to entail inflicting a moral wrong on his heirs?), Ross maintains that "no general rules can . . . be laid down" to supplant particular, circumstantial judgment. Citing Aristotle, he concludes, "This sense of our particular duty in particular circumstances, preceded and informed by the fullest reflection we can bestow on the act in all its bearings, is highly fallible, but it is the only guide we have to our duty."[43]

Although Ross is addressing matters of individual moral conduct rather than public policy, his account is no less applicable to ethical dilemmas that arise in that broader field. Consider the complex problems we face in bioethics today. Where should the lines be drawn regarding biomedical-genetic research and its applications in such areas as genetic manipulation, the use of mood-altering medications, and cloning? Can we effectively distinguish, as many would wish, between (allowable) "therapeutic" cloning

42. For a more recent account of moral judgment arguing (in response to Rawls) that it is inherently tied to particular circumstances and to the accumulated moral wisdom that derives from civilization's collective experience, see David Wiggins, "Neo-Aristotelian Reflections on Justice."

43. Ross, *Right and the Good*, 41–42. The preceding sentence cites Aristotle *NE* 1109b23 and 1126b4 for the observation, "the decision rests with perception." In passing, I note how Ross's admonition to consider the full range of circumstances and likely consequences of an act before deciding what we ought to do is reminiscent of Sidgwick's counsel. Thus Rawls's labeling of Ross and Sidgwick as representing alternative schools of thought exaggerates their difference. In fact, Sidgwick thought of his work as reconciling utilitarianism and intuitionism (*Methods of Ethics*, xiii, xxii–xxiii, 496).

and (prohibited) reproductive cloning, or will the former inevitably lead to the latter? Will the use of human embryos even for the former aim tend to promote a merely utilitarian view of human life? Should scientists be encouraged to seek to lengthen our life span indefinitely, or would that generate a host of new problems that few have thought about, transforming the very structure of human and familial life? Surely any reasonable resolution of these issues will entail not only thorough reflection on long-term consequences but also a balancing of various goods (e.g., health vs. the preservation of human dignity) in a manner that Rawls would call "intuitionistic." But how would substituting a simple set of principles make a satisfactory resolution any easier?[44]

What gives Ross's account of moral reasoning a particular relevance to the American political tradition is that it embodies the same outlook that underlies the common-law jurisprudence that long shaped our political institutions and our collective understanding of justice. As James Stoner observes, while it is a maxim of the common law that the judge reasons his way to general principles out of the particular empirical data—that is, the facts of the case before him, as well as the record of previous relevant precedents—the resultant principles were traditionally understood, in America as well as in Britain, as an attempt to articulate the community's collective, developing understanding of what *is* right, not merely as constructions by a judge of what seemed to him and like-minded peers an "appealing" set of principles. In other words, contrary to Oliver Wendell Holmes Jr., and the school of "legal realism" that he spawned, the common law is not merely "judge-made" law: if it were, it would have no moral sanction. At the foundation of our common-law tradition is an outlook of moral realism that Rawls will explicitly reject in *PL* by calling his theory a form of "constructivism."[45]

Before entering into the details of Rawls's theory and its derivation, I have pointed out certain difficulties in his initial approach to the problem of justice. I have also argued that his case against utilitarianism and intuitionism, on which he grounds his call for a new theory about justice, rests on a certain distortion of those rival doctrines. In the next chapter I turn to Rawls's elaboration of his second principle of justice.

---

44. For an impressive example of ethical reflection on these issues, see Leon Kass, *Life, Liberty, and the Defense of Dignity.*

45. Stoner, *Common Law Liberty,* chap. 1. Contrast Dworkin's denial, in his reconstruction of Rawls's theory, that common-law precedents are to be viewed by judges as embodying "glimpses into a moral reality" (*Taking Rights Seriously,* 161.)

CHAPTER 2

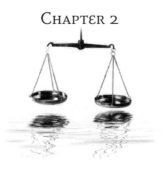

The Second Principle of Justice

I.

As we have seen, Rawls initially addresses justice by abstracting not only from the existence of constitutions and governments but from human nature itself. Starting neither by considering the conflicting claims about justice that arise in actual political communities (as was done, for instance, in book 1 of Plato's *Republic* and book 3 of Aristotle's *Politics*) nor by analyzing the core of human nature that arguably underlies and in a sense precedes human society, as was done by social-contract theorists such as Hobbes, Locke, and Rousseau, Rawls constructs a theory derived from "our" considered judgments of what is fair or just and "our" vision of a just social order. Only later will he treat the structure of a just political regime, defined as one that conforms to the theory.

In the second chapter of *Theory*, Rawls undertakes to elaborate and defend his two principles, without yet demonstrating that they would be chosen in the original position. After restating the principles in a more elaborate but still "provisional" form (*Theory*, 52–53), he focuses on developing the second one, which specifies the conditions under which social and economic inequalities—that is, inequalities in goods other than "basic liberties," which must first be made equal for all—may be rendered legitimate. Throughout, Rawls continues to stress the need for principles of justice to be "clear and simple" (*Theory*, 78).[1] The two principles together reflect a more general conception of justice according to which "all social values—liberty and opportunity, income and wealth, and the social bases of self-respect—are to be distributed equally" unless their unequal distribution serves "everyone's advantage" (*Theory*, 54).

The second principle has two aspects: a mandate of "fair equality of opportunity" and the difference principle. Fair equality of opportunity differs from simple equality of legal opportunity ("careers open to talents") by requiring not only that positions of greater privilege or wealth be formally open to all, but that all individuals "have a fair chance to attain them." Hence those with equal levels of ability and motivation "should have the same prospects of success" regardless of their initial social position. To this end, economic institutions must be regulated in ways Rawls thinks "familiar enough" not to need elaboration, other than emphasizing "the importance of preventing excessive accumulations of property and wealth and of maintaining equal opportunities of education." Furthermore, schools, "whether public or private, should be designed to even out class barriers" (*Theory*, 63).

Rawls judges this "liberal conception" of equal opportunity to be clearly preferable to "the system of natural liberty," which makes no provision for assisting those from disadvantaged backgrounds to rise, other than offering public schooling.[2] Nonetheless, the liberal conception "intuitively" still seems deficient by itself, since even if it eliminates "the influence of social contingencies" on people's life prospects, "it still permits the distribution of wealth and income to be determined by the natural distribution of abilities and talents" among human beings, an outcome that "is arbitrary from a moral perspective." Moreover, "at least as long as some form of the family exists," the goal of equal opportunity can be only imperfectly achieved, since "even the willingness to make an effort . . . and so to be deserving in the ordinary sense is itself dependent upon happy family and social circumstances," which only some individuals enjoy (*Theory*, 64).[3]

1. For other references to simplicity in chapter 2, see *Theory*, 54, 72, 79, 80, 81, and 93; see also 453–54, where simplicity is represented as the major advantage of analyzing justice from the standpoint of the original position.

2. Rawls seems to have borrowed the term "system of natural liberty" from Adam Smith's *Wealth of Nations* by way of Sidgwick, though he makes no reference to Smith in this connection, and it is unclear whether or in what sense Rawls himself regards it as natural. (Recall his earlier, offhanded reference to "natural rights.")

3. Rousseau argued the moral irrelevance of people's natural talents in *Emile, or, On Education*, bk. 4, 245: "the good man can be proud of his virtue because it's his," whereas the "intelligent man" did nothing to acquire his intellect or talent. But neither Rousseau nor his pupil Kant inferred from this principle that society should aim to

According to Rawls, "we" are no less "troubled" by the influence of "natural chance" on people's distributive shares than by the arbitrary effect of "social contingencies" on them. This sentiment becomes the ground of Rawls's "democratic conception" of justice, which aims to treat everyone equally as "moral person[s]" whose "share in the benefits of social cooperation" is independent of their social or natural "fortune." The democratic conception combines fair equality of opportunity with the difference principle. That principle (Rawls's major innovation) holds that "the higher expectations of those better situated" in society "are just . . . only if they work as part of a scheme which improves the expectations" of its "least advantaged" members (*Theory*, 64–65).[4] In other words, because it is impossible to equalize all people's life prospects, the next-best solution is to prohibit anyone from enjoying a greater share of social and economic goods unless his gains also somehow profit the less fortunate. The commitment to such a system is the necessary entailment in Rawls's view of conceiving society "as a cooperative venture for mutual advantage" (*Theory*, 73–74).

II.

Deferring questions about the moral attitude Rawls presupposes that "we" hold, I turn to his introductory discussion of the "primary goods" in

---

compensate for the arbitrariness with which nature distributes her gifts. Rather, both concluded (Rousseau partly rhetorically, Kant with utter seriousness) that moral virtue is of infinitely greater worth than either talent or the external goods it enables one to acquire, and that a just society will be devoted to protecting the equal rights and hence dignity of its members. As I shall observe, Rawls's attempt to elevate the just over the good sits uneasily, by contrast, with the value he attributes to external ("primary") goods.

Closer to Rawls's thesis is Mill's representation of remunerating human beings in accordance with "natural difference[s] of strength or capacity" (as distinguished from motivation) as "an injustice," albeit one that must be tolerated given people's "selfish" nature until they have been entirely "regenerated" through moral education (*Principles of Political Economy*, bk. 2, chap. 1, sec. 4, 211–12). On the tension between Mill's utilitarianism and the Lockean natural-rights teaching on which the United States was founded, see Marc Plattner, "Capitalism," 325–32.

4. Cf. Mill, *Principles of Political Economy*, bk. 5, chap. 2, sec. 2, 805, on "the true idea of distributive justice" as consisting "not in imitating but in redressing the inequalities and wrongs of nature." Rawls's first intimation of the difference principle (without using that term) came in his 1963 "Constitutional Liberty" article, but there it remained in an unresolved tension with his previous assertion that inequalities should "work to the advantage of every person" participating in an institution rather than only of the least advantaged (*CP*, 76, 82).

terms of which people's well-being is to be compared.[5] One of the methodological advantages of justice as fairness over utilitarianism according to Rawls is that it "asks less of our judgments of welfare." Although applying the difference principle requires us to identify "the least advantaged representative man," we need not determine the *degree* of his disadvantage, whereas utilitarianism requires comparing the utility scales of different individuals to ascertain whether some people's gains are large enough to outweigh others' losses (*Theory*, 78–79). Additionally, interpersonal comparisons are made easier in Rawls's scheme by calculating "expectations of primary social goods." Primary social goods "are things which it is supposed a rational man wants whatever else he wants," and of which "he would prefer more . . . rather than less." "In broad categories," the primary goods are "rights, liberties, and opportunities, and income and wealth," along with "a sense of one's own worth," which Rawls postpones for later consideration (*Theory*, 79).[6]

Rawls's account of primary goods depends on a view of the good to be elaborated later in *Theory* according to which "a person's good is determined by what is for him the most rational long-term plan of life" (*Theory*, 79). Rawls supposes that everyone has a "rational plan" that "schedules" his activities so that he can satisfy his various desires "without interference." Even in this initial sketch, we again note the abstractness of Rawls's account of human life: does anyone actually live this way? Is anyone— even the most absolute of tyrants—so fortunate that he can fulfill all his desires without interference? Is the central obstacle to achieving one's good really a "scheduling" problem? Rawls has evidently designed his

5. I pass over Rawls's digression illustrating the difference principle with a series of graphs and introducing such terms as "chain connection" and "close-knitness" (*Theory*, 65–73). Neither the graphs nor the technical concepts prove to have any bearing on his account of justice. Rawls acknowledges that even if the conditions for chain connection among the interests of different classes do not hold, the difference principle would still apply (70–71).

6. Rawls never actually explains how the reasoning in the original position could provide for self-respect, aside from claiming that it does so by supporting the equal "basic liberties." He subsequently describes the possible need to adjust the index of primary goods to promote self-respect as an "unwelcome complication" best left to hypothetical legislators at a later stage of application of the difference principle (478–79). In reality, there is no evident reason that a utilitarian could not employ Rawls's notion of primary goods, if it were thought desirable to do so; indeed, Brian Barry observes, utilitarians like Bentham already did "take primary goods of the kind Rawls describes as surrogates for want-satisfaction" (*The Liberal Theory of Justice*, 55). A utilitarian would probably argue, however, that it is more useful, in setting economic policy, to try to determine people's actual degrees of desire for particular goods rather than rely solely on Rawls's vague categories. Presumably Rawls himself would not deny the usefulness of such calculations, assuming that the constraints of justice have been satisfied.

account of the good not so much with a view to describing how people live, as for the sake of excluding judgments of the substantive content of their lives: justice as fairness does not assess "the relative merits of different conceptions of good." Since everyone is guaranteed the right to pursue his plan of life so long as it conforms to the dictates of justice, "once the whole arrangement is set up . . . no questions are asked" about the actual levels of "satisfaction or perfection" people attain under it (*Theory*, 80–81).

We should remind ourselves here of the way in which a liberal polity like the United States already affords its citizens the opportunity largely to live as they please, without imposing a particular way of life on them within the broad limits set by law. But justice is not the only ground of the constraints that our government (or any government) imposes on people's pursuit of their good. In prohibiting such allegedly "victimless" crimes as drug abuse and prostitution, even a liberal regime ordinarily sets certain limits with a view to promoting the requisites of decent human life, on the understanding that not everyone is sufficiently rational to avoid activities that are ruinous to the common well-being and to human dignity. Rawls has not said, of course, that justice is the only criterion of good government. The only other prerequisites he has acknowledged for a "viable human community," however, are "coordination, efficiency, and stability" (*Theory*, 5), none of which seems to cover the sorts of case I have cited. In fact, as I shall observe further on, Rawls specifically maintains that justice prohibits interference with people's individual life plans, however irrational or degrading they may seem, so long as they do not violate others' liberties. The merits of such an understanding remain to be demonstrated.

III.

Having propounded the difference principle, Rawls next must define the "least fortunate group" for purposes of applying it. He identifies that group as consisting of those "least favored by each of the three main kinds of contingencies" in the acquisition of primary goods, having less advantaged "family and class origins" than others, lesser "natural endowments," and inferior "fortune and luck in the course of life" (*Theory*, 83).[7]

We wonder in passing how people can be compensated in advance for bad luck over the course of their lives, when that course is not yet known;

7. In his final account of the difference principle in *JF* (59), Rawls specifies that the least advantaged are simply "those belonging to the income class with the lowest expectations."

but Rawls does not pause to address this difficulty.[8] An additional oddity is that Rawls specifies that the least advantaged, for purposes of the difference principle, should be assumed to have "physical needs and psychological capacities" that are "within the normal range, so that the questions of health care and mental capacity do not arise," since he wants to avoid "prematurely introducing matters that may take us beyond the theory of justice" and is concerned that "these hard cases can distract our moral perception by leading us to think of persons distant from us whose fate arouses pity and anxiety." Even as a provisional move, this exclusion seems curious, because one would think that those suffering from severe mental and physical handicaps are far more disadvantaged than those who are merely born into poverty or who lack the IQ to make it into college, and hence the seriously disabled should be first in line for any compensation to be distributed for faring poorly in nature's "lottery."[9] In fact, Rawls immediately acknowledges the inevitability of "a certain arbitrariness in actually identifying the least favored group," defending his procedure by pleading "practical considerations" and the limits of philosophy's capacity to make fine distinctions (*Theory*, 84). Still, he "assume[s] that the persons in the original position understand these matters." This seems an awfully heavy burden to lay on those persons, who are to represent all of us in their choice of principles of justice: if Rawls by his acknowledgment cannot avoid arbitrariness and imprecision, how accurate or reliable could their decisions be? Dare we put our fates, so to speak, in the hands of unknown persons faced with problems of information that their own creator represents as beyond him?

These passages in which Rawls acknowledges the artificiality and vagueness of his definitions fortify the impression that he is more concerned with securing his readers' agreement on a set of principles to guide their judgment than with ensuring the solidity of the foundations those principles rest on. According to Rawls, "social wisdom" entails adopting "clear and simple principles" (*Theory*, 78). A long line of distinguished

---

8. In *JF* (139) Rawls explains that in a just "property-owning democracy," as distinguished from unjust "welfare-state capitalism," rather than redistribute income "to those with less at the end of each period," by ensuring "widespread ownership of productive assets and human capital (that is, education and trained skills)" government can enable the less advantaged to do "their full share" on terms consistent with their self-respect, instead of being merely "objects of our charity and compassion." But his acknowledgment in the same context of the additional need "to assist those who lose out through accident or misfortune" indicates the disconnect between real human disadvantage and the merely hypothetically "least advantaged" class (those with the lowest incomes) who are to benefit from the difference principle.

9. Cf. Barry, *Liberal Theory*, 55–57.

political, legal, and ethical theorists, to the contrary, warns against such simplification. The very concept of equity as a necessary corrective to the strict rule of law, or of fixed legal principles, stems at least as far back as Aristotle and has a long provenance in Anglo-American common law.[10] In ethical matters, W. D. Ross observes, "loyalty to facts is worth more than a symmetrical architectonic or hastily reached simplicity."[11] When it comes to designing political institutions, the authors of the American Constitution learned from Montesquieu that complex structures were needed to secure individual liberty, since "simple" government amounts to despotism.[12] During the founding era, both John Adams and James Madison defended the complexity of American political systems against the abstract schemes of "theoretic" politicians.[13] Perhaps most relevant is the classic statement of Edmund Burke (responding to the theorists of the French Revolution), denying that any political doctrine can be assessed in "the nakedness and solitude of metaphysical abstraction." Circumstances, Burke argued, are what give every political principle "its distinguishing color and discriminating effect. The circumstances are what render every civil and political scheme beneficial or noxious to mankind."[14]

In the sharpest contrast to Burke, Rawls holds that accepting his principles commits us "to discard as irrelevant" to justice "much of the information and many of the complications of everyday life," thus eliminating the need to keep track of "the endless variety of circumstances and the changing relative positions of particular persons" (*Theory*, 76). But how, then, would we even be able to identify who, at any particular moment, is truly least advantaged and hence continues to merit compensation?

What Rawls has in mind, we shall see, are institutions and public policies that ensure that the least advantaged, whoever they may be at any time, benefit from the successes of the more advantaged. Given the admitted imprecision in his definition of the least advantaged as well as his arbitrary exclusion of the most severely handicapped from that category, however, it is unclear how such a result can be assured. Wouldn't it be advantageous, in any event, for social policy to take as much account as possible of "the complications of everyday life" to achieve its ends? For

10. Cf. Plato *Statesman* 294a ff; John Locke, *Two Treatises of Government*, 2, chap. 14; Schaar, "Reflections on Rawls' *Theory*," 161.

11. Ross, *Right and the Good*, 23. Schaar properly takes Rawls to task for "abolish[ing] human complexity in the interests of quasi-mathematical theory" ("Reflections on Rawls' *Theory*," 160.) See also Wiggins, "Neo-Aristotelian Reflections," 503.

12. Montesquieu, *The Spirit of the Laws*, bk. 5, chap. 14, 60, 63.

13. See Adams's *Defence of the Constitutions of Government of the United States of America*; Hamilton, Madison, and Jay, *The Federalist*, No. 10, 49.

14. *Reflections on the Revolution*, 7.

instance, don't we need to consider the actual gradations of disadvantage among the less well-off members of society, rather than single out one group to profit from the gains of the more fortunate on what Rawls acknowledges is the uncertain assumption that if the least well-off benefit, "every other representative man" does as well (*Theory*, 70)?

A further difficulty that is already visible in Rawls's project arises from his having described "the social bases of self-respect" as one of the primary goods in which inequalities are allowable only if they benefit the least advantaged (he subsequently calls self-respect "perhaps the most important primary good" [*Theory*, 386])—yet postponing his treatment of it until much later, after the principles of justice have been fully formulated. Here, we are driven to reflect on what truly fosters self-respect and on whether any sort of redistributive scheme can possibly promote it. Do people who receive welfare benefits to mitigate the effects of poverty or unemployment typically respect themselves more as a result? Don't we respect ourselves rather for our own genuine achievements?[15] For that matter, isn't it likely that self-respect is less dependent on one's economic status than on such things as the consciousness of doing one's job well, having friends, and enjoying a degree of romantic success and the blessings of conjugal happiness, the "social bases" of which Rawls (sensibly) does not propose to equalize? From what Rawls represents as a moral standpoint, doesn't the fact that some people are born with movie-star looks seem no less arbitrary than the fact that others are born with, or acquire, entrepreneurial skills? If this is the case, but such arbitrariness is an inevitable fact of life, just how great a contribution can Rawls's principles make to human happiness and self-respect, even if their internal difficulties can be resolved?

IV.

Rawls appears untroubled by such considerations. Instead, he is concerned with covering his left flank, so to speak, by "forestall[ing] the objection" that "the principle of fair opportunity . . . leads to a meritocratic society" (*Theory*, 86). To the contrary, he emphasizes, the difference principle dictates that undeserved inequalities in people's "natural endowment[s]" be "compensated for." Hence he suggests that "in pursuit of this principle greater resources might be spent on the education of the less

15. This is not to deny that there are valid reasons for a proper policy of public assistance to the poor, albeit one that would help them so far as possible to become self-sufficient and therefore have the opportunity to acquire greater self-respect.

rather than the more intelligent," at least in "the earlier years of school." Yet the difference principle has enmeshed Rawls in a difficulty here: if the ultimate outcome of spending more on educating the *more* talented were to maximize the ultimate well-being of the less advantaged (thanks to what we might call the "difference tax" on their gains), then such a priority would seem to be called for. (And wouldn't more talented children who come from disadvantaged backgrounds be especially deserving of support?) Apparently sensing the problem, Rawls backtracks by saying that if "the long-term expectation of the least favored" is indeed improved "by giving more attention to the better endowed, it is permissible" (*Theory*, 86–87).[16] Still, he stresses that a society based on the two principles will be very different from a meritocratic one, wherein "there exists a marked disparity between the upper and lower classes" in wealth and "organizational authority"; "the culture of the poorer strata is impoverished while that of the governing and technocratic elite is securely based on the service of the national ends of power and wealth"; and "equality of opportunity means an equal chance to leave the less fortunate behind in the personal quest for influence and social position" (*Theory*, 91).

Rawls does not specify whether he thinks there is any actual society that tends in this direction, though some readers will undoubtedly interpret it— plausibly, in view of some of his later remarks—as a (rather crude) criticism of the contemporary United States. But whether this was his intention or not, it is worthwhile at this point to compare Rawls's account of the entailments of justice with the one already present in the American constitutional tradition. At the time of the founding, statesmen as diverse as Jefferson, Hamilton, and John Adams espoused the goal of government by the "natural aristocracy" and the expectation that the Constitution would help to achieve that result.[17] What was meant by the term was that under a system of individual liberty and republican government, in which all officeholders derive their positions directly or indirectly from the consent of the people as expressed in elections, the only way to achieve and retain public office is to demonstrate to the electorate the conduciveness of one's public activities

16. On the ways in which applying the difference principle to public education not only fails to offer meaningful policy guidance but also disregards research findings (notably, the Coleman Report) challenging the assumption that variations in educational attainment are chiefly the result of unequal educational resources, see Schaar, "Reflections on Rawls' *Theory*," 154–55.

17. See, e.g., Jefferson to John Adams, October 28, 1813: "that form of government is the best, which provides the most effectually for a pure selection of [the] natural aristoi into the offices of government" (*Life and Selected Writings*, 633). See also, on how the Constitution "affords a moral certainty" that the presidency will be "filled by characters preeminent for ability and virtue," Hamilton, Madison, and Jay, *The Federalist*, No. 68, 382.

to their well-being. Similarly, the opportunity that a system of economic liberty gives all individuals to advance their fortunes by labor and investment profits the whole community, as John Locke and Adam Smith argued, since their self-regarding activities increase the common stock of wealth.[18] (As the supply of goods produced grows, their price drops and hence their accessibility to the broader population increases.)

What prevents such a system from constituting a mere "meritocracy," in the pejorative sense given the term by Michael Young in the novel Rawls cites in this regard (*Theory*, 91), is precisely the protection that the Constitution provides to the rights of every citizen, regardless of his talents, and the deference to popular will that is mandated by the republican system of government.[19] If one needed evidence that this system benefits not only the people as a whole but also the least advantaged in Rawls's sense, we need only consider the millions of immigrants, most of them from the poorer strata of their countries of origin, who have striven to attain these shores, often at great risk, to enjoy the benefits of what they perceive to be the land of opportunity. Moreover, if we define the least advantaged more broadly, to include those victimized by serious mental and physical handicaps, there can be little doubt that America's provision for them is among the most generous in the world.[20] (Consider, in addition, how agricultural

18. See Locke, *Two Treatises*, bk. 2, chap. 5; Smith, *An Inquiry into the Nature and Causes of the Wealth of Nations*, bk. 3, chap. 4; bk. 4, sec. 2, par. 9; Hamilton, Madison, and Jay, *The Federalist*, No. 12, 2nd par.

19. Rawls appears to have missed the point of Young's novel, which is aptly summarized by Bernard Williams as "the feeling that a thorough-going emphasis on equality of opportunity must destroy a certain sense of common humanity" owing to an overemphasis on competitive success. For Williams the alternative ideal of "equality of respect . . . urges us to give less consideration to those structures in which people enjoy status or prestige, and to consider people independently of those goods, on the distribution of which equality of opportunity precisely focuses our, and their, attention" ("The Idea of Equality," 129–30.) In other words, Williams's argument applies more or less directly against Rawls's own emphasis on "fair equality of opportunity"—even though Rawls proceeds in the next note to express indebtedness to Williams's essay for his understanding of the problem. Rawls unpersuasively contends that his difference principle solves the problem by "transform[ing] the aims of society" so as to serve the less advantaged (*Theory*, 91), when its emphasis on the increase and distribution of primary goods would actually exacerbate the problem described by Williams. On the "inner contradiction" of socialism in this regard, see Bertrand de Jouvenel, *The Ethics of Redistribution*, 11–14, 47–48.

20. For instance, while U.S. health care spending in 2001 was $3,858 per capita, the highest figure in the world, amounting to $15,432 annually for a family of four, the typical such family spent only about $4,000 on medical insurance, deductibles, and co-pays that year, with the bulk of its medical expenses being covered by employers, the government, and insurance firms instead. While nationalized health care systems in Canada and Europe typically will not pay for heart bypass operations for senior citizens, Medicare provides them at almost any age, with thousands being performed each year (Gregg Easterbrook, *The Progress Paradox*, 96–97).

and medical research in which the United States is the world leader contributes to alleviating problems of hunger and disease throughout the globe.) If, as Rawls surmises, there is a "chain connection" among different classes' well-being (*Theory*, 70), why not recognize how policies of liberty that enable some few to grow rich through labor, entrepreneurship, and investment inevitably raise everyone's standard of living—without the need for superimposing the difference principle? (In the oft-quoted words used by President Kennedy in support of his tax cut, "a rising tide lifts all boats.")[21]

Rawls, as we have seen, finds the constitutional scheme wanting because it allows the more talented, or those born into wealth, to prosper without guaranteeing that some share of every gain they make will benefit the least advantaged. But what possible guarantees could be provided other than those that our constitutional system already embodies to ensure that the rich cannot use their wealth to tyrannize the poor, and that opportunities remain open for all, so that as society's wealth increases, that of the

21. The effect of entrepreneurial capitalism in raising the standard of living of the poor is seen no less, when it is allowed to operate, in the so-called Third World than in more developed nations. On the vast contribution to employment and the rise of living standards made by private "knowledge industries" in contemporary India since the liberalization of its economy, see, Gurcharan Das, *India Unbound;* see also Hernando De Soto, *The Other Path.* On the contrast between high economic growth in former Communist nations that adopted extensive market-oriented reforms during 1989–2004 and the severe declines in those that did not, see Leszek Balcerowicz, "The Wealth of Nations."

22. The percentage of Americans living below the official poverty line dropped from 22 percent to 12 percent between 1959 and 2004. While 25 percent of American households were considered "low income" in 1999 because their incomes were under $25,000, by that standard 40 percent of households in Sweden, Europe's model "welfare state," would fall into the low-income category. Large majorities of those currently defined as poor by the U.S. census own such conveniences as automobiles, air conditioners, color televisions, VCRs, and microwave ovens. Because of their higher per capita gross national product, Americans are able to spend some $9,700 more annually on consumption than their European counterparts (see Robert E. Rector and Kirk A. Johnson, "Understanding Poverty in America"; "Europe vs. America," *Wall Street Journal* editorial [reporting the results of a study by two Swedish economists]). In fact, when noncash government transfer payments such as food stamps and housing subsidies, as well as the Earned Income Tax Credit, are taken into account, the actual share of Americans living under the poverty line in 2004 was estimated by the census bureau as 8.3 percent; the percentage drops below 5.1 percent when government estimates of nonreported income, as well as the value of Medicaid, are included (see U.S. Bureau of the Census, "The Effects of Government Taxes and Transfers on Income and Poverty: 2004"; Douglas Besharov, "Poor America." On the gross underestimation of the increase in living standards among the poor over the past several decades by the "official" poverty rate, owing to defects in the standard used by the census bureau, see Nicholas Eberstadt, "The Mismeasurement of Poverty."

poor does as well?[22] As Rawls's inconsistency on the subject of education spending priorities indicates, there is no way of knowing in advance whether the genetically least advantaged ("the less intelligent") will profit most by having more spent on their education rather than on the training of the more talented whose professional and economic success can ultimately enhance the well-being of their less able peers. Given that the most intelligent are by definition a minority, the democratic nature of our polity, combined with the sentiment of compassion that is a characteristic attribute of modern democratic peoples, ensures that the educational well-being of the multitude and even of the retarded is unlikely to be sacrificed on the altar of assisting future entrants to Harvard. Is the good of the less advantaged therefore promoted in any substantive way by Rawls's continually reminding them that "no one deserves his greater natural capacity nor merits a more favorable starting place in society" (*Theory*, 87), especially since even his own theory allows the more advantaged to profit from these "undeserved" assets to an in-principle unlimited extent, so long as they pay the difference tax? (In other words, Rawls too "permits the distribution of wealth and income to be determined by the natural distribution of abilities and talents," the very phenomenon that he cited as his objection to the "liberal" understanding of equality.) As for merely conventional advantages such as inherited wealth or social standing, has any American—or any significant thinker since the end of the feudal age—ever believed that some people do "deserve" their "more favorable starting place"? Is it even meaningful to ask whether anyone "deserves" his natural capacity, any more than Marilyn Monroe deserved her generous natural endowment or some people deserve to be born with red hair?

Rawls also seems to exhibit a certain confusion regarding the notion of natural aristocracy, since he acknowledges it as "a possible interpretation" of his two principles, but rejects it on the ground that it allows people's "distributive shares" to be unfairly influenced by "natural chance." Yet in the formulation that Rawls gives to this ideal, according to which besides the establishment of "formal equality of opportunity," "the advantages of persons with greater natural endowments are to be limited to those that further the good of the poorer sectors of society" (*Theory*, 64), it seems practically indistinguishable from Rawls's second principle, which also

---

Although there is a significant "underclass" in this country (as in major European nations), its problems are rooted in such pathologies as unwed motherhood, truancy, crime, and drugs, rather than in "distributional" deficiencies of the sort that the difference principle addresses.

allows those better endowed by nature to receive greater rewards than others do. (Of course, traditional advocates of the notion of natural aristocracy justified that ideal by its conduciveness to the good of society as a whole, not merely that of an arbitrarily defined class called the "least advantaged.")

I hasten to add that in principle, a serious argument can be made, as it was by Rousseau and by some Antifederalists, that the people as a whole (not just the least advantaged) are better off in a simple and relatively egalitarian society, where neither great talents nor large fortunes are cultivated and where the nation offers few temptations to great ambition. In such a society, arguably, the people are more than compensated for a lower standard of living by a greater feeling of personal independence and civic solidarity. It is questionable whether such an argument has much applicability in the modern world, where the spread of technology and mass communication makes the isolation that Rousseau believed necessary for such a society a near impossibility. But in any event, because of its formal character, Rawls's difference principle provides no ground for assessing this claim. If anything, the fact that his list of primary goods favors wealth-maximization implies a choice against it.

There is in fact a sense in which contemporary American society is threatened by the rise of a narrowly "meritocratic" ethos, but the danger is quite different from the one identified by Rawls. As social critics such as Christopher Lasch and David Lebedoff observe, and as the passions aroused by the 2004 election (and subsequent Supreme Court nominations) indicated, America is increasingly characterized by a split between a rationalistic "elite" who owe their success to technical knowledge, bureaucratic expertise, or prominence in the media or entertainment worlds, and who espouse an ethos that is cosmopolitan and morally libertarian, and the greater number of ordinary citizens who adhere largely to traditional religious, moral, and patriotic beliefs—including the belief that it is the individual's, not the government's, primary responsibility to provide for his and his family's needs—beliefs toward which the new elite expresses an often-undisguised scorn. Typically unable to advance their libertarian and antireligious "reform" program through the representative political process, members of the social elite have enjoyed far greater success through the undemocratic means of having it read into our Constitution by an activist judiciary, in conjunction with the influence of self-styled "public interest" lobbies on the administrative process.[23] This division

23. See Christopher Lasch, *The Revolt of the Elites*; David Lebedoff, *The Uncivil War*.

exemplifies the concerns of Rousseau and the Antifederalists about the potential rise of a new sort of aristocracy whose personal ambitions, combined with their moral and religious skepticism, might trump the concern for democracy and undermine the moral foundations it presupposes. On these issues, we shall observe, Rawls, despite his professions of concern for democracy and equality, sides with the new elite, in opposition to the principles of constitutional, representative government.

V.

One other unacknowledged difficulty to be noted in Rawls's second principle of justice is the potential conflict between his interpretation of "fair equality of opportunity" and the difference principle. In emphasizing that the former rule entails limiting the development of "excessive" accumulations of property, Rawls seems to point toward a Brandeisian policy of rigorous enforcement of antitrust laws, even at the cost of reducing economic efficiency (and thus the funds available to benefit the least advantaged). Indeed, he elsewhere asserts the unacceptability of even a capitalist welfare state that offers "generous" welfare provisions and supplies all citizens' "basic needs," since unlike a "property-owning democracy" it ostensibly "permits a small class to have a near monopoly of the means of production" (*JF*, 139; see also *Theory*, xv). But don't large merchandising firms like Wal-Mart elevate the living standards of poorer people by making a wide variety of goods available to them at lower prices than smaller independent stores can offer? Should the government break up large automobile, steel, or software companies merely to broaden the class of people who own them? (This would entail imposing high tariffs to exclude competition from more concentrated and efficient foreign firms, thus further increasing domestic prices, while ultimately increasing unemployment thanks to retaliatory tariffs imposed by other nations.) In fact, in the United States, market concentration in some areas of the economy has proved fully compatible with widespread ownership of the means of production by means of employee pension funds and retirement accounts.[24] Similarly, the continuing success of startup businesses (especially, today, in the computer and biotech fields, as well as in more pedestrian retail enterprises) demonstrates

24. More than half of all American households owned stock, either directly or through pension plans, by the end of the 1990s (Ramesh Ponnuru, "Investor Class, Investor Nation," 28).

the compatibility of large-scale industrial capitalism with widespread opportunity for individual entrepreneurship as well.[25]

Rawls gives no evidence of having thought of these issues; he seems simply to assume, despite overwhelming evidence to the contrary, that a policy focusing on wide dispersion of ownership of industrial and commercial firms will somehow improve rather than worsen the economic well-being of the less advantaged. As with his remarks on education spending, Rawls writes as if a "theory" of justice can give us fairly specific policy direction before considering the relevant empirical information as a statesman, or anyone wishing to proffer him useful advice, must do.

It is perhaps reassuring that Rawls, in defending his theory against the appearance that it is "unfairly biased" in favor of the least advantaged, stipulates that "the more advantaged have a right to their natural assets, as does everyone else," since "this right is covered by the first principle under the basic liberty protecting the integrity of the person" (*Theory*, 88–89). (Without that stipulation, would the less advantaged have a claim to the bodily organs of their better-endowed peers?[26]) Yet not only does Rawls reiterate that nobody deserves his "native endowments" or "starting place in society," he adds that it is "problematic" whether anyone deserves "the

25. On the coexistence of large industrial enterprises in Western economies in spheres where the scale of operation requires it with a multitude of smaller enterprises that do some three-quarters of the economy's total work, see Nathan Rosenberg and L. E. Birdzell Jr., *How the West Got Rich*, chap. 9. The authors emphasize as well how the West's continued technological innovation depended on a "decentralization of enterprise" that accommodated the "prickly individualism" of innovators, and diffused "the authority to make economic decisions . . . into a multitude of enterprises of diverse size, ownership, internal structure, and situs," in contrast to the "hierarchical control of industrial technology" that characterized the Soviet economy and impeded its growth (267)—but also in contrast, I add, to a Rawlsian mandate to break up large industrial enterprises, even where the nature of their work dictates such a scale.

26. Cf. Nozick, *Anarchy, State, and Utopia*, 206. Our assurance on this score must be qualified by Rawls's raising the possibility on the next page of adopting "eugenic policies, more or less explicit" to equalize people's "natural assets" (*Theory*, 92). While leaving such questions aside, Rawls raises no principled objection to the suggestion—implicitly inviting another theorist who shares his commitment to the least advantaged to develop it. Nor are we adequately reassured by Rawls's caveat "that it is not in general to the advantage of the less fortunate to propose policies which reduce the talents of others" (92), since this is a mere maxim of prudence rather than a moral principle—hardly the kind of guarantee one expects from a supposed champion of human dignity and the elevation of justice over utility. (Rawls objects to the utilitarian case against slavery precisely because of its conditional character [137].) Considering Rawls's curious "conjecture" that "in the long run" so long as a society takes steps "to preserve the general level of natural abilities" (how?) while preventing "the diffusion of serious [genetic] defects, . . . we would eventually reach a society with the greatest equal liberty the members of which enjoy the greatest equal talent," it is probably fortunate that he chooses "not [to] pursue this thought further" (92–93).

superior character" that leads us "to cultivate our abilities," since "such character depends in good part upon fortunate family and social circumstances in early life for which we can claim no credit" (*Theory*, 89). That one's character is typically shaped to a significant degree by familial upbringing is undeniable, but to suggest that for that reason one's character is undeserved compels us to ask, if people don't deserve their own character, what ground of desert can there ever be?[27]

Remarkably, in view of his having criticized utilitarianism in chapter 1 of *Theory* for failing to "take seriously the distinction between persons," Rawls represents his difference principle as "an agreement to regard the distribution of natural talents as in some respects a common asset and to share in the greater social and economic benefits made possible by the complementarities of this distribution" (*Theory*, 87).[28] It is telling that he subsequently adds, "*From a suitably general standpoint*, the difference principle appears acceptable to both the more advantaged and the less advantaged individual" (*Theory*, 89 [emphasis added]). What has enabled Rawls thus far to give his principles the appearance of answering to "our" sense of justice is that he has left them at such an extreme level of generality that, as the education spending example illustrates, they point to no particular policy consequences. Nor does Rawls buttress the difference principle when he represents it as expressing "the principle of fraternity"—that is, "the idea of not wanting to have greater advantages" unless they also benefit "others who are less well off."[29] Although Rawls calls this a "natural meaning" of the term, he provides no source, and the example he chooses hardly supports it: he claims that family members "commonly do not wish to gain unless they can do so in ways that further the interests of the rest" (*Theory*, 90). Does anyone know a family like

27. On the logical impossibility of eliminating or compensating for all "undeserved" claims as Rawls wishes, so that the very ground of "desert" would somehow be deserved, see Michael Zuckert, "Justice Deserted"; Nozick, *Anarchy, State, and Utopia*, 225–26. See also, on the misunderstanding that underlies Rawls's inference "that because the distribution of talents is morally arbitrary, special rewards for their possession and use are improper" (unless they are compensated for), Yack, *Problems of a Political Animal*, 256–59.

28. Rawls added the qualification "in some respects" in the revised edition of *Theory* (here and on p. 156), apparently hoping to deflect some of the criticism this proposition had received. It hardly resolves the contradiction with his earlier critique of utilitarianism. (Similarly, Rawls omits from the revised edition his original account of justice as fairness as entailing an agreement "to share one another's fate" [*Theory* 1st ed., 102; cf. *Theory*, 88], perhaps recognizing that people can never literally share one another's fate, but thereby further undercutting the rationale for the difference principle.)

29. In a later and starker formulation, Rawls explains that under the difference principle, "*however willing people are to work* to earn . . . greater shares of output, existing inequalities must contribute effectively to the benefit of the least advantaged. Otherwise the inequalities are not permissible" (*JF*, 64 [emphasis added]).

this: one in which Dad lacks interest in winning a tennis tournament unless there's a cash prize he can spend on the kids, and Junior avoids doing well in school because he fears it will make Sis jealous?[30] (It sounds about as realistic as Rawls's previous account of a rational plan of life as enabling one to fulfill all his desires "without interference.")

In any event, it is doubtful that the family, constituted by natural bonds of affection, represents an adequate model for conceiving political society. (Just as Aristotle warns against blurring the difference between the two, Locke's case for the doctrine of natural freedom and equality specifically rests on a denial that the two forms of association can be equated.)[31] Rawls himself acknowledges that "it is unrealistic to expect" "ties of sentiment and feeling" among citizens comparable to those within a family. Nonetheless, he maintains that if "the ideal of fraternity . . . is interpreted as incorporating the requirements of the difference principle," it is "not impracticable" but is rather "a perfectly feasible standard" (*Theory*, 90–91). But this argument is circular: it amounts to saying that if we agree to identify the meaning of fraternity with the dictates of the difference principle, then the difference principle embodies the ideal of fraternity.

In fact, even the principle of "fair equality of opportunity," the moral foundation of Woodrow Wilson's New Freedom and the subsequent New Deal and War on Poverty, is far from an adequate guide to public policy. Although most Americans agree that government should take broad steps to assist individuals coming from disadvantaged backgrounds to rise in accordance with their natural talents and motivation—both as a matter of justice and for the sake of the nation's good—common sense recognizes, as Rawls himself acknowledges, that this principle can never be fully achieved. Even if government were able somehow to compensate for all advantages that accrue to certain individuals from having wealthier parents, some children will inevitably benefit from having parents who are more loving or more talented (or simply from having two parents who remain married to one another). Beyond differences in upbringing, of course, each person's success and happiness in life are inevitably affected in an infinite variety of ways by sheer luck, in ways that far surpass the

---

30. Even if what Rawls meant was that nobody wants to gain at the expense of other family members, a glance at the scholarly literature on marital relations and sibling rivalry, or consideration of classic literary works portraying the rivalry of fathers and sons, should suffice to refute this account of the "typical" family. Cf. Nozick, *Anarchy, State, and Utopia,* 167, on how the implausibility of Rawls's difference principle when applied to the family casts doubt on its appropriateness for a broader society.

31. Aristotle *Politics* bk. 1, chap. 1; bk. 2, chaps. 2–4; Locke, *Two Treatises,* bk. 2, chaps. 6–7, and sec. 112.

influence of wealth or natural talent: some enjoy good health, others suffer debilitating illness or die at an early age; some are lucky in love, others aren't; some have the good fortune to be born in a free and prosperous country like the United States, others are practically doomed to misery from being born under wretchedly oppressive dictatorships in Zimbabwe or North Korea. While a polity like the American one can and does provide superior medical care to those residents who can't afford to pay for it, offers free education and a multitude of social services to its poorer citizens, and donates billions of dollars annually in foreign aid and contributions to international relief agencies (alongside private contributions to these ends), it cannot literally rid the world of poverty, disease, tyranny, civil war, and other forms of human suffering.

None of this means that America shouldn't continue doing what it can to alleviate these problems. But it does put the problem of justice in its proper perspective. Not only can the opportunities even of America's own citizens never fully be equalized, but at some point programs adopted in the name of equal opportunity prove to be either self-destructive (by undermining the motivation of their supposed beneficiaries to help themselves, damaging the nation's economic prosperity and hence reducing the resources available to the poor, weakening citizens' motivation to practice private charity, and/or subjecting the lives of everyone, not least the poor, to a morass of demoralizing bureaucratic regulation) or simply ineffectual. Although equality of opportunity (unlike Rawls's difference principle) has a broad intelligibility, when the term is used to signify something beyond legal equality of opportunity, or freedom from arbitrary discrimination, it is a slogan, not an attainable goal or therefore a meaningful guide to policy. In a liberal polity, citizens, through their elected representatives, decide how far they are willing to tax themselves to pay for programs to increase the opportunities of the less well-off, and how far such programs may be carried without infringing on the people's rights to liberty and the fruits of their legitimately acquired property, to say nothing of more pressing national needs such as defense. It is not evident how Rawls's principle of fair equality of opportunity would improve on this process.[32]

A Rawlsian may respond that even though the arbitrariness of nature and fortune can never fully be overcome, Rawls's fair-equality-of-opportunity doctrine at least encourages us to strive harder in that direction,

32. On the limitations of equality of opportunity as a principle of justice, cf. Wiggins, "Neo-Aristotelian Reflections," 502–4, as well as Williams, "Idea of Equality." The historical novelty of the doctrine of equality of opportunity, originated in the U.S. by Theodore Roosevelt and Herbert Croly (along with Woodrow Wilson), is noted by Harvey C. Mansfield, *Manliness*, 96–97.

thus promoting the quest for justice. However, to make this claim overlooks the threat to the *attainable* goal of securing people's equal natural rights, as specified in the Declaration of Independence (along with its corollary, the principle of *legal* equality of opportunity or nondiscrimination), that results from Rawls's blurring the differences among inequalities that arise from nature, political institutions, and just plain luck.

Rather than ground the assessment of particular political regimes on nature, as the Declaration does, Rawls maintains that what is unjust about "aristocratic and caste societies" is that their "basic structure . . . incorporates the arbitrariness found in nature" (*Theory,* 87–88). This argument is confused. No thoughtful observer from Aristotle to the present ever maintained that the fixed conventional inequalities found in so-called aristocracies, let alone caste societies, are derived from any natural differences between rulers and the ruled. To the contrary, what is unjust about such regimes is that they arbitrarily allocate privileges among individuals without regard to any demonstrable difference in desert. Similarly, the core liberal argument against discrimination on the basis of such attributes as race and religion is that these characteristics have no correlation with natural human capacities. By holding that inequalities in people's natural talents (and their fruits) are no less arbitrary than inequalities in the privileges and opportunities that nonliberal regimes allow them, Rawls is effectively saying that such purely artificial differences in treatment are no *more* arbitrary than those that result from people's natural talents and degrees of motivation. In this way Rawls weakens the case for challenging the justice of hereditary caste societies, since not even he believes that the effects of "the natural lottery in native assets" among human beings can be eliminated (*Theory,* 89). Rawls's renunciation of nature as a ground or standard of justice is not a promising route for liberalism.

I have dwelt on the problems inherent in Rawls's "fair equality of opportunity" mandate at what may seem a premature stage because Rawls never pursues it much beyond his initial statement in chapter 2 of *Theory;* he is more interested in elaborating his difference principle as well as the ostensible policy consequences of his first principle. At this point I pass over the discussion of "principles for individuals" in the last two sections of chapter 2, since it doesn't add significantly to Rawls's account of justice. I turn next to his derivation of the two principles from the original position in chapter 3.

CHAPTER 3

"Choosing" Principles of Justice
in the Original Position

I.

In the third chapter of *Theory*, Rawls elaborates his account of the original position and undertakes to demonstrate that the parties in that situation would choose his two principles over alternative conceptions of justice. He compares his use of the original position to the economist's practice of describing "a simplified situation . . . in which rational individuals . . . choose among various courses of action in view of their knowledge of the circumstances" (*Theory*, 102–3). But there is this distinction: while an economist tries to explain how markets operate "by assumptions about the actual tendencies" influencing human behavior, the original position incorporates "conditions which it is widely thought reasonable to impose on the choice of principles" to guarantee that the results are morally acceptable (*Theory*, 104–5).

Rawls surely understates the difference between designing a simplified model of human behavior to clarify the consequences of various situations and incentives in actual life and adopting such a model merely to impose whatever restraints we wish on human choices. The former sort of abstraction is a necessary tool of a predictive economic science, given the multitudinous circumstances that affect collective human behavior in the real world, just as natural scientists conduct controlled experiments to single out the effect of particular substances or operations. In each case provisional assumptions are needed to compensate for our lack of direct access to the causal relations under investigation. But it remains obscure why human beings should wish to have principles of justice chosen for them under simplified, highly abstract conditions, when the essence of moral reflection—as suggested by Sidgwick, Ross, and Aristotle—seems to demand the fullest attention to the particulars of human existence, direct acquaintance with which (through biographical, historical and comparative studies, judicial opinions and philosophic treatises, as well as reflection on our own experience) *is* available to us.[1]

Of course, in ordinary life we often rely on rules of thumb to simplify moral decision making (e.g., "don't lie"). But since in hard cases, and especially in dealing with justice, these commonsense rules sometimes conflict (how far should the precept of rewarding desert be followed as opposed to that of alleviating need?), we recognize the need to consider the particular circumstances before deciding which rule to follow. By contrast, Rawls wishes to exclude information from the very process of defining principles of justice.

To understand Rawls's thinking here it is helpful to consider his friend Brian Barry's account of his own enterprise in *Political Argument*, for which he acknowledges Rawls's early work as an inspiration. In reaction against the logical positivist T. D. Weldon's contention that correct political appraisals depend on "intensive study of the facts," which in Weldon's view explained away "the questions of traditional political philosophy," Barry preferred to treat political philosophy as based on "values such as freedom or equality" that have "incompatible" implications.[2] (In this respect, Barry's position appears to recapitulate the fact-value distinction that is central to the positivism he rejects.) Like Rawls, Barry aimed to combine analytical philosophy with "analytical politics," understood as "simplify[ing] the complex reality of a situation by picking out certain aspects of it and then building a model relating these aspects" as economists do.[3] This would considerably reduce the political philosopher's need to accumulate factual knowledge about politics and therefore his dependence on "writers on political institutions and statesmen" whom Weldon represented as final authorities. If successful, Barry's enterprise, like Rawls's, might restore political theorists to the position of influence they once enjoyed—without requiring them to undertake the sort of detailed empir-

---

1. Cf. Aristotle *NE* 1142a12–14, 1141b15–24, 1143b6–14.
2. Barry, *Political Argument*, xxiv, xxxv, xxxvi–xxxviii.
3. Ibid., 290–91.

ical and historical inquiry that thinkers such as Aristotle, Cicero, Machiavelli, Locke, Montesquieu, and Rousseau had pursued as a prelude to their writing. But like Rawls, Barry never demonstrates why such simplification is necessary or useful for understanding political life.

The closest historical precedent for Rawls's notion of the original position is the accounts of a pre- or nonpolitical "state of nature" given by such social-contract philosophers as Hobbes, Locke, and Rousseau, to which Rawls alluded in chapter 1. But those philosophers held such an abstraction from the everyday condition of life to be necessary because law, custom, and established government ordinarily conceal from us the fundamental reasons that make government essential, and thus they obscure the criteria by which the legitimacy of existing regimes should be measured. Hence Hobbes argues that since, in the absence of government, our most pressing need, and the precondition of any other good we may seek, would be security, the true criterion of political legitimacy is whether a particular government provides us with that protection without which life would be "solitary, poor, nasty, brutish, and short." In this regard Locke's decisive modification of Hobbes is to argue that, on the basis of Hobbes's own premises, we need not only to have our life, liberty, and property secured against the depredation of other private individuals but some institutionalized means of protection against arbitrary government itself. Rousseau, in turn, arguing that the very conflict of interests that makes government necessary among civilized human beings is a consequence of our socialization away from the truly natural, quasi-animal condition, lays down still stricter criteria of political legitimacy, demanding that government not only protect our rights but also give us some simulacrum of the natural autonomy without which human life, however secure, would be miserable.

This is not the place to address the controversy among these thinkers, let alone ask whether it even makes sense, contrary to Aristotle, to define the natural human condition as a nonpolitical one that we are unlikely to encounter in actual life. What bears emphasis here is that in none of these cases was the state of nature a free construct, reflecting the conditions a given philosopher happened to think it reasonable to impose on the choice of governmental institutions. If that is all the description of a nonpolitical condition entailed, who would care about it or think it should be taken into account in our political deliberations? Rather, the state of nature is intended to be just that: an account of what life would be like in the absence of government (and in Rousseau's case, of society), *given* human nature. Each philosopher's account of it is, in Hobbes's phrase, an "inference made from the passions" of man as we know him (or, as Rousseau would put it, from the fundamental motions of the human heart), and we are invited to confirm its validity by looking into ourselves as well as observing the behavior of our fellows.[4]

By contrast with the aforementioned philosophers, Rawls, who seems to have no place for nature in his system other than as a source of "arbitrariness" that must be compensated for,[5] believes he can freely construct the original position in whatever way he deems morally acceptable, knowing in advance the consequences he wants to derive from it. (In his words, "we want to define the original position so that we get the desired solution" [*Theory*, 122].) He does begin his construction on a note of realism, however, borrowing from Hume an account of the "normal conditions" that both require and facilitate human cooperation, entailing "a conflict as well as an identity of interests." Thus, each person is better off under a scheme of social cooperation than if he had to live on his own, but each aims to maximize his own share of the resultant benefits (*Theory*, 109). (Hume, however, is describing the actual circumstances of human life, not a hypothetical original position.)[6]

Rawls then describes the "objective" and "subjective circumstances" of the original position. The former include the stipulations that "many individuals coexist . . . on a definite geographical territory," that they have "roughly similar . . . physical and mental powers" such that none can "dominate" the others, all are "vulnerable to attack," and that there is a "moderate scarcity" of resources. The subjective circumstances include people's having "roughly similar needs and interests" but also diverse "conceptions of the good," associated with "a diversity of philosophical and religious belief, and of political and social doctrines" (*Theory*, 109–10).

Rawls claims to make "no restrictive assumptions about the parties' conceptions of the good except that they are rational long-term plans." (As in

4. See Hobbes, *Leviathan*, chap. 13, par. 10; introduction, pars. 3–4.

5. I leave aside Rawls's rhetorical references in *Theory*, chapter 9 and later writings to people's "nature as free and equal moral persons," since they are ungrounded in any substantive analysis of human nature. In *PL* (18–19) Rawls will acknowledge having formulated his "idea of the person" to "go with" a conception of society ostensibly derived from the democratic tradition: in other words, instead of designing the just society to fit human nature, he conceives human beings to fit his notion of justice, in the manner of Procrustes.

6. In the texts to which Rawls alludes, Hume simply refers to the fact that justice is necessary because of people's selfishness and the natural scarcity of goods in comparison with human wants and possible because of their capacity for moderation and (limited) generosity; he makes no reference to "distributing" the benefits of social cooperation, as if he agreed with Rawls that it is up to us to design the rules of society de novo (see *Enquiry Concerning the Principles of Morals*, bk. 3, chap. 1, 188; *Treatise of Human Nature*, bk. 3, pt. 2, sec. 2, 494–95).

his previous account of rationality, Rawls uses the term solely in an instrumental sense: a rational person has "a coherent set of preferences," ranks alternative choices by how well they serve his aims, and "follows the plan which will satisfy more of his desires" and has the greater likelihood of success [*Theory*, 124].) Thus besides conflicts of personal interest, the parties to the original position may have "spiritual ideals" as "irreconcilably opposed" as those of "saints and heroes." However, so as not to make the principles of justice "depend upon strong assumptions," Rawls postulates that the parties are mutually disinterested (*Theory*, 109–12). That is, in order to show that the principles result from people's rationally pursuing their individual goals or interests, Rawls wants to avoid appearing to stack the deck by assuming that the parties are already motivated by a concern for justice.[7] Additionally, Rawls stipulates that being rational, the choosing parties do "not suffer from envy," so long as the differences between their fortunes and those of others "do not exceed certain limits" or result from injustice or uncompensated "chance" (*Theory*, 124). (These qualifications effectively undermine the stipulation, for what envious person doesn't believe that the reason for his lesser fortune is injustice or arbitrary chance?)[8]

The most remarkable feature of Rawls's original position is the veil of ignorance, which was briefly introduced in chapter 1. To guarantee that the original position generates just principles, Rawls explains, "we must nullify the effects of specific contingencies which put men at odds and tempt them to exploit social and natural circumstances" to favor their own interests. Hence the parties in the original position must be prevented from knowing how the alternatives they choose among will affect their particular cases. Thus Rawls specifies that no one knows his social or economic class, his natural capacities, his view of the good or plan of life, or "the special features of his psychology such as his aversion to risk." Nor do the parties know "the particular circumstances of their own society," including its economic or political situation or "level of civilization and culture." They don't even know what generation they belong to (*Theory*, 118). (Note that these stipulations effectively nullify the description of the parties to the original position as having diverse and partly conflicting interests as well as a diversity of religious and moral beliefs: if they are unaware of their particular interests and beliefs, the effect is no different

7. In *PL*, as discussed in chapter 10 below, Rawls alters this condition—and does stack the deck—by adding that the parties are equally motivated by a desire to express their "moral power" of acting justly.

8. I address Rawls's response to "the problem of envy" thematically in chapter 9 below.

from their all having the same ones).[9] The parties' choice is to be guided solely by their knowledge of "the general facts about human society," including "political affairs and the principles of economic theory . . . the basis of social organization and the laws of human psychology" (*Theory,* 119). In addition, since the parties lack knowledge of their conceptions of the good, Rawls postulates that they accept the notion of primary social goods that he introduced in explaining the difference principle and that they consequently prefer more rather than less of such goods as "rights, liberties, and opportunities, and income and wealth" (*Theory,* 79, 123). Even though "it may turn out, once the veil of ignorance is removed, that some of them for religious or other reasons may not, in fact, want more of these goods," Rawls judges it rational "from the standpoint of the original position . . . to suppose that they do want a larger share, since in any case they are not compelled to accept more if they do not wish to" (*Theory,* 123).

Rawls believes that "the veil of ignorance is so natural" that many others must have thought of it (*Theory,* 118n). But it isn't difficult to grasp why none of the great social-contract philosophers adopted such a device. As I have observed, their goal was to uncover the most powerful motives that are present in human nature so as to provide a firm and reliable criterion of legitimate government. Far from wanting to limit the knowledge either of their readers or of the parties they depicted as agreeing to withdraw from the state of nature by establishing government, they sought to base political choices on the fullest awareness of the essential facts of human and political life.[10] Although their accounts of the state of nature, like Rawls's original position, serve to simplify the decision-making problem, these philosophers show us why the perspective of that condition should be decisive for us, without asking us to forget anything we know.

Because they were seeking to ground their political doctrines on nature, rather than concoct an artificial situation that would generate principles they found intuitively appealing, the modern social-contract philosophers

---

9. In fact, Rawls emphasizes how the original position situation generates "unanimity" (*Theory,* 121, 232–33, 494–95). See also note 52 below.

10. Nor is the veil "implicit" as Rawls maintains in Kant's categorical imperative, which requires us to test a possible moral maxim by its consequences "if it were a universal law of nature" (*Theory,* 118n): Kant simply asks us to imagine whether a world governed by the maxim would be a satisfactory one, without our having to pretend that we have somehow forgotten our identities (Kant, *Foundations of the Metaphysics of Morals,* pt. 2, 38 [Akad. ed. 421]).

The contrast between Rawls's use of the social contract and its use by Hobbes, Locke, and their successors has been noted by several other commentators. See Anderson, "Antipolitical Philosophy," 43; Allan Bloom, "Justice: John Rawls vs. the Tradition of Political Philosophy," 651–53; Leon Craig, "*Contra* Contract".

had no need to adopt the arbitrary motivational assumptions that Rawls makes about the parties to the original position. Hobbes, for instance, indeed represents human beings in the state of nature as roughly equal in their physical and mental powers, as well as vulnerable to attack, as Rawls does. But Hobbes's assumption is grounded in certain essential truths about human nature: the limitlessness of our wants, which creates a conflict of interest among us; and the fact that no matter how much stronger or smarter some may be than others, all are naturally equal in the practically most decisive respect, vulnerability to being killed by anyone else.[11] These facts give us the strongest incentive to agree in our own lives to regard ourselves as bound to obey any government that provides us with the security that is our utmost need. Nor, of course, did Hobbes or his successors need to make any assumptions about people's liability in the state of nature to feelings of envy or their holding diverse "political and social doctrines": if the one thing most needful for our enjoying any other earthly good is security, it is eminently rational to subordinate one's freedom to act on what Hobbes calls "private opinions" for the sake of stable government. By contrast, despite the cursory nod to realism contained in Rawls's reference to the parties' vulnerability in the original position, he never tells us how vulnerable they are or *why* they are vulnerable. (Nor do we learn the extent of the "moderate scarcity of resources" that is said to exist.) As a consequence, Rawls, unlike Hobbes, provides no criterion for assessing the urgency of the agreement that the parties to the original position are to arrive at.[12] In sum, Rawls does not seem to take the "objective circumstances" of the original position all that seriously.

Beyond the arbitrariness of Rawls's assumptions about the parties' circumstances, motivation, and knowledge, these assumptions embody numerous inconsistencies that make it difficult to conceive how they could serve as a basis for deliberation. To begin with, it is hard to see how any genuine complementarity of needs and interests, or "mutually advantageous cooperation," could exist among human beings whose aims were "irreconcilably opposed." Nor can we imagine how persons whose aims in life might turn out to be "wealth, position, and influence, and the accolades of social prestige," as the parties to the original position must allow

---

11. See Hobbes, *Leviathan*, chap. 13; similarly, Locke, *Two Treatises*, bk. 2, chap. 9.

12. As Leon Craig puts it, "Hobbes threatens you with death" if you do not agree to obey a sovereign capable of rescuing humanity from the state of nature, "Rawls threatens to call you unjust" ("Traditional Political Philosophy and John Rawls's Theory of Justice," 39). The abstractness of Rawls's account of the original position renders his ostensible derivation of the difference principle from it vulnerable to Nozick's witty critique (*Anarchy, State, and Utopia*, 183–229).

(*Theory*, 111), could be immune to envy, since these aims are essentially relative ones. If the parties to the original position are designing principles for a society whose members may be envious, must they not take that possibility into account? Conversely, if the conceptions of the good that the principles allow human beings to pursue include those of saints and heroes, isn't the assumption of mutual disinterest in the original position an unrealistic one? Isn't it inherent in the life of a saint or hero to take a considerable interest in how his fellows live? Furthermore, how can Rawls assume that would-be saints and heroes would choose a society that was organized to maximize people's share of primary goods such as personal freedom and wealth? If one aspires to live in a society where holiness or heroism are likely to flourish, the maximization of wealth, or of freedom to live as one likes, is more likely a detriment, and it is hardly a reply to say that the individual can always forego them if he chooses.[13] Nor is Rawls's notion of rationality at all clear: why is it rational to seek to satisfy the greatest number of one's desires, rather than to emphasize a single aim that one regards as most important?

In addition to the foregoing problems, several aspects of the veil of ignorance appear superfluous, given Rawls's description of the parties to the original position. If their powers are roughly equal, why must they be kept ignorant of their particular abilities, since, as in Hobbes's or Locke's state of nature, no one is in a position to impose his wishes on his fellows anyway? Why should they be unaware of the circumstances of their society, especially considering that Rawls himself will subsequently hold that the ordering of his two principles presupposes that the society adopting them has reached a certain level of economic and cultural development?

Still greater difficulties emerge when one tries to imagine the parties actually reasoning under the veil. Rawls himself anticipates the objections that "the exclusion of nearly all particular information" makes the original position difficult to conceive and that "the veil of ignorance is irrational," since it would seem that "principles should be chosen in the light of all the

13. Later, in his discussion of justice between generations, as I note in chapter 5 below, Rawls himself will observe that "beyond some point" great wealth "is more likely to be a positive hindrance" to living well (*Theory*, 258). But his second principle contradicts this observation by organizing society on the premise that a rational individual prefers more rather than less of the primary goods including wealth. Similarly, in *JF* (63–64, 159), Rawls denies that his account of justice requires "continual economic growth over generations to maximize . . . the expectations of the least advantaged," citing "Mill's idea of a society in a just stationary state where (real) capital accumulation may cease." But he offers no criterion for determining when that state has been attained. And to the extent he retreats from the aim of maximizing primary goods, Rawls undermines the pretense that the choice of principles in the original position is based on a rational calculation of one's own good made under a veil of ignorance. If the absolute sum of wealth possessed by the least advantaged doesn't matter beyond some point, why should they care so greatly about their relative shares?

knowledge available" (*Theory*, 119–20). His now-familiar answer to the latter objection—that "simplifications" are needed "to have any theory at all" (*Theory*, 120)—seems clearly to make the methodological tail wag the substantive dog: if the price of having a theory of justice is to exclude highly relevant information, what's the value of substituting such a theory for our considered judgments in particular cases? As for Rawls's reply to the former objection—that we "can at any time . . . simulate the deliberations of this hypothetical situation, simply by reasoning in accordance with the appropriate restrictions" (*Theory*, 119)—what is in question is precisely whether it is possible for us to reason that way at all.

Consider: how can human beings have acquired any general knowledge, of the sort the parties in the original position are to employ, without deriving it from the study of particulars (awareness of which they are denied)? One cannot, for instance, have learned any "laws of human psychology" while remaining entirely ignorant of one's own psychology. But how, having derived one's knowledge from the awareness of particulars, could one forget the latter in order to simulate the deliberations of the original position? One might pretend or deceive oneself into believing that he had forgotten his particular beliefs and characteristics, but this wouldn't have the radically neutralizing effects Rawls wants. Moreover, even if one could somehow engage in this kind of temporary memory lapse, it is doubtful that one would have any meaningful general knowledge left with which to deliberate. Given the infinite variability and complexity of human affairs, it is not evident that there are significant and meaningful universal laws that determine human conduct in the way that the laws of physics govern purely material things. (At best, it is likely that political and social science can typically supply us only with probabilistic laws, or maxims, that apply "most of the time"; whether and how far they apply to any given situation will depend on a judgment of particular circumstances.[14]) Indeed, how, without a knowledge of particulars, would one even know to what things one's general knowledge referred?[15] (I invite any reader who believes these objections can be overcome to try reasoning in accordance with the veil of

14. Again, consider Aristotle's warning against seeking the same precision in the study of politics or ethics as in geometry (*NE* 1094b11ff). See also Herbert J. Storing, ed., *Essays on the Scientific Study of Politics;* Peter Winch, *The Idea of a Social Science and Its Relation to Philosophy,* 91–94; and James W. Ceaser, *Liberal Democracy and Political Science,* chap. 7.

15. The inseparability of general from particular knowledge thus constitutes a decisive objection to Rawls's subsequent "Kantian interpretation" of the original position, according to which the veil of ignorance "deprives the persons in the original position of the knowledge that would enable them to choose heteronomous principles," so that they "arrive at their choice together as free and rational persons knowing only that those circumstances obtain which give rise to the need for principles of justice" (*Theory,* 222).

ignorance, being careful to forget everything he knows about himself and his beliefs, and see what conclusions he comes up with.[16])

Revealingly, Rawls himself concedes only a few pages later that "when we try to simulate the original position in everyday life, . . . we will presumably find that our deliberations and judgments are influenced by our special inclinations and attitudes," which "it will prove difficult to correct for." Yet he denies that any of this affects the determination of the decision that the parties in the original position would arrive at. "It is another question," Rawls believes, "how well human beings can assume this role in regulating their practical actions" (*Theory*, 127). But if it is difficult or impossible to conduct ourselves in moral argument as the constraints of the original position require, how can it be any easier to simulate the reasoning in the original position?[17]

As a final aspect of the incoherence of the veil, consider the impossibility of squaring Rawls's proviso that the parties are ignorant of their conceptions of the good with his portraying them as pursuing various and conflicting conceptions of the good. What can it mean to know that one has a conception of the good without knowing what it is? How could one even explain to someone who lacked any conscious conception of the good what such a conception would be like? Moreover, as for the index of primary goods that Rawls wishes to substitute for people's conceptions of their good as a basis for deliberation in the original position, how can anyone be imagined to deliberate over their allocation when the description of these goods has been left almost entirely general and abstract ("rights and liberties, powers and opportunities, income and wealth")? To decide rationally how to allocate such goods, don't we (or the parties in the orig-

16. Some of the foregoing difficulties are noted in Schaar, "Reflections on Rawls' *Theory*," 149; B. Parekh, "Reflections on Rawls' *Theory of Justice*," 480–81; Robert Paul Wolff, *Understanding Rawls*, 131–32; and Benjamin Barber, "Justifying Justice," 295. In response to Barber's critique, which notes the impossibility of conceiving human beings who desire "primary goods" without knowing what particular things they want, Rawls explained that Barber had taken the original position "too literally" and insisted that any such psychological impossibility "would not affect" the use of the original position as a device for selecting principles of justice. ("Comments," 7). Rawls made no attempt to repair these problems in his subsequent writings, making one wonder how seriously he took the original position as a ground of his principles.

17. In *PL* (273–74) Rawls acknowledges that there is "no practicable way actually to carry out" the deliberative process he attributes to the original position, but he proceeds on the following page to repeat his claim that we can "enter" the original position "at any moment simply by conducting our moral reasoning about first principles in accordance with the stipulated procedural constraints." He also acknowledges the impossibility of "know[ing] what we would have been like had we not belonged to" a particular society (*PL*, 276), but he does not consider the implications of this concession for the possibility of reasoning under the veil of ignorance.

inal position) need more information: a right to do what? A power or opportunity for what? Is there a single substance called "power" or "opportunity" that we can imagine being divided up in some manner or other?[18] (When all is said and done, it appears that aside from liberty, "income and wealth" are the only substantive goods left on the list, implying a distinctly materialistic bias in Rawls's conception of the good.)[19]

III.

In the sequel to his account of the circumstances of the original position, Rawls professes to demonstrate that the two principles would be chosen in that situation over utilitarianism. Even given this limited range of alternatives, however, I shall observe that the decision Rawls attributes to the parties doesn't follow from the account he has given of their situation. Rather, the selection depends on certain ad hoc modifications Rawls makes to his description of the parties' psychology and the circumstances of the society

18. In *PL* (181, 291) Rawls elaborates the list of primary goods to include "basic rights and liberties," "freedom of movement and free choice of occupation against a background of diverse opportunities," and "powers and prerogatives of offices and positions of responsibility in the political institutions of the basic structure," along with income and wealth and "the social bases of self-respect." In turn, the "equal basic liberties" cover "freedom of thought and liberty of conscience, the political liberties and freedom of association," "the liberty and integrity of the person," and "the rule of law." These categories are further described in *JF*, 58–59. But the grab-bag nature of these lists of goods still leaves it hard to discern any way of choosing among them, aside from the ostensible "priority" of liberty over other goods.

Although Hobbes represents power as a common denominator among people's various private goals, he never pretends that it can be allocated among individuals in the manner Rawls suggests, but simply argues the necessity that authoritative power be concentrated in a sovereign capable of providing all individuals with security (*Leviathan*, chap. 11, par. 2; chap. 17, par. 13).

19. As Barber observes, since "Rawls ultimately rests his entire technical case" for interpersonal comparisons of well-being "on wealth and income alone . . . comparability has been won only by gutting the category primary good and leaving a shell called income behind" ("Justifying Justice," 303). On the secularist, materialistic bias of the original position, see also Craig, "*Contra* Contract," 73–74, 77; Wolff, *Understanding Rawls*, 75. Rawls subsequently responds to the charge that the representation of wealth as a primary good gives the original position a materialistic bias by distinguishing between the parties' desire for wealth and the desire to be wealthy, i.e., to have "far more wealth than the average person," which he postulates they do not seek ("Fairness to Goodness," *CP*, 272–73). But since the definition of wealth in a given society will vary with that society's resources, doesn't the desire to maximize one's own wealth entail wanting to have more than others? And doesn't the focus of the difference principle on redistributing wealth to the less advantaged teach those influenced by it that wealth is a more "objective" or real good than other aspects of our respective conceptions of the good?

for which they are choosing (in violation of the veil of ignorance) to engender his desired outcome.[20]

Rawls begins his account of the reasoning leading to the two principles by citing some "intuitive" considerations favoring them. Since, given the veil, there is no way for any of the parties to win special advantages, Rawls argues, the most reasonable opening move is for each to favor a principle requiring an equal distribution of all primary goods. But for the sake of "economic efficiency and the requirements of organization and technology," he immediately adds, it makes sense to modify the initial benchmark of equality to allow "inequalities in income and wealth, and differences in authority and degrees of responsibility, that work to make everyone better off." He recognizes, in other words, that people ordinarily need incentives of personal economic gain to motivate them to work and that the operation of any organized enterprise necessitates some sort of hierarchy. Thus, Rawls concludes that such inequalities should be allowed, so long as they are "consistent with equal liberty and fair opportunity" (*Theory*, 130–31).

The way in which Rawls has formulated the issue here, I submit, begs all the interesting questions. It is practically tautological to assert that if inequalities make everyone better off, people should accept them. Nor does any serious thinker maintain the possibility of a society without any economic inequality or organizational hierarchy. What is really at issue in the debate over inequality, however, is *how far* differences in wealth and authority, essential though they are to a society's overall well-being (and therefore to promoting the security and standard of living of the poor along with everyone else), are compatible with people's liberty and happiness. If thinkers as diverse as Plato, Rousseau, and some Antifederalist writers are correct, excessive inequalities in wealth undermine the sense of fraternity on which the people's loyalty and civic harmony depend.[21] If Rousseau is right, as I noted in chapter 2, even the encouragement of the development of individual talents in modern regimes weakens patriotism and civic virtue and produces an unhealthy private dependence of some citizens on others.[22] On the other hand, if the arguments of Locke, Mon-

---

20. Citing these "ad hoc adjustments," Wolff remarks that the original "bargaining game" Rawls purported to portray as occurring in the original position had to be "called on account of ignorance" (*Understanding Rawls*, 71, 119).

21. See Plato *Laws* 744d–745b; Rousseau, *Discourse on Political Economy*, in *"On the Social Contract" with "Geneva Manuscript" and "Political Economy,"* 221–22; "Centinel," letter #1, 16, and "Federal Farmer," letter #5, 60–62, in Herbert J. Storing, ed., *The Antifederalist*.

22. See Rousseau's *First Discourse* (*Discourse on the Sciences and Arts*) and *Letter to M. D'Alembert on the Theater* (trans. by Allan Bloom under the title *Politics and the Arts*); also Melancton Smith's warning in the debate of the New York Ratifying Convention against the threat of domination by the natural aristocracy under the Constitution, in Storing, ed., *Antifederalist*, speech of June 21, 1788, 340–41.

tesquieu, Hume, and the authors of *The Federalist* are sound, the unlimited opportunity for the acquisition of wealth by honest means not only improves everyone's material lot but also channels people's spiritual energies away from the destructive path of religious fanaticism and civic faction in the direction of a peaceful and tolerant political life, as well as the benefits of enlightenment.[23]

In chapter 5, Rawls himself stresses the need for (at least temporary) redistributive taxation to limit economic inequality. But nowhere does he acknowledge the tension between wealth maximization and civic or familial virtue as societal goals. Since this issue is left entirely open, it cannot be said that Rawls's "intuitive" argument for his second principle, as thus far described, settles any substantive point. Ordaining that inequalities should be accepted if they make everyone better off, without considering how far different kinds and degrees of inequality actually have that effect, offers no meaningful guidance.

Rawls next suggests that the parties to the original position would be likely to arrange the two principles in serial order—that is, one that gives priority to equal liberty and fair opportunity over allowable social and economic inequalities. Here again, instead of tracing out the parties' reasoning, Rawls simply provides his "intuitive idea" of it. Since the parties view themselves as free persons having "fundamental aims and interests" for the sake of which they "make claims . . . concerning the design of the basic structure of society," but do not know (thanks to the veil) the "particular forms" their interests take, he asserts, they must secure these interests (such as "the religious interest") by ranking the first principle, mandating equal liberty, ahead of the second. Rawls doesn't directly explain how we can know that they would want to impose this ranking, but he seeks to justify it by articulating "the notion of a free person." He describes free individuals as people "who do not think of themselves as inevitably bound to . . . the pursuit of any particular complex of fundamental interests," but who instead "give first priority" to preserving their liberty to "revise and alter their final ends." It follows according to Rawls that they will choose his two principles over utilitarianism to guarantee "their highest-order interest as free persons" (*Theory*, 131–32).

Once again Rawls's argument is tautological. It amounts to saying that people who prefer freedom to other goods will also prefer to be governed by principles that elevate freedom over other goods. Additionally, we

---

23. See Locke, *Two Treatises*, bk. 2, chap. 5, sec. 34 (the distinction between the "industrious and rational" and the "quarrelsome and contentious"); Montesquieu, *Spirit of the Laws*, bk. 20, chaps. 1–2; bk. 21, chap. 20; Hume, "Of Commerce" and "On the Populousness of Ancient Nations," in *Essays Moral, Political, and Literary*, 258–62 and 416–21.

wonder whether this account of the relation between people's freedom and their "final ends" is at all coherent or psychologically intelligible. If people's first priority is to retain the right to revise their final ends whenever they choose, it appears that *no* end is ever meaningfully final. In what sense can we speak of such individuals' expressing "devotion" to their ends (*Theory*, 132), as opposed to being devoted to their right to revise them? Doesn't devotion to an end, a cause, or another human being entail committing oneself not to desert them? Despite Rawls's pretense of making the deliberations in the original position independent of any particular conception of the good, hasn't he actually presupposed a particular, highly questionable view of the good without submitting it to critical assessment?[24]

The problem of the inherent bias of the way Rawls constructs the original position will dog his enterprise to the end. In the last section of *Theory* (507), Rawls will disclaim holding that "the family of conceptions it draws on is ethically neutral," choosing to "simply leave aside" this problem. Similarly, in *PL* (184–85) he asserts "that justice as fairness is fair to conceptions of the good . . . even though some conceptions are judged not permissible and all conceptions do not have the same chance to flourish" under it. And in *JF* (154), Rawls concedes that his procedure may not be neutral toward various conceptions of the good, since such neutrality is "impracticable," but he still insists that it is not "arbitrarily biased" against them— for whatever satisfaction that may provide to those whose favored views of the good "die out" under his system.

The curious notion of being "fair" to a conception of the good, as if it had a disembodied existence of its own, exemplifies the abstractness of Rawls's approach. Although Rawls sometimes acknowledges the imprecision of that terminology, explaining that he means "fairness to moral persons with a capacity for adopting" conceptions of the good (*CP*, 284; *PL* 184–85), his customary usage is not a mere slip, but it suggests the difficulty in his attempt to demonstrate that justice mandates a quasi-impartial treatment of various conceptions of the good, contrary to our ordinary understanding of that virtue. Is it really unjust to organize society so as to encourage worthier ways of life over less worthy ones? If what is in question is the initial ordering of society—before its members' "choosing" particular ways of life or conceptions of the good—in what sense can one be said to treat any of those members "unjustly" by encouraging them to pursue some ways of life rather than others?

24. See, on this point, Michael Sandel, *Liberalism and the Limits of Justice*, 19–22, 54–59, 177–83; Thomas Nagel, "Rawls on Justice," 7–10. I address Rawls's response to Sandel in *PL* in chapter 10 below.

Beyond this problem, the two principles uphold the priority of liberty only in a limited and conditional way, as we learn from the following paragraph, wherein Rawls explains that "the priority of liberty means that *whenever the basic liberties can be effectively established,* a lesser or an unequal liberty cannot be exchanged for an improvement in economic well-being," while when "social circumstances do not allow the effective establishment of these basic rights," they may be restricted "to prepare the way" for the ultimate elimination of such restrictions. Hence, "in adopting the serial order of the two principles, the parties [in the original position] are assuming that the conditions of their society . . . admit the effective realization of the equal liberties" (*Theory,* 132 [emphasis added]).

This assumption is the first of several breaks that Rawls allows to pierce the veil of ignorance. Rawls does not explain why the parties to the original position should be allowed to make this particular assumption about their society but not others. At the same time we note that the conditionality of the priority of liberty is a point on which Rawls agrees with the utilitarian thinker John Stuart Mill, who in *On Liberty* holds that his doctrine of liberty properly applies only to nations that have advanced sufficiently in culture to be "capable of being improved by free and equal discussion."[25] We wonder therefore whether Rawls's doctrine truly gives any more primacy to liberty than Mill's does.[26]

Rawls later elaborates on the conditionality of the priority of liberty by saying that "the equal liberties can be denied only when it is necessary to change the quality of civilization so that in due course everyone can enjoy these freedoms" (*Theory,* 475). He doesn't explain how this process would take place, other than to observe that actualizing the equal liberties may require "certain social conditions" and the fulfillment of "material wants" (*Theory,* 476). While it is plausible that a workable system of constitutional government presupposes a certain material base as well as such social conditions as a sense of national unity, Rawls ought to have distinguished those liberties it is reasonable to expect from any legitimate government (e.g., respect for property rights, freedom from arbitrary imprisonment or execution) from those that may be less universal in application. (It is precisely because of their universal applicability as well as their fundamental

25. Mill, *On Liberty,* "Introductory," 96–97.
26. Cf. *Theory,* 185, where Rawls judges Mill's arguments in favor of liberty to be inferior to his two principles because they depend on such conditional assumptions as "a certain similarity among individuals." As Barber notes, depending on where Rawls's threshold for the priority of liberty is set, "even Marx might be comfortable" with the result ("Justifying Justice," 303n). Rawls moves further in this direction, as will be noted in chapter 10 below, in *PL* and *JF* (see also Barry, *Political Argument,* xlii–xliii).

character that the philosophic founders of liberalism, Hobbes, Locke, and Montesquieu, distinguished the former rights as "natural.") As things stand, Rawls's open-endedness on the suspension of liberty has the unfortunate effect of buttressing the most common alibi given by despots throughout much of the world over the past century for denying their subjects any semblance of liberty.[27]

In the immediate sequel in chapter 3 Rawls further modifies his account of the original position to show that the two principles would be chosen therein. He suggests viewing those principles as "the maximin solution to the problem of social justice," meaning those one would choose "for the design of a society in which his enemy is to assign him his place."[28] Just after denying that the parties in the original position "assume that their initial place in society is decided by a malevolent opponent," Rawls reiterates that the two principles "would be chosen if the parties were forced to protect themselves against such a contingency," and expresses the hope that he has described the original position so as to embody the "special features" that make it rational to adopt the "conservative attitude" expressed by the maximin rule (*Theory*, 132–33). The three reasons favoring this attitude are (1) the fact that the veil of ignorance "excludes all knowledge of likelihoods"; (2) the assumption that the two principles guarantee everyone "a satisfactory minimum," such that there is "little reason for trying to do better" at the risk of winding up with a worse outcome; and (3) the assumption "that other conceptions of justice may lead to institutions that the parties would find intolerable," so that "it seems unwise, if not irrational . . . to take a chance" on them in place of the secure guarantees offered by the two principles (*Theory*, 134–35).

Far from reflecting the original position as Rawls previously described it, each of these contentions derives from ad hoc assumptions he has inserted that violate the supposed strictures of the veil of ignorance. Since the parties to the original position were said to possess general knowledge of political and economic theory, even while remaining ignorant of the circumstances of their particular society, it follows that they would have a "knowledge of likelihoods"—that is, of the probability that various social

27. For a recent illustration, consider the justification offered by Mark Rosenzweig, reference director for the Center of Marxist Studies and board member of the American Library Association, for the Castro regime's jailing of dissident librarians for terms of up to twenty-six years, for the crime of trying to operate independent libraries: "We cannot presume that all countries are capable of the same level of intellectual freedom that we have in the U.S." (quoted in Mary Anastasia O'Grady, "Cuba's Jailed Librarians Get No Succor from the ALA."

28. In *JF* (43n, 96–97), Rawls describes the maximin rule as decisive only in supporting the first principle, not the second.

consequences would follow from a given set of choices.[29] Nor does Rawls offer any reason for supposing that the two principles guarantee "a satisfactory minimum" or that other views of justice would generate unacceptable consequences. (To support the maximin rule, Rawls groundlessly assumes that the parties have "a conception of the good" such that they have little interest in gains beyond the "minimum stipend" that the rule guarantees [*Theory*, 134–35]—an assumption that violates not only the parties' ignorance of their conceptions of the good but also the motivational assumption underlying the difference principle that the prospect of earning larger gains will cause people to work harder, thus benefiting the less advantaged as well.)[30] In sum, there is no reason to think that decisions made under a veil of ignorance give more support to Rawls's principles than to any other view of justice. While Rawls might easily have dispensed with his rigmarole about the maximin rule and simply recommended the two principles as a safer bet than the utilitarian alternative, by his acknowledgment there is nothing inherently more rational about adopting such a conservative attitude over a riskier one.[31]

Rawls then adds yet another assumption to the parties' deliberations in the original position. In response to the objection that the difference principle seems arbitrarily to make "the justice of large increases or decreases in the expectations of the more advantaged . . . depend upon small changes in the prospects of those worst off," he explains that that principle assumes "a certain theory of social institutions." To wit, it presupposes "that in a competitive economy . . . with an open class system excessive inequalities will not be the rule," and "given the distribution of natural assets and the laws of motivation, great disparities will not long persist" (*Theory*, 136–37). Hence we need not fear that some people will get away with enjoying large gains while benefiting their less successful fellows in only minute ways.

Here again, Rawls has asserted as one of "the general facts of economics and psychology" (*Theory*, 137) a premise that is either tautological or highly debatable and therefore seems a dubious foundation for the reasoning that is to yield principles of justice. On the one hand, in the absence of any criterion of excessiveness, we cannot assess Rawls's claim about the absence of excessive inequalities in a just society. By historical standards, a country like the contemporary United States clearly enjoys a competitive economy and a fluid social hierarchy, without ever having been consciously shaped

29. Cf. David Lyons, "Nature and Soundness of the Contract and Coherence Arguments," 161–62; Wolff, *Understanding Rawls*, 163–64.

30. The latter point is noted by Barry, *Liberal Theory*, 97.

31. As noted by Barber, "Justifying Justice," 296–300. See also R. M. Hare, "Rawls' Theory of Justice," 102–7.

by the difference principle. On the other hand, if by "excessive" inequalities Rawls simply means large ones, there is plenty of evidence to contradict his claim that a competitive economy and open class system are incompatible with their persistence or even their growth. One need only contrast contemporary Japan, with its relatively rigid social hierarchy and extensive state direction of the economy, with the U.S. to see how conditions of freedom and openness may actually enhance the gap in monetary rewards between the most and least economically successful citizens.[32] (Rawls's claim that his theory is buttressed by knowledge of "the distribution of natural assets and the laws of motivation" is mystifying, since recent research has highlighted the "bell curve" of natural intellectual attributes among human beings.[33] As for other natural assets, neither Tiger Woods nor Julia Roberts would be likely to achieve quite the multiple of average earnings in Japan that they do in the U.S.)

Finally, we arrive at Rawls's weighing of the reasoning that would lead the parties in the original position to choose his principles over two alternatives: the principles of "average utility" and "classical utilitarianism." The somewhat arcane difference between those doctrines is that while the classical principle requires us to maximize "the absolute weighted sum" of representative individuals' welfare, the principle of average utility, which Rawls attributes to Mill and the economist Knut Wicksell, "directs society to maximize . . . the average utility (per capita)" (*Theory*, 139–40).[34] Rawls

32. Cf. Tocqueville, *Democracy in America*, vol. 2, pt. 1, chap. 8, 431, and John Schaar, "Equality of Opportunity, and Beyond," 231–32. Of course, in authoritarian political systems, whether they be feudal monarchies or contemporary dictatorships, even larger gaps in living standards between the few and the many can be maintained through some combination of law and custom (in the former) and the direct application of force (in the latter). These differences are transmissible over successive generations of the same family. But they are not strictly based on "economic" success.

33. Richard Herrnstein and Charles Murray, *The Bell Curve*.

34. Rawls's source for attributing the average utility principle to Mill (*Theory*, 140n) is Gunnar Myrdal's *The Political Element in the Development of Economic Theory*, which argues that Mill's "ideal is a population in which average happiness per head is maximized" (38). Myrdal presumably has in mind the chapter on "the stationary state" in *Principles of Political Economy* (pt. 4, chap. 6), wherein Mill argues that a "great increase" in the world's population is undesirable, since it would make people no happier and would reduce the opportunity for solitude as well as for minimizing necessary labor through the use of inventions to increase leisure rather than wealth (750–51). But nowhere to my knowledge does Mill ever argue in favor of advancing some people's happiness at others' expense for the sake of maximizing the mathematical average of utilities. On the contrary, in *Utilitarianism*, he remarks that all individuals "have a *right* to equality of treatment, except when some recognized social expediency requires the reverse" (chap. 5, 78; emphasis in original), which entails the priority of equal treatment to any sum or average of individual utilities (as distinguished from the common

plausibly judges that the latter principle would be more acceptable, since the classical view would encourage unlimited population growth (to maximize total utility) while guaranteeing only "a very low average of well-being" for each individual (*Theory*, 140–41).[35] His major reason for holding that the parties to the original position would reject the principle of average utility, in turn, is that by representing all persons as having "the same deep utility function," such that they value other people's satisfaction no less than their own, it conceives them "as having no definite highest-order interests or fundamental ends by reference to which they decide what sorts of persons they care to be." By contrast, since Rawls has "assumed that the parties do have a determinate character and will," even though they are unaware of their specific ends, they must greatly value the basic liberties covered by the first principle of justice that are requisite for enabling them to choose their aims and way of life. Hence they would prefer the two principles to the principle of utility (*Theory*, 152).

While doubting that any sensible person would choose to live in a society that was governed purely by the utilitarian principle (whether "classical" or "average"), we must question whether the foregoing argument demonstrates the superiority of Rawls's principles from the standpoint of the original position. It is difficult, to say the least, to imagine how the parties can be said to reason on the basis of "a determinate character and will" while remaining ignorant of their actual ends. How can the parties know, therefore, that they value the basic liberties above all other goods, let alone agree on Rawls's second principle?

---

good or "social expediency"). Thus Rawls misrepresents Mill's view (while preparing to accuse him of self-contradiction on this point in chapter 8). On the other hand, Mill's formulation shares with Rawls's principles an abstractness and open-endedness by comparison with the guarantees of equal rights grounded in nature that are embodied in the American constitutional system and the Declaration of Independence.

35. Rawls's one apparently unambiguous example of a thinker who adopted the classical over the average principle is Sidgwick, who argues that "if we take Utilitarianism to prescribe, as the ultimate end of action, happiness on the whole," as distinguished from the happiness of any particular individual, then "population ought to be encouraged to increase" to the point "at which the product formed by multiplying the number of persons living into the amount of average happiness reaches its maximum." Hence population growth would be encouraged even if it decreased the happiness of the original population, so long as their loss was outweighed by the happiness of the additional number (*Methods of Ethics*, 415–16). But Sidgwick states this position rather tentatively, as if he were simply extrapolating what he deemed a logical consequence of utilitarianism rather than a point he seriously advocates. And he offers this utilitarian calculation as a basis for calculating the general good of society, not as a formula for justice.

IV.

Rather than confront these difficulties, Rawls proceeds in the penultimate section of part 1 of *Theory* to lay out further arguments for the two principles on the basis of the maximin rule. According to the first of these arguments, the principles best enable human beings to weather "the strains of commitment," that is, the obligation to live in accordance with the demands of justice. The advantage of the two principles in this regard is that they not only protect people's basic rights but also help "insure" them "against the worst eventualities." Knowing that they will not have to sacrifice their own freedom merely to enhance others' good, the parties should be better able to abide by their agreement (*Theory*, 153–54).

A second argument for the two principles invokes "the condition of publicity," according to which "when the basic structure of society is publicly known to satisfy its principles for an extended period of time, those subject to these arrangements tend to develop a desire to act in accordance" with them. In this connection Rawls observes that utilitarianism "seems to require a greater identification with the interests of others than the two principles" do, since it may compel the less favored to sacrifice their own good for "the greater good of the whole." Not only are the two principles more realistic in embodying "a principle of reciprocal advantage," their public recognition better supports everyone's "self-respect." Each person's self-respect depends, according to Rawls, on the respect of others. The principle of equal liberty and the difference principle are certain to generate such respect, Rawls maintains, since (he reminds us) they entail treating people's natural abilities "in some respects as a collective asset so that the more fortunate are to benefit only in ways that help those who have lost out."[36] By contrast, the utilitarian principle would compel the less fortunate "to accept even lower life prospects for the sake of others," thus weakening their self-esteem (*Theory*, 154–57).

Rawls acknowledges that the foregoing arguments are "informal and not a proof" and presuppose "an appeal to intuition" as their basis. Moreover, his account of the tendency of the two principles to engender behavior that accords them depends on an account of "moral psychology" that will not be articulated (along with a fuller description of the grounds of self-respect) until part 3 of *Theory* (154, 156). And his case for rejecting the "principle of perfection" in the original position will not be presented until

---

36. In Rawls's earlier and (it appears) more precise formulation (*Theory*, 87), it was only the difference principle that embodies this view of people's individual abilities.

chapter 5. Nonetheless, since the pages I have just surveyed complete Rawls's explanation of the reasoning that would lead the parties in the original position to choose the two principles over either version of utilitarianism, this is an appropriate time to assess that account as a whole.

Surveying Rawls's entire description of the reasoning in the original position, we find, not surprisingly, that it has been circular. Having set out to design that situation to generate agreement on the principles he already favored on "intuitive" grounds, Rawls finds that it does so.[37] Yet as we have seen, it proved impossible to frame the original position so that the conditions in which the parties deliberated actually compelled them to settle on Rawls's principles. Hence, after laying out the circumstances in which principles were to be chosen, Rawls kept adding assumptions— about the need to avoid risk and hence pursue a maximin strategy; about the assurance that the two principles guaranteed a "satisfactory minimum"; about the unlikelihood of "excessive" inequalities in a properly organized competitive economy—that came out of nowhere.

Dispensing with an actual description of the deliberative process in the original position saves Rawls from confronting the incoherence of the veil of ignorance. As I noted, even though Rawls stresses the purely heuristic character of that device as a guide to moral reflection, it is literally impossible to simulate the reasoning that is supposed to occur behind the veil, reaching decisions on the basis of "general" knowledge while somehow forgetting all particular knowledge of one's own desires and beliefs and the character of one's society. Thus the pretense of trying to think as if we ourselves were under a veil of ignorance provides only the illusion of liberating us from our particular moral, political, and religious outlooks, without really having that effect. If readers find Rawls's principles plausible, this can only be because the principles were appealing to them all along.

The most fundamental fact that the veil conceals is that not all conceptions of the good are compatible, or even commensurable, with one another. Rawls himself acknowledged that the ideals of saints and heroes might be "irreconcilably opposed." Yet he apparently assumed that all such ideals could find their place within the same "just" social order, as if the pursuit of holiness or heroism might not entail making nonliberal demands on one's fellow citizens, and as if one's view of the good didn't necessarily have implications for what one conceives as just. Far from leaving open the

---

37. Hence Schaar's observation that after he poured so much ostensibly liberal economics and psychology into the original position, it was no great trick for Rawls to pour it out again ("Reflections on Rawls' *Theory*," 150).

opportunity for a broad diversity of ways of life, Rawls simply ruled out of order the wishes of those who aspire to found a society on God's will (unless God happens to have willed justice as fairness), on the pursuit of human greatness, or on openness to the serious pursuit of truth. The only people whose conceptions of the good are sure to be advanced by the two principles are those with the idiosyncratic motivation of the parties to the original position: mutually disinterested beings who "know" that the greatest possible sum of money and freedom to live as one pleases are good, but not that such things as virtue (aside from the supposed virtue of Rawlsian justice itself), honor, or holiness are good.[38]

Of course, the reader may respond, we already knew that a liberal polity, such as Rawls's theory presupposes, cannot be dedicated to the pursuit of holiness or self-sacrificing virtue. And Rawls himself will later acknowledge that some worthy forms of life inevitably "lose out in a just constitutional regime," reflecting Isaiah Berlin's observation that every social world excludes some goods.[39] What does it matter, then, if Rawls's account of the reasoning in the original position doesn't actually demonstrate the superiority of a liberal regime (for instance) to ancient Sparta or medieval France, so long as his conclusions promote liberalism?

It matters in at least two respects. First, by replacing the substantive argument for liberalism set forth by philosophers such as Locke and Montesquieu, based on an analysis of human nature, with an abstract and faulty set of arguments derived from his "intuitions," Rawls weakens the liberal cause, reducing it (following the pragmatists' path) to a foundationless, rationally indefensible "commitment." Second, Rawls's version of liberalism is far more dogmatically libertarian and materialistic than that of the great liberal philosophers, none of whom denied (as Rawls will in chapter 4) that a liberal regime may offer support to moral practices that make people capable of freedom and self-government. Thus Rawls weakens our capacity to defend liberalism against contemporary critics who charge it with undermining human dignity.[40]

---

38. Cf. Schaar's comment on the narrow range of conceptions of justice that Rawls allows to be considered in the original position, notably omitting the views of Plato, Aristotle, and Aquinas (ibid., 153).

39. "The Priority of Right and Ideas of the Good," CP, 462–63; PL, 197.

40. Consider Aleksandr Solzhenitsyn's eloquent condemnation of the excessive materialism and individualism of modern liberal/commercial society and the way that the mass media divert us from the things that matter in his 1978 Harvard commencement address entitled "A World Split Apart." One need not agree with all of Solzhenitsyn's charges to see in his remarks a forceful reminder of the elements of a good or truly human society that Rawls's original position diverts us from considering.

V.

What prevents Rawls from facing such issues as I have raised is his narrowly abstract conception of political and moral philosophy, which leads him merely to try to account for his original beliefs rather than rationally assessing their validity. Hence, instead of addressing substantive objections to his doctrine, Rawls juxtaposed it only with a politically irrelevant doctrine of abstract utilitarianism. We never needed the original position to show that it would be silly to agree to be governed by a principle that authorizes the redistribution of goods to maximize the average or total "utility" in a given society. And it is unthinkable that any government would ground its policies on such a theory.

We should recall at this point that in introducing the distinction between his theory and utilitarianism, Rawls explained that he had in mind only the ostensibly "classical" version of the latter doctrine as espoused by Bentham, Sidgwick, and the economists Edgeworth and Pigou (*Theory*, 28). By contrast, he set aside as irrelevant for his purposes the utilitarianism of Hume, who meant by utility simply "the general interests and necessities of society" (*Theory*, 28–29)—just as Mill appears to have done in *Utilitarianism*. If Hume's doctrine is free from the implausible claims of later utilitarian theorists, why not consider it in depth as a rival to justice as fairness rather than compare the latter only with abstract utilitarian principles that haven't had significant political influence? Isn't it eminently more sensible to hold that laws and social practices should serve the overall interest of one's country than that they should aim at maximizing the mathematical sum of individuals' utilities, even assuming such a sum could be calculated?[41]

Utilitarianism in its stricter sense (as developed by Bentham and James Mill) was a powerful tool of legal "rationalization" or reform, but it was hardly an adequate overall source of guidance for the governance of a society or the grounding of a way of life.[42] Indeed, Rawls himself, in one of his

41. Granted, from an authentically liberal or Lockean perspective such as that of the American founders, the principle of serving the common interest must be constrained by a prior consensus on the natural rights that government exists to secure, entailing a limit to the proper scope and purpose of government. I am not arguing for Hume's adequacy here, only for the superiority of his sensible and politic "utilitarian" doctrine to the abstract utilitarianism that Rawls uses as his foil.

42. The central difficulty of Bentham's doctrine, as Sidgwick observes, is its incapacity to establish an essential link between the collective utility that we are supposed to promote and our own individual interests, which we are (at least) no less entitled to pursue on the basis of the utilitarian principle. In *Outlines of the History of Ethics,* Sidgwick discusses Bentham's unsuccessful attempts to address this problem, first citing "the religious sanction" as an added inducement to moral conduct, but ultimately assuming (unpersuasively) that "the conduct most conducive to general happiness

earliest essays, acknowledged that the classical utilitarians were chiefly interested in using their principle as a ground for reforming social institutions, leaving it doubtful that their doctrine requires amendment to harmonize it with commonsense moral intuitions; he believed that they themselves recognized the need for the principle to be constrained by a qualification prohibiting the violation of people's equal rights.[43] In its later incarnation utilitarianism became an economist's device for assessing, in the abstract, the costs and benefits of alternative policies. It survives today as well in the ivory towers of Anglo-American philosophy departments, wherein scholars whose substantive political and moral judgments rarely differ develop competing theories to "explain" their judgments.[44] But it hardly constitutes an influential political movement or threatens to become one.

I submit that the real significance of Rawls's argument lies less in its putative refutation of utilitarianism than in its departure from the core tenets of constitutional, natural rights-based liberalism. Most important, although

---

always coincides with that which conduces most to the happiness of the agent" (242–44 [Sidgwick's emphasis]). The subtitle of Bentham's *Deontology* illustrates his naiveté in this regard: "Morality made easy; Shewing how Throughout the whole course of every person's life Duty coincides with interest rightly understood, Felicity with Virtue, Prudence extra-regarding as well as self-regarding with Effective benevolence" (119). The greater interest of the writings of John Stuart Mill and Sidgwick results from their having largely abandoned the "strict" utilitarian principle (in Mill's case, critically modifying Bentham's "felicific calculus" by admitting a distinction between higher and lower pleasures) and moving toward a more commonsensical (and Humean) identification of the collective utility with a liberal conception of the common good.

43. "Two Concepts of Rules" (1955), *CP*, 26, 33–34n; "Justice as Fairness," *CP*, 50–51. The writer Rawls cites who comes closest to exemplifying his foil, the utilitarian calculator for whom the utility principle may require trumping the premise of equality if people differ significantly in their capacity for happiness, is the nineteenth-century economist Francis Ysidro Edgeworth, author of *Mathematical Psychics* (vii). But Edgeworth's work is concerned with such issues as allocating the tax burden in the fairest and most efficient manner or arbitrating disputes over rents, and does not propose sacrificing some people's rights (e.g., by enslaving them) for the sake of maximizing social utility. See also Edgeworth, "The Pure Theory of Taxation," which Rawls himself cites in an earlier article as embodying the primacy of "equality as an initial principle," with inequalities allowable only if they make everyone better off ("Justice as Reciprocity," *CP*, 203n).

44. One contemporary philosophical exponent of utilitarianism observes that "the utilitarian addresses himself to people who very likely agree with him as to what consequences are good ones, but who disagree with him [only] about the principle that what we ought to do is produce the best consequences" (J. J. C. Smart, "An Outline of a System of Utilitarian Ethics," 14). See also Warnock, *Ethics since 1900*, 140, on the "surprising" hostility toward utilitarianism expressed by British philosophical writers, "many of whom would in their nonphilosophical moments turn out to be utilitarians of an enlightened liberal kind."

Rawls does not offer his chief justification for the difference principle until chapter 5 (on grounds having little to do with the original position), we cannot avoid remarking the highly questionable and illiberal premise on which that principle rests: that we should regard people's natural abilities "as a collective asset" whose fruits we are free to reallocate in accordance with the supposed dictates of justice (*Theory*, 156). As I noted in chapter 2, Rawls's collectivized vision of human capacities entails exactly the fault for which he reproached the utilitarian of disregarding "the distinction between persons" (*Theory*, 24, 163). How can it be just to particular individuals to tell them that they won't be allowed to achieve greater-than-average success in life (however measured) unless they compensate the less fortunate?[45] Why should Rawls hold that allowing highly talented and motivated individuals to advance in life somehow causes "those already less favored" by nature to accept "still lower life prospects" (*Theory*, 157): lower than what? In what way does one person's success by lawful means damage the life prospects of anyone else? Indeed, if, as the difference principle supposes, the natural assets of different individuals are to be regarded as commonly owned, even while their possessors retain them, why shouldn't it follow that the gains people make as a consequence of their talents (or other causes) are enjoyed no less in common, even as their acquirers most directly profit? In other words, why bother to redistribute them?[46]

Just as it is impossible literally to forget our conceptions of the good as Rawls ordains, the reasoning (such as it is) that underlies the choice of the difference principle embodies a separation between actual persons and

---

As for utilitarianism as a tool of economic analysis, it is potentially problematic for constitutional liberalism, but not for the reason given by Rawls. Rather, the difficulty arises when economists, inevitably violating their professions of value-neutrality, attempt to reduce more fundamental issues of politics and morality to matters of consumer preference—forgetting the ultimately instrumental relation of economics to politics (see Steven Rhoads, *The Economist's View of the World*, pt. 3; Joseph Cropsey, "What Is Welfare Economics?" and "On the Relation of Political Science and Economics," in *Political Philosophy and the Issues of Politics*, 19–43).

45. In an essay published three years later, Rawls distinguishes his proposal from "a head tax on natural assets" designed to reduce or eliminate income inequalities, holding that the latter policy "would be a drastic infringement upon freedom," while "society can [legitimately] say that the better endowed may improve their situations only on terms that help others" ("Some Reasons for the Maximin Criterion," *CP*, 231). But this distinction seems arbitrary: if the better endowed must compensate the less advantaged for developing their own talents, why shouldn't they also be taxed to compensate the less advantaged for the unearned difference in their capacities, which at least enable the more advantaged to enjoy greater leisure (by earning as much as others in less time)? (Of course, the problem would arise of how to measure undeveloped natural capacities.)

46. See Zuckert, "Justice Deserted," 482n.

their specific abilities and efforts that is not only unrealistic but unimaginable. The notion that because someone's success in life presupposes a scheme of social cooperation, he is obliged to compensate those who achieve less than he does for their supposedly lesser natural endowment, depends on the implicit attribution to human beings of an imaginary, formal existence that preceded their "acquisition" of distinct attributes and character traits—so that one can say that nature or fortune treated them unfairly by "giving" them lesser abilities than others. Outside of mythology (such as the ironic Myth of Er in Plato's *Republic*), nothing in our experience supports such an assumption.[47]

Perhaps what gives the original position an initial plausibility as a device of political reflection is the common exercise of wondering what it would have been like to be born into a different time and place, under a very different sort of political regime and culture, and asking yourself whether you would find it preferable to your present situation. Most Americans, tempted though some might feel by the lost glories of aristocratic grandeur, would in all likelihood opt for the present or the relatively recent past, recognizing (like the "conservative" parties to Rawls's original position) that mathematically, the odds are much greater that, if randomly plunked into seventeenth-century France, they would find themselves suffering the lot of poor peasants rather than assigned the lot of a noble lord.[48] Most of us, in other words, would agree with Tocqueville's judgment that justice, understood as securing the rights of all individuals, ultimately trumps the collective cultivation of splendor or excellence for a few. But again, this is not the procedure that Rawls has described in his account of the original position or the conclusion he derived from it. In comparing the justness or goodness of existing institutions with those of other times and places, we do not ordinarily pretend that our talents, beliefs, or views of the good are unknown to us. How could we? We neither purport to adopt a neutral position vis-à-vis our view of the good nor imagine that our particular natures are somehow the consequence of a "lottery" that needs to be compensated for. Instead, we assess the conduciveness of the institutions under which we live to our good as actual human beings. Whereas most Americans, regardless of economic or social status, are thereby led to

47. We do metaphorically speak of people's having been "dealt a bad hand" by nature or fortune when they suffer from serious physical handicaps or chronic diseases or die an untimely death, or when such misfortunes befall their loved ones. But it is easier, in thought, to separate a person's "real" being from his bodily condition (or the fortunes of those close to him) than from his own intelligence or motivation. And Rawls's theory, as we saw in chapter 2, is not intended to compensate those suffering from serious ailments or disabilities.

48. Cf. Montesquieu, *Spirit of the Laws*, bk. 14, chap. 9, for an argument against slavery on these grounds.

appreciate their good fortune to have been born (or become) citizens of a constitutional, liberal democracy, Rawls, we shall observe, continually denounces the supposed wrongs of the American regime by comparison with a purely imaginary model of justice.

It is not uncommon, unreasonable, or unsalutary, of course, for people who achieve success to think, upon encountering someone less fortunate or accomplished, "there, but for the grace of God, go I." That reflection can be the source of laudable acts of benevolence and charity, even if it often understates the contribution that a person's own efforts and sacrifices make to his achievements. Moreover, to deny that the more successful owe particular compensation for their success to the least fortunate is by no means to deny that since everyone's well-being depends on the prosperity, security, and liberty of his country, every citizen has a duty to promote his country's welfare, and governments appropriately require citizens to support their country through financial and nonfinancial means in rough proportion to their capacity. Contributing to the cost of universal public education, for instance, is in the long-range interest of the better-off; and it will be hard for a nation to retain the loyalty of poorer citizens if they think their government disregards their welfare.[49]

But it is one thing to emphasize citizens' duty to promote the common good and the need for government as well as private charity to assist those who suffer misfortune through no fault of their own; another entirely to presuppose that for anyone to be poorer than others is *always* something for which bad luck, rather than his own bad habits or lack of effort or providence, is responsible, and to prohibit anyone from gaining more than others except when he can prove that his gains benefit his less successful fellows.[50] (Indeed, the very term "less advantaged" misleadingly implies that all differences in people's success are the product of unearned advantages.)

In this light, there is little to be said for Rawls's contention that his principles best address "the strains of commitment." If sane human beings are unlikely to agree to be governed by a principle of maximizing the total or

49. Rawls's (sometime) libertarian colleague Nozick errs in the opposite direction in understanding such political obligations, by equating them with the mandate that one contribute to the cost of a public entertainment system that a majority of one's fellow citizens desire (*Anarchy, State, and Utopia*, 93–95). Nozick shares with Rawls an abstract approach to issues of justice that disregards the real problems of maintaining citizen loyalty in a democracy.

50. An earlier champion of progressive liberalism, Franklin Roosevelt, explicitly distinguished between those who exercised the "right to make a comfortable living" that government ought to secure them and those who effectively declined it owing to "sloth or crime" (Commonwealth Club Address, *Public Papers and Addresses*, 754). See, regarding the split between liberal elites and popular majorities on the extent to which welfare policy should take account of recipients' behavior, Steven M. Teles, *Whose Welfare?* chap. 4.

average utility, without regard to their own benefit, they are no more likely to accept having their abilities treated as a collective asset whose fruits they may enjoy only on condition of paying tribute to the least advantaged. Nor is it credible that the supposed beneficiaries of the difference principle, the least advantaged themselves, will feel heightened self-respect from knowing that they are to be the lifelong beneficiaries of mandatory economic redistribution.[51]

In the end, it should be apparent that Rawls's original position is a poor substitute for previous philosophers' accounts of the state of nature. By replacing the realistic, if narrowly conceived, human beings whom Hobbes and Locke depict in that condition with artificial "parties" who so little resemble us that they don't know their aims or abilities and have no interest (positive or negative) in their fellows, Rawls removes any motive we might have for caring about their ostensible decision. Such impossible beings can no more "represent" us than the robot R2D2 could. Nor, for that matter, is there any reason to regard the parties to the original position as plural rather than singular: since all are alike in their ignorance and passionlessness, and they engage in no actual dealings with one another, they are indistinguishable from a single calculating machine,[52] except that their ostensible calculations don't yield the desired results without the continued

---

51. In a 1982 essay Rawls specifies that "the least advantaged are, by definition, those who are born into and who remain in that group throughout their life," so that the prospect of social mobility offered by the principle of equal opportunity "is irrelevant" to the application of the difference principle ("Social Unity and Primary Goods," *CP*, 364). This seems a terribly pessimistic, not to mention demeaning, view for a liberal society to adopt, even for heuristic purposes.

52. Jürgen Habermas observes that since the parties to the original position choose the same principles for the same reasons, the process is "monological rather than dialogical." Rawls cites this observation in his "Reply to Habermas" in *PL* (383n), but he does not refute it by responding that it is "all citizens over time . . . who judge the merits of the original position as a device of representation and the principles it yields." While readers remain free to accept or reject Rawls's devices and principles, he never conducts a meaningful dialogue either within the original position or outside it among alternative substantive views of justice. Indeed, Rawls confirms Habermas's point by remarking that "the unanimity condition" imposed on the choice of principles "is suited even to express the nature of a single self" (*Theory*, 494).

Barry notes that one can replace the notion of the original position by asking "what principles an impartial person would adopt" (*Liberal Theory*, 13). Kukathas and Pettit similarly observe that "to follow Rawls's theory . . . you can think of yourself as the only relevant person making the choice in the original position" (*Rawls*, 21). See also Lyons, "Nature and Soundness," 151; Sandel, *Liberalism and the Limits of Justice*, 129–32; and Berkowitz, "Ambiguities of Rawls's Influence," 122. What remains in question is whether human beings can achieve the sort of superhuman impartiality to which Rawls aspires through any method whatsoever—notably (unlike Adam Smith's impartial spectator) in somehow forgetting their conceptions of the good.

fiddling of the machine's operator. Finally, because the parties are so unlike us, their decisions, unlike those of the inhabitants of Hobbes's and Locke's states of nature, carry no real sanction. Whereas Hobbes and Locke demonstrate *why* we are obliged to obey government, or government of a certain sort (to avert the terrors of the state of nature), Rawls must resort to a farfetched, formalistic "moral psychology" (discussed in chapters 7 through 9) to show why we should obey the dictates of justice as fairness.

Considering the nonhuman character of the parties to the original position and Rawls's inability to demonstrate that his principles are the outcome of any genuine process of deliberation in that situation, there was no reason for him to adopt this device at all. (In his earlier essays "Justice as Fairness" and "Constitutional Liberty," Rawls had done without it, simply asking us to imagine how human beings who were concerned to adopt a fair set of principles for regulating their society would reason [CP, 52–55, 59–63, 77ff].) Its only function seems to be a rhetorical one: simulating the supposed reasoning of a group of artificial persons is supposed to persuade us that we can somehow transcend our conceptions of the good (not a requirement in Rawls's earlier formulation), as well as make the bizarre foundations of the difference principle seem plausible. But this impression is illusory.

CHAPTER 4

A Just Constitution

I.

Part 2 of *Theory*, "Institutions," is devoted to describing a "basic structure" that satisfies Rawls's principles, thus showing that they are "workable" as well as constituting "a reasonable approximation to and extension of our considered judgments." While "the main institutions of this structure are those of a constitutional democracy," Rawls does not contend that such a political regime is the only just one (*Theory*, 171). (However, neither here nor in his other writings does Rawls identify an alternative regime that he would regard as just, and in *IPRR* [134] he remarks that his idea of public reason "does not engage" those who reject constitutional democracy.)

Just as Rawls emphasized the need for simplicity in enunciating principles of justice, at the outset of chapter 4 he outlines a "framework . . . to simplify" their application. He represents the development and application of these principles as occurring in four stages: (1) the selection of principles of justice in the original position (as already discussed); (2) a constitutional convention that establishes the powers of government and citizens' "basic rights"; (3) the legislative stage, where social and economic policies are adopted with a view to "maximizing the long-term expectations of the least advantaged under conditions of fair opportunity"; and

(4) "the application of rules to particular cases by judges and administrators," along with the determination of the extent to which citizens are obliged to obey laws that they deem unjust.[1] At each of the last three stages, elements of the veil of ignorance are successively lifted. Thus, although delegates to the constitutional convention remain ignorant of their personal attributes and conceptions of the good, they are allowed to know such "general facts about their society" as "its natural circumstances and resources" and "level of economic advance and political culture," so as to enable them to adopt "the most effective just constitution," that is, the one "that satisfies the principles of justice and is best calculated to lead to just and effective legislation." At the legislative stage, in turn, "the full range of general economic and social facts is brought to bear," though "bills are judged from the position of a representative legislator" who remains ignorant of "the particulars about himself" (*Theory*, 173–75). Only at the last stage, where rules are applied by judges and administrators and obeyed (or not) "by citizens generally," does everyone have "complete access to all the facts," though "the grounds and limits of political duty and obligation" will still have to be determined from the standpoint of the original position (*Theory*, 175).

While emphasizing that this four-stage sequence does not exemplify "the working of actual constitutions, except insofar as political agents are influenced by the conception of justice" it embodies, Rawls also asserts that it "is suggested by the United States Constitution and its history" (*Theory*, 172–73n). Yet it is difficult to discern any connection between the sequence and the actual history of our Constitution. No one at the 1787 convention, needless to say, proposed that delegates adopt a veil of ignorance to constrain their deliberations. Nor did anyone inside or outside the convention maintain that a just constitution should, or could, be devised in the absence of a known, if broad, conception of the good. Nor, finally, did the founders adopt Rawls's dichotomy between constitutional and legislative decision making, according to which the "principle of equal liberty is the primary standard for the constitutional convention," while the legislature chiefly concerns itself with "social and economic policies" (*Theory*, 174–75). A survey of the Constitution shows that its authors regarded the protection of property as an integral aspect of "the blessings of liberty" and the general welfare it was designed to secure: witness the prohibition of state legislation impairing the obligation of contracts, the authorization

---

1. Rawls later seems to blur the distinction between the constitutional and legislative stages by citing government-financed health care for the uninsured as an "important constitutional essential" (*PL*, 407).

of a patent office, and the Fifth Amendment's prohibition on the seizure of property without just compensation.[2] Conversely, there is no evidence that because the Constitution provided protection for liberty, its authors thought there was less need for continuing congressional or state legislative attentiveness to securing that end.

Of course, there is a fundamental difference of purpose between Rawls's four-stage sequence and the actual process of constitution- and lawmaking, since the former is intended to illustrate the application of Rawls's principles, with effectiveness only a subsidiary criterion. But given the priority Rawls attributes to justice, he clearly intends his model of a just constitution and political process to serve as a standard for assessing actual political regimes (*Theory*, 199). In this regard, we wonder how his dichotomy between justice and effectiveness as criteria for judging political institutions, as well as the four-stage sequence itself, can generate reasonable assessments. Leaving aside the difficulty of conceiving constitution-makers who can somehow (any more than the parties to the original position) forget their conceptions of the good, we note that Rawls assumes without argument that some constitution satisfying his principles would be "effective" (*Theory*, 173).[3] Then, he misleadingly characterizes "the political process as a machine which makes social decisions when the views of representatives and their constituents are fed into it" (*Theory*, 171–72). Omitted from this characterization is any account of political *deliberation:* the possibility that citizens or, more likely, their representatives may alter their political opinions and demands as a consequence not only of legislative logrolling but sometimes of being genuinely persuaded by advocates of alternative views.[4] To frame a government that would base its policies on such reflection as much as possible, so that "the deliberate sense of the majority," rather than transient popular whims, would govern us was a key

2. Rawls's deprecation of economic liberty in comparison to other forms of liberty follows the "preferred position" doctrine enunciated by the Supreme Court beginning in the 1930s. For a critique of that doctrine, see Thomas Schrock, "The Liberal Court, the Conservative Court, and Constitutional Jurisprudence."

3. In his later "Reply to Habermas," Rawls acknowledges assuming that a just constitution in his sense is "realizable," but he adds that even if it isn't, his model still provides "the aim of long-term political reform" (*PL*, 398). But since he never demonstrates that the institutions he mandates for a just constitution are compatible with its being effective, it hardly follows that those prescriptions would enable us gradually to better achieve Rawlsian justice over time, assuming that we wished to do so.

4. In *IPRR*, Rawls maintains that his concept of public reason provides a basis for deliberative democracy. As I shall note in chapter 12 below, however, all that concept does is exclude arguments grounded in particular religious or moral views (other than Rawls's own) from the public forum.

aim of the American founders.[5] By contrast, Rawls conceives the political process in the manner characteristic of contemporary "rational-choice" theory, which treats it simply as an alternative means to the market for satisfying people's idiosyncratic preferences in the most efficient manner (assuming in Rawls's case, of course, that the constraints of justice have first been observed).[6] In fact, Rawls disparages the democratic political process as "at best regulated rivalry" such that it lacks "even in theory . . . the desirable properties" of "truly competitive markets" (*Theory*, 199).

Rawls's mechanistic account of the political process is a consequence of his determination to make considerations of justice prior to, and dominant over, those of prudence or effectiveness. Clearly, a genuinely open-ended process of political deliberation cannot be limited in advance to questions of means as distinguished from ends: in considering issues ranging from taxation to welfare to foreign policy, we inevitably raise questions of justice and are influenced by somewhat differing interpretations of that virtue, as well as of the proper scope and meaning of liberty. Even though a written constitution like the American one is supposed to constrain particular legislative determinations, the very meaning of that document is worked out in practice through the political process, in which the legislative and executive branches no less than the judicial one share in the act of constitutional interpretation.[7] But to recognize that considerations of justice and constitutionality are necessarily interwoven with considerations of policy, and vice versa, would overthrow Rawls's representation of justice as prior to the good, so that its meaning can be fixed in advance of the adoption of a constitution, which in turn must constrain all subsequent political deliberations. This is not only an empirically misleading account of the political process, I suggest, but a potentially harmful one, inasmuch

5. See Hamilton, Madison, and Jay, *The Federalist*, Nos. 63 (352) and 71 (400). For a useful if perhaps overly sanguine account of the deliberative process in the American national government today, see Joseph M. Bessette, *The Mild Voice Of Reason.*

6. Rawls's distinction between his four-stage sequence and rational-choice theory on the ground that it "is part of a moral theory" rather than "an account of the working of actual constitutions," and therefore does not presuppose any views about human behavior comparable to the "individualistic assumptions" of economics (173n), does not address this issue.

7. Elsewhere Rawls himself emphasizes that constitutional interpretation is a task for all three branches of government, with the people themselves as the ultimate interpretative authority (*Theory*, 342; *PL*, 232; *JF*, 147). But he fails to appreciate the significance of this observation for his dichotomy between constitutional and legislative reasoning in the four-stage sequence, and elsewhere, as I shall note, he effectively invites courts to read his preferred principles into the Constitution, without regard to the text or popular wishes.

as it may encourage political actors to absolutize their particular partisan claims as inherently moral ones that cannot be compromised or moderated by considerations of prudence.[8] When beliefs about justice are severed from and given absolute priority over considerations of effectiveness, there is little room left for deliberation.[9]

Rawls himself concedes that the justness of particular legislation, especially regarding economic and social policies, is "subject to reasonable differences of opinion." Judgment in such cases "frequently depends upon speculative political and economic doctrines," and applying the difference principle precisely "normally requires more information" than is available. (This admission seems to qualify Rawls's contention in chapter 2 concerning the relative ease of applying the difference principle as compared with the principle of utility.) By contrast, he believes that "it is often perfectly plain and evident" when the liberties ordained by the first principle are being abridged (*Theory*, 174). Even if this were true, however, it would still leave open whether the abridgments were legitimate, since Rawls acknowledges that the first principle allows liberty to be restricted in some respects for the sake of the broader enhancement of other basic liberties (*Theory*, 213). Whether the line between legitimate and illegitimate restrictions of liberty is as clear as Rawls claims is one of the questions we must consider in assessing the remainder of chapter 4, which treats the constitutional provisions necessary to secure equal liberty.

II.

In describing the application of his first principle Rawls proposes to "bypass the dispute about the meaning of liberty," such as "the controversy between the proponents of negative and positive liberty," since this debate really concerns "the relative values of the several liberties when they come into conflict" (*Theory*, 176). Of course, the serious controversy about the meaning of liberty was always a substantive rather than a definitional one; but Rawls, remarkably, attempts to sidestep that controversy

8. Cf. Wiggins, "Neo-Aristotelian Reflections," citing the late Bertrand de Jouvenel's likely critique of Rawls for neglecting "the singular collocation that one encounters in sound practical reasoning of the specific and the universal, of executive questions and policy questions" (501). Also relevant is Mary Ann Glendon's warning about the detrimental effect of continually turning controverted political issues into claims about rights (*Rights Talk*). See also John Gray, *Enlightenment's Wake*, 22–23.

9. As I shall note in chapter 6, Rawls's mechanistic view of the political process leads him to encourage civil disobedience rather than constitutional representation as the proper check on policies that citizens find objectionable.

entirely, beyond urging that "the so-called liberty of the moderns" (i.e., individual freedom) "ought not to be sacrificed to political liberty," the "liberty of the ancients" as described by the nineteenth-century liberal writer Benjamin Constant (*Theory*, 177). Rawls then tries to narrow the problem by making a series of rather question-begging assumptions. He "assume[s]" that the basic liberties can be defined so that "the most central applications of each can be simultaneously secured and the most fundamental interests protected." He "assume[s]" it to "be clear for the most part whether an institution or law actually restricts a basic liberty or merely regulates it." And he holds that "some of the equal liberties may be more extensive than others, assuming that their extensions can be compared" (*Theory*, 178).

But how, then, do we resolve conflicts among the different forms of liberty when they do occur? Rawls's solution is simply to apply "the principle of equal advantage" through "marginal exchanges" among the various liberties. In other words, when faced (for instance) with a conflict between individual freedom and the principle of participation, or majority rule, we should modify the extent of the former "to the point where the danger to liberty from the marginal loss in control over those holding political power just balances the security gained by the greater use of constitutional devices" that limit popular power. In this way, we avoid having to "assess the relative total importance of the different liberties." Of course, Rawls acknowledges, "different opinions about the value of the liberties" will affect judgments about a just overall system. But "ideally," he concludes, "these conflicts will not occur, and it should be possible, under favorable conditions anyway, to find a constitutional procedure that allows a sufficient scope for the value of participation without jeopardizing the other liberties" (*Theory*, 202).

I think it evident that Rawls's ostensible method of resolving conflicts among different forms of liberty is no solution at all. Since people's opinions about the value of different liberties vary, is it not a fundamental task of "substantive political philosophy," as Rawls calls his enterprise in this context (*Theory*, 177), to address that controversy? How helpful is Rawls's advice to marginally increase one liberty to the point where it balances the loss of another, as if all sorts of liberty were homogeneous, commensurable, and quantifiable? Whether or not one is persuaded by Constant's argument that individual freedom is of greater value than political participation, doesn't his analysis add considerably more to our understanding of the issues, because of its substantive character, than Rawls's formalistic one? (Consider, for instance, the debate over the Patriot Act, enacted in response to the threat of international terrorism: does Rawls's discussion help us in any way to decide how far government should limit certain personal liberties for the sake of defending the freedom of the nation as a whole?)[10]

Rawls acknowledges that his opening remarks about liberty are "unhappily abstract." Hence he adds yet another assumption: "I shall assume that we have a clear enough idea of the distinctions [among 'the various liberties'], . . . and that in the course of taking up various cases these matters will gradually fall into place" (*Theory,* 179). He then refers us to the next sections, which discuss "liberty of conscience and freedom of thought, political liberty, and liberty of the person as protected by the rule of law," to "clarify the meaning of the equal liberties" and "the use of the criteria for limiting and adjusting" them (*Theory,* 180). I turn now to Rawls's account of "Equal Liberty of Conscience."

III.

Rawls opens this discussion by reminding us "that one of the attractive features of the principles of justice is that they guarantee a secure protection for the equal liberties." In a somewhat curious footnote, he cites the writings of Kant, John Stuart Mill, and "many other liberal thinkers" for the principle of "an equal right to freedom" (*Theory,* 180n). The oddity here lies in Rawls's seeming disregard of the original arguments for people's equal right to freedom in the writings of Locke and Rousseau, as well as the Declaration of Independence—apparently consigning them to anonymity among the "many" thinkers of whom it "may be claimed" that they asserted such a right. Instead, Rawls supplements his reference to Kant by citing a couple of articles from philosophy journals of the 1950s. As signified by his earlier offhand reference to the concept of natural rights, Rawls seems to regard arguments for liberty that are grounded in nature as merely a primitive precursor to the approach of Kant or, still better, the subsequent Anglo-American analytic tradition.

What, then, is Rawls's own mode of argument for equal liberty of conscience? He begins by asserting that "the question of equal liberty of conscience is settled. It is one of the fixed points of our considered judgments of justice" (*Theory,* 181). Precisely because of its certainty, the reasoning underlying that belief "can be generalized to apply to [the] other freedoms, although not always with the same force." The argument for equal liberty

10. The practical irrelevance of Rawls's doctrine of the maximization of liberty, both in *Theory* and in its revised form in *PL,* is forcefully noted by John Gray in *The Two Faces of Liberalism,* 70–82.

of conscience is simply that since (thanks to the veil of ignorance) the parties in the original position "do not know . . . what their religious or moral convictions are, or . . . the particular content of their moral or religious obligations as they interpret them," or even "know that they think of themselves as having such obligations" at all, "they cannot take chances with their liberty" by adopting a principle that would allow "the dominant religious or moral doctrine to persecute or to suppress others." To "gamble" on any other principle than equal liberty of conscience, Rawls holds, "would show that one did not take one's religious or moral convictions seriously, or highly value the liberty to examine one's beliefs" (*Theory*, 181).

Rawls himself anticipates the objection "that religious sects . . . cannot acknowledge any principle at all for limiting their claims," given the "absolute" character of "the duty to religious and divine law." Remarkably, however, he finds it "unnecessary to argue against" this objection, since even though a religious person might think he must convert others to his faith for the sake of their salvation, "an understanding of religious obligation and of philosophical and moral first principles shows that we cannot expect others to acquiesce in an inferior liberty," much less "ask them to recognize us as the proper interpreter of their religious duties or moral obligations" (*Theory*, 182–83).

If we take Rawls literally, he means that no one who advocates that government policies favor what he believes to be the true religion properly understands his religious obligations. What is in question here, it should be emphasized, is not merely religious "suppression" or "persecution" as these terms are ordinarily understood. Rather, beyond specifying that "the state can favor no particular religion" or penalize dissenting religious sects (*Theory*, 186), Rawls holds that in accordance with the principle of neutrality among conflicting moral beliefs, it must also avoid regulating people's conduct on the basis of any particular view of human excellence or dignity. Hence, as he later explains, government may not prohibit sexual relationships that are thought to be "degrading and shameful," because such judgments reflect "subtle aesthetic preferences" about which individuals may disagree (*Theory*, 291).

Rawls's prescription of strict governmental neutrality on issues of personal morality accords well with political beliefs that are widespread in the contemporary academy, as well as with the thrust of numerous Supreme Court decisions over recent decades—though even the Court has not (yet) pushed that principle to its logical limit (e.g., by striking down laws banning polygamy). (On the other hand, consistency would seem to dictate that Rawls specify that government not favor or encourage religion as such over atheism, a position he does not explicitly state, though the

Court has come close to adopting it.) But it surely adds nothing to the case for such neutrality to say that our hypothetical representatives in the original position, who don't even know that they have religious convictions, would adopt the principle lest they be accused of not taking "their" (unknown) convictions seriously. Indeed, in claiming that government must be firmly neutral among competing religious and moral beliefs on the ground that to do otherwise would improperly make some individuals the interpreters of other people's religious and moral duties, isn't Rawls setting *himself* up as the authoritative interpreter of everyone's religious and moral duties?[11]

As in chapter 3, to the extent that we can conceive the reasoning of the parties to the original position, I submit that Rawls has misrepresented its likely outcome. Let us leave aside Rawls's rather inscrutable statement that the parties "must choose principles that secure the integrity of their religious and moral freedom" since "they know . . . that they have obligations which they interpret in this way" even though "they do not think of themselves as having" "moral or religious obligations" (*Theory*, 181). (It is not evident why acting to "protect" one's convictions requires being ignorant that one believes he has such obligations: can there be a morality or religion that imposes no obligations? Is Rawls thinking of obligations other than religious and moral ones, and if so, what would their ground be? How could anyone know that he has obligations without knowing what they are?) Going only on the basis of the limited information that is available under the veil of ignorance, I suggest, the most likely decision that the parties would agree on is that whatever religion and morality appear, once the veil is lifted, to be the *true* ones, society should be guided by them. In other words, there is no way around the necessity for actual polities composed of living human beings—as distinguished from the artificial inhabitants of the original position—to address, collectively as well as individually, the question of how we ought to live. That question inevitably involves consideration of the human good in ways that transcend the issue of justice but which are prerequisite to an adequate account of what is just.

To say this is by no means, of course, to maintain that government should require human beings to conform to a heroic or puritanical morality or to the dictates of a particular religious faith. To the contrary, we ourselves, on the basis of the fullest historical experience (rather than a veil of

11. Cf. Barber, "Justifying Justice," 313–14; Victor Gourevitch, "Rawls on Justice," 494–98; and Gray's valuable distinction between Rawlsian neutrality and toleration properly understood in *Enlightenment's Wake*, 19–20.

ignorance), can appreciate the virtues of religious toleration and even a rel-atively nonintrusive governmental policy regarding morality.[12] In fact, the true religion may well appear to be, as most Americans believe, one that treats faith chiefly as a private matter and denies that governmental com-pulsion should be employed to support it, let alone suppress dissenters, just as it can plausibly be held that genuine morality presupposes that individuals be left a considerable latitude in their life choices, so as to pro-mote a sense of personal moral responsibility, as well as to avoid generat-ing unnecessary political controversy. But all this is to say only that the proper role of government with respect to religion and morality cannot be resolved on the basis of a purely abstract notion of justice. Rawls is placing far more weight on an idea of justice severed from, and given priority over, the human good (to say nothing of the holy), as well as considerations of political prudence, than it can bear.

It is in this light that we must consider Rawls's ostensible demonstration of the superiority of his contractuarian argument for freedom of con-science over the broadly utilitarian reasoning of John Stuart Mill, in the pages that immediately follow in *Theory*. After judging as "forceful" Mill's contentions that liberty best enables human beings to develop their capac-ities, and that it is also necessary for them to make informed choices, as well as being desirable in itself, Rawls objects that these arguments will not necessarily "justify an equal liberty for all." That is, in the absence of "familiar utilitarian assumptions" such as the "equal capacity for the activ-ities and interests of men as progressive beings," the advancement of certain ends might be found compatible with some people's "being oppressed, or at least granted but a restricted liberty." Rawls's contract view reflects the belief "that we have more confidence in the principle of equal liberty than in the truth of the premises from which a perfectionist or utilitarian view would derive it" (*Theory*, 184–85).

But has Rawls offered a superior ground for equal liberty of conscience? Why should the supposed fact that that principle would be chosen in an original position of equality matter to us at all, unless we presuppose that human beings *are* in some fundamental sense equal? In other words, doesn't Rawls's argument presuppose at least as much as Mill's a certain empirical observation about human nature? Does one ground the princi-ple of equal liberty at all by merely asserting that "we" have confidence in it? Has Rawls truly justified his claim, in the opening sentence of the next

12. Cf. Rawls's sensible observations (citing Tocqueville) on how the American prin-ciple of religious freedom contributes to the relative vitality of religion in this country, in *IPRR*, 166–168.

section, that "justice as fairness provides, as we have now seen, strong arguments for an equal liberty of conscience" (*Theory*, 186)?

It must be emphasized that although Rawls tries to buttress his position by representing the chief alternative to it as the abstract utilitarian doctrine that ordains maximizing the "net balance of the satisfaction of interests" in a society (*Theory*, 185), that doctrine is not the ground on which actual political societies have rejected the principle of strict governmental neutrality among differing religious and moral beliefs. What is in question rather is what the common good of a community (and in the case of religious beliefs, what is thought to constitute the divine commandment) appears to dictate.

IV.

The problems that result from Rawls's failure systematically to address the relation between the principle of liberty and society's common good become even more visible in the discussion that follows of "Toleration and the Common Interest" and "Toleration of the Intolerant." If Rawls's remarks on liberty of conscience push the neutrality principle to a doctrinaire extreme, his discussion of toleration, conversely, understates the threat to liberal tolerance from the propagation of fanatical and truly intolerant religious beliefs—dangers of which the events of 9/11 and beyond have offered us a terrible reminder.

Rawls holds that government may not limit liberty of conscience unless there is a "reasonably certain or imminent" danger of risk to "public order" (*Theory*, 185).[13] On this ground he rejects Rousseau's argument against tolerating religions that teach that "outside the church there is no salvation," based on the belief "that people would find it impossible to live in peace with those whom they regarded as damned." Such an "a priori psychological argument" cannot justify abandoning the principle of toleration, any more than Locke's judgment that toleration could not safely be extended to Catholics and atheists, since Rawls presumes that "a greater historical experience and a knowledge of the wider possibilities of political life would have convinced" these philosophers "that they were mistaken, or at least that their contentions were true only under special circumstances" (*Theory*, 189–90). Rawls himself is confident of the "psychological principle that those whose liberties are protected by and who benefit from a just constitution will, other things equal, acquire an allegiance to it over a period of

---

13. This formulation seems equivalent to the "clear and present danger" test for regulating freedom of speech that Rawls will reject in *PL*, as noted in chapter 11 below.

time," so that it will not be necessary to limit the propagation of intolerant religious doctrines except in those "special cases . . . when the tolerant sincerely and with reason believe that their own security and that of the institutions of liberty are in danger" (*Theory*, 192–93; note that this exception—along with the question-begging "other things equal"—potentially undermines Rawls's whole argument.)

Any survey of the history of relations among adherents of different religious sects in the West over the past millennium will demonstrate that it is far more Rawls's position than that of Locke or Rousseau that depends on an a priori psychology that is insufficiently grounded in "the wider possibilities of political life." The historical experience that Rawls believes refutes Locke's and Rousseau's arguments is clearly that of the modern liberal, commercial republic. Such regimes gradually arose in the West only over the past three centuries, following the apparent resolution of the theologico-political problem through a combination of rationalizing philosophic propaganda; the liberation of the pursuit of economic gain and technological mastery of nature from religious and moral restraint (causing the joys of material gratification in this life to divert popular multitudes from singlemindedly pursuing the promise of eternal bliss after death); and a populist political movement, itself rooted in the teachings of such thinkers as Locke and Rousseau, that overthrew the rule of church, nobleman, and king. Yet—as recent world events remind us—it would be unwise to assume that the "natural strength" of free institutions (*Theory*, 193) is such as to guarantee the inevitable continuing victory of liberalism over religious (or ideological) fanaticism. Even in England, the birthplace of modern constitutional liberalism, the triumph of religious toleration could never have occurred without the temporary repression of intolerant sects until such time as the secure establishment of limited, constitutional government and the development of a commercial policy that diverted people's energies from the pursuit of salvation to that of earthly gain overcame their intolerance. (Recall the English Civil War and the events that precipitated the Glorious Revolution of 1688.)[14]

Nearly all Americans applaud the triumph of toleration and the overcoming in the West of theocracy and violent religious strife. Moreover, Rawls himself, as we have seen, acknowledges that the preservation of free institutions may on rare occasions require temporary limits to toleration. Nonetheless, both his argument for religious toleration and his account of its limits are misleading, inasmuch as neither addresses the substantive grounds for toleration or the means by which governments must act to

14. See Harvey C. Mansfield, "Party Government and the Settlement of 1688"; Robert P. Kraynak, "John Locke: From Absolutism to Toleration"; Bloom, "Justice," 653–54.

build support for that principle, which may well include, in circumstances where such support is not already well-nigh universal, restricting the public advocacy of intolerant doctrines (such as fanatical Islamism today). Additionally, by seeming to equate liberty of conscience—literally, of private belief—with the right publicly to espouse one's convictions, or demand public religious "neutrality," Rawls threatens to blur the crucial line between governments that literally persecute religious minorities (at the extreme, by massacring or enslaving them) with those that merely exclude such minorities from public office (as England did until 1828) or that have nominal religious establishments (as England still does).

If Rawls's treatment of the religious issue remains too abstract and superficial to offer useful guidance, still less can we share his hope that his principle of equal liberty might ultimately "adjudicate" "between opposing moralities" (*Theory*, 194), a claim he will elaborate in *PL*. What ground can Rawls supply for persuading those who adhere to a particular moral code that they should abstain from seeking that government conform to and promote it, just because not everyone shares their beliefs? Isn't it one of the chief functions of the law, even in a liberal society, to serve as a teacher of moral decency?[15] It is one thing to try to moderate people's moral expectations of government and their fellow citizens, but another to demand that the principles they would allegedly acknowledge in an artificial original position override their moral beliefs whenever they conflict. Why should anyone regard Rawls's principles as "the kernel of political morality" (*Theory*, 194)? As in his treatment of religion, isn't Rawls, in the name of an ostensible neutrality, really demanding that everyone accept *his* moral code, without acknowledging its partisan character or the difficulties it entails?

V.

Following his account of liberty of conscience, Rawls next seeks to illustrate the implications of his first principle for "political justice." He lays down two criteria for a just constitution and apparently assumes that they can be made to coincide: it must embody "a just procedure satisfying the requirements of equal liberty" and should generate "just and effective" legislation (*Theory*, 194). Because of his implicit (but unexplained) assumption that a constitution embodying what he regards as the most just legislative procedure will also generate the justest and most effective results,

15. See Harry Clor, *Public Morality and Liberal Society*, chap. 2, especially 76–86; and, on the impossibility of the law's remaining strictly neutral on questions of the right way of life, in view of its pedagogical function, Mary Ann Glendon, *Abortion and Divorce in Western Law*, 139–40.

Rawls emphasizes the procedural aspect of political justice rather than systematically examining the kinds of institutional arrangement that tend in practice to promote justice.

The fundamental requirement of political justice as Rawls conceives it is that "all citizens are to have an equal right to take part in, *and to determine the outcome of*, the constitutional process that establishes the laws with which they are to comply" (*Theory*, 194). I have italicized the novel, and somewhat mystifying, aspect of Rawls's formula. What would it mean for every citizen to have an equal right to "determine the outcome" of a political process? While all adult citizens (or at least those without felonious criminal records) in a modern constitutional democracy typically enjoy an equal right to take part in that process, is it not inevitable that some individuals, by virtue of their natural abilities, the offices or jobs that they hold, or their popularity or wealth, will exercise more influence in shaping its outcome than others will? Indeed, as already suggested, is it not a leading criterion of good government that what Jefferson and Adams called the "natural *aristoi*," or those best equipped by nature to govern well, *should* have more such influence (subject to the consent of their fellow citizens) than others do?

Before elaborating the steps that must be taken to equalize citizens' political influence, Rawls lays out a set of general requirements that a constitutional democracy must meet to satisfy the "principle of participation." Besides a representative, legislative body through which "a firm majority of the electorate" can normally attain its goals, Rawls mandates a system of political parties that are not "mere interest groups" but rather "advance some conception of the public good." Additionally, "the precept one elector one vote" must be enforced so that "each vote has approximately the same weight in determining the outcome of elections," and legislative districts must be drawn by an "impartial procedure" to prevent gerrymandering (*Theory*, 195–96).

Although some of these mandates appear uncontroversial, we wonder how the stricture concerning political parties is to be applied: in any democratic system, won't each major party's program represent some combination of principled appeals and the pursuit of policies that would benefit particular groups in the electorate? Don't parties that are largely interest-based offer certain advantages, in terms of moderation and a disposition toward tolerance, over more ideologically based ones?[16] Additionally,

16. See Tocqueville, *Democracy in America*, vol. 1, pt. 2, chap. 2, 167–69; Edward C. Banfield, "In Defense of the American Party System," with Harry V. Jaffa, "The Nature and Origin of the American Party System." For a defense of partisan party politics against Rawls's "disdain," on the basis of Rawls's own premises, see Russell Muirhead and Nancy L. Rosenblum, "Liberalism vs. 'The Great Game of Politics.'"

while it is hard to say a good word on behalf of gerrymandering, we might question how far it constitutes a significant substantive evil, meriting inclusion in a theory of justice. We might wonder as well why a federal system of representation in which one branch, like the U.S. Senate, is elected on a geographic rather than populational base, should be regarded as illegitimate, despite its giving extra weight to inhabitants of less populous states. Above all, we observe anew how Rawls's four-stage sequence has tended to put concerns that are either abstract or trivial to the fore as aspects of constitutional design, while giving only cursory attention to the problem of structuring power to secure liberty and promote deliberation and executive leadership that was of primary concern to the authors of the American Constitution. Is it really helpful to our own political deliberations to model the process of constitutional selection as based purely on considerations of theoretical, procedural justice, as if the practical necessities of constructing government so as to support justice and the common good could be severed from and subordinated to such considerations? How can one articulate the shape that political parties or electoral systems should have without regard to how such institutions fit into a broader constitutional scheme?

Still more problematic are the proposals Rawls adds to secure what he calls "the fair value of political liberty" (*Theory,* 197). In his view political liberties "lose much of their value whenever those who have greater private means are permitted to use their advantages to control the course of public debate," enabling them "to acquire a preponderant weight in settling" issues that affect their interests (*Theory,* 198). Rawls offers no source for this assertion, which we can only regard as an exercise in pop sociology. If Rawls is purporting to describe the actual operation of polities like the United States (as he makes explicit in *PL*), his claim would seem manifestly to be belied by such phenomena as progressive income taxation, welfare, Social Security, and antipoverty programs, all of which tend to favor the class interests of the poor and the lower middle class far more than they do those of the rich. The persistence and overall growth of these programs attests in part to the fact that rich people don't necessarily vote in ways that support their economic interests (witness the plethora of wealthy donors to the Democratic Party in recent decades—not all of them motivated by the pursuit of special favors for their businesses). Perhaps more important, it also shows how a democratic franchise enables the multitude to counteract and often overcome whatever enhancement in per capita influence the wealthy enjoy.

Rawls, however, insists that numerous "compensating steps" must be taken "to preserve the fair value" of citizens' political liberties. "In a society allowing private ownership of the means of production, property and wealth must be kept widely distributed and government monies provided on a regular basis to encourage free public discussion." (What would the latter proposal mean: government-financed discussion groups? More NPR news programs? Is there any evidence that a country that allows a free press will find that political issues are not sufficiently debated without public subsidies? Should the government bribe citizens to spend their evenings discussing public policy rather than watching *The Simpsons*? What of the danger that government financing will be used to favor the outlook of the governing party?) Additionally, "political parties are to be made independent from private economic interests" through government subsidies that make them "autonomous with respect to private demands, that is, demands not expressed in the public forum and argued for openly by reference to a conception of the public good." Without such provision, Rawls believes, the "pleadings" of "the more advantaged social and economic interests . . . are bound to receive excessive attention," while "the less favored . . . withdraw into apathy and resentment" (*Theory,* 198).

Once again Rawls offers no evidence to support his speculations, which he uses to justify a sweeping program of making political parties into financial wards of the government that considerably exceeds what any mainstream advocate of public campaign financing has proposed. Curiously, while uncertain whether "private ownership of the means of production" should even be *allowed,* Rawls seems wholly unsuspicious of the likelihood of abuses of governmental power. His suggestion that subventions to parties might be "based on the number of votes received in the last several elections" would tend, we note, to freeze existing partisan alignments rather than encourage political change. (At the same time, the prospect of federal subsidies would encourage extremist organizations such as the Nation of Islam and the American Nazi Party to register so as to gain at least a small share of the spoils, thus using taxpayer funds to spread their messages of hate.) Rawls seems oblivious, moreover, to the possibility that demands expressed openly in a democratic forum may be no less self-interested, or based on no less partisan a view of the public good, than those that smaller groups may think it advantageous to advance privately.[17] In later writings

17. In a note Rawls explains that his remarks on the tendency of economic inequalities to undermine political equality "draw upon" the economist Frank H. Knight's *The Ethics of Competition and Other Essays* (*Theory,* 199n). But within the very pages Rawls cites, Knight expresses greater concern about the influence in democratic politics of the capacities for public persuasion and political organization, which he maintains are "more unequally distributed among men by nature than is economic ability or power of any other kind," "tend more strongly to cumulative increase through their own exercise," and correlate poorly with "competence to counsel and to lead" (*Ethics of Competition,* 296–97, 304–5).

Rawls proposes further restrictions on the political process, such as (unspecified) content-neutral "regulations of freedom of speech and of the press," to try to guarantee that it will "yield just legislation" (*JF,* 149–50). Presumably, the sheer fact that an existing political system fails to produce legislation that Rawls and like-minded partisans find just would prove the need for further fine-tuning of the electoral system until the desired result is reached.

In defense of the need for such ostensible reforms, Rawls offers a broad-brush criticism of democratic polities past and present, claiming that "historically one of the main defects of constitutional government has been the failure to insure the fair value of political liberty," since "disparities in the distribution of property and wealth that far exceed what is compatible with political equality have generally been tolerated." As a consequence, he asserts, social and economic inequities "may soon undermine whatever political equality might have existed," because when parties are dependent on private contributions, "the political forum is so constrained by the wishes of the dominant interests that the basic measures needed to establish just constitutional rule are seldom properly presented." Again Rawls offers no support or illustration for his claims, explaining that such questions "belong to political sociology" as distinguished from his enterprise of describing "an ideal arrangement" against which "actual institutions" may be judged (*Theory,* 199). But may not the assertion of an abstract ideal, combined with sweeping (though unsupported) denunciations of the alleged inequities of existing constitutional polities, weaken the cause of justice by engendering contempt for political regimes like that of the United States that in practice have tended best to promote it? (As we shall repeatedly observe, Rawls has an unfortunate habit of venturing beyond the sphere of "moral theory" to make a variety of questionable, partisan claims about the operation of actual political life, only to retreat from having to defend them by saying that the details aren't his business.)

The incoherence of Rawls's "principle of participation" is visible in the two criteria he propounds for judging the performance of representatives: although "responsive to the felt interests of the electorate," they must "seek first to pass just and effective legislation," and only secondarily "further their constituents' other interests" (*Theory,* 199–200). While no one would deny legislators' primary duty to pursue justice and the common good, this formulation passes over their need to accommodate their constituents' "felt interests" sufficiently to win reelection (and hence be able to continue pursuing justice).[18] Would it not be more fruitful to consider, with

18. More radically, a few pages later, Rawls asserts that "where issues of justice are involved, the intensity of people's desires should not be taken into account" at all, even

the American founders, how political institutions can be designed to reduce the likelihood that a majority of the electorate can, or may try to, compel its representatives to pursue unjust or foolish courses of action?[19] Might not that goal be best achieved, in part, through institutions whose ranks are filled by diverse means of election and appointment (not always conforming to the rule "one elector one vote") and that are designed to attract public officials of superior education and talent, as in the American Constitution?

In contrast to the foregoing (Federalist) view that highlights representatives' independent discretion, Rawls concludes this section of his discussion by expressing an expectation that is reminiscent of the Antifederalist perspective: while "in a well-governed state only a small fraction of persons may devote much of their time to politics . . . this fraction, whatever its size, will most likely be drawn more or less equally from all sectors of society" (*Theory,* 200). But what facts can ground this observation? In a modern representative republic with a diversified economy (one very unlike the small, relatively homogeneous society envisioned by the Antifederalists), is the average factory worker or small farmer just as likely to take an active part in politics or be elected to state or national office as persons whose occupations—in law, commerce, teaching, or other professions—bring them closer to the political arena and give them the sort of knowledge, rhetorical talents, and negotiating skills that equip them to represent their constituents' interests?[20]

In keeping with his abstract, mechanistic account of the political process, Rawls displays no appreciation of how the representative system of constitutional government devised by the American founders reconciles the principle of self-government with the need, in a large, diverse, commercial republic, for legislators, presidents, and professional civil servants having the sort of talents and understanding of complex issues that can come only from devoting full-time attention to them. As the authors of *The Federalist* observe, the founders' enterprise reflected an "honorable determination . . . to rest all our political experiments on the capacity of

---

though "as things are, legislators must reckon with strong public feelings" (*Theory,* 203; see also 395). The implied wish seems to be that some day legislators will be liberated entirely from having to attend to their constituents' opinions when they conflict with the mandates of Rawlsian justice (see chapter 7 below on Rawls's implicit support for judicial activism to advance his agenda in the face of a recalcitrant electorate). Rawls's sharp dichotomy between "the question of right" and that of "feasibility" (*Theory,* 203) only deepens the statesman's problem in the meantime.

19. See Hamilton, Madison, and Jay, *The Federalist,* esp. Nos. 10, 51, 63, 71, 78.
20. See ibid., No. 35, 182–85.

mankind for self-government."[21] But self-government is workable only if our public officials have sufficient discretion and independence from direct, plebiscitary control to work out policies that take account of the complexity of political issues and the need to balance various circumstances and popular demands. While an informed citizenry is highly desirable, it is neither necessary nor beneficial to bribe citizens to spend more time debating health care policies or the military budget. If they are dissatisfied with the government's policies, members of the government will find out soon enough—at the next election. Subsidized political discussions would merely heighten the influence of "activists" with time on their hands, while encouraging the illusion that difficult issues of national and international policy can be resolved on the basis of a little Internet surfing and TV watching.[22]

Thanks to the federal principle and the spirit of limited government, we should recognize, the American political system continues to provide far more opportunity to persons of merely ordinary talents to serve in government, or to contribute informally to political deliberations, *on the local level*, than do more centralized systems like the French one (to say nothing of nondemocratic polities). Through federalism and devolution, the citizens of a polity like the United States are able, as Tocqueville observed, to have their cake and eat it too: enjoying the national strength and economic prosperity for which large size is a near prerequisite and a considerable advantage (respectively) in the modern world, while maintaining the personal vigor and the spirit of liberty that are associated with small

21. Ibid., No. 39, 208; cf. David Epstein, *The Political Theory of "The Federalist,"* 5–7, 32–34, 119–25. As we shall observe, the theme of honor has no role in Rawls's political theory; it is replaced by the primary good of "self-respect."

22. Illustrative of these problems is the proposal by political theorists Bruce Ackerman and James Fishkin for a national "Deliberation Day" on which all but essential work would be prohibited and citizens would be paid $150 each to participate in guided group discussions of current issues (*Deliberation Day*). Since participation would (fortunately) be voluntary, the likely bias of those who would attend the community meetings where issues would be discussed following a viewing of televised candidate debates—i.e., "activists" and those in serious need of $150—is obvious. On the patronizing and fundamentally undemocratic character of the Ackerman-Fishkin proposal, its misunderstanding of the purpose of representative government, and evidence that the authors' trial runs for their ostensibly nonpartisan enterprise tended to push participants toward a left-liberal agenda, see Brendan Conway, "Just Think about It." As Yale political scientist Steven Smith observes, such calls for more ostensibly "deliberative democracy and . . . publicly funded days of national deliberation are merely watered-down versions of the populist assault on the Constitution," akin to the anticonstitutional populism that helped bring down the Weimar Republic (*Reading Leo Strauss*, 182).

republics.[23] It is far more natural as well as feasible for human beings to concern themselves with local issues in which they have a direct stake and firsthand knowledge, and in which they sense that their individual voices can make a difference (such as their schools), than for them to devote close attention to the details of national policy.

Although Rawls has nothing to say about federalism and local self-government, the centralizing effect of the policies he infers from the difference principle would only tend to weaken them (just as strict application of his one-man, one-vote rule would do). Moreover, through his doctrine of the "fair value" of political liberty Rawls devalues self-government as such. His principle of participation, he emphasizes, neither "define[s] an ideal of citizenship" nor prescribes "a duty requiring all to take an active part in political affairs" (*Theory*, 200).[24] Political liberty in Rawls's account seems to owe its chief, if not sole, value to its instrumental capacity to help each citizen secure his rightful share of the primary goods that government distributes; hence Rawls's claim that the more economic inequality there is, the lower the "value" of political liberty.[25] Is the right to participate in one's own governance, directly or indirectly, valuable only in proportion to the degree of economic equality one enjoys as a result? Why, then, even take the time to vote so long as you get your share of the spoils? Is political apathy really the consequence of a lack of public campaign financing, as Rawls contends, or rather of an individualistic attitude that causes the citizen to think less of what he owes his country than the reverse, along with the growth of a centralized national government too remote from the ordinary citizen for him to feel he can influence its actions? But what kind of citizenry is disinclined even to discuss public issues without a financial subsidy?

In the next section Rawls indeed affirms that equal political liberty is valuable "not solely [as] a means," since it serves to "strengthen men's sense of their own worth, enlarge their intellectual and moral sensibilities,

23. Tocqueville, *Democracy in America*, vol. 1, pt. 1, chap. 8, 149–54. See also William Schambra, "The Roots of the American Public Philosophy."

24. More emphatically, in his "Reply to Habermas," Rawls states that justice as fairness rejects any claim that "human beings achieve their fullest realization, their highest good" in political activity (*PL*, 420). Schaar notes that Rawls's vision of a largely apolitical citizenry governed by the two principles "sounds a lot like interest-group liberalism *cum* professional bureaucracy" and might be viewed "as the shortest road to that 'democratic despotism'" about which Tocqueville warned ("Reflections on Rawls' *Theory*," 162; cf. Wiggins, "Neo-Aristotelian Reflections," 500–502).

25. See also Rawls's claim that "the usefulness of our political liberties is far more subject to our social position and our place in the distribution of income and wealth than the usefulness of our other basic liberties" (*PL*, 328).

and lay the basis for a sense of duty and obligation" (*Theory*, 206). But this claim does not cohere with his foregoing argument. Here he asserts that the citizen "is expected to vote" and "have political opinions"; yet earlier he denied that citizens have any duty of active political participation. Now Rawls denies that the "time and thought" a citizen devotes to forming political opinions are determined by "the likely material return of his political influence," since political activity is "enjoyable in itself"; but how do we reconcile these claims with the doctrine of the "fair value" of political liberty or the supposed need to subsidize political discussions? (And can't Rawls find a higher or more persuasive ground for political participation than how enjoyable it is?) Finally, even in making the case for the intrinsic value of political liberty, Rawls insists that it "not [be] designed to satisfy the individual's desire for self-mastery" (*Theory*, 205). Why not?[26]

In the end, Rawls indicates that his case for what he calls equal political liberty is only a conditional one: he proceeds to explain how *unequal* political liberty can be defended on the basis of his principles, simply by arguing "that the inequality of right would be accepted by the less favored in return for the greater protection of their other liberties that results from this restriction" (*Theory*, 203). He cites without criticism Mill's contention that more intelligent or highly educated people should be given extra votes to enhance their influence, observing that Mill's argument shows "why political equality is sometimes regarded as less essential than equal liberty of conscience or liberty of the person" (*Theory*, 204–5). But how far, then, has Rawls added to the case for political liberty? (Recall his criticism of Mill's arguments precisely on the ground that they might not guarantee equal liberty for everyone.) Granted Rawls's acknowledgment that a restriction of some people's political liberties may be justified by its contribution to the greater security of their other freedoms, why not allow such a restriction if it contributes to their well-being in some other respect? (In fact, Rawls does just that in *PL* [7] by mandating that the basic liberties be subordinated to a prior principle requiring that citizens' "basic needs" first be met.) Do we not find a far stronger—because substantive—case for self-government in such works as Locke's *Second Treatise*, Rousseau's *Social Contract*, Pericles' funeral oration, and Lincoln's speeches, as well as Mill's writings?[27]

26. Contrast Rawls's later appeal to the virtue of "self-command," discussed in chapter 8 below. Or is "self-mastery" a misprint for "mastery," simply?

27. Consider Dworkin's argument that the right to liberty in Rawls's account of the original position is ultimately derivative from, and subordinate to, a prior right to equality, making liberal constitutional and social institutions dispensable to it (*Taking Rights Seriously*, 182–83).

VI.

In the remaining sections of chapter 4 Rawls sets forth three subsidiary clarifications of his first principle: its relation to the rule of law, the specific meaning of the priority of liberty, and the "Kantian interpretation" of that principle. His remarks on the importance and the specific content of the rule of law (including the need for laws to be promulgated and fairly administered, as well as the prohibition of bills of attainder and ex post facto criminal laws) are conventional and unexceptionable. But two odd aspects stand out. First, while acknowledging that "a coercive sovereign is presumably always necessary," Rawls adds that "in a well-ordered society sanctions are not severe and may never need to be imposed," a proposition he curiously describes as "Hobbes's thesis" (*Theory*, 211).[28] Is this a claim about justice, or merely a utopian ideal that is essentially tautological (in that a "well-ordered society" would by definition be free from crime)? Second, there is his insistence, derivative from the first principle's assertion of the priority of liberty, that restrictions of liberty are never justified except to promote an overall enhancement of "the basic equal liberties of the representative citizen," not for the sake of any other good (*Theory*, 213). It is difficult to assess this assertion, because Rawls does not provide any illustrations of a restriction of basic liberties that would be prohibited because it served some good other than liberty.[29] One implication, however, would

28. Neither the chapters Rawls cites in Hobbes's *Leviathan* nor the passages in two secondary works on Hobbes cited in the same note (*Theory*, 211n) just following this claim provide any support for it, so far as I can determine. Apparently the cited passages are meant only to support the noncontroversial point that "the existence of effective penal machinery serves as men's security to one another" (*Theory*, 211); but Hobbes never forecast a machinery so effective that it would deter or prevent practically all crime. Closer to the thesis are the utopian claims of Kant regarding a "perfect state" in his *Critique of Pure Reason* (B373), and Sidgwick's "hope that crime and its punishment will decrease and gradually disappear as the world improves" (*Methods of Ethics*, 283). In his *Social Contract* (bk. 2, chap. 5, 65) and *Discourse on Political Economy* (215), Rousseau also holds that the frequent application of criminal penalties is a sign of bad government, but their radical reduction presupposes the success of the legislator's sweeping transformation of people's outlook, through such devices as a civil religion, to cause them to identify with their country and revere its laws, as well as a strict censorship over mores (*Social Contract*, bk. 2, chap. 7; bk. 4, chaps. 7–8; *Discourse*, 216–19).

29. He provides two illustrations at *JF*, 47. First, "the equal political liberties cannot be denied to certain groups on the grounds that their having these liberties may enable them to block policies needed for economic growth and efficiency" (but presumably they could be denied if people's "basic needs" had not yet been met). Second, we cannot "justify a selective service act that grants educational deferments to some" on the ground that it provides incentives to those otherwise subject to conscription to seek further education: "Since conscription is a drastic interference with the basic liberties of equal citizenship, it cannot be justified by any needs less compelling than . . .

seem to be the invalidity of restrictions on the public advertisement and distribution of obscene materials, for the sake of fortifying what many thinkers have regarded as the moral prerequisites of a healthy republican order.[30] On the other hand, if such restrictions may be justified on the ground that they indirectly enhance citizens' basic liberties, it becomes hard to discern just what restrictions on liberty are disallowed by Rawls's principle at all.

In the next section, "The Priority of Liberty Defined," Rawls nonetheless reiterates that his two principles provide "the strongest arguments for freedom," in contrast to the "uncertain grounds" supplied by teleological principles. Not only do the principles "define an appropriate path between dogmatism and intolerance . . . and a reductionism which regards religion and morality as mere preferences," they also rely on "weak and widely held presumptions," encouraging the hope that they will be widely accepted (*Theory*, 214). As I have shown, Rawls's argument for liberty is in fact merely formal and is considerably weaker than the substantive argument provided by Mill, to say nothing of more profound liberal thinkers such as Locke and Montesquieu. And I have challenged Rawls's claim that his version of liberalism treats religion and morality as anything more than preferences, since the neutrality requirement embodied in the veil of ignorance reduces them to the level of merely idiosyncratic "conceptions of the good"; and to restrict the calculations of the parties in the original position to the maximization and proper distribution of so-called primary goods is in practice to elevate these things over religious and moral goods. Finally, Rawls has never demonstrated the need for a new set of arguments for freedom, at least outside the cloistered domains of certain philosophy departments.

The other element in this section that requires mention is Rawls's rather obscure distinction between what he calls "ideal theory"—that is, the selection of principles of justice based on the assumption (which he has relied on) "that they will be generally complied with"—and "nonideal theory," on which he offers only brief remarks, which concerns what to do under "less than favorable conditions." One confusing aspect of Rawls's distinction between ideal and nonideal theory is his classification of the constraints on liberty that derive from "natural limitations" (such as

---

the defense of these equal liberties themselves." Whatever the injustice of the latter policy, Rawls's criticism seems to confuse the reasons for conscription with the reasons for exemptions. (And what if military leaders judged that an educated army would offer a more effective defense force?) I cite the difficulties in each of Rawls's applications to suggest the limited utility of a bare assertion of the priority of liberty when it comes to concrete cases.

30. On the case for regulating pornography in a liberal regime, see Harry Clor, *Obscenity and Public Morality*, especially chap. 5.

restrictions on children's freedom) as belonging to "nonideal theory" (*Theory*, 217), when he had remarked more sensibly only two pages earlier that "the question of the justice of these constraints does not arise" precisely because they reflect "the more or less permanent conditions of political life" or "the human situation" (*Theory*, 215). Why should accommodations to the natural human condition, such as the incapacity of children to exercise properly the same liberty as adults, be classified as "nonideal," unless the "ideal" standard is one that ignores the actual character of human life even more than Rawls has done through the veil of ignorance?

More significant for Rawls's account of nonideal situations is the case in which it is argued that adults must be allocated unequal amounts of liberty (as distinguished from having the liberty of all restricted equally). Rawls judges that "in many historical situations a lesser political liberty may have been justified" by circumstances, reflecting the fact that "the various liberties are not all on a par," with political liberty being less vital than freedom from enslavement or religious intolerance.[31] Such a sacrifice of some liberties can be allowed, however, only for the sake of establishing conditions in which the restrictions can ultimately be abolished (*Theory*, 217–18). But how can such an outcome be guaranteed? How do we know that a stable, liberal republic can be actualized everywhere, even in the long run? Would it not be more prudent to acknowledge the superior legitimacy of nondemocratic regimes that conform to the rule of law and respect basic personal rights, as compared with those that violate such guarantees, whether or not it can be proved that the former will ultimately be transformed into constitutional democracies?

Even after asserting that neither "serfdom and slavery" nor religious intolerance were justifiable as unequal political representation might have been (as Burke believed) by the circumstances of eighteenth-century European society, Rawls then acknowledges that the former two practices might be "tolerable . . . when they relieve even worse injustices," as when the enslavement of prisoners of war is the only alternative to their slaughter. Still, he insists, no such considerations can justify hereditary slavery (*Theory*, 217–18).

---

31. By contrast, in his later "Reply to Habermas," Rawls insists that in justice as fairness "the ancient and modern liberties," or "public and private autonomy," "are co-original and of equal weight with neither given pride of place over the other" (*PL*, 412–13). Rawls's weak response to Habermas's charge that his version of political liberalism contains an "unresolved competition between ancient and modern liberties" is that it just requires "weighing the evidence one way or the other" to decide how to balance them (*PL*, 417)—which seems another way of saying that it leaves the competition unresolved. Rawls also judges that Habermas sketches his ideal "too broadly to foresee to what family of liberties" it would lead—but then admits, "I have not done much of this myself" (*PL*, 419).

But why not? If it is held that slavery might be justified as a substitute for the slaughter of captives, might not the authority of the conqueror to keep the captives' descendants in servitude be justified as an added incentive to avoid killing the captives? I cite this possibility not to argue in favor of hereditary (or other forms of) slavery, but only to suggest that Rawls's criteria for distinguishing between what is legitimate and what isn't again appear arbitrary or ad hoc, rather than following from his principles. Similarly, how can Rawls know that some measure of religious intolerance, in the form of the Test Acts, wasn't a necessity in eighteenth-century Britain (as previously noted), given the possibility of an attempted forcible Catholic restoration and renewed religious strife?

Rawls's brief account of nonideal theory represents an attempt to give his principles of justice a more realistic application. But if the principles themselves are exceedingly abstract, the compromises that Rawls acknowledges may be necessary to accommodate the nonideal (i.e., real) world are effectively open-ended, again undermining his claim to provide a firm foundation for liberty. Rawls supplies no sufficient reason for accepting the compromises he finds tolerable while rejecting others such as those I have suggested under all circumstances.

In the concluding section of chapter 4 Rawls represents his first principle and its priority as grounded in a "Kantian interpretation" of justice. But as with the construction that Rawls previously labeled "Hobbes's thesis," this interpretation depends on a highly selective use of Kant's writings: indeed, he concludes by remarking (circularly) that "the Kantian interpretation is not intended as an interpretation of Kant's actual doctrine but rather of justice as fairness" (*Theory*, 226).[32] However, Rawls maintains that his "empirical" interpretation of Kant's moral view reveals its "characteristic structure" more effectively than Kant's own presentation did, by identifying the choice of the parties to the original position as reflecting their "desire to express their nature as rational and equal members of the intelligible realm" (*Theory*, 225).

It would take me too far afield to assess Rawls's use of Kant, which several scholars have shown distorts that thinker's doctrine.[33] Two points must suffice here. First, given the nonhuman character of the parties to the

32. In the following section Rawls explains that he "detached" Kant's doctrine from its metaphysical foundations to show it "more clearly" and "relatively free from objection" (*Theory*, 233). But in consequence, Rawls's doctrine is hardly Kantian in any serious sense.

33. See, for instance, Oliver A. Johnson, "The Kantian Interpretation"; Susan Meld Shell, "'Kantianism' and Constitutional Rights"; Sandel, *Liberalism and the Limits of Justice*, 35–40; Devin Stauffer, *Plato's Introduction to the Question of Justice*, 7–9; Bloom, "Justice," 756–57.

original position, as well as the fact that Rawls could elicit a "decision" from them only by smuggling all sorts of question-begging assumptions into his account of that situation, Rawls has no ground for claiming that obeying the principles ostensibly derived from that situation somehow expresses our "nature." Second, whereas Kant's categorical imperative in its various formulations imposes severe duties on the individual—that he treat other human beings always as ends, not merely as means; that he act always on the basis of maxims that he could rationally will to be universal laws—Rawls's principles impose no such duty on anyone. In fact Rawls baldly asserts that Kant's doctrine, properly interpreted, "leads not to a morality of austere command but to an ethic of mutual respect and self-esteem" (*Theory*, 225).[34]

Whereas Kant's teaching is intended to fortify human dignity by emphasizing our capacity to overcome selfish interest out of reverence for the moral law that our reason prescribes, it is hard to know what justifies our mutual respect and self-esteem in Rawls's scheme. That question must be addressed when we consider part 3 of *Theory*. First, I address Rawls's prescriptions for economic justice and his treatment of the duty of law-abidingness in the remainder of part 2.

34. Rawls supports this interpretation with references to Kant's discussion of moral education in his *Critique of Practical Reason* and a four-page section of Lewis White Beck's commentary on that work, neither of which justify Rawls's reading. In the former, Kant stresses the need to inculcate the young with a love of virtue unmixed with any regard to their own happiness or welfare, so that the grown man will fear most "to find himself . . . worthless and contemptible in his own eyes" (*Critique of Practical Reason*, 160, 165). The other source Rawls cites in this note, Williams's "Idea of Equality" (116), specifically denies that the transcendental, Kantian conception of humanity can "provide any solid foundation for the notions of equality . . . or of equality of respect" (*Theory*, 225n).

Rawls's inclination to substitute a morality of self-gratification for Kant's stern teaching is further indicated by his subsequent promise that members of his well-ordered society will be liberated from the burden of "oppressive conscience" that unreasonably interferes with people's "spontaneity and enjoyment" (*Theory*, 428–29).

CHAPTER 5

Economic Justice

I.

Chapter 5 of *Theory*, "Distributive Shares," describes an economic system conforming to Rawls's second principle. At the outset Rawls emphasizes his agnosticism regarding the comparative justness of free-market and socialist economies, holding that either one might be compatible with his principles (*Theory*, 228).

The first section of this chapter, "The Concept of Justice in Political Economy," contains one of Rawls's most important statements about the intention of his theory and its relation to people's conceptions of the good. Rawls stresses the significance of the choice of an economic system as a means not only of satisfying people's present wants but of shaping their future desires, thereby "determin[ing] in part the sort of persons they want to be as well as the sort of persons they are." Since the choice of economic institutions presupposes a conception of the good, it must "be made on moral and political as well as on economic grounds" (*Theory*, 229).

Although Rawls properly highlights the moral and political significance of economic institutions, there is a potentially misleading abstraction in his representation of social and economic "systems" as if they were independent objects of choice. To the extent that actual human beings get to "choose" an economic order, they do so through the political process. Yet, as in his prioritizing of society over government in chapter 1, Rawls's reference to an economic system as "regulat[ing]" such matters as production and distribution (*Theory*, 235) blurs the fact that it is governments that lay down economic regulations, while perceived human need largely determines (within the limits set by law) what is produced and how it is distributed or paid for. Of course, there is a considerable variety in the conceptions of need held among different political societies, though they are not infinitely variable. But Rawls's representation of economic systems as somehow independently chosen to determine what we "want to be" severs the processes of economic and political decision making (despite his assertion of their connectedness), as if the choice of a political regime, such as the American people made in 1787–1788, does not already entail favoring certain sorts of economic institutions rather than others. (Rawls wants to maintain this severance to leave the choice between free-market institutions and socialist ones entirely open.)

The problem deepens in the sequel, where Rawls asserts the compatibility of society's influence on people's wants and self-understanding with the "objectivity" of his account of justice. By deriving that account from the original position, he explains, he sought to provide an "Archimedean point," independent of existing desires, from which society's basic structure can be appraised. In response to the objection that his doctrine still depends on existing aims in its formulation, Rawls argues that it makes "only the most general assumptions" about the parties' goals in the original position, "namely, that they take an interest in primary social goods, [which] . . . men are presumed to want whatever else they want." Hence he denies that his theory derives justice from aspirations that reflect current social arrangements: though justice as fairness presupposes a view of the good, "within wide limits this does not prejudge the choice" of what we become (*Theory*, 230).

As we have seen, contrary to this claim, the original position as Rawls interpreted it sets rather narrow bounds to human possibility. All ways of life that depend on living in a society collectively dedicated to religious faith or the pursuit of military glory, or even that require limitations on degrading sexual practices, are excluded. Meanwhile, the doctrine of primary goods inevitably implies, despite Rawls's disclaimers, that the greater people's wealth, the better off they are. Indeed, now that the two principles have been established, Rawls becomes more explicit about the limits they set to conceptions of the good. Not only must the social system discourage desires for "inherently unjust" things, or wants that entail violating just arrangements, since such desires "have no weight" or "value"; just institutions must be designed "to encourage the virtue of justice," thereby defining "a partial ideal of the person." This ideal establishes society's "long range aim" without regard to its present members' "particular desires and needs." But even though justice as fairness resembles perfectionism in embodying an ideal that limits people's goals, Rawls emphasizes that its standard is based only on the requisites of justice, not on any more specific (hence more restrictive) view of human excellence (*Theory,* 230–31).

This defense is unpersuasive. Rawls's ultimate aim, it will be recalled, is to devise an account of justice that "we" will find intuitively satisfying and that will largely conform to the particular judgments that "we" already make intuitively.[1] What reason is there to think that the "we" from whose perspective a theory of justice is thereby assessed are any more transhistorical beings than a "we" on whose judgments of human excellence a model of the good society might be based?[2] And is it not highly doubtful that "our" judgments about justice can be made independent of our judgments of goodness, so as to elevate the former over the latter?[3]

The chief aim of political philosophy, as understood from antiquity through at least the late eighteenth century, is to achieve an objective account of the good society, including the nature of justice, one that transcends the prejudices of a given time and place. The philosophic formulators of the modern doctrine of natural right, most obviously Locke, endeavored to enunciate a popularly accessible standard of right that can be used to assess the legitimacy of any government, thereby arming what Locke calls the "weak hands of justice" with the power of popular majorities.[4] Rawls's contract approach to justice, as well as his endeavor to formulate that virtue in terms of simple principles, is loosely modeled, we have seen, on the Lockean project of abstracting from existing, conven-

---

1. As Rawls puts it even more explicitly in *PL* (25–26), the ultimate test of the procedure in the original position is "what we regard—here and now—as fair conditions" for specifying "the terms of social cooperation," as well as its yielding a "conception of justice that we regard—here and now—as fair" and reasonable.

2. In chapter 9, Rawls expressly cites the historically transitory character of all views of justice and their claims to validity. Thus by his own account, his principles no more transcend our contingency and historicity than do the current desires he represents as irrelevant to justice (*Theory,* 480).

3. The source that Rawls cites in this context regarding the influence of economic systems on people's individual aspirations (*Theory,* 229n) actually argues the impossibility of a system's being truly impartial among alternative visions of the good (Barry, *Political Argument,* 76–77).

4. Locke, *Two Treatises,* bk. 2, chap. 16, sec. 176. See also the preface to Rousseau's *Second Discourse,* criticizing previous definitions of natural right as too sophisticated to be accessible to unlearned multitudes (*Discourse on the Origin and Foundations of Inequality,* in *First and Second Discourses,* 94–95).

tional political opinions so as to derive justice from people's most fundamental, universal needs. But because Rawls avoided basing his original position on an empirical consideration of human nature, he cannot plausibly claim that his perspective is in any sense "Archimedean." It may be, of course, that Hobbes and Locke also failed to achieve such a perspective, as such critics of their state-of-nature doctrine as Rousseau maintained; but they at least supply plausible criteria for distinguishing what is natural in human desires from what is merely conventional and hence essentially malleable, in a way that Rawls makes no effort to do.

Rawls's present remarks about how a just social system must discourage "unjust" desires bring out the greatest danger of his approach. Doesn't his demand that society's aim be settled without regard to its present members' wishes evince a highly authoritarian impulse?[5] When Rawls asserts that "there is no place for the *question* whether men's desires to play the role of superior or inferior" might justify autocratic institutions, or of whether some religious practices might seem so degrading as to justify prohibiting them (*Theory*, 231; emphasis added), is he not adopting an antiphilosophical if not autocratic posture himself? Doesn't Rawls risk a dangerous self-righteousness in assuming that human desires can be neatly categorized into those that are and are not "inherently unjust," the latter being dismissed without further consideration?[6]

The foregoing problems are ultimately the consequence of Rawls's assumption that political institutions can be designed to give justice priority over the human good. Even though Rawls has not demonstrated that his account of justice is independent of his own understanding of the good, he has used the pretense of such independence to avoid having to justify that understanding.[7] Contrary to his claims, we must ask whether

---

5. This demand recalls Socrates' ironic account in Plato's *Republic* (540e–541a) of the decisive precondition for establishing a just city: the expulsion of all inhabitants over the age of ten. Plato thereby provides his ultimate indication of the impossibility of achieving perfect justice and the dangers of the utopian spirit itself. Rawls, by contrast, is utterly serious about wanting to refound society in a way that disregards its members' existing wants and beliefs.

6. Contrast Aristotle's argument at the outset of the *Nicomachean Ethics* that every human activity is directed at some good, and see the references in note 16 to chapter 7 below. Rawls adopts a slightly more nuanced moral psychology in part 3, where he acknowledges that the unjust and the bad man (but not the evil one) pursue things that are intrinsically good, but do so in the wrong way or to a wrong extreme (*Theory*, 385). But Rawls never integrates that qualification into his account of justice, and his later remarks, as I will observe, still embody some of the problems I note here.

7. Although Rawls attempts to demonstrate "the good of justice" in part 3 of *Theory*, that demonstration will prove to be purely formal rather than resting on a realistic analysis of human nature.

the desire for some form of superiority over others is not inextricably con-nected with the aspiration to human greatness.[8] Doesn't the pursuit of holiness, similarly, often entail setting limits to even the peaceful (public) religious practices of others, such as devil worship? (This, certainly, is the teaching of the Hebrew Bible, the New Testament, and the Koran.) While extreme care must be taken to prevent these wishes from being expressed in politically harmful ways, can we reasonably dismiss the desires them-selves as having "no value"? If constitutional liberalism is to be defended, must we not rather endeavor to show how it is compatible with the human aspirations toward excellence and holiness, reasonably expressed? What mandate can a constitutional, republican government have to discourage all desires that conflict with Rawls's conception of justice? Because Rawls, in emphasizing how the social system shapes people's wants and aspira-tions, makes no distinction between conventional and natural desires, does he not, however inadvertently, offer a dangerously open-ended recipe for tyrants and fanatics who seek to reengineer human nature to their specifications?[9]

Seeing none of this as problematic, Rawls instead observes hopefully that a well-ordered society will be "homogeneous," in that its members' moral judgments, like those of the parties to the original position, will tend toward unanimity. Thus, he concludes, even though justice as fairness rests on an individualistic foundation, it provides "a central place for the value of community" (*Theory*, 232–33).[10] This exaltation of a community based on unanimity (to be elaborated in chapter 9) corresponds to Rawls's earlier labeling of the disagreements about justice that characterize exist-ing liberal societies as a defect to be corrected. Again, we wonder how far

---

8. Consider Hamilton's reference in describing the presidential office in *The Federal-ist*, No. 72 to the love of fame as "the ruling passion of the noblest minds" (405). The presidency as Hamilton conceives it was designed to attract candidates who aim to achieve and demonstrate their superiority, while the constitutional structure channels their ambition in ways that serve the public good.

9. Cf. Marx's call in *The German Ideology* for "the alteration of men on a mass scale" to generate "communist consciousness" and "found society anew"; similarly, the demand for a "total loss of humanity" for the sake of its "total redemption" in the introduction to *Contribution to the Critique of Hegel's "Philosophy of Right*" (both in Robert C. Tucker, ed., *The Marx-Engels Reader*, 193 and 64).

10. In chapter 9, Rawls radicalizes this claim of unanimity to celebrate the fact that in his well-ordered society everyone will "find satisfaction in the very same thing" (*The-ory*, 461–62). Although in *PL* he retreats from the claim in favor of a more modest "over-lapping consensus," the retreat, I will observe, is more rhetorical than substantive, since Rawls retains the mandate that moral and religious concerns founded in particu-lar views of the good (other than Rawls's own, unacknowledged one) may have no direct influence on public policy.

Rawls's project is truly a liberal one. Rawls's ostensible corrective to individualism seems to leave no room for human individuality.

II.

Rawls next introduces his account of the economic institutions mandated by the difference principle in a section headed "Some Remarks about Economic Systems" that elaborates his agnosticism on the relative merits from the standpoint of justice of free-market and socialist systems (*Theory*, 235). Rawls believes that both sorts of regime "normally allow for the free choice of occupation and of one's place of work"; "only under command systems of either kind" is "this freedom . . . overtly interfered with" (*Theory*, 239). Rawls provides no example of a private-property economy that is also a "command system"; presumably, the reference is to premodern and non-Western systems that have limited economic opportunity on the basis of hereditary class or guild restrictions. More important, he fails to cite a socialist system that allowed most people a freedom in the choice of employment comparable to that offered in free-enterprise nations. Nor does Rawls supply evidence to justify his denial that there is any "essential tie between the use of free markets and private ownership of the instruments of production" (*Theory*, 239). Certainly Rawls's discussion of these themes would have been improved, and his agnosticism might have been modified, had he considered empirical examples rather than relying on abstract definitions of economic systems.[11]

Rawls reiterates this agnosticism in the following section, "Background Institutions for Distributive Justice." Although he chooses to illustrate the

---

11. Barry, whose *Liberal Theory* helped publicize Rawls's *Theory*, finds the book's "significance" to lie in its stating liberalism in a form "compatible with socialism" (166), as if merely denying the connection between economic freedom and other forms of liberty constituted a theoretical breakthrough. Amy Gutmann, similarly, explains that Rawls's omission from his list of basic liberties such "capitalist market freedoms" as the rights "to own commercial property, to appropriate what one has produced, [or] to inherit or to pass on one's possessions" exemplifies "the integration of socialist criticism into liberal theory," generating "a liberalism that pays a moral tribute to the socialist critique" and thus can win Rawlsian principles the support of "left-liberals" ("The Central Role of Rawls's Theory," 339). Indeed, going beyond his professed agnosticism about the comparative merits of free-enterprise and socialist systems, in *JF* Rawls judges that Marx's view that no regime that allows private ownership of the means of production can be just may be "in good part true," although "the question is not yet settled" (178).

On the philosophical reasons (rooted in the nineteenth-century utilitarian rejection of Locke's natural-rights doctrine) for the disaffection of contemporary intellectuals with the free-enterprise system, see Plattner, "Capitalism," 327–32.

economic regime mandated by the two principles by reference to a "property-owning democracy" rather than a socialist system, he emphasizes that he has done so only because such a regime "is likely to be better known." (Does he mean that it will be better known to his Western readers, or that nothing remotely resembling a "liberal socialist" regime has ever existed?) He stresses that his articulation of an ideally just property-owning system "does not imply" that its actual "historical forms are just, or even tolerable"—appending only the pro forma qualification that "of course, the same is true of socialism" (*Theory,* 242).

Rawls repeatedly reminds us that his theory "does not by itself favor" either free enterprise or socialism (*Theory,* 248, 249), and that "in theory anyway, a liberal socialist regime" can satisfy his principles of justice just as well as one based on private property (*Theory,* 248–49). Aside from Rawls's failure to provide any example of a liberal socialist regime, we are struck by the contrast between his unwillingness to consider the actual consequences of socialism and his unsubstantiated pronouncements concerning the tendency of excessive inequalities of wealth in private-property regimes to destroy the "fair value" of political liberty, as well as his remark that "the injustice of existing institutions" is so great that "steeply progressive income taxes" might be needed to correct them (*Theory,* 245–47). (Rawls's only hesitation about the merits of a socialism that would abolish "all market institutions" concerns its tendency toward bureaucratization, but he hedges even this reservation by reminding readers that the superiority of the price system presupposes "the necessary framework" [*Theory,* 248].) Why ignore the clear historical record showing the inherent link between socialism and despotism, while implying that political liberty has lost its value for citizens of constitutional republics like the United States simply because large (though typically quite fluid) inequalities of wealth exist among them? (In the words of that experienced observer Leon Trotsky, "in a country where the sole employer is the state," government's power to deny employment to its opponents "means death by slow starvation.")[12]

For the American founders, as for the liberal philosophers who guided them, the protection of people's "different and unequal faculties of acquir-

---

12. *The Revolution Betrayed,* 283. In 2004 the Marxist despot of Belarus, Alexander Lukashenko, used his power over state-owned companies to guarantee himself the status of president-for-life: employees "who demonstrate[d] a lack of loyalty face[d] being fired, without a chance of finding another job" (Anna Dolgov, "Belarus Vote Is Seen as Pivotal").

For a thorough demonstration "that the Soviet experiment turned totalitarian not *despite* its being socialist but *because* it was socialist," since socialism "is the ideal formula for totalitarianism," see Martin Malia, *The Soviet Tragedy,* 498 (emphasis in original).

ing property," which means particularly protecting the wealth of those who have lawfully acquired it (and thereby, the opportunity of those who aspire to do so) against potentially tyrannical majorities who might seek to seize it, was a fundamental end of government.[13] This was so not only as an element of justice, and not only as a means of fostering economic growth that raises everyone's standard of living (hence satisfying Rawls's difference principle), but also because private property serves as a "fence" around other aspects of individual liberty.[14] Precisely because the difference in the amounts and sorts of productive property people acquire is one major source of diversity in human opinions, fostering a free and diversified economy is a key element in *The Federalist*'s well-known solution to the problem of faction.[15] Additionally, the accumulation of private fortunes, some part of which is often used to support educational and other charitable institutions, creates independent centers of power that help mediate between an otherwise quasi-omnipotent, centralized political authority and the mass of the citizenry.[16]

By contrast to the founders, Rawls displays a remarkable naïveté about the dangers of granting government, even in an economy based on private property, a broad authority to reallocate private wealth and ownership of the means of production in accordance with his vision of justice. He offers a schematic account of governmental institutions regulating the economy as consisting of four branches: (1) the allocation branch, which "keep[s] the price system workably competitive . . . prevent[s] the formation of

13. Hamilton, Madison, and Jay, *The Federalist*, No. 10, 46. Besides the sources cited in note 23 to chapter 3 above, see Locke, *Two Treatises*, bk. 2, chap. 1, 3; bk. 2, chap. 5; and bk. 2, chap. 11, 138; Jefferson, Second Inaugural Address, in *Life and Selected Writings*, 344, and letter to Samuel Dupont de Nemours, April 24, 1816, in Gilbert Chinard, ed., *Correspondence of Jefferson and Du Pont de Nemours*, 258.

14. On the inherent link historically between the security of private property and individual and political liberty, see Richard Pipes, *Property and Freedom*. See also Rousseau, *Discourse on Political Economy*, 230–31, on "the right of property [as] the most sacred of all the rights of citizens, and more important in certain respects than freedom itself" on account of its connection to self-preservation, its greater susceptibility to usurpation, and its status as "the true basis of civil society"; and Harvey C. Mansfield, "On the Political Character of Property in Locke," 33–38.

15. See *The Federalist*, No. 10; Martin Diamond, *The Founding of the Democratic Republic*, 70–78; Epstein, *Political Theory of "The Federalist*," 72–80.

16. See Jouvenel, *Ethics of Redistribution*, 27–28, 37–44, 67–78; Milton Friedman, *Capitalism and Freedom*, chap. 1. On the danger of "democratic despotism," see Tocqueville, *Democracy in America*, II.iv.6–7. Rawls's lame response in *Theory* (287–88) to Jouvenel's contention that great fortunes should be allowed (among other reasons) because they promote cultural excellence is that this argument could not be accepted in the original position because the parties lack "an agreed on criterion of perfection"—something Rawls denied them, in circular fashion, precisely to prevent their considering such arguments! (On this issue, see also Friedrich Hayek, *The Constitution of Liberty*, 125–30.)

unreasonable market power," and imposes "suitable taxes and subsidies and . . . changes in the definition of property rights" to correct "the failure of prices to measure accurately social benefits and costs"; (2) the stabilization branch, which aims to promote "reasonably full employment"; (3) the transfer branch, which is to maintain the "social minimum" to the maximal benefit of the least advantaged; and (4) the distribution branch, which imposes taxes not only to finance "public goods" and "make the transfer payments necessary to satisfy the difference principle" but also "to preserve an approximate justice in [citizens'] distributive shares by means of taxation and the necessary adjustments in the rights of property." In the latter capacity it aims "gradually and continually to correct the distribution of wealth and . . . prevent concentrations of power detrimental to the fair value of political liberty and fair equality of opportunity" through such devices as inheritance and gift taxes (*Theory*, 244–45).

Clearly, Rawls's overall framework for government's economic responsibilities is modeled on the practice of contemporary welfare states like the United States. But in contrast to the American system and even its West European counterparts, the account Rawls gives of these responsibilities is strikingly vague and open-ended. Regarding the allocation branch, for instance, we must ask, who decides what constitutes "social costs" that must be compensated by means of taxes and subsidies? How far may government go in altering the definition of property rights? (A cursory examination of the complexity of the current American tax code—despite what proved to be an all-too-temporary simplification in 1986—would give any sober observer pause before thinking that a democratic government [or any other government] is likely to use the broader power Rawls would assign it in a rational or just fashion.)[17]

No less problematic is the authority Rawls would give to the distribution branch. Regarding inheritance taxes, we should recall that for most of the twentieth century, until the federal tax reductions adopted in 2001 (which are scheduled to expire in 2011), the United States, along with many state governments, levied quite heavy taxes on bequests exceeding $1 million (previously, $600,000), without generating a major contribution to federal revenues. One reason for the relatively modest receipts is that the law offered the wealthy various means of reducing estate taxes through devices like educational trusts for their descendants (without such devices, Congress would probably not have been willing to retain the high nominal

---

17. As of 2005 the federal tax code numbered six thousand pages or 2.8 million words, while leaving open a practically infinite number of issues to be resolved by the courts. See "Taxing Words," *Wall Street Journal*, editorial. The same column estimates the total including implementing regulations at nine million words.

rates in the first place).[18] But in addition, as federal records indicate, contrary to Rawls's hopes, there simply are not enough huge estates around such that even if their total proceeds were redistributed among all families living below the official poverty line, the latter would have gained all that much.[19] More important, over the long run, punitively high taxes reduce the incentive for those with already high savings to continue working and investing in new enterprises (hence providing jobs for others) and even encourage them to migrate with their wealth to countries with lower rates (as tennis star Bjorn Borg, for instance, left Sweden for Monaco).[20]

In these respects, as well as on account of the economic dislocations resulting from the breakup of family-owned businesses with each generation, high estate taxes would likely violate the difference principle, which authorizes economic inequalities that profit the least advantaged. Indeed, Rawls expressly holds that unequal inheritances "are no more inherently unjust than the unequal inheritance of intelligence" and are "permissible" so long as they benefit the least advantaged and do not abridge "liberty and fair equality of opportunity" (*Theory*, 245). In other words, Rawls's second principle by itself no more mandates "steeply progressive" taxes on income or estates than it does a flat income or sales tax and the abolition of all estate taxes: without empirical investigation of the sort Rawls never undertakes, it cannot be known which scheme will most benefit the least advantaged. In fact, by 2005, eleven nations, including Russia and Greece,

18. For instance, when Joseph Kennedy, the father of the president and of the current Massachusetts senior senator, died, the family's fortune was estimated to amount to some $300 million to $500 million; yet the family paid only $134,330.90 in taxes, thanks to the money's having been placed in "an intricate web of trusts and private foundations": Peter Schweizer, *Do as I Say (Not as I Do)*, 81 (citing Michael Jensen, "Managing the Kennedy Millions," *New York Times*, June 12, 1977).

19. As of 2002 (the first year of the gradual reduction in rates enacted in 2001) the estate tax raised $26.5 billion, or less than 1.43 percent of federal revenues; for 1995 the figure had been $14.7 billion, less than 1.7 percent of revenues. There were 98,356 taxable estate tax returns in 2002, with a total gross value (not tax yield) of $211 billion. Of course reported estates were significantly lower than the total wealth accumulated by the richest individuals, reflecting various means of legal tax-avoidance including charitable donations and trusts. Several studies found that net receipts from the estate tax were no higher than the costs to the economy from the resultant tax-avoidance activity (i.e., largely the employment of estate lawyers), while total tax revenues would ultimately increase as a result of higher investment if the estate tax were abolished. William W. Beach cites the influence of *Theory* as largely responsible for recent academic support of "intergenerational wealth taxation," though he goes on to show that such policies actually contradict the goal of benefiting the less advantaged ("The Case for Repealing the Estate Tax"; the 2002 figures were supplied to the author by Mr. Beach).

20. On the disincentive effects of estate taxes on savings and investment, see Gary Robbins, "Estate Taxes: An Historical Perspective."

had adopted uniform, flat income tax rates, recognizing that the revenue lost from cutting higher rates would be more than made up for by increases in overall national income available for taxation—to say nothing of the large savings from eliminating the costs of compliance with more complex tax codes.[21] Additionally, by prohibiting the rich from passing much of their wealth on to their heirs, confiscatory estate and gift taxes encourage the well-off to pursue a hedonistic way of life (spend it all now since you can't pass it on to your children) rather than inculcating morally attractive habits. Prominent liberal and progressive economists and legal scholars, including Joseph Stiglitz, later chairman of President Clinton's Council of Economic Advisers, have criticized heavy estate taxes for this reason.[22]

The broad responsibilities Rawls assigns to the distribution branch also exhibit an unconcern about the threat to liberty from the concentration of political power when government is given an open-ended mandate to impose taxes and restrict property rights to promote whatever public officials deem a proper distribution of wealth. Significantly, Rawls himself offers no meaningful definition of such a distribution, noting only that determining the limit of allowable economic inequality "is a matter of political judgment guided by theory, good sense, and plain hunch, at least within a wide range" (*Theory*, 246).[23] If Rawls himself cannot explain how

21. "The World Is Flat," *Wall Street Journal* editorial.

22. Cited by Beach, "Case for Repealing the Estate Tax"; see also Edward J. McCaffery, "The Uneasy Case for Wealth Transfer Taxation," and excerpts from McCaffery's testimony before the Senate Finance Committee, June 7, 1995, cited by Beach.

Even a prominent liberal think tank headed by former advisers to President Clinton that opposes repeal of the estate tax acknowledges the need for reforms that would permanently raise the estate-tax exemption per couple to $5 million and exempt family farms and businesses worth less than $8 million from paying the tax (Center for American Progress, *Repeal/Reform of the Estate Tax*).

23. Schaar astutely observes that a "society built on Rawlsian principles will require a technically trained elite managing the agencies of distribution," and there is no reason to think "that such an elite will remain any more 'just' and responsible than other previous priestly classes known to history" ("Reflections on Rawls' *Theory*," 166n).

As precedent for Rawls's notion that government needs "gradually and continually to correct the distribution of wealth" one might consider James Madison's assertion of the need to moderate party conflict in a republic "by the silent operation of laws, which, without violating the rights of property, reduce extreme wealth towards a state of mediocrity, and raise extreme indigence towards a state of comfort." But Madison penned these words at a time when the American South was still characterized by large estates based on slavery, when Virginia had only recently abolished the laws of primogeniture and entail that preserved those estates intact over generations, and when the inherently fluctuating character of wealth based on commerce and industry was not yet fully appreciated, except by Hamilton and his supporters. Decades later, Madison observed that "in Governments like ours a constant rotation of property results from the free scope to industry, and from the laws of inheritance" ("Parties," *National Gazette,*

to identify an acceptable distribution of wealth, isn't his delegation to government of the responsibility to define and enforce it a recipe for arbitrary authority rather than for justice?

Although Rawls is never clear on the policies that should be adopted to enforce the difference principle, we recall that in *JF* (139) he denies advocating a policy of continuous income redistribution, as distinguished from government-mandated dispersion of ownership of the means of production (presumably, through the breakup of estates as well as vigorous antitrust enforcement) and the provision of adequate education and training to the less advantaged. Yet since such policies could just as easily have been derived from the doctrine of "liberal equality" that Rawls found insufficient, it is hard to know what the difference principle adds. Indeed, while remarking in *Theory* that steeply progressive taxes may temporarily be needed to correct excessive inequalities, Rawls suggests that once those taxes have had their effect, they will no longer be necessary, as estate taxes and antitrust laws prevent the return of such inequalities. (He favors replacing the graduated income tax at that point by a strictly proportionate tax on consumption [*Theory*, 246–47].) But this expectation, too, is unsubstantiated.[24]

Rawls gives no evidence of having thought through the causes that generated economic inequalities under liberal regimes in the first place, or whether there is an essential connection between the economic freedom that allows the development of great fortunes and the unrivaled prosperity of the U.S. (including most of its less well-off citizens). His abstract representation of economic "systems" as independent objects of choice leads him to reify "inequalities," as if they were chiefly causes rather than results of individual economic behavior within a framework of law and government that guarantees liberty. While Rawls's friendly libertarian rival Nozick doesn't tell the whole story either, there is certainly merit to his charge that Rawls misleadingly treats a society's wealth as if it fell like "manna from heaven," rather than being produced by individuals, and to his point that any system in which people are free to choose their jobs and spend their

---

January 23, 1792, and letter to William Barry, August 4, 1822, both in *James Madison, Writings,* 504 and 792). (The mention of inheritance laws undoubtedly refers to the abolition of primogeniture and entail. See Tocqueville, *Democracy in America,* vol. 1, pt. 1, chap. 3, 46–50).

Regarding the incapacity of critics of economic inequality to specify a "fair" distribution of wealth, and the real reasons underlying their distress, see Irving Kristol, "About Equality," in *Two Cheers for Capitalism,* 171–87.

24. Hence the argument of two of Rawls's critics on the Left that he underestimates the need for continuous redistributive policies to achieve his goal of permanently reducing economic inequality (Richard Krouse and Michael McPherson, "Capitalism, 'Property-Owning Democracy,' and the Welfare State," 94–99).

money as they wish will tend to upset any imposed "pattern" of income and wealth.[25] As if playing a game—"create your own society"—Rawls thinks he can modify a piece called "economic inequality" at will and without any untoward side effects. Like the originators of various failed experiments in confiscating "surplus" wealth (the most visible of which today is Castro's Cuba), Rawls thinks there will be an endless supply of golden eggs even after the goose's demise.

As regards the actual economic consequences of a free-enterprise system like the American one for the poor, the inequalities that so trouble Rawls and like-minded social commentators appear far different when one considers their causes and their fluidity over time. Rather than displaying anything resembling a fixed socioeconomic hierarchy, American society continues to exhibit the sort of social and economic mobility that so impressed Tocqueville some 170 years ago. As the economist Thomas Sowell notes, studies that have tracked individual Americans over a period of years "have found that most do not stay in the same quintile of the income distribution for as long as a decade" and that "only 3 percent of the American population remained in the bottom 20 percent for as long as eight years. More who began in the bottom 20 percent had reached the top 20 percent by the end of that period than remained where they were."[26] Of course, those who are born to rich parents start life with major advantages, while the poor have greater hurdles to climb. But over the longer term as well, studies have demonstrated considerable flux in familial wealth.[27]

While economists have recorded an increase in wage inequality among American workers beginning the 1970s, that inequality, as one study reports, "mainly reflects increased economic rewards for schooling and skills," in turn generating "a strong increase in the proportion of young people enrolled in postsecondary schooling."[28] In other words, such inequal-

25. Nozick, *Anarchy, State, and Utopia,* 149, 160–61, 198–99.

26. Sowell, *The Quest for Cosmic Justice,* 38–39. See also Bruce Bartlett, "Class Struggle in America?" 34, and W. Michael Cox, "It's Not a Wage Gap but an Age Gap" (citing the University of Michigan Panel Survey on Income Dynamics).

27. For statistics showing the considerable proportion of larger fortunes in America that derive from the individual's own efforts rather than inheritance, see George Gilder, *Wealth and Poverty,* 55–56; John C. Weicher, "Increasing Inequality of Wealth?" 23–24. Even a report alleging an increase in inequality of household wealth beginning in the 1980s attributes it to the higher capital gains received by wealthier families as the result of a rising stock market, rather than from inheritances, the influence of which was "qualitatively unimportant" (James P. Smith, "Why Is Wealth Inequality Rising?" 93–96, 111). On the tendency toward "rapid convergence between generations" in wage differentials, rather than persistent inherited differences, see also Finis Welch's introduction to *The Causes and Consequences of Increasing Inequality,* 2–3.

28. Marvin H. Kosters, *Wage Levels and Inequality,* 48.

ities had the effects both of increasing economic productivity and encouraging young people to seek higher education, thus seemingly satisfying Rawls's difference principle. Furthermore, the same study finds, when nonwage benefits (such as health insurance) are taken into account, the average worker's real total pay during the preceding twenty-five years "increased by more than 25 percent."[29] Another study found that efforts by European governments to reduce wage inequality led to higher unemployment among low-skilled workers than in the U.S., since European employers would have less of an incentive to hire such workers, for whom government mandated higher pay than the market would justify.[30] The high long-term unemployment rates in France resulting partly from extensive state-mandated protections afforded to those who hold jobs were a major cause of the rioting that swept immigrant neighborhoods in the fall of 2005.[31] Meanwhile, wage differentials in the United States have become more meritocratic, in a sense that even Rawls would presumably approve, in that wage and education gaps between men and women, and between blacks and whites, have narrowed, so that differences correlate more with skill and effort and less with gender or race.[32]

Public opinion surveys confirm that most Americans continue to regard their country as a land of opportunity. Eighty percent of Americans in a recent poll believe it is possible for someone who starts out poor in this country to become rich through hard work.[33] By contrast, as noted previously, Rawls specifies that the least advantaged for purposes of his theory are those born into the lowest income class who remain there throughout their lives. His theory thus appears particularly ill-suited for a society as dynamic as the United States: relatively few of the least advantaged are likely to remain in that condition long enough to "benefit" from his difference principle, even if it were adopted!

Statistics on economic inequality commonly cited to demonstrate the supposed disappearance of widespread opportunity in America are often misleading in several ways, not only by omitting fringe benefits from wage calculations, as well as the effect of government transfer payments,

29. Ibid. See also Kevin M. Murphy and Finis Welch, "Wage Differentials in the 1990s." As of 2005, worker compensation (including benefits) was about 27 percent higher than it had been twenty-five years earlier (Stephen Moore, "The Wages of Prosperity").

30. Francine D. Blau and Lawrence M. Kahn, *Wage Inequality*, 25–26.

31. See Marcus Walker and John Carreyrou, "French Labor Model Fuels Riots"; Joel Kotkin, "Our Immigrants, Their Immigrants."

32. Donald R. Deere, "Trends in Wage Inequality in the United States," 23–28.

33. Bartlett, "Class Struggle in America?" 37 (citing *New York Times* polling data from March 2005). See also "Wealth," *The American Enterprise*, 61.

but also by disregarding age differences in income (including those among various ethnic and racial groups) and overlooking the consequences of widespread immigration, which make it appear that millions of Latinos, for instance, remain "at the bottom" over time, when new waves of poor immigrants have taken the place of those who formerly occupied that status a decade or more earlier but have since risen in economic status, contributing to our economic dynamism.[34] According to one study, when the increased immigration of the 1980s and 1990s is factored out, the entire supposed rise in economic inequality during that period disappears, as does much of the poverty problem.[35] (In another "simplification" that distorts his perspective, Rawls elsewhere chooses to "abstract from" immigration "to get an uncluttered view" [*PL*, 136n]—much as one might chop down the trees to get a clearer view of the forest.)[36]

Again, Rawls's disregard of the widespread opportunity for economic advancement as well as political and personal freedom for ordinary individuals in societies with free-market economies like the United States is belied by the millions of (mostly poorer) immigrants, both legal and illegal, who flock to these shores each year. Did any boat people ever strive to make it into Communist Vietnam, or did other immigrants hungering for freedom dodge electrified fences and machine-gun fire to escape from capitalist oppression to "liberation" in the former Soviet bloc? Why do so many thousands risk death to enter the U.S. from Central America and China today?

Of course, the continuing existence over the past several decades of an "underclass" in America, consisting largely of families headed by single mothers dependent on welfare whose children grow up in neighborhoods rife with crime, drugs, and gang warfare, and in an environment that discourages the quest for academic success, is this country's greatest social

34. Between 1978 and 2002, the percentage of foreign-born Americans nearly doubled, from 6.2 percent to 12 percent. Meantime, median family incomes among immigrants rose by some ten thousand dollars for every decade that they lived in the U.S., demonstrating that they were not remaining "at the bottom" (see "French Lessons," *Wall Street Journal* editorial).

35. Steven Camarota, "The Impact of Immigration on the Size and Growth of the Poor Population in the United States" and "Importing Poverty," cited in Easterbrook, *Progress Paradox*, 11–12. See also Sowell, *Quest for Cosmic Justice*, chap. 1, and *The Economics and Politics of Race*, chap. 6; Linda Chavez, *Out of the Barrio*, 101–13; and Kristol, *Two Cheers*, 199–202, 239–40.

36. In fairness, Rawls does address this issue in *LP*: if we somehow guarantee the rights of all citizens throughout the world, eliminate famines, and overcome population pressure supposedly caused by gender inequality, "the problem of immigration . . . is eliminated" (9). (We may be in for a long wait.) Meantime, as Hayek pointed out, the principle that poorer citizens are automatically entitled to a share of the earnings of their better-off peers would heighten anti-immigrant sentiment (why share the spoils with newcomers from abroad?) (*Constitution of Liberty*, 101).

problem.[37] (Similar classes largely composed of ethnic minorities are found in most Western European nations with more elaborate governmental welfare systems.) But Rawls offers no reflection on the causes or possible remedies for this problem. (In his only allusion to welfare dependency, Rawls attributes it to the failure of society to provide all citizens with sufficient "productive means" such as "education, and trained skills" and implausibly suggests that the failure results from the concentration of wealth under capitalism [*JF*, 140].)

In the foregoing remarks I do not claim to have settled particular issues of economic policy, such as whether estate taxes should be abolished. I have simply highlighted the groundlessness of Rawls's sweeping pronouncements on economic "injustice"; his lamentable lack of appreciation of the benefits of a free-enterprise economy from the standpoint of all citizens, including the less advantaged; and the lack of connection between his vague policy recommendations and the difference principle. That principle provides no more meaningful guidance for economic policy than Rawls's first principle of justice did for resolving issues of political and personal liberty. In his eagerness to articulate "simple" principles of justice, Rawls ended up depriving them of substantive content. But Rawls thought they sufficed to justify his partisan judgments, without the need of empirical investigation or sufficient understanding of how our economy operates.

III.

Rawls next broadens his theory to include what he acknowledges may seem "a somewhat far-fetched application" of it to the problem of "justice between generations" (*Theory*, 258). He conceives the question of justice in this instance as one of determining the amount that any generation is obliged to save rather than consume, so that "each generation receives its due from its predecessors and does its fair share for those to come" (*Theory*, 254). The "just savings principle" requires the parties in the original position (who don't know which generation they belong to) to consider "how much they would be willing to save at each stage" of the advance of civilization, "on the assumption that all other generations have saved, or will save, in accordance with the same criterion." Different rates of saving, Rawls surmises, are appropriate for different stages of civilization, until the point where "just institutions are firmly established and all the basic liberties firmly realized," at which time no further net savings are required

37. For a classic journalistic portrayal, see Ken Auletta, *The Underclass.*

(*Theory*, 254–55). Rawls emphasizes that "the last stage at which saving is called for is not one of great abundance," since "justice does not require that early generations save so that later ones are simply more wealthy":

> It is a mistake to believe that a just and good society must wait upon a high material standard of life. What men want is meaningful work in free association with others . . . within a framework of just basic institutions. To achieve this state of things great wealth is not necessary. In fact, beyond some point it is more likely to be a positive hindrance, a meaningless distraction at best if not a temptation to indulgence and emptiness (*Theory*, 255–56).

As I noted in chapter 3, this observation about the limited importance of wealth for happiness or justice, although it is one of Rawls's most sensible remarks about human well-being, implicitly contradicts the assumption on which the reasoning in the original position was based that a rational human being prefers more rather than less wealth, as well as other primary goods. If the goodness of wealth is limited, shouldn't this fact have played a role in those deliberations? Indeed, doesn't the observation cast doubt on the terms by which Rawls defined the least advantaged for purposes of the difference principle (which he says must be combined with the just savings principle to determine the proper rate of societal accumulation [*Theory*, 258])?

With respect to the broader issue of justice among generations, the notion that each generation owes a debt to its predecessors, which it can repay only by maintaining or improving that legacy for its successors, has been given eloquent expression in modern times by Edmund Burke and Abraham Lincoln. For Burke, that principle reflects the fact that civil society, properly understood, is a partnership among generations, and therefore, no generation is free simply to tear up the existing social order to suit its own convenience.[38] Similarly, Lincoln, notably in the Gettysburg Address (prefigured by the opening paragraph of his 1838 Lyceum address), stresses the duty of each generation of Americans to preserve for its successors the legacy of freedom and justice bequeathed by the founders and the patriots of 1776. For Burke and Lincoln, our debt to our predecessors entails an obligation to restrain the pursuit of present pleasures or fancies for the sake of the common good and a readiness to sacrifice even our lives to perpetuate our country's free institutions.

By contrast, Rawls's limitation of his treatment of justice among generations to the relatively trivial issue of the rate of savings reflects a highly

---

38. See Burke, *Reflections on the Revolution*, 84–85, 149.

constricted view of the political problem. While Rawls might agree with Burke and Lincoln about our broader obligation to later generations, he makes no mention of the issue, allowing his readers too easily to delude themselves that they have fulfilled that duty when they have ensured that their society's savings rate is sufficient "to improve the standard of life of later generations of the least advantaged" (*Theory*, 258). Although, to interest the parties to the original position in the welfare of their successors, Rawls suggests conceiving them as representing "family lines . . . who care at least about their most immediate descendants" (*Theory*, 255), he curiously limits the form of that care to improving the economic situation of the least advantaged among them, as distinguished from securing the blessings of liberty to posterity. (Even the economic duty is not one that "the less favored" in the present generation have any obligation to fulfill [*Theory*, 258], and it is limited in time to generations before the final stage, when justice has been achieved.) Thanks to his confidence in the inherent stability of just institutions (*PL*, 347–48), Rawls apparently does not believe that once a just political regime has been established, any significant effort will be required to maintain it in the face of domestic or foreign enemies or moral decay. All this seems reflective of a kind of naively Hegelian belief in the "end of history" that Rawls does nothing to justify.[39]

Additionally, it is not even evident that the issue of the savings rate is properly a subject for justice, or one that requires public supervision for the sake of future generations. The enormous prosperity achieved in recent centuries by nations organized on the basis of free enterprise has been the result largely of private rather than public investment.[40] In a country that respects property rights and the rule of law, investors do not ordinarily need to be prodded or commanded by government to save; they do so to obtain market rates of return (and thereby provide for their immediate descendants and for their own old age). Nor is it apparent that governments are well qualified to ascertain the "proper" rate of savings, let alone channel investments in the most valuable direction; the economic disaster of communism and the sclerotic Japanese economy of recent decades should have demonstrated this lesson. Rawls's account of justice among generations is a "solution" in need of a problem.

39. On Rawls's Hegelianism, see note 5 to chapter 13 below.

40. This is not to deny the contribution that publicly funded roads, airports, schools, etc., made to our prosperity. But such public projects are hardly what distinguish the prosperous free-enterprise nations from their impoverished socialist or statist peers. And the very funds that financed those facilities in the free world came, of course, from tax revenues deriving from the wealth generated by private economic activity.

Of course, it is well recognized that countries that can afford to do so have an obligation to invest public funds in the education of the young, but citizens typically do so not so much out of a perceived duty to abstract justice as out of concern for their own offspring and for the perpetuation of their nation's prosperity and culture. As Rawls himself acknowledges, the question of "how the burden of capital accumulation and of raising the standard of civilization and culture is to be shared between generations seems to admit of no definite answer" (*Theory*, 253). But it is doubtful that he makes the question any easier to answer, or fortifies people's sense of duty in this regard, when he reduces it to the problem of maximizing the welfare of "later generations of the least advantaged" rather than of society as a whole.

One further contrast may be drawn between Rawls's and Lincoln's conceptions of the duty of each generation to its successors. The highest duty that most citizens can perform for a free country in times of peace, Lincoln suggests in the Lyceum address, is scrupulously to obey its laws, even unjust ones. Only through the inculcation and practice of a civil religion of law-abidingness, Lincoln holds, can the people adequately fortify their nation against the twin dangers of mob rule and Caesarean despotism.[41] By contrast, Rawls suggests that disagreements over the proper level of a nation's savings, of all things, are a suitable occasion for citizens to disobey the law through "acts of civil disobedience or conscientious refusal" (*Theory*, 261). Although Rawls has acknowledged how difficult it is to specify or agree on the proper savings level, he invites citizens to violate the law of the land whenever they don't happen to agree with the public's decision on this matter! For Rawls, unlike Lincoln, being "a democrat" simply means believing that a democratic constitution best tends to "yield just and effective legislation." It does not entail regarding "the public decision concerning the level of savings" (or, apparently, concerning any other issue) as "sacrosanct," to the point of commanding one's obedience until and unless the law embodying that decision is changed through constitutional means (*Theory*, 261). There can be little doubt about the judgment Lincoln would have made of this sort of legacy.[42]

41. Springfield Lyceum Address, *Collected Works of Abraham Lincoln*, 1:112–16. On Lincoln's project of shaping a popular civil religion that would support liberal-democratic institutions, see Jaffa, *Crisis of the House Divided*, especially chaps. 9–10, and Glen R. Thurow, *Abraham Lincoln and American Political Religion*.

42. As an alternative means of overriding decisions by the people's elected representatives about the rate of savings, Rawls suggests an appeal to the judiciary, which could correct those decisions by appealing to Rawlsian principles of justice that might "be more or less explicit in the constitution" (*Theory*, 261). In other words, Rawls would extend the imperial tendencies of the American judiciary by inviting judges to tell elected officials what they must do to compel a "just rate of savings."

Meantime, Rawls does not mention one aspect of governmental economic decisions wherein insufficient regard for subsequent generations (as well as today's working people) is increasingly displayed by the American government: the disposition to saddle them with mounting federal debt to finance large and open-ended spending programs to benefit senior citizens (notably the 2003 extension of Medicare to cover drug prescriptions, which trustees for the program estimated could cost up to $7 trillion over the next seventy-five years). Many of those seniors are more prosperous than the workers who will have to pay the bill.[43]

Considering the issue of economic "justice among generations" from a wider perspective, Rawls's professed agnosticism about the relative merits of socialism and free enterprise, and his repeated disparagements of the latter, threaten to do an injustice to later generations in a manner that Nathan Rosenberg and E. L. Birdzell Jr. warn against in their study of the sources of the modern Western world's wealth: weakening the likelihood that the free-enterprise system that generated that wealth will survive the efforts of misguided intellectuals and politicians to redirect it to serve purposes of their own. It was easy enough for Rawls, from his perch at Harvard, to depreciate the significance of "a high material standard of life," just as many of his academic peers continue to do. But what of the many Americans who don't yet enjoy a standard of living like Rawls's? Are their living conditions more likely to be improved by the perpetuation of a free-enterprise system, or by the pursuit of that will-of-the-wisp "liberal socialism"? Does the evidence suggest that ordinary people are more likely to benefit from continued economic growth under a free-enterprise system, or from fighting for their "share" of their more successful fellow citizens' gains as the difference principle encourages them to do? As Rosenberg and Birdzell observe, one likely reason that West German workers' wages during the Cold War were far higher than those of their East German counterparts was that "high real wages may [have been] a low priority goal of government planners" in the putative "workers' state," while high wages were "presumably an important goal of West German workers," and West Germany's free political as well as economic institutions made it necessary as well as feasible for that goal to be achieved. By contrast, the authors remark, "judging the efficiency of Soviet society by its comparative success in serving worker or consumer welfare may be like judging the efficiency of

---

43. See Edmund Andrews and Robert Pear, "Entitlement Costs Are Expected to Soar"; and, on the broader problem, Jagadeesh Gokhale and Kent Smetters, *Fiscal and Generational Imbalances.* As of 2006 unfunded future entitlement liabilities had climbed to some $80 trillion ("The Entitlement Panic," *Wall Street Journal* editorial).

a feudal society by statistics relating to the welfare of the serfs."[44] In practice, as any sober and reasonably informed observer could have explained to Rawls, the power that socialism puts in the hands of governments practically guarantees that it will be used to feather the nests of the rulers—whether in the old Soviet empire or in the various socialist despotisms that remain in Africa and a few other nations like Cuba and North Korea.[45]

There is one other fundamental respect in which human generations of our time and the future (for the first time in the history of the human race) may be said to have a vital obligation to their successors: to forego and legally prohibit the use of the tools that biotechnology now threatens to make available to undertake a radical reconstruction of the human psyche itself, in the exercise of what the biologist Edward O. Wilson calls "volitional evolution." If anything, Rawls's tentative speculations about eugenics only encourage this sort of development. (Indeed, his exhortation that we work to overcome the moral arbitrariness of nature would seem to require it.) But as Adam Wolfson observes, "there is something immoral and tyrannical about one generation of human beings experimenting upon and changing the essence of humanity for all succeeding generations."[46] One might expect a thinker who professes to be concerned with upholding our status as "equal moral persons" to give consideration to this issue, but Rawls unfortunately does not (even in his later writings). It is certainly a more critical problem than trying to set the "just savings rate."

IV.

Following his treatment of intergenerational justice Rawls addresses the argument that "inequalities in wealth and authority violating the second principle of justice may be justified if the subsequent economic and social

---

44. Rosenberg and Birdzell, *How the West Grew Rich*, 323–24, 334.

45. As David Landes observes, the worst aspect of the disastrous Soviet socialist "command economy" was the rulers' contempt for the people themselves, exemplified in the regime's last years by the Chernobyl disaster and the authorities' attempted coverup. Meanwhile, in Africa, he notes, the outcome of newly independent governments' vast schemes of "social engineering" was that "the richest people are heads of state and their ministers" (*The Wealth and Poverty of Nations*, 496–98, 504). On the economic disasters that African nations suffered as a result of the socialism their leaders originally learned at Western institutions such as the London School of Economics, exemplified by the havoc Julius Nyerere wreaked in Tanzania, see Joshua Muravchik, *Heaven on Earth*, chap. 8.

46. Wolfson, "Biodemocracy in America," 27. See also Francis Fukuyama, *Our Posthuman Future*, and Kass, *Life, Liberty, and the Defense of Dignity*. Kass notes the insufficiency of the notion of "personhood," which Rawls borrows from Kant, for meeting "the challenge of bioethics," because of its abstract opposition between human life and nature and consequent severance of mind and body (16–17).

benefits are large enough." This argument is suggested both by John Maynard Keynes's contention that "the immense accumulations of capital built up before the First World War" could only have been achieved thanks to an inegalitarian social system that placed the bulk of the increased income in the hands of a frugal upper class that preferred to invest rather than consume it; and by the claim of such thinkers as Burke and Hegel that a country's well-being requires a hereditary governing class bred to public service and a sense of aristocratic honor (*Theory*, 263–64). It is noteworthy that despite his commitment to the priority of equal liberty and opportunity, Rawls does not reject either claim. Instead he simply indicates the proper form those arguments would have to take to accord with his principles. In Keynes's case it would be necessary to show that "while there were many ostensible injustices in the system, there was no real possibility that these could have been removed and the conditions of the less advantaged made better" by directly combating the inequalities (*Theory*, 263–64). With respect to the issue raised by Burke and Hegel, "it is not enough to argue . . . that the whole of society including the least favored benefit from certain restrictions on equality of opportunity"; rather, it must be shown that without those inequalities, "in the long run anyway the opportunities of the disadvantaged would be even more limited" (*Theory*, 265).

Rawls excuses himself from weighing these arguments for "overriding the principle of fair equality of opportunity in favor of a hierarchical class structure" by saying that such matters "are not part of the theory of justice" (*Theory*, 265). Once again, we wonder about the value of a theory that abstracts from such substantive issues. Additionally, we must question the significance of the ostensible correction Rawls makes to Burke's and Hegel's arguments. How can one meaningfully distinguish between inequalities that benefit "the whole of society including the least favored" and those without which the opportunities of that class would be even more limited? Could the opportunities of the least advantaged possibly be enhanced by policies that damaged the society of which they are members? And why hold that restrictions on equal opportunity are legitimate only if they enhance the opportunities ultimately available to the least advantaged, rather than benefiting them in some more substantive way (say, by making it more likely that their country has a political leadership sufficiently capable to supervise and direct its diplomacy and defense effectively)?

After expressing his disinclination to "pursue these complications further," Rawls acknowledges that even if all other barriers to fair equality of opportunity were eliminated, differences in "the internal life and culture of the family" might still influence children's motivation, their educational performance, and consequently their prospects of success. Since Rawls has defined the second principle to require "equal life prospects" only among those "similarly endowed and motivated," variations in how different families within the same social class shape their children's aspirations would mean that while fair equality of opportunity may exist among classes, "equal chances between individuals will not" (*Theory*, 265). Rawls refers us to part 3 of his book for further reflection on "how far the notion of equal opportunity can be carried"; but he displays no doubt, such as we may experience, regarding the value to anyone of an "equality" that holds only among social classes but not within them, assuming that this distinction is even intelligible. (If familial advantages enhance the individual's ability to rise, why assume he will remain in the same class at all?) Once Rawls has challenged the legitimacy of all socioeconomic inequalities that derive from an "unearned" basis, including even people's genetic inheritances, it seems inconsistent (albeit prudent) for him to stop short of trying to overcome inequalities in life prospects that derive from unequal parental upbringings as well.

Rawls concludes his discussion of these issues of priority by restating his principles of justice in their fullest form. I quote the crucial portions here:

> First principle: Each person is to have an equal right to the most extensive total system of equal basic liberties compatible with a similar system of liberty for all.
>
> Second principle: Social and economic inequalities are to be arranged so that they are both:
>
> (a) to the greatest benefit of the least advantaged, consistent with the just savings principle, and
> (b) attached to offices and positions open to all under conditions of fair equality of opportunity.
>
> First priority rule: The principles of justice are to be ranked in lexical order and therefore the basic liberties can be restricted only for the sake of liberty.
>
> Second priority rule: The second principle of justice is lexically prior to the principle of efficiency and to that of maximizing the sum of advantages; and fair opportunity is prior to the difference principle (*Theory*, 266).[47]

Acknowledging that these principles and priority rules are still "incomplete," and that in application to the real world the latter "will no doubt fail" so that "we may be able to find no satisfactory answer at all," Rawls exhorts us "to try to postpone the day of reckoning as long as possible, and

---

47. For Rawls's revision of the two principles in *PL* (cited as "better" in the revised edition of *Theory*, xii), see chapter 10 below.

try to arrange society so that it never comes" (*Theory*, 267). It is hard to know what to make of this advice.

V.

Immediately after restating the two principles, Rawls endeavors to demonstrate that the account of distributive justice in the second principle, which includes "a large element of pure procedural justice," properly takes priority over the "common sense precepts of justice," such as the belief that people's efforts or social contributions should be rewarded. "From the standpoint of the theory of justice," Rawls explains (tautologically), "the two principles of justice define the correct higher criterion" for weighing these precepts (*Theory*, 267–68). More specifically, he challenges the "common sense" assumption "that income and wealth, and the good things in life generally, should be distributed according to moral virtue." Rawls denies that such a principle would be chosen in the original position, since "there seems to be no way of defining the requisite criterion [of desert] in that situation." (Here again, his reasoning appears circular, since he chose to arrange the original position in that manner.) Distinguishing between "moral desert and legitimate expectations" (the latter defined as the outcome of a system of just institutions), Rawls observes that "the principles of justice that regulate the basic structure and specify the duties and obligations of individuals do not mention moral desert, and there is no tendency for distributive shares to correspond to it" (*Theory*, 273).

At one level any defender of the free-enterprise system must acknowledge that there is no necessary tendency within it for the most virtuous human beings to receive the greatest monetary rewards, any more than a system of free elections guarantees that the most meritorious candidates will win. Historically, the movement toward free enterprise reflected an awareness that trying to regulate economic transactions through government-mandated "just" prices and wages resulted in arbitrary rules that hampered economic growth and the general prosperity, as well as individual opportunity, just as hereditary political regimes assigned positions of power on the basis of at most a presumptive "virtue."[48] But while the free-enterprise system commits us to accepting as legally just whatever outcomes result from voluntary exchanges, it hardly follows that we must accept a system of "pure procedural justice" even if it has *no* tendency to

48. See Hobbes, *Leviathan*, chap. 15, par. 14 ("The value of all things contracted for is measured by the appetite of the contractors"), and chap. 21, par. 6, last sentence.

reward merit. The original argument for the modern commercial republic stressed its tendency to promote not only economic gains but also certain moral virtues: thrift, industry, probity, and tolerance.[49] A merely procedural defense of free enterprise cannot suffice: a citizenry that becomes persuaded that "capitalism" chiefly rewards such attributes as dishonesty and selfishness ("the profit motive"), along with sheer luck, is unlikely to support it, whatever its contribution to their prosperity.[50]

By contrast to the classic argument for free enterprise, Rawls not only disclaims any tendency within his system for moral desert to be rewarded, he even denies that more industrious individuals *ought* to receive greater rewards, since a person's effort "is influenced by his natural abilities and skills" as well as "the alternatives open to him." "The better endowed," Rawls maintains, "are more likely, other things equal, to strive conscientiously, and there seems to be no way to discount for their greater good fortune" in this respect (*Theory*, 274).

Unless the first clause of the sentence last quoted is interpreted tautologically (the very disposition to "strive conscientiously" being an advantageous "endowment"), there is little reason to think it true. May not poor people, other things equal, be more likely to strive to advance themselves, since they have a greater need to than those who are born rich? Isn't there something degrading, moreover, in dismissing a person's effort to better his condition as just an "unearned" and morally arbitrary asset like any other? Carried to its logical extreme, as John Kekes points out, Rawls's position so elevates the sheer precept of need over that of moral worth (*Theory*, 274) as

49. See Montesquieu, *Spirit of the Laws*, bk. 5, chap. 6; bk. 20, chaps. 1–2; bk. 21, chap. 20, 389–90; Tocqueville, *Democracy in America*, vol. 2, pt. 3, chap. 10, 565; vol. 2, pt. 3, chap. 11, 571; Jerry Z. Muller, *Adam Smith in His Time and Ours*, chaps. 7–10; James Q. Wilson, "Capitalism and Morality."

50. This point has been eloquently argued by Irving Kristol, see "Horatio Alger and Profits" and "When Virtue Loses All Her Loveliness," in *Two Cheers for Capitalism*, 84–89, 257–68. Responding to Rawls's account of "pure procedural justice," Wiggins remarks, "it is not an accident that human beings have always made it a requirement on human justice that one should be able to see as just that which really is just" ("Neo-Aristotelian Reflections," 506; see also Gourevitch, "Rawls on Justice," 504–6 and 516–17). Rawls's ungrounded confidence in a merely procedural defense of economic systems is mirrored by his colleague Nozick's denial that the argument for free-market arrangements should be grounded on any claims that they somehow correspond to desert or are conducive to people's substantive good (*Anarchy, State, and Utopia*, 158–59). It was Rawls's attempted severance of institutional from substantive justice that also won him Hayek's praise (*Law, Legislation, and Liberty*, vol. 2, xiii, 100, 183n). By regretting only that Rawls had used the term "social justice" (vol. 2, 100), Hayek indicated that he had misunderstood Rawls's central aim. See Hayek, *Constitution of Liberty*, 93ff, for a similarly problematic statement; and for a critique, see Plattner, "Capitalism," 329–32.

On the analogous problem of American courts' having substituted an ideal of "pure" procedural justice for that of substantive justice, particularly in criminal proceedings, see Macklin Fleming, *The Price of Perfect Justice*.

to imply not only that a poor mugger has just as strong a title to societal rewards as an equally poor working mother whom he victimizes, but that if she rises in economic status thanks to her industry, she owes the mugger a share of her earnings, since her very disposition to work hard constitutes an unearned "natural asset" for which he deserves compensation![51]

It is difficult to comprehend in this instance how Rawls can contend that the difference principle corresponds to or plausibly extends "our" (or almost anyone's) moral judgments. It is far less obviously "one of the fixed points of our moral judgments that no one deserves his place in the distribution of natural assets" (*Theory*, 274)—assuming that the "we" in question represents a broad cross section of human beings, past or present—than that (as Rawls acknowledges) we tend to believe or at least wish that "the good things in life . . . should be distributed according to moral desert" (*Theory*, 273). Every sensible person recognizes that the latter expectation is frequently bound to be disappointed. But Rawls offers no reason for simply setting aside that expectation in favor of his idiosyncratic dictum regarding the undeservedness of natural assets, including the determination to strive to better oneself, and society's supposed duty to reward the less industrious at the expense of their harder-working peers.

Rawls tries to finesse this issue in two ways. First, he argues that in "a well-ordered society . . . in which institutions are just and this fact is publicly recognized," it can be assumed that all individuals "have a strong sense of justice, an effective desire to comply with the existing rules and to give one another that to which they are entitled." Consequently, "we may assume that everyone is of equal moral worth" (*Theory*, 274–75). Since this response is purely abstract and hypothetical, it does not answer the objection I have raised (nor does Rawls explain why an equal disposition to act justly, even assuming it existed, should trump all other claims to "primary goods"). Moreover, if even in Rawls's ideal society, people differ in their dispositions toward just conduct, as is suggested by his acknowledgment that penal laws will still be needed,[52] why not regard differences in the sense of justice itself as unearned "natural assets," so that society, contrary to the assumption of the law, ought to go out of its way to reward criminals (extending Kekes's point) by way of compensation for their lack of a moral sense?

---

51. Kekes, *A Case for Conservatism*, 181–83. For a comparable illustration, see Anderson, "Antipolitical Philosophy," 49. Consider also Nozick's comment that "the unexalted picture of human beings" that Rawls provides here sits uneasily "with the view of human dignity" it is supposed to uphold (*Anarchy, State, and Utopia*, 214).

52. Rawls reiterates here that such laws would be needed in a well-ordered society only on account of "the assurance problem" (*Theory*, 277); but of course the very need for the law to be penal implies that some human beings would be tempted to violate it without the threat of punishments to deter them.

Rawls's second response is a definitional one. Since "in a well-ordered society individuals acquire claims to a share of the social product by doing certain things encouraged by the existing arrangements," he argues, the just system "allots to each what he is entitled to *as defined by* the scheme itself," and "the principles of justice . . . *establish* that doing this is fair" (*Theory*, 275–76 [emphasis added]). But if a sense of justice is in some sense natural to human beings—as Rawls maintains in part 3—it is unlikely that its dictates can simply be remade to conform to a particular theorist's definition of fairness. (And if the criterion of fairness is a consequence of Rawls's principles, how do we establish the fairness of the principles themselves?) When Rawls compares the acceptance under his system of the fact that "there is . . . no tendency for distribution and virtue to coincide" to our accepting that in a game, the more skillful or determined team sometimes loses (*Theory*, 276), he surely underestimates the difference between what is at stake in the cases of civil justice and of play—to say nothing of the fact that participation in a game is wholly voluntary in a way that citizenship is not.[53]

To conclude this point, under any political and economic system, the nature of things ultimately compels our acceptance of the truism that, as regards the fate of individuals, "life isn't fair." The typical premodern response to this fact on the part of philosophers and religious teachers was to educate human beings to recognize that since the greatest goods (wisdom, virtue, and holiness) are not those for which we literally compete with other people, and other substantial joys (love, friendship, the beauties of nature, and parenthood) are available to most or all of us, there is little point in lamenting that one has achieved a lesser share of wealth or fame than others. By contrast, a key element of the modern argument for free enterprise, as seen in the fifth chapter of Locke's *Second Treatise*, consists in diverting people from contending over which group "deserves" to have more, in favor of accepting a system in which everyone is ultimately better off as the result of having the (in principle) unlimited opportunity to acquire wealth (in varying degrees) through labor and investment. But neither of these solutions is available to Rawls. As we have seen, his second principle requires us to assess a social order by the way it "distributes" primary goods, rather than by its conduciveness to human excellence, piety, or substantive well-being. But unlike Locke, he cannot argue that his difference principle actually benefits anyone, except, perhaps, someone who has the good/bad fortune to belong to the "least advantaged." If justice has an

---

53. Cf. also Rawls's comparison of our agreement to reason in accordance with the strictures of the original position to our performing a role in a stage play, in *PL*, 27.

entirely artificial character, such that Rawls can define it as he wishes, it is hard to see why anyone should feel bound to promote it.[54] And isn't it strange, after Rawls's sweeping, yet unsupported, denunciation of the alleged injustice of existing inequalities, to hear him trumpet the fact that his preferred system offers only a "procedural" justice, without any correlation to people's merit or effort?

The most seriously misleading aspect of Rawls's endeavor to define "disadvantage" so broadly that even those blessed with the *motivation* to get ahead are ipso facto among the "privileged" who lack any inherent title to the fruits of their achievement is that a free society that allows everyone the legal opportunity to advance doesn't only "reward" inborn motivation; it encourages and stimulates the development of such motivation. There is little reason to think that motivation is determined by a person's genes to the degree that intellectual or athletic ability are. Showing poor people that they are capable of advancing their situation through effort encourages them to do so; treating them as helpless victims of fortune who are "entitled" to a share of their more industrious peers' gain has the opposite effect. Rawls's difference principle doesn't merely violate justice; it tends to undermine the sort of character that encourages just behavior as well as self-reliance, the pursuit of education, and work that contributes to the common good.

VI.

Rawls devotes the last two sections of chapter 5 to comparing his principles of justice to two alternative theories: "Mixed Conceptions" and "The Principle of Perfection" (*Theory*, secs. 49–50). Mixed conceptions of justice

54. On one occasion Rawls went even further in teasing out possible implications of the difference principle, expressing openness in principle to the economist R. A. Musgrave's proposal of a "lump sum tax on natural abilities" to compel the more talented to work harder so as to benefit the least advantaged. In Rawls's original judgment the proposal "is not an interference with liberty until it infringes upon the basic liberties," and Rawls is uncertain "when this happens" (*CP*, 252–53). Passages such as these (along with his sanctioning in *JF* [149–50] and in *PL* of "regulations of freedom of speech and of the press" to ensure their "fair value") should give pause to those who regard Rawls as a partisan of liberty. (As noted previously, in another paper published the same year, as well as in *JF*, Rawls did describe a head tax on natural assets as a "drastic infringement" of liberty, hence presumably something disallowed by his first principle [*CP*, 231; *JF*, 158]. It is unclear why Rawls expressed seemingly opposed judgments in two contemporaneous essays, unless the difference is that in the latter remark he is referring to a head tax that aims to "reduce or eliminate" income inequalities, whereas Musgrave's proposal was simply an extension of the difference principle. But even Rawls's hedging on the issue indicates a shakiness in his commitment to individual liberty as normally understood.)

combine Rawls's first principle with some rule other than the difference principle for allocating social and economic goods, such as a combination of the principle of average utility with the provision of a "social minimum" (i.e., a "safety net") (*Theory*, 278).

It is in the context of asserting the superiority of justice as fairness over mixed principles that Rawls offers his chief argument for the difference principle. Remarkably, its superiority is said to lie mainly in its simplicity, or "the comparative ease with which it can be interpreted and applied," since (as Rawls maintained in chapter 2) it requires us only to determine which policies favor the interests of the least advantaged, rather than the utility functions of all individuals (*Theory*, 281). Additionally, he argues that whereas "in everyday life we often content ourselves" with balancing "common sense precepts" in light of the facts of a situation, an admonition merely to "exercise one's judgment" in weighing the various legitimate ends of public policy fails to offer "an articulated conception of justice" (*Theory*, 279). Similarly, the "vagueness" of the notion of seeking to advance society's overall well-being is "troublesome," since it is always debatable how far one group's gains outweigh another's losses (*Theory*, 282).

The great advantage of the difference principle over conventional precepts of public policy according to Rawls is that it is not only easier to apply but offers greater "clarity" in its demands (*Theory*, 282). Because "it is a political convention of a democratic society to appeal to the common interest," but "we cannot assume that government affects everyone's interest equally," and since "it is impossible to maximize with respect to more than one point of view," Rawls concludes that it is "natural, given the ethos of a democratic society, to single out" the least advantaged and to "further their long-term prospects in the best manner consistent with the equal liberties and fair opportunity." Hence the difference principle constitutes "a reasonable extension" of the convention of aiming at the common good "once we face up to the necessity of adopting a reasonably complete conception of justice" (*Theory*, 280–81). In other words, Rawls rejects as insufficient the maxim "promote the common good" because it could entail benefiting some societal groups more than others on one occasion, and favoring other interests at another time, without offering any clear rule as to which group should primarily benefit. (Farm legislation particularly benefits farmers, labor legislation assists workers, small-business loans favor businessmen, etc.) Just as the two principles as a whole were formulated with a view to simplicity, the difference principle is devised to give concrete content to the common interest by defining it in a particular way, thus saving government the trouble of having to judge which groups specially deserve to benefit from each particular policy. But can any reasonable person be persuaded by

Rawls's argument to define or identify the common interest as the maximal benefit of the least advantaged just to keep things simple?[55] (Analogously, it might simplify the task of medicine to define "bodily health" as the maximum strength of people's big toes. But what value would a science of medicine have if it were based on that premise?)

Rawls's argument embodies a curious set of logical leaps. Since it is indeed a convention of democratic societies, and perhaps of all nondespotic political regimes, to appeal to the common advantage rather than a single class's interest as a ground for public policies, it hardly follows that we can reasonably expect the generality of citizens to agree on a set of social and economic policies that will consistently favor only the least advantaged (however defined), which effectively means *ignoring* the common interest. Only because Rawls demands an unrealistic, quasi-mathematical standard of rigor for judging the impact of public policies can he infer, from the fact that government policies do not equally affect all people's interests, that we must single out one class to have its gains maximized. A more empirical and sensible view of the policy process would accept as sufficient the fact that while most domestic policies favor some groups more than others, in a well-organized republican regime that rests on the consent of the governed (especially one large enough, and with an economy complex enough, to ensure a multiplicity of factions forming shifting political alliances, following the argument of *The Federalist*, No. 10), the people will have a sense that on the whole public policy tends to serve the common good (including their own), rather than that one group is consistently favored.

---

55. Although Rawls also maintains "that the policies in the justice of which we have the greatest confidence . . . tend in [the] direction" of the difference principle (*Theory*, 281), in *JF* (132–33) he will concede that the principle may "have little support in our public culture at the present time," though he still thinks it is "worth studying" since it is "essential to democratic equality." But the concession further indicates the remoteness of justice as fairness from "our" considered judgments, assuming that the "we" being consulted are a cross section of the American electorate. Interestingly, in his earlier, pre-*Theory* writings, instead of the difference principle Rawls had offered the less extreme (although still hard to operationalize) requirement that an inequality must serve "the advantage of *every* party engaging" in a given social practice ("Justice as Fairness," *CP*, 50; "Constitutional Liberty," *CP*, 76 [emphasis added]). The grounding of the difference principle in the need for methodological simplicity was apparent in the 1967 essay "Distributive Justice" where Rawls first introduced it (*CP*, 134–40). On the curious path that led Rawls to the difference principle, see Wolff, *Understanding Rawls*, 58–59. By contrast, Rawls's precursor, the British liberal-socialist theorist L. T. Hobhouse, despite calling for confiscatory inheritance taxes and other largely impractical policies aimed at overcoming economic inequality, was content to hold that individuals may justly earn larger rewards so long as "society also is enriched by them" (*The Elements of Social Justice*, 164–65).

The only other ground besides simplicity that Rawls proffers in *Theory* for maximizing the welfare of the least advantaged rather than striving to promote the good of society as a whole is the hypothesis that there is a "chain connection" in the well-being of all individuals other than those at the top, such that improvements in the lot of the least advantaged inevitably benefit (almost) everyone else (*Theory*, 67–68). But Rawls acknowledges that he has no evidence for this proposition, which seems neither demonstrable nor plausible (increased welfare payments for the poor are typically resented more by blue-collar workers than by multimillionaires). In fact, as I noted in chapter 2, Rawls has the real chain connection backwards: when society as a whole benefits, the least advantaged normally do as well, and it is difficult or impossible in the long run to benefit the latter at the expense of the society to which they belong.

In his earlier article on "Distributive Justice" Rawls had offered a more substantive reason for choosing the difference principle over aiming to maximize the common good. He objected to Hume's justification of "the institutions of justice," including the laws regarding property and contracts, as serving everyone's interest over the long run (even though the rich make out better than the poor), on the ground that such an argument could justify such an unjust institution as slavery, since even slavery, ostensibly, is a better condition than anarchy (*CP*, 134–35). In fact, neither Hume nor Hobbes (the original natural-rights, social-contract theorist) maintains, and Locke expressly denies, that slavery is preferable to anarchy. When we refer to a nation's common good, we ordinarily mean the good of its citizens as a whole. Rawls never grasps the point of the liberal state-of-nature doctrine, which perpetually invites the individual to ask whether the treatment he receives from government is worth the sacrifice of his natural freedom. That doctrine rests on our natural self-assertiveness or sense that "I'm just as good as you are." If human beings are by nature free and equal—that is, no one is marked out by nature to rule anyone else without his consent—then no one may ever justly be enslaved. Regarding such a "hypothetical benchmark" as the state of nature as "irrelevant to the question of justice" (*CP*, 135), Rawls fails to recognize that it offers the surest foundation for securing all people's rights, precisely because it is founded on nature, unlike his purely abstract original position.

Nor is it the case that the difference principle offers even the methodological advantages Rawls claims. To show the relative "ease" with which that principle can be applied, he observes that the least advantaged group "can be identified by its index of primary goods, and policy questions can be settled by asking how the relevant representative man suitably situated would choose" (*Theory*, 281). But just how easy are those tasks? How do we balance deficiencies in wealth, social status, and physical and mental health against each other? (To define the least advantaged solely in economic terms, as Rawls typically does, would only raise the issue of why economic disadvantages should have priority over other forms of inferiority.) Even if we could satisfactorily identify the least advantaged, should we be asking how "the relevant representative man" would choose for them, or what policies are in fact most likely to benefit them? And how do we construct an "index" of primary goods? If it were as easy as Rawls supposes to improve the lot of the less advantaged, wouldn't the United States and other wealthy democracies, at least, have long ago solved such problems as poverty, drug abuse, and educational underperformance, recognizing their effect on the common good?

Aside from the unlikelihood that justice can be reduced to a set of principles that can somehow determine government's policy priorities in each circumstance, I note that by making the good of the least advantaged the sole criterion of the sorts of social and economic inequality that a just society can allow, Rawls has disregarded the problem of democratic consent. Whatever the artificial parties to the original position might be thought to decide, it is unlikely that the citizens of any actual political community will ever accept the difference principle as their standard of justice. That principle, no less than utilitarianism, embodies what we might call the individualistic fallacy: the notion that the concept of the common good can be replaced by a sum of individual "utilities" or "satisfactions" (however distributed), and that individual citizens can be induced to forsake their own interests not for the sake of their country as a whole, in which all have a stake, but merely because some theory calls for reallocating benefits to other persons. In the process of rejecting the straw man of abstract utilitarianism, Rawls has effectively instructed statesmen that as far as justice is concerned, they need not worry about the overall good of their societies, so long as their policies benefit the least advantaged. For good reason, it is unlikely that any democratic politician will choose to run under this banner.

VII.

Turning to "the principle of perfection" (sometimes labeled "perfectionism"), Rawls notes that it resembles justice as fairness in that each doctrine promotes "an ideal of the person," without regard to the satisfaction of wants that are incompatible with it. But justice as fairness, he reminds us, does this without introducing a standard of human excellence that is "prior" to justice itself (*Theory*, 287).

Rawls has little difficulty disposing of "the strict perfectionist conception" that mandates organizing society "to maximize the achievement of human excellence in art, science, and culture," a doctrine he attributes to Nietzsche (*Theory*, 285–87).[56] His response is simply to recall that the parties in the original position lack a known conception of the good embodying a criterion of human excellence. Being unaware, thanks to the veil of ignorance, of their particular "moral and religious interests and other cultural ends," but unwilling to accept any restriction of their freedom to pursue such ends, the parties can only agree on the greatest-equal-liberty principle (*Theory*, 288).

Rawls's entire argument against the principle of perfection is circular: the principle has "failed" only because he defined the original position to ensure its failure. Only if we are convinced, as Rawls is, that we have a surer grasp of justice (understood as entailing the equal right of all individuals to pursue their idiosyncratic life plans) than we do of the criteria of human excellence, will we be persuaded by his argument against "perfectionism"—a doctrine to which he gave no serious consideration anyway.

Again, there are good reasons that modern liberal regimes are prevented from directing citizens to pursue a particular standard of perfection. (The most important is the theocratic legacy of premodern Christianity.) But the reason Rawls finds the traditional liberal case for limited government in this regard wanting emerges more clearly when he explains his rejection of a "more moderate" form of perfectionism, which treats human excellence as "but one standard among several" for assessing social institutions, to be balanced against other criteria by intuition (*Theory*, 286). If we allow people's conduct to be restricted on any ground besides its interference with others' "basic liberties," he warns, we will be "tempted to appeal to perfectionist criteria in an ad hoc manner." Hence, for example, when it is urged that government restrict "certain kinds of sexual relationships" on the ground that they are "degrading and shameful . . . we are likely to be influ-

---

56. Doubtless Nietzsche would be surprised to learn that he identified the sum of human greatness with the advancement of "art, science, and culture," especially given his lament that the modern conception of science has undermined the foundations of genuine human excellence (see especially *On the Advantage and Disadvantage of History for Life*). The only sources Rawls lists for the doctrine he attributes to Nietzsche are a few page citations (plus one quotation) from a couple of secondary sources (*Theory*, 286n).

On the confused character of Rawls's account of the "perfectionist" position, disregarding the fact that serious arguments for rewarding excellence derive from its conduciveness to the common good, see Gourevitch, "Rawls on Justice," 493–94.

enced by subtle aesthetic preferences and personal feelings of propriety," as well as "sharp and irreconcilable" "individual, class, and group differences." Hence, Rawls concludes, "it seems best to rely entirely on the principles of justice" he has ordained to determine the limits of government action, since they "have a more definite structure" (*Theory*, 291).

Just as in his treatment of religious liberty, Rawls reasons from the sheer fact of disagreement about the truth to the conclusion that a just society must be organized according to his own version of the truth—here, pushing to an extreme the Millian principle that nobody's freedom should be restricted except insofar as it interferes with other people's liberty. But Rawls's case is even weaker regarding the moral issue as compared with the religious one, and it certainly goes beyond anything that Mill himself would have found reasonable.[57] We wonder whether Rawls himself has thought through the implications of his assertions. How far is government obliged to go in legalizing such activities as prostitution, polygamy, public nudity, incest, or bestiality, that do not infringe on others' liberty to do as they please? Most civilized peoples throughout the ages have thought restrictions on sexual behavior to be necessary for the sake of what we call human dignity, not merely on account of "subtle aesthetic preferences." By contrast, despite asserting that his principles express our worth as "moral persons," Rawls seems unconcerned with the question of what sorts of regulation may be needed to make human beings seem worthy of having their rights respected, in the way that we do not typically regard other life-forms as having rights.[58]

Lest someone object that in citing constitutional protection of such practices as bestiality and incest as following from Rawls's interpretation of his first principle, I am being unfair, since Rawls never mentions such lurid activities, I stress that (1) Rawls nowhere excludes them from the principle, and these are the sort of sexual practices that are most widely thought to be degrading and shameful; (2) even if Rawls wouldn't want to draw these consequences from his doctrine, others surely will, especially in view of his emphasis on the "uncompromising" character of justice (*Theory*, 3); and (3) it is precisely Rawls's failure to consider such concrete issues that

57. For instance, Mill opposed a public system for the medical inspection of prostitutes on the ground that such a practice would weaken the law's disapprobation of prostitution (Sheldon Amos, *Prohibition, Regulation, and Licensing of Vice in England and Europe*, 54).

58. For Rawls, the notion of human dignity, like the idea of natural rights, is merely an optional rhetorical flourish: "we can say *if we wish* that men have equal dignity" (*Theory*, 289; emphasis added). Similarly, he refers in a note regarding the Hart-Devlin debate on governmental restrictions of sexual conduct to "the so-called enforcement of morals" (*Theory*, 291n), as if there were no true moral issue involved at all.

weakens his version of liberalism and prevents casual readers from considering whether it truly reflects their judgments in "reflective equilibrium." (In fact, Rawls's dictum would seem to guarantee as well the right to practice consensual cannibalism—contrary to the decision of a German court in a notorious case in 2006.)

Again, aside from Rawls's own apparent inclination in favor of moral libertarianism, his utmost concern appears to be the elimination of controversy. Because people's "feelings of propriety" differ, and their differences on moral issues sometimes seem "irreconcilable," Rawls concludes that the only reasonable solution is to rule in the name of justice that the libertarian side of the debate must win. Those who believe that the maintenance of lawful liberty for all depends on preserving a certain standard of moral decency may doubt that Rawls's resolution to this sort of controversy is—to use his term—"fair." Just whose "common sense convictions" does it "match" (*Theory*, 292)?[59]

The manner in which Rawls's objection to allowing considerations of human excellence to enter into judging the proper extent of liberty—the danger that government will thereby use perfectionist criteria "in an ad hoc manner"—passes over fundamental issues of substance in the name of supposed methodological precision recalls his implausible attempt to give concrete "content" to the precept of serving the common good by reducing it to benefiting the less advantaged. Why, as Ross or Aristotle might ask, should popular governments avoid judging such issues on an ad hoc or case-by-case basis in formulating legislation, rather than being bound in advance to conform to the abstract principles that Rawls has mandated? And why, for that matter, should sexual liberties be given sacrosanct status in Rawls's scheme when economic liberties are not? Rawls's failure to address such issues in constructing a supposedly comprehensive theory suggests that as soon as he thought he had found a way of writing his policy preferences into his principles, he figured his philosophical task was done.

Rawls does make one effort to show that the consequences of "doing without a standard of perfection" are "acceptable" (albeit without regard to the moral issue): government may create a special "exchange branch" that provides public funds for the arts and sciences, subject to the (admit-

59. In chapter 7 Rawls restates as a fundamental objection to utilitarianism the possibility of its authorizing "harsh repressive measures" against religious or sexual practices that people regard as "an abomination," assuming that "the real balance of advantages in the long run" favored such measures (*Theory*, 395). But why should society disregard the long-range advantages to its civic health of measures that prohibit abominable sexual practices?

tedly difficult) requirement of unanimous consent among all those who contribute to it (*Theory*, 249–50, 291).[60] This branch would be free to "assess the merits of these public goods on perfectionist principles," since no one would be taxed to finance them without his consent. It is hard to know why, if the agency couldn't use any tax money that donors didn't specifically allocate for this purpose, its existence would serve any purpose at all, since private foundations already do the same thing. Still, while "the claims of culture can be met in this way," Rawls emphasizes that "the principles of justice do not permit subsidizing universities and institutes, or opera and the theater, on the grounds that these institutions are intrinsically valuable"; "taxation for these purposes can be justified only as promoting directly or indirectly the social conditions that secure the equal liberties" and "the long-term interests of the least advantaged" (*Theory*, 291–92).

Doubtless, inventive grants officers at colleges and other cultural institutions can make the case that courses in geology or performances of Verdi indirectly enhance liberty or benefit the least advantaged; but it remains unclear why government may freely impose taxes on the bulk of the population to serve only that class while being prohibited from using any funds to promote higher education or culture as intrinsic goods for the citizenry as a whole. In any event, given the impossibility of truly severing the interests of the least advantaged from those of the society to which they belong, all that Rawls's qualification would seem to entail in practice is that every time government subsidizes such activities, it must add a caveat to the effect that it isn't maintaining that education or culture have any intrinsic value, but is acting only with the interests of the least advantaged in mind.

In conclusion, I note that when Rawls revisits the theme of public support for science and culture in *JF* (151–52), he passes over the issue of financing them through the exchange branch, perhaps recognizing the superfluity of such a device. But he still observes, hedgingly, that justice as fairness "puts in question whether society can allocate *great* public resources to pure science," philosophy, or the arts, "*solely* on the grounds that their study and practice realizes certain great excellences" (*JF*, 151–52, emphasis added). No longer ruling this practice out entirely, Rawls nonetheless stresses that "it is far better to justify" public financing of such enterprises with reference to "political values" such as "public health and preserving the environment, or . . . (justified) national defense," rather

---

60. While acknowledging "very real difficulties" in conceiving how the exchange branch would operate, Rawls chooses, as he frequently does, to "leave aside these problems" (*Theory*, 250).

than "perfectionist" ones. In a note, however, he adds that his version of political liberalism allows allocating public funds "to preserve the beauty of nature" not only for the sake of "political values" but also for "the good of wildlife" as an independent value (*JF*, 152n). Just government, it appears, has a freer hand to promote the good of animals than that of human beings! But in the end, Rawls concedes that once "fundamental justice" has been achieved, "a democratic electorate may devote large resources to grand projects in art and science if it chooses." Partisans of public support for these pursuits may feel grateful for this last-minute concession. Still unspecified, however, is how government will allocate funds to support culture, even for "political values," without invoking what Rawls calls "perfectionist" criteria—that is, ranking the merit of different applications. As we shall see in part 3, Rawls holds it a mandate of justice that no one who devotes himself to counting blades of grass should be made to feel that his activity is inferior to that of, say, an accomplished violinist.

These changes of mind on matters of detail, along with Rawls's characteristic, hedging "great" and "solely" (italicized above), suggest that even after decades, his theory retained an ad hoc character that sits poorly with the dogmatic character of his pronouncements.[61]

---

61. In his adulatory review of *CP*, however, Jeremy Waldron observes that the early essays that show Rawls "formulating and reformulating the ideas that were to figure finally" in *Theory* "provide a salutary example for those of us who write more impulsively" ("The Plight of the Poor in the Midst of Plenty," 5). He does not explain why Rawls then had to publish so many essays after *Theory* to clarify or reformulate his doctrine and its intent. Perhaps the most striking evidence of a certain impulsiveness that continued to characterize Rawls's writing, or at least the work of his copy editors, is his explanation in *PL* (xviii n) of the task that still remained before him: "a number of errors and revisions need to be made in the way the structure and content of justice as fairness was presented in *Theory*" [*sic*].

CHAPTER 6

Civil Disobedience vs. the Right of Resistance

I.

Chapter 6 of *Theory*, "Duty and Obligation," falls into two parts: an introductory pair of sections (nos. 51–52), discussing the principles of "natural duty" and fairness, and the remaining sections (nos. 53–59), which address the extent to which citizens of a reasonably just society are obliged to obey the law or the decisions of the majority, or are justified or even obliged to engage in civil disobedience or "conscientious refusal." The first part, which lacks significant substantive content, merits only brief comment. Beyond his affirmation that from the standpoint of his theory, "the most important natural duty" is to support and promote just institutions (*Theory*, 293), Rawls's major innovation in the first section is his description of "the duty of mutual respect"—that is, the respect due to each person "as a moral being." The novelty here lies in Rawls's assertion that such respect entails "see[ing] the situation of others . . . from the perspective of their conception of the good." Rawls maintains that the parties to the original position would acknowledge such a duty because they recognize (as he previously argued in chapter 3) that human beings "need to be reassured by the esteem of their associates," since "their self-respect and their confidence in the value of their own system of ends cannot withstand" other people's "indifference" or "contempt." Besides, "the cost to self-interest" from respecting other people's ends is small compared to the benefit of guaranteeing their support for one's own sense of worth (*Theory*, 297).

Let us first note the questionableness of Rawls's denial that anyone's self-respect or confidence in his aims can withstand other people's disregard or scorn. Surely, the individuals we most admire are not those whose self-estimation or confidence in their ends—assuming the ends themselves to be respectable—is so dependent on the approval of others as Rawls maintains.[1] Granted that most of us require the esteem of some of our fellows, we also endeavor to train young people to *resist* undesirable peer pressure.

Beyond this point, we must ask whether it is either psychologically possible or genuinely helpful (or respectful) to others to consistently see things from the perspective of their conception of the good, without assessing its content. Are we to try to appreciate a career criminal's or drug addict's way of life from the standpoint of his view of the good rather than our own? Wouldn't we benefit such people far more by trying to correct their outlook?[2] To pick a different sort of example, is it reasonable to demand that a religious believer treat alternative religious views that he regards as false with the same sympathetic appreciation as his own faith? (This is not an argument against respecting other people's religious beliefs, within broad limits. It is an acknowledgment that an adherent of one faith cannot be expected to regard the world from the perspective of someone with fundamentally different beliefs.) Is it even truly *respecting* other people or their beliefs to think that they can't possibly regard their ends as worthy unless we show appreciation for them? (How would Rawls explain the survival for so many centuries of a religious minority such as the Jews amid societies that did far worse than express contempt for them?)[3]

In part 3 of *Theory*, I shall observe, Rawls carries the duty of respecting people's diverse conceptions of the good to remarkable lengths. At this point I simply note the tension between this argument and Rawls's denial in the preceding section that in rejecting the "principle of perfection" as a

1. Consider Frederick Douglass's scornful denial that segregationists had any capacity to degrade him, as recounted by Booker T. Washington in *Up from Slavery*, 16.

2. Cf. Pierre Manent, *A World Beyond Politics?* 191–96, contrasting the contemporary demand of equal regard for all lifestyles with the original Kantian mandate of respect for human dignity; Clor, *Public Morality*, 152–53. On why liberal toleration does not dictate sympathetic respect for all beliefs, see Isaiah Berlin, "John Stuart Mill and the Ends of Life," in *Four Essays on Liberty*, 184.

3. Although Rawls might respond that members of such religious minorities can depend on their coreligionists for expressions of respect, that fact would hardly support his inference that we are obliged to express respect (in his extended sense) for the conceptions of the good held by all members of a pluralistic society.

standard of justice he was denying the existence of vast differences in the excellence of various activities and accomplishments (*Theory,* 288). And I pose the question whether anyone would feel that his sense of self-worth was fortified as a consequence of knowing that people "respected" his ends, whatever they might be, just as much as they respected anybody else's ends. What can the term "respect" mean when it is used in this way?[4]

For now, I turn to Rawls's account of the extent and limits of citizens' obligation to obey the law. Rather than intersperse my summary of his argument with critical comment, I shall first summarize this entire portion of the chapter, postponing most of my analysis to the sequel.

II.

At the outset, addressing the situation of "a nearly just society" with "a viable constitutional regime," Rawls reasonably observes that democratic government requires us to appreciate the limitations of each person's knowledge, as well as of his sense of justice, so as to establish "an effective legislative procedure." Hence, he concludes, "our natural duty to uphold just institutions binds us to comply [even] with unjust laws and policies" under such a regime, so long as the injustice does not "exceed certain limits." Among these limits are the requirements that "in the long run the burden of injustice should be more or less evenly distributed" over different social groups, "the hardship of unjust policies should not weigh too heavily in any particular case," and no one's basic liberties should be denied. Sensibly, Rawls concludes, "we have a natural duty of civility not to invoke the faults of social arrangements as a too ready excuse for not complying with them" (*Theory,* 310–12).

Rawls proceeds to describe the role of the majority-rule principle in an "ideal" political procedure. Just laws and policies, he explains, "are those that would be enacted by rational legislators . . . who are constrained by a just constitution and who are conscientiously trying to follow the principles of justice." Even "under ideal conditions," legislators would need to vote on proposed legislation (rather than aim at unanimity), since their conclusions about the best policy will often differ. A law or policy is to be

4. Admittedly, a Rawlsian view of the duty of respect has become more widespread, witness events such as the "Gay Pride" celebrations to which public officials are expected to render homage. While ethnic "pride" events are intelligible, in that participants can reasonably boast of their particular cultural heritage, what can it mean to take pride in one's sexual practices or orientation? (Cf. Manent, *A World Beyond Politics?* 196.)

deemed "sufficiently just" if "when we try to imagine how the ideal procedure would work out, we conclude that most persons taking part in this
procedure . . . would favor" the policy. Rawls emphasizes that in this procedure "the decision reached is not a compromise . . . between opposing
parties trying to advance their ends," but results from an earnest attempt
"to find the best policy as defined by the principles of justice." (He does
not explain how the need for compromise could be disregarded by representatives who are accountable to their constituents.) He also acknowledges that we cannot assume that even "if many rational persons were to
try to simulate the conditions of the ideal procedure . . . a large majority
anyway would be almost certainly right." Nonetheless, "an ideally conducted discussion among many persons is more likely to arrive at the correct conclusion," and this would be true even among perfectly impartial
legislators, since shared discussion helps overcome the limits of each law-
maker's knowledge and reasoning (*Theory*, 313–15). Under these circumstances, so long as a law is "within the range of those that could reasonably
be favored by rational legislators conscientiously trying to follow the principles of justice," the majority's decision "is practically authoritative,
though not definitive" (*Theory*, 318).

It is hard to discern what this account of an ideal legislative procedure
adds to our understanding of the criteria of just policies. To simulate the
decisions of an ideal legislature in Rawls's sense seems indistinguishable
from asking whether a particular law promises to be beneficial and conforms to the principles of justice. Hence there seems no point to conceiving
laws as generated by an ideal legislature composed of many persons
rather than by a single legislator, which means using our own judgment of
the best policy that fits the two principles. On the other hand, to the extent
that Rawls intends his account as a model for the operation of actual legis-
latures, it is clearly inapplicable, since it is impossible for a democratically
accountable legislative body to place an absolute priority on following
Rawls's principles, without accommodating its constituents' perceived
interests or moral beliefs.

Be this as it may, Rawls next proceeds to sketch a theory of civil disobedience that is to apply under "a legitimately established democratic authority." He defines civil disobedience "as a public, nonviolent, conscientious"
violation of law aimed at engendering a change in the government's policies. It expresses a "considered opinion" that the government has failed to
observe the principles of social cooperation. As Rawls defines it, civil disobedience must be grounded on the principles of justice that "regulate the
constitution and social institutions" rather than on "personal morality or

... religious doctrines." By practicing civil disobedience a minority compels a democratic majority to consider "whether it wishes to have its actions construed" as "persistent and deliberate violation[s]" of justice or chooses instead to acknowledge the minority's "legitimate claims." Civil disobedience operates within an underlying "fidelity to law," as shown by the perpetrator's "willingness to accept the legal consequences" of his conduct. It is thus "far removed from organized forcible resistance" (*Theory*, 319–22).

Unlike civil disobedience, conscientious refusal is "noncompliance" with a law or administrative order, motivated not by the desire to appeal to the moral sense of the majority but by an unwillingness to commit an act one regards as morally wrong. Hence it may be based on religious or moral principles rather than political ones. In this context Rawls suggests that pacifism should be "treated with respect and not merely tolerated," since "it accords reasonably well with the principles of justice," despite the pacifist's unwillingness to fight in a just war (assuming there can be such a thing). "Given the tendency of nations, particularly great powers, to engage in war unjustifiably," pacifism "conceivably compensates" for people's "weakness in living up to their professions," "alerting citizens to the wrongs that governments are prone to commit in their name" (*Theory*, 325).

Having distinguished civil disobedience and conscientious refusal, Rawls then explains the circumstances in which each practice may be justifiable. Viewing civil disobedience as a political act addressed to the community's sense of justice, he judges it reasonable "other things equal, to limit it to instances of substantial and clear injustice, and preferably to those which obstruct the path to removing other injustices." Hence there is a presumption in favor of restricting it "to serious infringements of the first principle of justice" and to "blatant violations" of fair equality of opportunity. Even though "it is not always easy to tell whether these principles are satisfied," Rawls maintains that "it is often clear" that "the basic liberties" are being infringed. Hence we can identify the practice of discrimination against particular minorities through restrictions on voting, officeholding, property ownership, and travel or the repression of religious groups as fundamental wrongs even without any "informed examination of institutional effects."

By contrast, since violations of the difference principle are harder to identify, and the complexities of social and economic issues make it "difficult to check the influence of self-interest and prejudice," Rawls judges that tax laws, for instance, should not ordinarily be violated unless they clearly abridge one of the basic liberties: "the resolution of these issues is best left to the political process provided that the requisite equal liberties are secure" and "a reasonable compromise can presumably be reached." (Here, compromises in the legislative process are allowable.) Additionally, civil disobedience is usually "a last resort" after "normal appeals to the political majority . . . have failed." Moreover, even assuming the above tests have been met, there are circumstances in which "justice may require a certain restraint": for instance, if many groups have "an equally sound case" for civil disobedience, but simultaneous disobedience by all of them might engender "serious disorder" that would undermine a just constitution's "efficacy." There may be "a limit on the extent to which civil disobedience can be engaged in without leading to a breakdown in the respect for law and the constitution, thereby setting in motion consequences unfortunate for all." Thus Rawls suggests that various oppressed minorities reach an understanding to coordinate their actions so that the limit isn't exceeded. Finally, the question remains whether it is prudent to practice civil disobedience in a particular situation or whether it might only provoke the majority to "harsh retaliation." But the theory of justice "has nothing specific to say about these practical considerations" (*Theory*, 326–30).

By contrast with civil disobedience, the issue of conscientious refusal according to Rawls typically involves questions of international justice and law. Anticipating his later enterprise in *The Law of Peoples*, Rawls indicates how the original position might be extended to encompass international relations, arriving at such principles as national self-determination, the right of a nation to defend itself against attack, and the duty to abide by treaties so long as they are consistent with the other principles of international justice. The conscientious refusal to comply with governmental commands based on these principles rests on a "political conception" of justice "and not necessarily upon religious or other notions." Hence a soldier may refuse to participate in acts that he believes violate the principles governing just military conduct (*Theory*, 331–33). Additionally, anyone may conscientiously refuse to comply with the military draft during a particular war on the ground that his country's war aims, such as "economic advantage or national power," are unjust. In fact, should the aims be "sufficiently dubious and the likelihood of receiving flagrantly unjust commands . . . sufficiently great, one may have a duty and not only a right to refuse." Therefore instead of an "unworldly" "general pacifism" Rawls recommends "a discriminating conscientious refusal to engage in war in certain circumstances." Such an attitude may prevent governments from fighting unjust wars; and "given the often predatory aims of state power, and the tendency of men to defer to their government's decision to wage war, a general willingness to resist the state's claims is all the more necessary" (*Theory*, 334–35).[5]

The final section of chapter 6 addresses the overall role of civil disobedience within a constitutional, democratic polity that is "nearly just." Rawls represents this practice as "one of the stabilizing devices of a constitutional system, although by definition an illegal one." "A general disposition to engage in justified civil disobedience" stabilizes a well-ordered or nearly just society, he believes, not only by obstructing unjust governmental policies but "by strengthening men's self-esteem" by giving them an alternative to submission to such policies (*Theory*, 336–37). Rawls even suggests that just as the modern recognition of the sovereignty of the people, as expressed through elections and other constitutional forms, represented an advance over medieval constitutionalism, "the theory of civil disobedience supplements the purely legal conception of constitutional democracy" (*Theory*, 338).

Rawls anticipates the objection that this theory is unrealistic because it presupposes that the majority has an effective sense of justice to which those who conscientiously disobey can appeal. While acknowledging "much truth" in the contention that human beings are moved by "the desires for power, prestige, wealth, and the like" more than by justice, he responds by reminding us that he has "assumed throughout that we have to do with a nearly just society" that is governed not only by a constitutional regime but by "a publicly recognized conception of justice." Unless "those who perpetrate injustice can be clearly identified and isolated from the larger community," or "the sentiment of justice of those not engaged" in injustice can be marshaled against it, he acknowledges, "the wisdom of civil disobedience is highly problematic," since "the majority may simply be aroused to more repressive measures." Under those circumstances courts may fail to "take into account the civilly disobedient nature of the protester's act" by reducing or suspending the penalty as they should (*Theory*, 338–39).

Fortunately, Rawls now explains, the achievement of a nearly just society doesn't require that all citizens accept the same principles of justice. Rather, he observes—prefiguring the revision of his theory in *PL*—that

5. For a likely source of Rawls's remark about the predatory character of governments, see Kant, "Perpetual Peace," 1st. sec., art. 4, 95. But Kant, unlike Rawls, attributes the "warlike inclination of those in power" to an instinct apparently rooted in human nature as such (ibid.), and he denies that citizens even have a right to rebel against tyrannical government, let alone disobey particular laws or policies that they deem unjust, including judgments of the justice of particular wars (ibid., app. 2, 126–27).

there can just as easily be an "overlapping consensus" among citizens' conceptions of justice, provided that they "lead to similar political judgments" (*Theory*, 340).

Once again Rawls acknowledges "definite risks in the resort to civil disobedience," including the possibility that it will engender anarchy. Indeed, "up to a certain point it is better that the law and its interpretation be settled than that it be settled rightly." And "in a state of near justice there is a presumption in favor of compliance in the absence of strong reasons to the contrary." Nonetheless, every citizen is responsible for assessing his country's policies in light of his own interpretation of the principles of justice and for deciding conscientiously when he ought to disobey a law on that basis. While "there is no way to avoid entirely the danger of divisive strife," Rawls concludes, "if justified civil disobedience seems to threaten civic concord, the responsibility falls not upon those who protest but upon those whose abuse of authority and power justifies such opposition" (*Theory*, 341–42).

III.

The remark last quoted echoes John Locke's *Second Treatise* in a way that actually brings out what is novel, and deeply problematic, in Rawls's doctrine of civil disobedience. Just as Rawls rhetorically asks "who is to decide" the proper interpretation of the principles of justice and answers "all are to decide, everyone taking counsel with himself" (*Theory*, 342), Locke famously asked "who shall be judge?" when violent resistance is called for against an oppressive sovereign and responded, "the people shall judge."[6] Similarly, Rawls's contention that the responsibility for any threat to civic concord resulting from justified civil disobedience lies with those in authority whose abuses provoked such resistance echoes Locke's contention that the true "rebel" is not the people who overthrow an oppressive government, but the sovereign whose misconduct provokes a return to the state of war into which human beings fall when a legitimate government no longer exists.[7]

The chief differences between Locke's teaching on this score and Rawls's are threefold. First, Locke offers a relatively clear (and self-enforcing) criterion for when resistance is justifiable and indicates that government has

6. Locke, *Two Treatises*, bk. 2, sec. 240. As Robert Goldwin points out, neither Locke nor the Declaration of Independence describes the just deposition of a tyrannical or incipiently tyrannical government as a "revolution" ("Is There an American Right of Revolution?").

7. Locke, *Two Treatises*, bk. 2, sec. 226.

every right to repress and punish unjustified resistance; Rawls by contrast offers only the vaguest sort of criteria and underestimates the dangers of encouraging widespread lawlessness as a result of his teaching. Second, Locke is offering a rationale for the *collective* exercise of a right of (potentially violent) resistance against unjust government, while Rawls is justifying an individual right to disobey laws or commands issued by a "nearly just" government. Third, Locke never speaks of a right to disobey particular laws or commands under a "nearly just" government; the choice between obeying a government and seeking to overthrow it is an all-or-nothing one, with the latter option not to be exercised (in the language of the Declaration of Independence) for "light and transient causes." Locke's doctrine, like that of the framers of the Declaration who followed him in this regard, has a coherence and realism that Rawls's teaching lacks.

For Locke and the authors of the Declaration, the right of human beings to resist and overthrow oppressive governments follows from the very purpose of government: to secure the natural rights of those who live under it. As the Declaration states, when government becomes oppressive of the rights it was instituted to protect, it is the people's right and duty to "alter and abolish" it and to replace it with another that in their judgment seems most likely to secure their rights. Locke is emphatic, however, that the right to resist government must be a collective one. The very defect of the state of nature that makes government necessary is the absence of a recognized legislator with the capacity to make laws that are binding on all citizens, a judge to apply them impartially, and an executive able to enforce them. From Locke's perspective it is therefore incoherent to speak of an individual citizen's having a right to disobey whatever laws or commands he happens to deem unjust. It is the obscurity of the particular dictates of the "law of nature" (which obliges us so far as possible to preserve all of mankind as well as ourselves), as well as the unreliability of any inherent sense of justice among human beings who are "no strict observers" of it, that makes it necessary to give up our right to interpret and enforce the natural law to a sovereign who is charged with preserving, so far as possible, the lives, liberties, and properties of all of his subjects.[8] Although Locke's initial description of life in the state of nature in the *Second Treatise* seems considerably milder than Hobbes's, his second account in chapter 9 makes clear, as a close analysis of the first account would also demonstrate, that without government human existence would in fact be a condition of war of every man against every other in which life is solitary,

8. Ibid., bk. 2, sec. 123.

poor, nasty, brutish, and short.[9] Hence Locke judges that anyone who undermines a legitimate government is guilty of the greatest of crimes.[10]

By contrast with Locke, Rawls, as we have seen, makes no attempt to consider what life without government would be like. Consequently, he underestimates both our need for government and government's inherent fragility. In contrast to Lincoln's endeavor to inculcate a civil religion of law-abidingness, Rawls encourages people "to resist the state's claims." His chief response to the threat that widespread civil disobedience will culminate in anarchy—his having assumed the existence of a "nearly just society"—begs the question of how such a society can be built up in the first place or maintained in the face of threats to its perpetuation. Here, Rawls's only answer is to resort once more to an abstract "moral psychology" that maintains, this time, that citizens' knowledge that they have a right to disobey whatever laws they deem unjust will stabilize their society by enhancing their self-esteem. He offers no evidence to document this unlikely claim. The best he can say for his approach is that "with reasonableness, comity, and good fortune, it often works out well enough" (*Theory*, 342)—to which one can only respond, well enough for what?

Turning to the criteria by which we are to judge whether resistance to government is called for, Locke is straightforward: it takes no great acuity, he maintains, for the people to "see and feel" that the security of their rights to life, liberty, and property is being undermined by the sovereign.[11] In fact, Locke emphasizes that the people need not and should not wait to resist until the sovereign has actually established a tyranny over them (that might be too late). Rather, in language repeated in the Declaration of Independence, when "a long train" of abuses has manifested the sovereign's intention or "design" of making himself a tyrant, the people are called on to overthrow him.[12]

What, then, guarantees that Locke's own doctrine won't incite frequent bouts of anarchy, making all governments dangerously insecure? Outwardly, his chief response, echoed in the Declaration, concerns the people's supposed natural conservatism: they are more prone to endure abuse

9. Consider as well Locke's remark (in the context of denying the existence of innate moral principles) that "robberies, murders, rapes, are the sports of men set at liberty from punishment and censure" (*An Essay Concerning Human Understanding*, pt. 1, chap. 3, sec. 9). See also Leo Strauss, *Natural Right and History*, 202–51; Richard Cox, *Locke on War and Peace*.

10. Locke, *Two Treatises*, bk. 2, sec. 218.

11. Ibid., bk. 2, sec. 209. In practice, the constitutional security against governmental oppression consists in the requirement that government ordinarily adhere to the rule of law and the separation of powers, as well as the mandate that taxes be approved by the people's elected representatives (bk. 2, secs. 135–42, 212–22).

12. Ibid., bk. 2, sec. 210.

than to rebel against it. The deeper reason for that conservatism, however, is that since government retains full authority to employ force to suppress any rebellion, and to punish unsuccessful rebels with appropriate severity, no sensible citizen is likely to join an uprising unless he perceives an oppression not only so severe but so widespread that he can reasonably expect a considerable portion of his fellow citizens to enlist in the effort—and not many to fly to the side of the sovereign.[13]

In comparison with Locke, Rawls offers a far vaguer test for legitimizing resistance. In his words, civil disobedience is authorized whenever one believes that government has violated "the principles of social cooperation among free and equal men" (*Theory*, 320). Yet Rawls acknowledges that even a set of rational legislators who were motivated by a concern for justice would not be likely to arrive at unanimous agreement on particular policies, hence the need for majority rule. There is at least as much reason to expect widespread disagreement among the citizenry at large about the fairness of various policies: that's why political debate so often concerns issues of justice. Isn't Rawls's advocacy of civil disobedience, despite the mild qualifications he sometimes adds (such as the duty "normally" to comply with moderately unjust laws under a nearly just regime), an open-ended invitation to citizens to disobey the law whenever they don't happen to agree with it? How could democratic government, or any form of government, be maintained on this basis? (Consider the American election of 1800, the first election in the world in which one political party or faction peacefully handed over power to another with which it disagreed over fundamental principles. How would the Federalists have responded to Jefferson's election had they been schooled in Rawls's doctrine of civil disobedience?)[14]

13. Ibid., bk. 2, sec. 168; bk. 2, secs. 30–34; bk. 2, sec. 208. Locke specifically denies the legitimacy of resistance to duly constituted authority as long as it is possible to appeal to the law for redress of one's grievances (bk. 2, sec. 207).

14. Contrast Jefferson's enunciation in his First Inaugural Address of the principle of "absolute acquiescence in the decisions of the majority," under constitutional procedures designed to ensure that the majority will be "reasonable," with Rawls's counsel (*Life and Selected Writings*, 322, 324). Jefferson's view is echoed in Lincoln's First Inaugural Address (*Collected Works of Abraham Lincoln*, 4:268), describing a constitutionally guided majority, whose government must be responsive to "deliberate changes of popular opinions and sentiments," as "the only true sovereign of a free people"; and in his "Message to Congress in Special Session," July 4, 1861 (4:439), citing the importance of demonstrating that "there can be no successful appeal" beyond the outcome of an election "except to ballots themselves, at succeeding elections." See Jaffa, *New Birth of Freedom*, chap. 1, on how the peaceful transfer of power in 1800 initiated "the transformation of the right of revolution into the right of free election" under a constitutional regime, the legacy that Lincoln subsequently undertook to defend (30). That legacy was still visible in the contrast between the response of disappointed Democratic partisans to the outcome of the 2000 American presidential election and the behavior of the losing candidate and his supporters in the 2006 Mexican presidential election.

Rawls contends, we recall, that though it is hard to assess violations of the difference principle (hence alleged violations do not typically justify disobedience), it is "often clear" that the "basic liberties" mandated by the first principle and the fair-opportunity clause of the second are being abridged. But even if this were the case, such that it did not take "an informed examination of institutional effects" to identify egregious discrimination against particular minorities, this is not simply the question that has to be answered to determine whether particular limitations of liberty or opportunity are justified, by Rawls's own precepts (as I noted in chapter 4). Even Rawls acknowledges that the practice of toleration mandated by the first principle can be extended to the intolerant only "as far as the safety of free institutions permits" (*Theory*, 340). Thus, to determine whether civil disobedience is truly justified, by Rawls's account, it isn't enough to note that the liberty of one group has been limited more than that of the rest of the population: we must also determine whether that restriction was justified by the particular circumstances that occasioned it. Can such questions be properly resolved without a factually informed examination? (Consider the controversy over the Bush administration's plan following the September 11 attacks to try certain foreign terrorists in military tribunals: aside from constitutional questions, to be resolved by the courts, how well equipped is the average citizen to judge this policy? Would the cause of justice or freedom be well served by encouraging anyone who disagrees with the government's policy to break the law in order to express his opinion, rather than relying on democratic processes to seek to change it?)

The thousands of cases that are brought in federal and state courts each year charging violations of people's constitutional liberties—many of them manifestly frivolous—indicate how far the United States, let alone any other large and diverse nation, is from reaching a unanimous consensus on the proper extent of such rights. Of course, to identify a violation of Rawls's "fair equality of opportunity" principle would be harder still, especially since Rawls himself can hardly be said to provide a perspicuous account of it. Finally, once we have endorsed the practice of civil disobedience, how are we to limit it to cases that Rawls would endorse, rather than extending it, say, to persons who refuse to pay income taxes on the ground that graduated income taxation (as some eminent authorities have maintained) is unjust since it arbitrarily discriminates among individuals, or who claim that the federal income tax is unconstitutional? (Many more extreme examples might be imagined.) Once the cat of civil disobedience has been let out of the bag, how can Rawls claim the authority to limit whose backyard it may wander into? (It is exemplary of his abstract perspective that Rawls's only extended account of potential problems arising from the practice of civil disobedience concerns the hypothetical situation in which many groups have "an equally sound case" for practicing it, and hence have to time their protests so as not to overload the system. Can anyone imagine such a situation and resultant agreement actually occurring?)

Rawls seems not to appreciate that citizens on both sides of many issues feel no less strongly that their view is right and the opposing one wrong. If those on one side feel free to break the law when it goes against them, possibly inducing the government to succumb to their demands, why shouldn't the others do so in response? How will such controversies end in the absence of an overwhelming consensus on the duty to obey the law regardless of one's private opinions? Isn't the proper recourse to a perception of injustice under a constitutional-democratic regime in almost all circumstances to make use of the lawful channels for political change that the Constitution provides, while being mindful that others won't necessarily see things your way, leaving you the option of either accepting that fact or emigrating to some other country the laws of which seem more attractive to you?

The very notion of civil disobedience, as such scholars as Herbert Storing and Steven Schlesinger have argued, is a theoretically confused halfway house between outright revolution and lawful democratic change.[15] Its chief tactical successes—notably, those of Gandhi's followers in India and civil rights demonstrators in America during the 1950s and early 1960s—occurred in dealing with regimes so structured that the moral scruples of the people as a whole generally constrained the government's response and ultimately dictated its surrender to the demonstrators' just demands.[16] But those scruples need to be seen as themselves the fruit of long traditions of constitutional governance and popular law-abidingness, which even peaceful resistance to law can have the effect of eroding. In both cases the protesters were driven to nonlegal methods because they

15. Storing, "The Case against Civil Disobedience," in *Toward a More Perfect Union,* 236–58; Steven R. Schlesinger, "Civil Disobedience."

16. Analogously, the "Velvet Revolution" that overthrew the Czechoslovak Communist dictatorship succeeded (in contrast to the failure of the "Prague Spring" two decades earlier) only because the Soviet occupying regime had already been persuaded, thanks to its inability to compete militarily and economically with the United States, to end its military support for Central European satellite regimes. The widespread, peaceful demonstrations against the unpopular Iranian theocracy in 2003 failed to engender any significant change in that regime. But in both the Czech and Iranian cases, as in the Indian one (and in subsequent peaceful uprisings against despotisms in Georgia, Ukraine, and Kyrgyzstan), the protestors' goal was regime change, not merely a selective change in the laws, and the nondemocratic character of those various regimes offered no effectual, legal means of change.

were excluded from the full rights of citizenship (in the American South, by racial discrimination, including the denial of constitutionally author- ized voting rights, and in India, by the refusal of the British to grant inde- pendence) that are the ordinary mode of democratic political change. (Indeed, since the goal of the Indian movement was to overthrow British rule entirely, it was a tactical variant of the Lockean right of resistance.) By contrast, civil disobedience, understood as a generalized right to disobey whatever laws one finds "sufficiently" unjust, threatens to erode the moral capital built up over centuries that not only causes people normally to be law-abiding but also underlies the tolerance and respect for other people's rights that a liberal society presupposes.[17] Greater historical and philo- sophic reflection might have caused Rawls to consider why none of the great liberal thinkers or statesmen ever enunciated such a doctrine.[18]

Not only does Rawls underestimate the difficulty of resolving disagree- ments among alternative views of just policy (such that nobody will ever be fully satisfied with all of his government's policies), it apparently never occurs to him that someone might challenge the laws on the basis of a fun- damentally mistaken, not to say pernicious, view of justice. Why assume as Rawls apparently does that whenever a minority undertakes to challenge a majority decision, the minority's judgment must be at least partly right?[19]

17. Even in the case of American civil rights demonstrators, despite the justness of their cause and the honorableness and prudence of Martin Luther King Jr.'s leadership, the evolution from the peaceful protests of the King years to the race riots and some- times violent antiwar protests of the 1960s serves as a cautionary tale about the danger- ous precedent-setting effect of disobedience to law—as foreseen in Lincoln's Lyceum address. (Cf. Rawls's own cautionary remarks about the fragility of a constitutional democratic consensus in *PL*, 228 and 316, cited in chapter 11 below.)

18. When it comes to defiance of the law on behalf of a cause that is less attractive to him—opposition to abortion—Rawls sings in a different key, urging opponents that "forceful resistance is unreasonable" since "it would mean attempting to impose by force their own comprehensive doctrine that a majority of other citizens who follow public reason, not unreasonably, do not accept" (*IPRR*, 170). Presumably, "forceful resistance" here includes the attempted obstruction of abortion clinics, a tactic that is no more forcible than some of the methods used by civil rights and antiwar protestors of the 1960s whose goals and, apparently, their tactics Rawls approved.

19. It is worth recalling that during the same era in which Henry David Thoreau first enunciated the doctrine of civil disobedience, based on his denial of the authority of law to override his personal conception of just conduct, South Carolina senator John C. Calhoun was propounding his own doctrine of the "concurrent majority" as a neces- sary means of "peaceably" resisting governmental abridgements of the rights of "minorities"—his core concern being the defense of the interests of southern slave owners against federal interference with their "peculiar institution" (Calhoun, *A Dis- quisition on Government*, in *Union and Liberty*, 12–14, 28–30). While on opposite sides of the slavery controversy, Calhoun and Thoreau agreed in their essentially illiberal chal- lenge to the legitimacy of constitutional, democratic government.

The ultimate check on frivolous or poorly justified resistance to the government in Locke's system, I have observed, is the threat of severe punishments to unsuccessful rebels. By contrast, even though Rawls initially defines civil disobedience in part with reference to the perpetrator's "willingness to accept the legal consequences" of his actions, he holds that the punishments should normally be mild, and he even endorses Ronald Dworkin's suggestion that the penalties be suspended entirely (*Theory,* 339). Thus there would be nothing to deter ostensibly peaceful lawlessness.

The other critical difference between Rawls's doctrine of civil disobedience and Locke's and the Declaration's principle of resistance to oppressive government is, as I have noted, that the latter is the product of a collective judgment, while the former is only a matter of individual opinion or sentiment. According to Locke, and the patriots of 1776, to defy the established government and law is a momentous act to be undertaken only after long deliberation, not only because of the risk of punishment, but also out of awareness of how far everyone's well-being normally depends on the maintenance of a system of law. By contrast, Rawls's appeal to the sovereignty of each individual's "interpretation of the principles of justice" (*Theory,* 342) evinces little awareness of the difficulty of forming a nation of individuals into a coherent political whole.

Under a constitutional, republican regime like the American one, in which all officeholders derive their authority, directly or indirectly, from the people themselves; in which the powers of government are constitutionally limited, and the limits are enforced through the separation of powers, buttressed by checks and balances among the branches of government, thus protecting against the danger of majority tyranny; and in which the constitutional rights of citizens are specifically guaranteed, and enforceable in courts of law, one may plausibly maintain, as Lincoln did, that even the doctrine of the right of resistance has no proper application. Contrary to Rawls, it is constitutional government itself that is the ultimate safeguard of our rights.[20]

One contemporary, nominally constitutional-democratic regime regularly illustrates the consequences of engendering the belief that the appropriate way for citizens to reverse government policies that they don't approve is through (mostly) civil disobedience: France. Lacking both a tradition of popular respect for law as strong as that which exists in America and a policy-making process as open to the constitutional expression and accommodation of public grievances as the American one, the French habitually resort to paralyzing acts of widespread "resistance," ranging

20. See remarks by Lincoln cited in note 14 above.

from highway blockades by truck drivers protesting the price of gasoline, to street riots aimed at deterring the National Assembly from modifying state pensions in the face of a fiscal crisis, and "strikes" and blockades by university students resisting changes in the labor laws aimed at reducing unemployment.[21] The French reliance on nonlegal challenges to government policies reflects a perceived lack of effectual constitutional representation in the policy process. But how different is the often high-handed attitude of French officials toward the citizenry from the principle Rawls laid down in chapter 4 that "where issues of justice are involved, the intensity of people's desires should not be taken into account" (*Theory*, 203)?[22] (And if popular resistance in France is sometimes a bit more violent than Rawls would approve, doesn't that just signify how strongly felt the people's grievances are?) As *New York Times* reporter Craig Smith observes, France's "long tradition of often violent demonstrations and paralyzing strikes . . . is largely tolerated by the broader population, which has a cultural mistrust of government even as it retains a deep dependency on the state," making it even harder than in the U.S. for government to curtail people's "entitlements" no matter how costly they become.[23] But as the *Wall Street Journal* observed of the student demonstrations in 2006, "When the thousands on the street assert the right to make laws for the millions, a country loses its right to call itself a 'democratic republic.'"[24]

IV.

The same problems that arise in Rawls's civil-disobedience doctrine mar his teaching about conscientious refusal. International law and the U.S.

---

21. See Craig S. Smith, "French Strike against Cuts in Pensions Jams Traffic"; John Carreyrou, "At French Utility, Union Wages War to Guard Its Perks."

22. On the moral issue of capital punishment, for instance, public opinion surveys regularly show majority support for its restoration in France and other European nations (as well as Canada) whose political leaders have effectively kept the issue "off the agenda." See Jeremy Rabkin, "Courting Abroad," 30; T. Alexander Smith and Raymond Tatalovich, *Cultures at War*, 242–44. Doubtless, Rawls would approve.

By way of imitation, as it were, the Massachusetts legislature twice in recent years avoided allowing a properly submitted popular petition for a constitutional amendment to prohibit same-sex marriage to be voted on, a prerequisite to its being placed on the ballot by refusing to consider the petition, until judicial pressure compelled it to do so. In the interval between the two occasions (2002 and 2006) on which the legislature adjourned without voting on the petition (so as to spare legislators from possible voter wrath for opposing it), the state's Supreme Judicial Court instituted same-sex marriage by judicial fiat under the pretense of constitutional interpretation, likewise evincing a Rawlsian attitude toward popular self-government.

23. Smith, "French Premier Considers Easing Job Law."

24. "The Decline of France."

Uniform Code of Military Justice already mandate noncompliance with any order that violates the recognized laws of war, such as the commission of atrocities against civilians. And in a democratic polity like the United States, wars can be conducted only under the leadership of a popularly elected president and with the support of the people's elected congressional representatives. Yet Rawls wants to encourage defiance of such democratic decisions by calling on individuals to resist the draft whenever they happen to believe that the war's aims are "economic advantage or national power" rather than self-defense or justice, and he calls widespread readiness to "resist the state's claims" a "necessary" element of justice, as well as a salutary "affront to the government's pretensions" (*Theory*, 334–35). But who is "the state" in a democratic polity except the people themselves? Who is "the government" but the people's elected representatives and those who serve under them? Do we not rely on elected representatives (rather than plebiscites conducted through home computers) to make fundamental decisions such as those of war and peace, precisely on the assumption that a professional deliberative body and chief executive, advised by an extensive staff, should be better able to make those judgments more wisely—subject to the voters' verdict in the next election—than the average man in the street? How would Rawls's doctrine of selective conscientious objection have worked during a war when the nation's very survival and freedom were clearly at stake—say, the Civil War or World War II? How, indeed, would Rawls assess the draft riots that occurred in the North during the Civil War: a justified protest against the Union's "predatory" objectives or a selfish unwillingness to answer the nation's call in time of need?[25] Would Rawls also encourage soldiers to desert whenever they come to doubt the legitimacy of their government's war aims? Similarly, when Rawls observes that conscription may not be justified "by any needs less compelling than those of national security" (*Theory*, 333), who determines what our country's security requires? Did the Korean War qualify? What of American participation in World War I? Or, to choose an example from another democratic country, should Israeli soldiers who opposed their government's decision to remove Jewish settlements from Gaza in 2005 have refused to obey their commanders' orders or gone AWOL?[26] Is there any plausible alternative to having a recognized, legitimate, popularly accountable government make the final decision in all such cases?

25. This is not to deny the folly of the policy that helped precipitate the riots—allowing wealthier individuals to buy their way out of military service (which had an effect comparable to the student deferments of the 1960s in biasing the class effect of the military draft in a manner incompatible with democratic mores).

26. See Michael B. Oren, "A Soldier's Story."

There are certain exceptional cases where we may excuse or even admire the actions of democratic citizens who peacefully violated the law to counteract a grave injustice perpetrated against others who were not represented in the political system. Two such examples are the individuals who operated the Underground Railroad in antebellum America, in violation of the Fugitive Slave Law, and Swiss citizens who broke laws during World War II that prohibited assisting Jewish refugees from Nazi genocide. But such cases of justifiable resistance on behalf of legally excluded minorities, in a constitutional democracy with a universal franchise, are fortunately quite rare, and their exceptional nature prevents their being subsumed under any general rule. To propound doctrines like Rawls's is far more likely to engender unjustified disobedience to any laws that somebody doesn't happen to agree with.

The need to elevate the laws in the eyes of the people if a republican regime is to survive has been recognized by democratic statesmen from Pericles to Lincoln and by philosophers as diverse as Plato and Rousseau. By contrast, Rawls's doctrine of civil disobedience is an unwarranted swipe at the very notion of constitutional government. He is correct to observe that in the American regime the ultimate interpreter of the Constitution is not any branch of the government (including the judiciary), but the electorate as a whole (*Theory*, 342). But the Constitution already provides a means for the citizenry to express its understanding of that document: through peaceful and law-abiding political activity, culminating in elections.[27] As Socrates argues in Plato's *Crito*, when a political regime offers each citizen the right to criticize laws that he deems unjust, to try to persuade his fellow citizens to change them, and to emigrate freely with his family and possessions if he thinks he can get a better deal elsewhere, he incurs a binding obligation to obey the laws, including those he disapproves of, if he chooses to remain. This is a matter of simple reciprocity, since we inevitably benefit from the law-abiding behavior of our fellow citizens, who doubtless have plenty of quarrels of their own with the law. Rawls shows himself quite sensitive to the "free-rider" problem in purely abstract contexts (*Theory*, 113, 236–39, 499), but not when it comes to the elemental duties of citizenship. Similarly, when compelled to acknowledge the limitations of available ways of life in his own model of a well-ordered society, he counsels those who find it objectionable that they will have to make their peace with it, since "no society can include within itself

27. The Republican victory in the 1860 presidential election was inspired in part, of course, by resistance to the *Dred Scott* decision, while the 1936 election buttressed Franklin Roosevelt's successful effort to overcome the Supreme Court's opposition to his New Deal legislation.

all ways of life," much as we may "lament" that fact (*JF*, 154). In dealing with actually existing constitutional democracies, however, Rawls cannot accept the notion that we are almost always obliged to limit ourselves to law-abiding modes of political activity, and he counsels his readers to break the law whenever they feel "sufficiently" justified in doing so. In a word, this attitude is unjust.

CHAPTER 7

"Goodness as Rationality," Self-Respect, and Rawlsian Jurisprudence

I.

In chapter 7 of *Theory*, which introduces part 3, "Ends," Rawls elaborates his conception of "goodness as rationality." Having heretofore relied on a "thin theory" of the good—that is, the doctrine of primary goods—to develop his account of justice, Rawls now aims to provide a "full theory" so as to demonstrate that justice is "congruent" with our good, or that "being a good person is a good thing for that person" (*Theory*, 347–49).

Just as Rawls's overall approach to justice is indirect or abstract, comparing rival theories rather than confronting substantive human opinions about it, the core of his account of the good is another theory, goodness as rationality. The indirection or formalism of Rawls's description of the good is necessitated by his understanding of justice, according to which society should be officially agnostic about the relative value of different ways of life, so long as they are just.

In Rawls's account, a person's good is determined by his "rational plan." A rational plan is one that conforms to "the principles of rational choice" and that a person would choose "with full awareness of the relevant facts and after a careful consideration of the consequences" (*Theory*, 358–59). Happiness is subjective: people's rational plans vary depending on their talents and situations, and "different individuals find their happiness in doing different things."[1] A happy person is someone who is "more or less" successfully executing his rational plan and "reasonably confident" that it can be completed (*Theory*, 359). In turn, the principles of rational choice include (1) selecting the most efficient, cost-effective means to one's ends; (2) preferring the most inclusive plan, which will enable one if possible to achieve all his desired aims rather than only some of them; and (3) choosing the plan that is likeliest to succeed. Even in formulating long-term plans of life, when we do not yet have all the desires that various plans encourage, we can still "choose" our future desires by deciding to do something now "that we know will affect" them (*Theory*, 361–62, 364–65).

This account of human life is curiously remote from our everyday understanding. Surely we don't often think of ourselves as "choosing" our future desires, either directly or indirectly. While our present choices undoubtedly affect our subsequent desires, that is hardly likely to be the point of our choices. Nor do we often "plan" our lives in quite the calculating way Rawls describes, despite his citation of various scholarly "writers" to that effect (*Theory*, 358n). (It doesn't seem to leave much room for falling in love, answering God's call, or life's various other adventures as well as misfortunes. And the emphasis on "success" puts a premium on not setting one's sights too high—recalling the timid attitude of Rawls's risk-averse parties to the original position.[2]) In fact, Rawls himself stresses that his notion of goodness as rationality attributes no "special value to the process of deciding" which plan to follow: "there is even nothing irrational in an aversion to deliberation itself providing that one is prepared to accept the consequences" (*Theory*, 367). It is simply "left to the agent himself to decide what

---

1. Rawls's subjectivism about the good broadly mirrors the liberal tradition. See, e.g., Hobbes, *Leviathan*, chap. 11, 1st par.; Locke, *Essay Concerning Human Understanding*, pt. 2, chap. 21, secs. 54–55; and the Lockean phrase *pursuit of happiness* in the Declaration of Independence. But not only does Locke emphasize in the *Essay* (pt. 2, chap. 21, secs. 56–70) the need for careful calculation of the means to one's long-range happiness, in *Some Thoughts Concerning Education* he propounds a view of the human good that is considerably less relativistic than Rawls's (consider, e.g., his condemnation of gambling [sec. 207]. See also Nathan Tarcov, *Locke's Education for Liberty*).

2. Cf. Wolff, *Understanding Rawls*, 137–41; and Yack, *Problems of a Political Animal*, articulating Aristotle's understanding as follows: "The human good . . . is not something that we choose or make for ourselves," but is a function of "the particular way of life that human beings, as a species and as individuals, happen to be capable of living" (258). Similarly, although "the way in which we react to moral training will contribute . . . to the shaping of our moral character . . . we never face a moment during which we can subject our lives and character to that favorite figment of modern moral philosophers' imagination, a rational 'life-plan'" (248).

. . . he most wants" and to rank his ends accordingly (*Theory*, 366). "It is not inconceivable that an individual, or even a whole society, should achieve happiness moved entirely by spontaneous inclination," without any forethought (*Theory*, 372). (We wonder whether that possibility is conceivable, assuming that we are thinking of a truly human happiness.)

The deeper incoherence in Rawls's account of rationality arises from his endeavor to give the term a purely instrumental meaning, yet employ it as a criterion for assessing people's choices. After all, if rationality is purely a matter of choosing what one prefers—all such preferences being equally valid—and there is no inherent value to the process of deliberation, what ground does Rawls have for saying that it is inherently more rational to choose effective rather than ineffective means to one's ends, to try to satisfy the greatest number of one's desires, or to select the plan that is likeliest to succeed? According to Rawls, so long as a person "does the best that a rational person can do with the information available" about his desires and the likely means of their fulfillment, even if he errs because of mistaken beliefs or insufficient knowledge, he "is not to be faulted for any discrepancy between his apparent and his real good" (*Theory*, 366–67). But if there is nothing inherently irrational about avoiding deliberation entirely, so long as we are ready to accept the consequences, on what ground can a person be faulted even if he turns out to be unwilling to accept those consequences, but rather laments them? (If we say it's unreasonable for him to lament consequences that he could have averted, he need only respond that this is what he prefers to do.) To speak reasonably about the human good, do we not need to engage in substantive consideration of what that good consists in, at least within a broad range?

The fundamental defect in the notion of instrumental rationality (derived from Max Weber), is that it arbitrarily assumes that the process of reasoning must stop short of assessing people's particular ends. If we can agree that in the deepest sense all people's ultimate (earthly) goal, as Aristotle asserts (and as Rawls's definition presupposes [*Theory*, 359]), is happiness (*eudaimonia*)—specifically, a more or less continuous and enviable (i.e., genuinely human) happiness rather than a mere collection of quanta of pleasure—how can we know that human reason is incapable of assessing which ways of life are more likely to achieve that aim? (Contrary to Rawls's argument in chapter 9, which will be discussed later, this by no means entails that there is only one acceptable way of life, that all people are equally capable of achieving the greatest goods, or that governments should compel people to pursue one single way of life or conception of the good.) To assume that only people's choice of means, not their ends, can be rationally assessed amounts, in Leo Strauss's words, to a recipe for "retail sanity and wholesale madness."[3]

Consider a concrete example that is connected to important public policy debates. Most of us recognize that among the essential components of a good life, especially in a liberal society like the American one, are certain attributes that give one a degree of self-sufficiency: personal virtues such as industry, thrift, sobriety, courage, self-control, responsibility (including for one's offspring), and prudence; an education that provides one with useful skills and the capacity to serve capably in various economic, charitable, and civic associations; and the civic virtues that contribute to an intelligent patriotism and a capacity to deliberate reasonably about public affairs. The chief obstacle that prevents many members of today's underclass from rising to such self-sufficiency and civic capacity, it is often observed, is a "culture of poverty" that causes people to overvalue immediate gratifications (excessive material consumption, promiscuous sex, drug abuse, alcoholism) at the expense of their long-term capacity to support themselves, their families, and their community.[4] Most of us would say that those who make these poor choices are acting unreasonably. Yet on Rawls's account, it appears, anyone who persuasively says, "I don't care about the future, I just want to enjoy the present," is acting no less rationally than one who works to achieve an education, to save money, and to develop the other attributes that will make him an esteemed member of his community. Of course Rawls himself maintains that a rational person, once he has chosen a plan, should be "able to adhere to it" and "resist present temptations and distractions that interfere with its execution" (*Theory*, 367), but why so, if his goal is simply to live for the day?

It is hard to believe that Rawls, if pressed on this issue, wouldn't agree that it is objectively better for young (and older) people to be steered away from wastefulness, self-indulgence, promiscuity, and drug abuse in favor of the range of skills and virtues I have mentioned. But neither his account of the good nor his treatment of what he calls distributive justice—which

3. Strauss, *Natural Right and History*, 4. Strauss proceeds in chapter 2 to refute the assumption that this sort of value relativism supports liberalism. Cf. Bloom, "Justice," 658–59. For a thorough critique of the notion of instrumental rationality as espoused by the economist Herbert A. Simon (cited by Rawls, *Theory*, 367n), see Herbert J. Storing, "The Science of Administration," in *Essays on the Scientific Study of Politics*, especially 69–81, 117–23, 147–49. And see the discussion in chapter 10 below of Rawls's Weberian representation of the issues that led to the American Civil War as constituting an unbridgeable "impasse," contrary to Lincoln's understanding.

4. See, e.g., Isabel Sawhill, "The Behavioral Aspects of Poverty"; Lawrence M. Mead, *The New Politics of Poverty*; John H. McWhorter, *Losing the Race*.

represents the poor as helpless victims of social inequity, their disadvantaged situation to be redressed by largely unspecified redistributive policies—takes account of that fact. Indeed, it is the ideology of nonjudgmentalism that Rawls represents as a dictate of justice that arguably underlies the deepest social pathologies of today's underclass. As social analysts at least as far back as Adam Smith have recognized, the "anything goes" attitude regarding "lifestyle" choices that Rawls encourages his (mostly well-off) readers to infer from his first principle of justice tends to generate the chief problems of the least advantaged, to which he mistakenly represents his second principle as a solution.[5] It is as if Rawls took literally Kant's dictum that the only unqualifiedly good thing is a good will, but concluded that all one need do to demonstrate one's service to justice is express the wish that the disadvantaged be favored, without considering whether the advice one proffers is likely to have that result.[6] Like the audience and participants at a Live 8 rock concert on behalf of increased foreign aid to Africa—who display little or no interest in analyzing the actual causes of African poverty—Rawls, and the partisans of his difference principle, are passionate about an abstraction, feeling that their mere righteous indignation against deprivation somehow makes them better people.[7]

In *LP* (106, 108–9, 116–17), Rawls will refrain from advocating a global redistribution of resources to benefit poorer countries on the sensible ground that a people's political culture is a greater determinant of its economic success than the amount of natural resources it starts with, and pro-

---

5. See Smith, *The Wealth of Nations*, bk. 5, chap. 1, sec. g, par. 10. On the ruinous effect of the 1960s ideology on the poor, see Myron Magnet, *The Dream and the Nightmare*; Theodore Dalrymple, *Life at the Bottom*; Mead, *New Politics of Poverty*, 251–59; Joel Schwartz, *Fighting Poverty with Virtue*, 200–203 (summarizing the findings of several prominent social scientists); Melanie Phillips, "What about the Overclass?" On Rawls's misconception of the problem of contemporary poverty, see Mead, *New Politics of Poverty*, 238–39; and Shelby Steele, *A Dream Deferred*, chap. 2.

6. In this respect Rawls's difference principle has the same appeal to today's social elites as racial quotas: supporting it makes them feel good while costing them nothing, so they have little interest in investigating whether it actually serves or harms its supposed beneficiaries. On the detrimental effect of so-called affirmative action on its ostensible beneficiaries, see McWhorter, *Losing the Race*; Shelby Steele, *The Content of Our Character*, chap. 7. Especially illuminating are Thomas Sowell's examinations of the international effects of preferential policies throughout the world: see most recently his *Affirmative Action Around the World*. Each of the aforementioned studies is relevant to assessing Rawls's approach to poverty, even though he never discusses affirmative action, since they display the negative consequences of treating the disadvantaged as a helpless class whose life prospects can be improved only through governmental assistance. See also Gray, *Enlightenment's Wake*, 20–23; Baumann, "Affirmative Action," 86–87.

7. See Anthony Daniels, "Expensive Talk," for a lucid analysis of this phenomenon.

viding more money alone might only obstruct needed reforms. Why doesn't he consider the implications of this insight for the problem of domestic poverty? If the primary cause of poverty in America is a cultural one—that is, a "cycle of dependency"—it is hard to see how Rawls's principles will do anything but exacerbate it.

Instead of confronting these issues, Rawls supplements his "purely formal" account of deliberative rationality with another element of goodness as rationality that he labels "the Aristotelian Principle." He postulates as a basic motivational principle that "human beings enjoy the exercise of their realized capacities (their innate or trained abilities)," the enjoyment increasing with the "complexity" of an activity.[8] Rawls surmises that this principle may be correct because "complex activities . . . satisfy the desire for variety and novelty of experience" and "evoke the pleasures of anticipation and surprise." He believes that it "accounts for many of our major desires" (*Theory*, 374–75). If so, it follows that "it will generally be rational" to develop our capacities (*Theory*, 376). At the same time, Rawls stresses, the Aristotelian Principle does not favor "any particular kind of activity" (*Theory*, 377). And even if the principle doesn't hold for everyone, "the idea of a rational plan still applies" to them. For instance, for someone "whose only pleasure is to count blades of grass," the definition of the good as the satisfaction of a rational plan "forces us to admit that the good for this man is indeed counting blades of grass," "surpris[ing]" as such a case might be (*Theory*, 379).

Since Rawls's definition of the good in terms of each person's (instrumentally) "rational plan" thus "does not require the truth of the Aristotelian Principle" (*Theory*, 380), we wonder why Rawls introduced this device at all. Whether or not it "accounts for" the things that human beings view as good, as Rawls maintains, it has no evident connection to the theme of justice. Apparently it is intended to show that his view of the good is somehow compatible with our commonsense recognition that some activities are intrinsically more worthwhile than others, even though his judgment of grass counting contradicts that belief. (Although Rawls contends that the Aristotelian Principle is linked to the good of self-respect, which in turn is central to "the moral psychology underlying justice as fairness" [*Theory*, 380], we shall see that he ultimately interprets the principle in a wholly relativistic manner.)

---

8. Rawls calls this "the Aristotelian Principle" despite acknowledging that Aristotle never states it, because it "seems . . . appropriate" in view of what Aristotle says in his *Ethics*. Notwithstanding Rawls's long footnote on this subject (*Theory*, 374n), he does not demonstrate that the principle is any more Aristotelian than the precept he previously labeled "Hobbes's thesis" was Hobbesean. Cf. Bloom, "Justice," 659–60.

II.

Some of the most deeply problematic aspects of Rawls's understanding of the good and its relation to justice emerge in the following section, "The Definition of the Good Applied to Persons." His initial aim is to show how goodness as rationality (unlike the thin theory of the good) can account for our moral judgments. The most plausible way to do this, Rawls suggests, is to define a good person as "one who has to a higher degree than the average person the broadly based properties . . . that it is rational for persons to want in one another" (*Theory*, 381–82). The members of a well-ordered society, Rawls reminds us, will all have "the fundamental moral virtues, that is, the strong and normally effective desires to act on the basic principles of right." (Curiously, Rawls seems to reduce the whole of moral virtue to one's disposition toward justice, omitting such excellences as courage and moderation.) But at the same time, he maintains, it will be "rational for each person to act" on those principles "only on the assumption that for the most part the principles are recognized and similarly acted on by others" (*Theory*, 382–83).

Herein we see the most obvious and fundamental departure of Rawls's account of justice from that of his sometime model Kant—as well as that of Aristotle and any other philosopher who regarded morality as having an independent dignity and worth rather than a merely instrumental value. In Kant's account, it is by acting in accordance with their self-given moral law that human beings demonstrate their transcendence of the merely "phenomenal" world of mechanical causation. The worth of moral conduct for the agent is not contingent on whether other human beings act justly: like the biblical Golden Rule, the categorical imperative commands us to act without regard to the expectation of concomitant rewards from others.[9] Similarly, Aristotle represents the morally virtuous human being as acting for the sake of the noble or honorable, not of any "rational" plan

---

9. See Kant, *Foundations of the Metaphysics of Morals*, pt. 2, 57 (Akad. ed. 438–9). In chapter 8, Rawls rejects the doctrine "that the highest moral motive is the desire to do what is right and just" for their own sake as "irrational," claiming that it gives "the sense of right" a status like the mere "preference for tea over coffee." Rawls believes that his own doctrine better represents the sense of justice as a desire "to act on principles that rational individuals would consent to in an initial situation which gives everyone equal representation as a moral person" (*Theory*, 418). Aside from the fact that this still presupposes a desire to do what is right for its own sake, it is belied by Rawls's acknowledgment in the text I am presently discussing that it wouldn't be rational to act justly in his sense unless one can expect almost everyone else to do likewise.

for reciprocal gain from other people's virtuous conduct. In fact, Aristotle expressly distinguishes reciprocity from justice in the strict sense.[10]

By making the goodness of just conduct for an individual depend on whether his conduct is reciprocated, Rawls implicitly adopts the conventionalist view espoused in antiquity by the Sophists, and in modernity by the most influential contractuarian theorists, Hobbes and Locke. As the latter thinkers demonstrate, it is possible to develop a more or less plausible grounding for justice and right on this basis. But that grounding depends on an explicit appeal to individual self-interest under liberal institutions rather than to the intrinsic rewards of just conduct: the doctrine that Tocqueville called "self-interest rightly understood."[11] By contrast, Rawls seeks to have it both ways: espousing a "Kantian interpretation" of the original position according to which "the desire to do what is right and just is the main way for persons to express their nature" so that it constitutes "a fundamental element of their good" (*Theory*, 390), yet acknowledging that justice in his sense isn't really "good for" an individual unless it is arranged to serve his interests.[12] Indeed, in introducing his account of the original position, Rawls had held that "the absolutely best for any man is that everyone else should join with him in furthering his conception of the good. . . . Or failing this, that all others are required to act justly but that he is authorized to exempt himself as he pleases" (*Theory*, 103), thus representing justice, as Glaucon does in Plato's *Republic* (358e–359b), as a purely conventional compromise, however necessary, of the individual's good.

The contradiction deepens when Rawls adds that "it would not be rational to want" some people to be so superior in such "natural assets" required for the practice of virtue as "intelligence and imagination, strength and endurance," which are desirable "in the appropriate degree . . . from a social point of view," that their superiority would "jeopardize" just institutions (*Theory*, 383). Rawls's position here is reminiscent of Aristotle's observation in the *Politics* that justice cannot exist between persons whose merit is vastly dissimilar, so that someone who too greatly surpasses his fellow citizens in virtue would need either to be made absolute

---

10. Aristotle *NE* 3.7, 1115b10ff, 1115b22ff; 5.5, 1132b21ff.

11. Tocqueville, *Democracy in America*, II.ii.8. See also Harvey C. Mansfield, "Self-Interest Rightly Understood." In an early version of his theory, Rawls related it to the Sophists' doctrine ("Justice as Fairness," *CP*, 55–56).

12. Later Rawls maintains that the virtues are good for their possessor as well as for others, but he explains the former benefit only by citing the shame and loss of esteem we will feel if we lack virtue (*Theory*, 390–91), thus continuing to give a purely conventional ground to its goodness. The contradiction is noted by Gourevitch, "Rawls on Justice," 491n; see also 489–90.

ruler of the city or exiled from it, and in the *Ethics,* that friendship is impossible between persons who differ greatly in excellence.[13] But Aristotle is explicit that the desirability of the greatest possible excellence for the agent himself is not in question; although moral virtue is a mean between two extremes, there is no mean with regard to the *possession* of virtue.[14] The same would hold true, surely, for characteristics such as intelligence, strength, and endurance: who would want to have less of them merely so others won't fear that one's superiority endangers ostensibly just institutions? Must we not therefore question Rawls's definition of a good person in terms of his having higher-than-average qualities "that it is rational for persons to want in one another," when it turns out that rationality supposedly requires that he not have those properties in too great a degree? Can human excellence properly be reduced to only those qualities that benefit people other than their possessor?

Like Kant but unlike Aristotle, Rawls sharply distinguishes in this context between moral virtues and "natural assets," the latter defined as "natural powers developed by education and training." Departing also from Kant—who identified moral conduct as that which is motivated purely by rational respect for the moral law, rather than by sentiment—he then defines the virtues as "sentiments and habitual attitudes leading us to act on certain principles of right." Rawls equates "the fundamental moral virtues" with the desire to act justly (in his sense) alone (*Theory,* 382–83) and defines "a good act" as one "which advances and is intended to advance another's good (his rational plan)" (*Theory,* 385).[15] But why is it rational to dedicate oneself to serving other people's ends? And doesn't serious consideration of the human good entail attending to virtues other than justice?

Rawls concludes this section by distinguishing various cases of the lack of moral worth: "the unjust, the bad, and the evil man." Here again his psychology is highly abstract and therefore dubious. Rawls explains that the unjust person "seeks dominion for the sake of aims such as wealth and security which when appropriately limited are legitimate," just as "the bad man desires arbitrary power because he enjoys the sense of mastery" and the resultant "social acclaim," again having an inordinate desire "for things

---

13. Aristotle *Politics* 3.13, 1284a2ff; *NE* 9.3, 1165b23ff. Another possibility is that the man of surpassing excellence would conceal his superiority through the practice of Socratic irony, since a philosopher (like the equitable man, *NE* 1137bff) is not concerned with obtaining his full share of "primary goods."

14. Aristotle *NE* 1107a6–7, 22–26.

15. Although Rawls explains that he means "good act" here "in the sense of a beneficent act," he does not identify any other sort of moral goodness beyond that which serves others, not oneself.

which when duly circumscribed are good." By contrast, "the evil man aspires to unjust rule precisely because it violates what independent persons would consent to in an original position of equality," aiming thereby to demonstrate his superiority and affront other people's self-respect. "What moves the evil man," Rawls claims, "is the love of injustice," in the form of being recognized as the author of other people's "degradation" (*Theory*, 385–86). Once again, Rawls provides no examples to illustrate these distinctions, which seem more or less arbitrary. Does anyone differentiate in ordinary life between the unjust man and the bad one on Rawls's grounds? More fundamentally, does his account of the evil man's motivation adequately explain it? Surely Rawls doesn't mean that notoriously evil men have reflected on what others would "consent to in an original position of equality" and tried to violate their expectations for that reason. But is there even any clear distinction between human beings who act unjustly for the sake of mastery and those who aim to degrade others? May there not rather be a continuum in human motivation, such that even the most wicked human beings pursue some things that are intrinsically good (renown, wealth, security) but in a wrong way and to an excessive degree by comparison with other goods?[16] As in chapter 5, where he dismissed desires for unjust things as "of no value," Rawls adopts too simple a dichotomy between good and evil desires or goals. It need not lessen the gap between good and evil as such to acknowledge that their psychological roots cannot neatly be dichotomized.

Rawls's incapacity to comprehend the psychology of the tyrant or evil-doer has the same cause as the abstract and implausible character of his account of the good life as the outcome of a "rational" plan. Like today's utilitarian rational-choice theorists, he overlooks the crucial political passions that are irreducible to mere calculation, such as the love of honor and glory, the fear of God, the pursuit of vengeance, and the indignation that lies at the core of the passion for justice itself.[17]

III.

Rawls's substitute for honor is something that sounds more democratic, "self-respect," which he represents as "perhaps the most important" primary good. As he explains, it has two aspects: a person's "conviction that

16. Consider Aristotle *NE* 1094a1ff, 1129b1ff, and *Politics* 1267a10ff; Joseph Butler, *Sermons*, #1, 208, in Selby-Bigge, ed., *British Moralists*, 204–5, and Rousseau, *Emile*, bk. 2, 243: "No one does the bad for the sake of the bad."

17. On liberal societies' need for a sense of honor, see Sharon Krause, *Liberalism with Honor*.

his conception of his good, his plan of life, is worth carrying out" and his "confidence in [his] ability . . . to fulfill" his aims. Given the importance of feeling that our plans have value, it follows that "the parties in the original position would wish to avoid at almost any cost the social conditions that undermine self-respect" (*Theory*, 386). With reference to the first element of self-respect, Rawls explains, two conditions must be satisfied: "having a rational plan . . . that satisfies the Aristotelian Principle" and "finding our person and deeds appreciated . . . by others who are likewise esteemed and their association enjoyed." Plans that conform to the Aristotelian Principle, entailing "activities that display intricate and subtle talents and manifest discrimination and refinement," are more likely to elicit other people's admiration. And persons who esteem their own activities as the result of their conforming to the Aristotelian Principle are more likely to applaud their fellows' attainments, generating a situation in which people's activities are "rational and complementary," forming a single overall scheme of activity that "all can appreciate and enjoy" (*Theory*, 387).

We wonder at this point about the hypothetical grass counter, whose happiness was said to be independent of the Aristotelian Principle. Now, however, Rawls removes whatever elitist tinge might have seemed to color that principle by explaining that its application "is always relative to the individual and therefore to his natural assets and particular situation." "It normally suffices" for an individual's self-esteem that "there is some association . . . to which he belongs and within which the activities that are rational for him are publicly affirmed by others." (A grass-counters' club?) Thus even though people's capacities vary, a well-ordered society contains "a variety of communities and associations" whose members "each have their own ideals appropriately matched to their aspirations and talents." It doesn't matter that "judged by the doctrine of perfectionism [i.e., the notion that there are objective standards of achievement] the activities of many groups may not display a high degree of excellence"; "the absolute level of achievement, even if it could be defined, is irrelevant." All that matters is that "the internal life of these associations is suitably adjusted" to their members' "abilities and wants," providing each with "a secure basis for the sense of worth." By rejecting the principle of perfection, the parties to the original position thus prepare a foundation for "recogniz[ing] the good of all activities that fulfill the Aristotelian Principle" so long as they are just; such "democracy in judging each other's aims is the foundation of self-respect in a well-ordered society" (*Theory*, 387–88).

Let us pause to consider whether this account of a well-ordered society is at all realistic. To begin with, as I have previously argued, it isn't true that self-respect in any proper sense is as dependent as Rawls maintains on how we are regarded by others. But even if it were, it is unlikely that persons whose abilities and achievements were quite limited would gain in self-esteem from knowing that the overall society of which they were members had officially adopted a policy of judging all aims to be equally valuable. It is already the case, of course, especially in a large and pluralistic society like the United States, that most people who lack the opportunity or capacity to get elected president or play professional football, respectively, can still enjoy opportunities for fulfillment and achievement on a smaller scale by serving on the boards of civic associations or playing pickup ball games on the weekend. But we don't normally pretend that the different levels of achievement are incomparable. In fact, most people don't seem to be deeply troubled by knowing that their deeds do not yield them the celebrity or wealth of the highest achievers in various respected fields of endeavor. (Indeed, we are often inspired in our endeavors by the models of the greatest achievers—even at the trivial level of pretending to be Michael Jordan while playing school-yard basketball.) Most human beings would be insulted, however, to be told that from the public standpoint, their endeavors are no more valuable than a life devoted to grass counting! In other words, common sense supplies us with a pluralistic but not relativistic or entirely open-ended understanding of the most fundamental human goods and the most worthy sorts of achievement. Of course, how the different goods and ways of life are ranked varies to some extent from one political culture or religious code to another. But there is unlikely to be a society in which the vocations of statesman, soldier, priest, doctor, sage, and athlete are not highly regarded; in which being able to support oneself and one's family by honest labor is not respected; and in which the notion that someone merits admiration for counting blades of grass would not be dismissed as ridiculous.

While Rawls apparently invented the Aristotelian Principle to offer a nonhierarchical substitute for the rankings of activities that human beings customarily make, it cannot serve that function. We can imagine all sorts of "complex" activities or "feats of ingenuity and invention" (*Theory*, 374) that will elicit admiration from almost no one. It is surely not true that the most complex work of art, scholarship, or athletic achievement is ipso facto the best one. (Joe DiMaggio was admired for playing center field in a way that made it look easy.) Nor can our assessments of various accomplishments be severed from awareness of the substantive ends that they serve.

My suggestion is that a constitutional, liberal republic like the United States already provides citizens with both a secure foundation for their sense of dignity—their status as legally free and equal citizens—and ample opportunities to acquire the real satisfactions of life (family, friends, basic comfort, and the chance to contribute to one's community and country), without the need for anything like Rawls's ostensibly democratic, but really patronizing, ethos. The teaching of the Declaration of Independence is not that all individuals' talents and achievements are equally estimable, but that no inequalities among human beings are so great that any group or individual is entitled to rule others without their consent. It is this principle that legitimate government exists to secure the equal rights of the governed that ultimately guarantees to the citizens of a liberal regime a proper equality of respect. But it would violate our right to liberty, and certainly not buttress anyone's respect, if we were required to adopt Rawls's abstract, relativistic standards for judging one another's achievements.[18]

IV.

Rawls confirms the conventionalist character of his view of justice and his relativistic view of the good in the discussion that concludes this section, concerning the opposite of self-respect: shame. He holds that "it is our plan of life that determines what we feel ashamed of, and so feelings of shame are relative to our aspirations." More specifically, "someone is liable to moral shame when he prizes as excellences of his person those virtues that his plan of life requires and is framed to encourage." In other words, there is nothing intrinsically shameful; it all depends on the individual's life plan, as influenced by the principles of justice he is persuaded to accept. (The subjective character of the shameful helps explain Rawls's having judged it unjust for any society to ban religious or sexual practices that it finds degrading, a judgment he will repeat in the next section.) But can the sense of shame plausibly be explained, as Rawls endeavors to do here, as mainly the sense of failure "to do what is right" as determined by "the Kantian interpretation of the original position" (*Theory*, 390–91)? Are the moral standards that influence our conduct as malleable as Rawls supposes?

In the concluding section of chapter 7, Rawls represents the very "indeterminacy" of the individual's good—beyond the primary goods, which

18. Susan Shell points out that Rawls's account of self-respect directly contradicts the teaching of his putative model Kant ("'Kantianism' and Constitutional Rights," 158). Compare, for instance, Kant's argument that the misuse of one's sexual faculties to the point of "abandon[ing]" oneself "entirely to an animal inclination" makes the individual "a loathsome thing, and thus deprives [him] of all self-respect," with Rawls's demand that we show equal respect for all "life plans" and avoid restricting what we regard as degrading sexual practices (Kant, *The Metaphysical Principles of Virtue*, pt. 1, sec. 1, 86–87 [Akad. ed. 424–25]). Kant, unlike Rawls, has a substantive notion of the grounds of self-respect.

must be defined so that all individuals desire them to some extent (*Theory*, 393)—as a decisive advantage of justice as fairness over utilitarianism. Because the utilitarian aims to maximally satisfy the preferences of the members of a given society, Rawls observes, he may be compelled to accede to an "abhorrence" the majority feels for religious or sexual practices that it regards as abominable, even though they "cause no social injury." By contrast, under Rawls's doctrine, "this problem never arises," since "the intense convictions of the majority," whenever they violate the antecedently established principles of justice, "have no weight" or "value" anyway. "To have a complaint against the conduct and belief of others," Rawls holds, "we must show that their actions injure us, or that the institutions that authorize what they do treat us unjustly," as determined by the principles we would agree to in the original position. Recapitulating the position he took at the outset of chapter 5, Rawls stresses that in his theory "the grounds of liberty are completely separate from existing preferences," and the principles of justice constitute "an agreement not to take into account certain feelings" when judging others' conduct. Since justice isn't presumed "to maximize the fulfillment of rational plans," its content is unaffected by the failure to give substantive content to the good, as it would be if the goal, as in utilitarianism, were to maximize people's happiness (*Theory*, 395).

Here, then, is the real purpose of Rawls's formalistic account of the good. That account must be formal, not only because Rawls believes that relativism about the good is a mandate of justice, but also to deter anyone from asking, how far does Rawls's just society actually promote my good? The ostensible superiority of justice as fairness to utilitarianism in this regard lies simply in its refusal to consider how far the just society serves people's substantive good.[19]

As I have emphasized, from the standpoint of the real political world in which concrete issues of justice are debated each day, the utilitarianism that Rawls represents as the chief alternative to his theory is a straw man. In actual political life, the debate over justice is intertwined with the question of what policies best serve a people's common good, not an abstract sum of individual preferences.[20]

In a liberal regime like the United States, the core meaning of the common good is set in advance as securing the natural rights of individuals.

19. In fact, since utilitarianism as a tool of welfare economics aims at maximizing the satisfaction of individual preferences, not at generating the maximum of happiness as measured by some external, objective standard, the "indeterminacy" of the good seems no more intrinsic a difficulty for it than for Rawls's theory.

20. Cf. Aristotle *Rhetoric* 1358b 33ff; Yack, *Problems of a Political Animal*, 174.

Over our country's history, indeed, the scope of the responsibilities assigned to government (at all levels) has been broadened to include such goods as education, medical research, a wider social "safety net" for the poor and elderly, and space exploration.[21] But even with this expanded view of government's responsibility, the question of which policies best achieve the public good, as well as the specific content of our rights, continues to be a matter for deliberation by the people's representatives and by the citizenry at large. While the sum of policies arrived at through the constitutional-democratic process is inevitably a messy one that cannot be reduced to the dictates of any particular theory, such is the democratic (nay, human) condition. If government were to announce that henceforth it would focus its concern on actualizing an abstract theory like Rawls's, giving it priority over the people's substantive good—following Kant's dictum, *fiat justitia, pereat mundus*—it would be unlikely to elicit the people's consent for very long (probably no longer than if it announced a policy of maximizing the "net balance of satisfaction").

In itself, the issue between justice as fairness and utilitarianism is too abstract to have any meaningful political consequences one way or the other. What is of far greater moment is that under the guise of challenging the utilitarian view, Rawls radically reconceives the task of liberal statesmanship in a way that can only be deleterious to the preservation and prosperity of liberal regimes. This can be seen in the closing pages of chapter 7 in two ways. First, by denying that a people may justly prohibit religious or sexual practices that they regard as abominations unless it can be proved that such practices injure other citizens, Rawls loads the dice (in a way that was prefigured, but never pushed to such an extreme, by Mill's *On Liberty*) to guarantee an outcome that is morally libertarian, not to say libertine. It is practically impossible to prove that a neighbor who practices prostitution, bestiality, consensual cannibalism, or ritual religious orgies directly injures me. But it is certainly plausible that a society in which such practices are

---

21. Historically, the original utilitarians such as Bentham contributed to the development of the modern welfare state through their critique of the Lockean doctrine of natural rights (dismissed by Bentham as "nonsense on stilts") and the concomitant notion of limited government. But the issue between Rawls and the utilitarians has little connection to that dispute, since Rawls hardly takes the notion of natural rights more seriously than Bentham did, and since he is no partisan of limited government in the economic sphere, while his various qualifications to the "priority" of liberty (elaborated in *PL*) similarly depart from the authentic liberalism of the American founders. In fact, as Marc Plattner observes, Rawls's difference principle (as well as his agnosticism on the issue of free enterprise versus socialism) actually derives from the utilitarian tradition represented by Mill rather than the Lockean natural-rights position ("Capitalism," 330–31).

accepted as lawful and therefore legitimate will have such a weakened sense of human dignity (thanks to the habit of regarding other human beings as mere tools for one's private gratification) as to undermine people's disposition to respect the rights of others or their willingness to forego private pleasures when their country's survival requires it. It will undoubtedly be harder to rear children properly under such circumstances. But according to Rawls's understanding of a just society, government is effectively forbidden to interfere with these practices. Is it not a curious understanding of morality that the "unjust" action to be guarded against is legislative interference with prostitution or bestiality? Should we want to liberate people from a sense of shame regarding such conduct, rather than encourage that sense so as to promote a more decent standard of behavior?[22]

The other way in which Rawls's teaching is destructive of liberal statesmanship, as I noted in chapter 4, is through his radical dichotomy between a statesman's duty to enact just legislation and any constraint he may be under to serve his constituents' wishes. While acknowledging that the people's "prevailing social attitudes" may "tie the statesman's hands," Rawls stresses that his theory requires us to "move toward just institutions as speedily as the circumstances permit irrespective of existing sentiments" (*Theory*, 395–96). What statesmen learn from Rawls is that they should do their best to effectuate his view of justice, with as little regard as possible to constituent opinions or wishes that conflict with it. It is thus misleading for Rawls to represent his view of justice as a democratic one that gives priority to a liberty that includes political freedom. What we see, rather, in the American context today, is a recipe for judicial and bureaucratic usurpation of the people's right to self-government in the name of what the people "should" favor. Only life-tenured judges, in fact, are likely to feel capable of rewriting the Constitution to give effect to whatever contemporary moral theories they happen to find appealing. Rawls himself, whatever his original intentions,

---

22. As Clor puts it, in denigrating on behalf of the right to equal public esteem "the ethical importance of the substantive ends or goods for which persons might choose to live," Rawls's doctrine "undermines good character by liberating from social restraint attitudes, conduct, and lifestyles inimical to the maintenance of good character and its communal supports" (*Public Morality*, 165). Contrast Kant's mandate that the government secure the conditions of public decency, e.g., by prohibiting public prostitution, so as to avoid violating people's moral sensibilities (*The Metaphysical Elements of Justice*, pt. 2, sec. 1, 49, 92 [Akad. ed. 325]).

On the toxic moral effect on children (and adults) of today's anything-goes mass media "culture," reflecting judicial determinations to interpret the "speech" protected by the First Amendment to encompass such products as computer games featuring dismemberment and sexual humiliation, see the essays by scholars representing diverse political orientations in Diane Ravitch and Joseph P. Viteriti, eds., *Kid Stuff*; and Diana West's review, "All That Trash."

came to recognize this: Brian Anderson observes that "in his later writings, Rawls increasingly looked to liberal judges to achieve justice, mirroring the Left's own tendency in recent decades to rely on activist courts to win the battles it could never win at the ballot box."[23]

Just as Rawls's rule against restricting people's sexual practices promises to weaken the civic and moral attitudes on which the preservation of liberal self-government depends, his radical separation between promoting justice and serving the people's interests as they conceive them (rather than attempting to harmonize the two, as a statesman must do) threatens to weaken respect for constitutional government itself. Such a disparagement of republican statesmanship was exhibited on both sides of the slavery controversy in the decades preceding the Civil War, from Henry David Thoreau's deprecation of government, voting, law, majority rule, and the "mere" politician typified by Daniel Webster to Roger Taney's attempt on specious constitutional grounds to overturn congressional prohibitions on the extension of slavery in *Dred Scott v. Sanford*.[24] The precedent is not encouraging.

V.

Rawls concludes chapter 7 with an elaboration of his transformative aims. He acknowledges that the terms "right" and "good" may not "normally be used" as he has defined them. But his theory doesn't require that such correspondence be established. Instead, Rawls argues, it suffices that after digesting his theory, "we can acknowledge these interpretations as suitable renderings of what on reflection we *now* wish to maintain" (*The-*

---

23. Anderson, "Antipolitical Philosophy," 51; see also, on Rawls's open-ended recipe for judicial governance, Clifford Orwin and James Stoner Jr., "Neoconstitutionalism?" 447–50). In *JF* (162) Rawls decides against including the difference principle in a constitution, given the difficulties courts would face in trying to interpret and enforce it. Nonetheless, he deems it "a constitutional essential" that society assure "a social minimum covering at least the basic human needs," a standard sufficiently "obvious, or at any rate . . . open to public view" that courts should be able to assess its fulfillment. One can imagine the consequences once judges were given an open-ended mandate to impose the provision of whatever they regarded as a necessary social minimum on recalcitrant legislators (and taxpayers). See also chapter 11 below regarding Rawls's endeavor in *PL* to read his principle of the "fair value" of political liberty into the Constitution.

For the Kantian roots of Rawls's deprecation of jurisprudence that aims chiefly to preserve the established system of law rather than to reinterpret or supplant it on the basis of a deeper moral understanding ostensibly possessed by philosophers, see "Perpetual Peace," Second Supp., 115, and app., sec. 1, 119.

24. See Thoreau, "Civil Disobedience," 222–23, 226–29, 232–34, 238–39. For the Kantian origin of Thoreau's disparagement of politicians who temper the pursuit of purely moral goals by considerations of expediency, see "Perpetual Peace," app., sec. 1, 118.

ory, 396 [emphasis added]). Rawls of course realizes the unlikelihood that many citizens will spend their time delving into his writings to assess his doctrine, let alone alter their judgments to correspond to it.[25] So the "we" for whom he is writing must be the sort of judicial and intellectual elites who are likely to study his theory and exercise their influence to give it effect, reordering the foundations of constitutionalism and public policy while paying lip service to established constitutional principles.

The thrust of Supreme Court decisions over the past several decades shows that judges hardly needed Rawls's encouragement to use their power of constitutional interpretation to rewrite the Bill of Rights into a vehicle of moral libertarianism, enunciating new constitutional rights to abortion, pornography, and, at the state level, gay marriage, while "protecting" our freedom against such ostensible threats as nondenominational prayers at school commencement ceremonies and displays of the Ten Commandments in courthouses. Similarly, as noted earlier, Rawls's depreciation of economic liberties in comparison with other rights echoes the "preferred position" doctrine enunciated by the courts (without constitutional grounding but in harmony with the trend of "progressive" liberalism) since the 1930s. But while Rawls cannot personally be held responsible for eroding the traditional moral standards that Tocqueville, among others, deemed essential to the preservation of lawful freedom, the spread of his doctrine in law schools (both directly and through his influence on other jurisprudential writers) has certainly enhanced our judges' confidence in disregarding popular moral beliefs and legislative determinations in the name of their own, often idiosyncratic, notions of "autonomy" and human dignity. As Michael Walzer observes, the enthusiastic reception of *Theory* in American law schools reflects the fact that "judicial review is the crucial institutional device through which the philosophical conquest of politics" by Rawls and his imitators in the world of ostensibly liberal legal scholarship, such as Bruce Ackerman and Ronald Dworkin, is given effect.[26] Another (sympathetic) scholar, Alan Ryan, remarked back in 1993 that *Theory* had "shaped the way teachers in every American law school talk about

25. In *JF* (121), Rawls calls it a "fantasy" that his writings will become "known in the public culture." He is not being unduly modest: one can safely surmise, given his prose style alone, that a large majority of the 300,000+ purchasers of *Theory*, as well as his other writings, were college students for whom the books were mandatory course readings. (As for foreign audiences, many were presumably encouraged to read *Theory* under the misapprehension that it constituted a guide to understanding the principles of American liberty, as in Richard Parker's remarkable suggestion that it "formulates as well as any book to date the principles of justice expressed by the [American] Constitution" ["The Jurisprudential Uses of John Rawls," 270].)

26. Walzer, "Flight from Philosophy," 43.

rights," adding that "through the invisible medium of Supreme Court clerks and the more visible medium of the Harvard, Yale, Stanford, Chicago, etc. law reviews, Mr. Rawls' ideas have crept into the law of the land," encouraging lawyers and judges to "keep pushing the envelope of the Constitution" so as to expand what they regard as Americans' "civil liberties," while simultaneously disparaging property rights as if they had less of a connection with justice (and hence, lesser constitutional status).[27]

To cite one instance of what Walzer and Ryan are describing: As early as 1977 NYU law professor David A. J. Richards argued that Rawlsian "contractarian theory" fully justified the "countermajoritarian" character of judicial review, interpreted in a very broad sense. Whereas Hamilton, in *The Federalist*, No. 78, had argued for the federal courts' authority to invalidate laws that violated the "manifest tenor" of the Constitution, so as to preserve the constitutional structure on which our rights and well-being depend, Richards drew the following lesson from Rawls:

> Majority rule is not the basic moral principle of the constitutional order. The basic moral principles are the principles of justice, including the principle of greatest equal liberty. Majority rule is justified only to the extent that it is compatible with this deeper moral principle. To the extent that judicial review enforces the requirements of a greatest equal liberty in a way that majority rule cannot, judicial review is morally justified.[28]

27. Ryan, "How Liberalism, Politics Come to Terms." Another commentator, Frank Michelman, questions Ryan's account of Rawls's jurisprudential influence on the ground that by the time *Theory* first appeared such Supreme Court justices as William Brennan had already "produced the basic doctrinal ingredients for a liberalized American constitutional law" ("Rawls on Constitutionalism and Constitutional Law," 408). But this judgment underestimates the extent to which the post-*Theory* court radicalized such notions, encouraged by Rawls's writings, as the supposed constitutional invalidity of generalized, nondenominational public expressions of support of religion (see *Lee v. Weisman* [1992]) and of laws criminalizing homosexual sodomy (*Lawrence v. Texas* [2003]), along with the continuing depreciation of property rights (*Kelo v. New London* [2005]). And by Michelman's own proposed test, whether the Court would reverse its position on the constitutionality of comprehensive legislative regulation of campaign finance expenditures in accordance with Rawls's mandates, it appears that "Rawls's ideas —his *distinctive* ideas, his ideas where it counts—have indeed crept into the law of the land" (420, Michelman's emphasis; see chapter 11 below on the campaign finance issue).

28. *The Federalist*, No. 78, 434–45; Richards, *The Moral Criticism of Law*, 50–51. In his application of Rawlsian theory to the Constitution, Richards rejects (for instance) all legal regulation of obscene publications on the ground that it violates the "moral purpose of the First Amendment—to secure the greatest equal liberty of communication" (67).

On the influence of *Theory* on American jurisprudence, see also Shell, "'Kantianism,' and Constitutional Rights," 149–52; Harvey C. Mansfield, *America's Constitutional Soul*, 33–34; and note 53 to chapter 11 below.

While America's founders were not simple majoritarians, the constitutional structure they created was intended to enable the people's "deliberate sense" to prevail. In fact, Hamilton's argument for judicial review in *The Federalist*, No. 78 hinges on the belief that the judiciary is the "least dangerous" of the three branches, having "neither force nor will, but merely judgment," and on the expectation that judges will be bound in their decisions to follow "strict rules and precedents," so that it is not their will (let alone their intuitions), but the collective will of the people as expressed in the Constitution itself, that will prevail through judicial interpretations of that document.[29] While constitutional and statutory interpretation inevitably entail a wide latitude for judgment, the guiding aim of that judgment is supposed to derive from the Constitution, along with legal precedent, rather than from any "moral theory" invented by professors. By contrast, Richards would justify rule by irresponsible judges in the name of Rawls's "equal liberty" principle.

Even more instructive than Richards's remarks is a 1979 essay by Rutgers law professor Richard Parker that explains why *Theory* was received still more "enthusiastically" by lawyers than by scholars of philosophy or political theory. According to Parker, lawyers read *Theory* "as an exciting reaffirmation" of the "constitutional and personal values" that they already held. Since according to Parker the Constitution "must be interpreted to give expression to our own [i.e., present-day lawyers'] best vision" of justice, rather than what that document's authors or ratifiers may have believed, he anticipates that even Rawls's difference principle (which underestimates the weight that "most Americans, including lawyers" presently believe should be given to "moral desert based on effort") may "in time be accepted" as a constitutional requisite (which can then be imposed by judges without regard to legislative determinations or popular wishes). While "some social philosophers and political theorists complain" that Rawls "has begged all the interesting questions," Parker observes that lawyers, who "already believe what Rawls assumes about equality and human nature," are more "willing to grant Rawls all of his basic premises" rather than demand that he demonstrate them, being eager to get on with the work of "translat[ing] Rawls's conception of justice into principles of constitutional law" and applying those principles "in complex factual settings." Besides, even academic lawyers find Rawls more "accessible" than such political philosophers as Kant and Rousseau. In other words, why should lawyers, already "self-selected into American law schools" and predisposed to agree with Rawls's principles, have to undergo the tedium of

29. *The Federalist*, No. 78, 433, 435–36, 439.

studying difficult philosophic texts, when (as Rawls reminds them) they already "know" what they need to about the dictates of justice and have more urgent work to do in rewriting the Constitution to accommodate their beliefs?[30]

Parker's discussion, along with the remarks of Ryan and Walzer, helps illuminate the reasons that prominent law professors such as Dworkin, Ackerman, Richards, Jeremy Waldron, and Martha Nussbaum have been among Rawls's most ardent advocates and imitators in the American academy. Their eager acceptance of Rawls's project exemplifies how the aspirations of the top tier of the American legal profession have been transformed from the time when Tocqueville praised the influence of lawyers in our regime as a conservative, moderating counterweight to democratic passions, by virtue of lawyers' habitual love of order and precedent and of empirical, common-law reasoning, into a claim to rule our country.[31] The means of achieving that goal is to read assorted "rights" into the Constitution (rights to abortion, same-sex marriage, or welfare payments, for instance) on the ground that such rights follow from the supposed moral "logic" of that document, regardless of whether its authors and ratifiers ever intended to establish those rights (and also despite, or rather because of, the refusal of the people's elected representatives to enact them through legislation).

Those who make this sort of argument do not even pause to ask whether it makes sense to seek a unifying theoretical logic in a charter of government, several elements of which (such as the compromises with slavery in the original document and the composition of the Electoral College) cannot be understood without reference to the political circumstances that may have necessitated them (in the former case), or to the continuing prac-

---

30. Parker, "Jurisprudential Uses," 270–79.

31. Tocqueville, *Democracy in America,* vol. 1, pt. 2, chap. 8. While the literature on today's judicial activism is vast, two book titles—the first by a West Virginia judge who largely approves of the development, the second by a Harvard law professor who questions its implications—will illustrate its extent: Richard Neely, *How Courts Govern America;* Mary Ann Glendon, *A Nation under Lawyers.* See, especially, chaps. 6–8 of Glendon's book on the renunciation of the traditional ideal of judicial impartiality in favor of political partisanship, enabling judges "to taste and enjoy the once-forbidden fruits of emancipation from the constraints of statute, precedent, Constitution, or tradition" (152), and chap. 10 on the growth of "one-sided advocacy in the guise of scholarship" in leading law schools, leading to the attempted substitution of a "Professors' Constitution" for the written one we enjoy (206, 218–19).

It should be mentioned that unlike the other Rawlsian law professors mentioned above, Nussbaum was a distinguished philosophical scholar before joining the University of Chicago law faculty; perhaps the move reflected a growing ambition on her part to shape the development of American institutions.

tical necessities of constitutional, federal government. If the Constitution fails to conform adequately to the moral beliefs of contemporary philosophical scholars and law professors, this only shows how philosophically, politically, and morally backward its authors were; hence any evidence of the founders' intentions, as reflected in the specific language they adopted, need not obstruct today's judges from effectively rewriting it through "creative" reinterpretation. In this manner, while the form of the constitutional text remains, its substantive content will have been replaced by a collection of left-liberal political preferences or "intuitions," woven together into an ostensibly coherent and allegedly more just whole through a grand, or at least impressively abstract, theory like Rawls's.[32]

The way that Rawls's influence harmonizes with the tendency of today's judges to claim a right to rule on the basis of their putatively superior moral insight may be seen in two passages of the "centrist" plurality opinion of the Supreme Court in *Planned Parenthood v. Casey*. First, three justices grounded the right to abortion in a supposed constitutional right "to define one's own concept of existence, of meaning, of the universe, and of the mystery of human life" and, consequently, "the attributes of personhood"— a right nowhere enunciated in our founding documents, but reminiscent of Rawls's doctrine of the "autonomous" self (elaborated in chapter 9 of *Theory*). Second, they maintained that the American people's self-understanding as a law-abiding people requires them to acknowledge the Court's authority to "speak before all others for their constitutional ideals."[33]

In both *Theory* and *PL*, Rawls himself (drawing on the distinguished constitutional scholars Alexander Bickel and John Agresto) sets forth a more moderate view of the Court's role, observing that "the final court of appeal" in interpreting the Constitution "is not the court, nor the executive, nor the legislature, but the electorate as a whole" (*Theory*, 342; cf. *PL*, 232). Unfortunately, the abstract and dogmatic account of justice that Rawls seeks to read into the Constitution, coupled with his dismissal of popular wishes or moral opinions that contradict his theory, leaves little room for the people actually to exercise their right of self-government or constitutional interpretation. (Even the remarks just quoted are set forth by Rawls to justify civil disobedience rather than constitutionally structured republican government. And in 1997, in further encouragement of judicial rewriting of the Constitution to advance his agenda, Rawls signed

32. For an eloquent critique of this process, see Robert Bork, *The Tempting of America*, chaps. 9–11.

33. *Planned Parenthood v. Casey*, 505 U.S. 833 (1992) at 851, 867–68. On Rawls's contribution to today's "judicialized politics," as well as his influence on the Court's notion of "personhood" in the *Casey* opinion, see Carrese, *Cloaking of Power*, 4, 249.

the "Philosophers' Brief" urging the Supreme Court to enunciate a constitutional right to physician-assisted suicide, subsequently explaining his view by saying that he felt that each individual "should be able to decide these questions [for himself] as a free citizen."[34] He offered no justification for denying the people's right to decide such questions through the political process, as the Constitution allows.) Thus the effectual truth of Rawls's doctrine is a recipe for irresponsible government-by-judiciary. Judges encouraged by Rawls (and the other theorists he has inspired) to impose a "higher" vision of justice on a recalcitrant, because insufficiently enlightened, citizenry will hardly be deterred by counsels of moderation and respect for the constitutional text.[35] When one combines Rawls's disparagement of ordinary citizens' moral opinions with his patronizing depiction of them as incapable of esteeming themselves adequately unless they are reassured that all achievements however trivial are equally praiseworthy, the picture that emerges is far more reminiscent of the sort of democratic despotism feared by Tocqueville than of a proud, active citizenry such as the American founders envisioned.[36]

34. "*Commonweal* Interview with John Rawls," *CP*, 617–18.
35. Consider Justice Antonin Scalia's contrast in his dissenting opinion in *Casey* (996) between the Court's Nietzschean vision of itself as "leading a Volk who will be 'tested by following'" its guidance with "the somewhat more modest role envisioned for these lawyers by the Founders."
36. See Carrese, *Cloaking of Power*, 249–51.

CHAPTER 8

The Sense of Justice

I.

The last two chapters of *Theory* concern the theme of "stability." Chapter 8 explains how people acquire a sense of justice and is intended to show that they will do so to the greatest extent in a society governed by justice as fairness. Chapter 9 in turn will demonstrate that the sense of justice is "congruen[t]" with our good, so that "both work together to uphold a just scheme" (*Theory*, 397). Since much of chapter 8 is tangential to Rawls's theory, my treatment will be relatively brief.

At the outset Rawls reminds us that a well-ordered society must not only advance its members' good but must be regulated by a view of justice that everyone accepts. He then emphasizes that since his principles "are consented to in the light of true general beliefs" about human society, they don't require the support of "theological or metaphysical doctrines," let alone the supposition of "another world that compensates for and corrects the inequalities" of this one (*Theory*, 397–98).

We cannot avoid remarking the sweeping character of Rawls's denial that justice requires theological or metaphysical support, thereby dismissing out of hand the beliefs of philosophers from Plato to Kant, along with the Western theological traditions.[1] The need for a deeper grounding of justice has commonly been thought to reflect the gap between the just and the individual's self-interest, a gap that Rawls professes to fill through his account of their "rational" congruence.[2] But if we recall the process by which Rawls's two principles were established, it is hard to find his assertion about their basis in truth plausible. Not only were the principles derived from a purely imaginary situation—the original position—the "knowledge" that the parties in that condition employed was severely restricted by the veil of ignorance, which deprived them (or, more important, us who try to simulate their deliberations) of any grounds for genuine understanding. The principles were selected not for their truth as such, but only because they derived from our supposedly intuitive beliefs about a fair selection process, as well as the likelihood that they would generate judgments "we" would find satisfying—even though "our" beliefs were never submitted to critical examination. Thus there is no reason to regard the principles as any more grounded in fact than Plato's "noble lie," a device that Rawls mentions would be ruled out by his ostensibly rational grounding of justice (*Theory*, 398n).[3]

It isn't surprising, then, that when Rawls undertakes to demonstrate the stability of his conception of justice, he again relies on a set of admittedly "speculative" theories (*Theory*, 399) rather than an empirical consideration of political life or human psychology. He claims (without citing any references) that "most traditional doctrines hold that to some degree at least"

1. See also George Washington's admonition in his Farewell Address against supposing "that morality can be maintained without religion" (*George Washington: A Collection*, 521; Vincent Phillip Munoz, "George Washington on Religious Liberty"). Rawls himself will cite Patrick Henry's assertion of the need for religious support to civic morality in *PL* (liv n) and *IPRR* (164).

2. Sidgwick, more genuinely empirical and philosophic than Rawls, acknowledges that although narrow selfishness is likely to interfere with the individual's happiness, "some few selfish persons appear at least to be happier than most of the unselfish"; hence he judges that only if one could believe that utilitarian morality is supported by divine sanctions (a proposition about which he remains uncertain) could everyone's individual interest be truly united with the goal of "universal happiness" (*Methods of Ethics*, 506).

3. It is also difficult to reconcile Rawls's claim with his previously having denied any inherent "value to having true beliefs" in executing "rational plans," remarking the potential benefits of "useful illusions" in that regard (*Theory*, 368). Why should civic orders be prohibited from relying even on false religious beliefs for support, if individuals are not to be discouraged from self-delusion in pursuit of their plans?

The denial that justice requires metaphysical grounding prefigures Rawls's representation of justice as fairness in *PL* as a purely "political" doctrine that is independent of all "comprehensive" philosophical or moral views. In that work (as discussed in chapter 10 below), Rawls himself retreats from the claim that his doctrine is grounded in truth.

human beings "acquire a desire to act justly when we have lived under and benefited from just institutions" (*Theory*, 399; note the hedging qualification "to some degree").[4] After drawing a somewhat obscure distinction between "two main traditions" of thought regarding the process of moral learning and the extent to which the principles of justice "spring from our nature" and thus harmonize with our good, Rawls sets the issue aside to describe "the course of moral development as it *might* occur in a well-ordered society" based on justice as fairness (*Theory*, 401–4 [emphasis added]). His actual aim is not to prove that justice as fairness would be stable but only to show that it is at least as stable as alternatives like utilitarianism (*Theory*, 401). It is hard to know how far Rawls can show even this, since his argument relies on a view of moral development that has been "designed to fit" his account of justice and "presupposes the plausibility if not the correctness" of that theory (*Theory*, 404). In sum, he hardly promises an unbiased test of even the limited proposition he has laid out.

There is little reason to attend to the details of Rawls's treatment of the stability of justice as fairness. In the next six sections of chapter 8 (sec. 70–75) he provides an abstract and largely hypothetical account of the process of moral learning that has no bearing on that issue, inasmuch as it addresses the development of a sense of justice as such, not the relative stability of different views of justice. But two points merit mention. First, in the process of distinguishing two forms of "the morality of principles . . . one corresponding to the sense of right and justice, the other to the love of mankind and to self-command," Rawls maintains that the moralities of "the saint and the hero" harmonize fully with "the norms of right and justice," since they entail simply pursuing those norms to a higher or supererogatory degree (*Theory*, 419). He represents the content of self-command as consisting in "fulfilling with complete ease and grace the requirements of right and justice," especially "in actions presupposing great discipline and training." Under the rubric of self-command, Rawls thereby collapses into a commitment to justice such virtues as courage, magnanimity, and self-control that for writers such as Aristotle and Adam Smith (Rawls's source for the term "self-command" [*Theory*, 419n]) have an independent dignity and worth for

4. Peter Berkowitz notes that Rawls's claim that the mere fact of living under just institutions tends to dissolve people's propensity to injustice is a contemporary manifestation of the Enlightenment illusion of the inevitability of moral progress, a conceit that the events of the past century ought to have refuted (*Virtue and the Making of Modern Liberalism*, 25). As Barber observes, Rawls seems unable to decide "what sort of reality the rules of justice are intended for," the hypothetical realm that manifests people's supposedly "instinctively virtuous inclinations," the purely self-interested world of the parties to the original position, or the actual world that is characterized by competition and conflict ("Justifying Justice," 314–15).

the individual himself.[5] As noted in the previous chapter, Rawls does not show himself to have reflected adequately on the relation between justice and other aspects of human excellence.

Second, just as his abstract moral psychology exhibits insufficient understanding of the man of surpassing excellence, Rawls offers an unpersuasive account of the human being at the other end of the moral scale, the crudely selfish individual, when he proceeds to maintain that "barring self-deception, egoists are incapable of feeling resentment and indignation," since their selfish conduct deprives them of any ground for objecting to similar behavior by others (*Theory*, 427). The qualification "barring self-deception" is the question-begging kicker here. Most egoists, we can surmise, do not think of themselves as being selfish. Rather, they believe they are claiming what is rightfully theirs. If they demand far more than they are willing to allot to other human beings—even to the point of being horrible tyrants like Stalin, Hitler, or Saddam Hussein—it is because they think they are that much superior in merit to the people they oppress.[6]

Doubtless such evil men are radically wrong in their self-assessments. But to demonstrate this would require some substantive account of human desert and the human good, based on our natures, such as is set forth in Aristotle's *Politics* and *Ethics*, on the one hand, and the teachings of such liberal philosophers as Locke, on the other. If Aristotle is correct, what is

5. In fact, Smith emphasizes the tension between justice and self-command, noting that "war is the great school both for acquiring and exercising" the latter and that "great warlike exploit . . . sometimes interests us" and commands esteem even when "undertaken contrary to every principle of justice" (*Theory of Moral Sentiments*, pt. 6, chap. 3, secs. 7–8, 239). The truly heroic aspect of self-command that Smith emphasizes is lacking in Rawls's account, and indeed in his whole representation of virtue as reducible to justice.

On Rawls's reduction of the virtues to a disposition to follow his preferred rules of justice, cf. Alasdair MacIntyre, *After Virtue*, 119. At the end of chapter 8, Rawls acknowledges that "many aspects of morality [are] left aside" in a theory of justice like his, but he does not elaborate other than to recommend kindness toward animals (*Theory*, 448).

6. Consider Alan Bullock, *Hitler: A Study in Tyranny*, 394: "Hitler never forgave the humiliation" he suffered from Czech president Eduard Benes's successful resistance to his original demands (which had been designed to be unacceptable [390]), "and from it sprang the venomous hatred with which he referred to President Benes, and an inflexible determination to obliterate the very name of Czechoslovakia."

Although Rawls repeatedly cites Rousseau's *Emile* to illustrate his view of moral learning (*Theory*, 402–3, 406n), he overlooks Rousseau's account in that work of the genesis of unjust indignation, and the radical steps that would be needed in order to tame it; the derivation of Rousseau's epigraph from Seneca's *Of Anger* suggests the centrality of this issue for him (*Emile*, bk. 2, 88, 96, 99; bk. 3, 243–44; 481n2). Earlier, Rawls had acknowledged that "those who act unjustly often do so with the conviction that they pursue a higher cause," but he expressed confidence that his well-ordered society would tend to "eliminate or at least to control" such inclinations (*Theory*, 215).

truly blameworthy in selfishness as commonly understood is that the selfish person has such a low conception of his good that he believes it consists simply in having as much as possible of such things as wealth and power (in other words, Rawls's primary goods). By contrast, Aristotle observes, the virtuous man is in a deeper sense the most selfish human being, since he seeks to possess the greatest amount of what is truly good.[7] The greatest of goods, for Aristotle as for Plato's Socrates, is wisdom (or its pursuit), a good that cannot be gained at anyone else's expense. The second-best way of life in Aristotle's account is that of the honorable gentleman—at the peak, the magnanimous man—who similarly understands his good in a way that does not typically entail doing injustice to others.

Unlike Aristotle's account of virtue, as we have seen in the preceding chapter, Rawls's understanding of justice—leaving aside his boilerplate rhetoric about "expressing our natures as free and equal human beings"— is merely instrumental. It isn't worthwhile to be just unless you know that everyone else will behave justly. But if so, then as Glaucon argues in Plato's *Republic*, why not have things even better, assuming you are clever and courageous enough, by successfully pursuing a life of injustice while you take advantage of other people's justice?

The danger of Rawls's argument here is twofold. First, by again encouraging us to think that the critical human divide is between the just and the selfish, Rawls potentially encourages a kind of moral fanaticism, such that anyone who is sufficiently convinced that he is just can peremptorily dismiss other people's claims as having, in Rawls's words, "no value." Such abstract moralism can hardly contribute to the reasonable resolution of political controversies either domestic or foreign. Second, because Rawls writes as if merely warning that anyone who acts unjustly will be deprived of the goods of "friendship, affection, and mutual trust" (*Theory*, 428) will normally suffice to dissuade people from injustice, he encourages readers to underestimate the need for forceful sanctions to achieve the necessary deterrence. (Hence Rawls's claim that "relations of friendship and mutual trust, and the public knowledge of a common and normally effective sense of justice" can substitute for Hobbes's sovereign as a support for justice [*Theory*, 435].)[8]

7. Aristotle *NE* 9.8, 1168b28–33. The same principle underlies the Socratic thesis that truly wrong action is incompatible with wisdom.
8. Some may argue that Rawls's vision constitutes an inspiring "idealism." To the contrary, as we are taught by Machiavelli, to encourage decent human beings to adopt a utopian outlook makes them the dupes and victims of the cleverly unscrupulous. One need not be a Machiavellian or Hobbesean to appreciate this lesson, which is elaborated in *The Federalist*, among many other classic works of liberal political philosophy: see Hamilton, Madison, and Jay, *The Federalist*, No. 51, 290 ("if men were angels . . .")

At the conclusion of his account of the moral sentiments, despite having previously called on the notion of self-command to buttress his doctrine, Rawls asserts that "our existing moral feelings may be in many respects irrational and injurious" because of the exaggerated "resentment and indignation, feelings of guilt and remorse," and "sense of duty and the censure of others" that they call forth, at the expense of "spontaneity and enjoyment" (*Theory*, 428). In other words, it seems that too much of a sense of shame, or even of duty, might be bad for you! (How do we reconcile this remark with the priority Rawls wants to give to justice over the individual's good?)

I have argued that Rawls's difference principle and his dismissal of desires that don't fit his theory tend to encourage rather than to moderate feelings of resentment and unjust indignation. Additionally, his wish to soften our feelings of guilt, remorse, and duty, combined with his emphasis on the dependence of our self-esteem on other people's valuing our "life plans" however trivial they may be, again indicates how remote Rawls's moral code is from the teaching of Kant, just as it is from Aristotle's account of magnanimity and Smith's notion of self-command, despite his citing these authorities for support.[9] (A glance at America's mass media "culture" over the past four decades should reassure anyone who worries that we currently suffer from an excessive sense of shame.)

II.

Following Rawls's long windup—the excursus on moral psychology that occupies most of chapter 8—his delivery, the demonstration of the "relative stability" of justice as fairness is anticlimactic. After asserting, on the basis of abstract psychological "laws" that have nothing specifically to do with justice as fairness, that "there seems to be no doubt" that it is "a

---

and No. 1, 3 (on energetic government as essential for "the security of liberty"). On why, in constructing a government, "every man ought to be supposed a knave," see also Hume, "Of the Independency of Parliament," *Essays Moral, Political, and Literary,* 42; and cf. Machiavelli, *Discourses on Livy,* bk. 1, chap. 3 (1st sentence). Neither Hume nor *The Federalist,* however, adopts quite the sour tone of Rawls's remark in chapter 9 about people's "often squalid" behavior (*Theory,* 499).

9. Cf., for instance, Kant, "Idea for a Universal History with Cosmopolitan Intent," in *Political Writings,* Third Proposition, 43–44: "It seems that nature has worked more with a view to man's rational *self-esteem* than to his mere well-being. . . . [N]ature does not seem to have been concerned with seeing that man should live agreeably, but with seeing that he should work his way onwards to make his own conduct *worthy* of life and well-being" (first emphasis Kant's, second one added).

reasonably stable moral conception," Rawls undertakes to demonstrate its superiority in this regard only to one alternative, utilitarianism. His argument is simply that because the various priority rules in justice as fairness, along with the difference principle, reinforce the principle of reciprocity—we naturally tend to support a system that treats us justly and buttresses our self-esteem—we are more likely to support a social order based on justice as fairness than a utilitarian regime, where we risk having our liberty or welfare sacrificed to increase the societal balance or average of utility (*Theory*, 436–37). By contrast to justice as fairness, Rawls maintains, utilitarianism weakens "the self-esteem of those who lose out," generating "self-hatred." Under Rawls's principles, on the other hand, not only might we identify with others' good, but our sense of justice will be strengthened by "the clarity of the moral conception and the attractiveness of its ideals" (*Theory*, 438). As further witness on behalf of his theory, Rawls even brings in Mill, citing the observation in *Utilitarianism* that as civilization advances human beings increasingly recognize the need for "the interests of all . . . to be consulted" as evidence that Mill himself renounced the utilitarian principle, albeit without realizing his self-contradiction, and would have favored something like the difference principle (*Theory*, 439).

I need not reiterate the artificiality and political irrelevance of the issue between Rawls's theory and his versions of the utilitarian alternative. The contradiction Rawls purports to discover in Mill exists only because Rawls has speciously attributed to him (as noted in chapter 3) the outlandish thesis that society should be organized to maximize the total or average utility of its members, when in fact Mill meant by "utility" as a standard for ethics nothing other than a society's common good, and he specifically mandated in *Utilitarianism* that all individuals' rights must be equally respected. More to the point, there is no reason to think that Rawls's principles best evince society's concern for the well-being of all its members, let alone that they are "perspicuous" (*Theory*, 438–39). As has been noted, Rawls's abstract first principle provides far less support for liberty than did Mill's *On Liberty* (to say nothing of more profound philosophic texts), while the difference principle requires all human beings except the least advantaged to forego any economic gains they might make unless they benefit that class. And all this only on the ground that "parties" from whom practically every element of humanity had been removed, acting on a peculiarly Rawlsian notion of rationality, would supposedly choose these principles in a hypothetical position of equality. (As previously noted, Mill offered a precedent for the grounding of the difference principle by describing the "true idea of distributive justice" as entailing the redress of nature's "inequalities and wrongs," but he never asserted anything like that principle, with its misleading impression of quasi-mathematical precision, any more than the abstract principle of "average utility.")

The theme that Rawls treats under the heading of stability is actually one of the most fundamental issues of political philosophy: how does one induce human beings voluntarily to subordinate their natural self-interestedness to the good of their community, to the extent that the common welfare requires it? Perhaps the profoundest modern thinker to address this issue was Rousseau, who feared that the effect of the ostensibly liberalizing teachings of Hobbes, Locke, and other Enlightenment thinkers was to undermine the moral and customary ties that made it possible for citizens to transcend selfishness, trading their birthright of civic freedom for the pottage of wealth and a specious refinement. He lamented that modern politicians, schooled by the principles of the Enlightenment, had lost the art of shaping the human heart so as to cause men to love their duties, relying instead on the mere carrot of self-interest combined with the threat of punishment.[10] In moderated form, Rousseau's emphasis on the importance of *moeurs* in supporting republican government was elaborated by his pupil Tocqueville. One can find serious reflections on the theme of engendering an attachment to the nation and its good as well in the writings of Jefferson and Lincoln, as I have noted, as well as in *The Federalist*.[11]

By contrast to these writers, Rawls never seriously addresses the problem of harmonizing the individual's interests and passions with the welfare of his country, because he never considers it part of his task to engage in an empirical examination of political life or human nature. Instead, after constructing his abstract notion of justice, he "demonstrates" its feasibility by postulating an account of human nature to fit it. Were the issue not so serious, we would be tempted to apply Robert Frost's judgment of free verse: "playing tennis without the net."

III.

The last section of chapter 8 concerns "the basis of equality," that is, the features that human beings share that entitle them to be treated fairly (*Theory*, 441). According to Rawls these features are twofold: people's capacity to have a conception of their good as expressed by "a rational plan of life"

10. See Rousseau, *The Government of Poland*, chaps. 1–4, especially 4–5; *Discourse on the Sciences and Arts*, 50–51; *Social Contract*, bk. 2, chap. 12, 77; bk. 4, chap. 7, 123; *Discourse on Political Economy*, 215–17; Burke, *Reflections on the Revolution*, 68.

11. See Hamilton, Madison, and Jay, *The Federalist*, No. 49; also Walter Berns, *Making Patriots*.

and their capacity for a sense of justice. He emphasizes that nothing beyond a "minimum" is necessary to constitute this "moral personality"; the requirement of these two capacities is "not at all stringent." Hence, "we cannot go far wrong in supposing that the sufficient condition is always satisfied." Indeed, a greater than minimal moral capacity, far from entitling some people to greater rewards than others, is simply "a natural asset like any other ability" (*Theory*, 442–43).[12]

In contrast to the Declaration of Independence, Rawls denies that there is any "natural feature with respect to which all human beings are equal." But he finds this no obstacle to grounding the claim to equal justice on people's "natural attributes": all one need do is limit the relevance of those attributes to certain "range propert[ies]" rather than taking account of possible inequalities in people's moral capacity (*Theory*, 442–45). This seems another way of saying that to the extent we can read nature as favoring equality, rely on it; to the extent nature doesn't support equality, ignore it.[13] It is hard to take this argument seriously as a grounding for equal natural rights. And it seems highly inconsistent for Rawls even to attempt to ground the claim to equal rights on people's natural attributes, when the whole point of his difference principle is to "compensate for" or overcome the arbitrariness of the way in which people's natural assets are "distributed." That inconsistency does not deter him, however, from suggesting that his theory can serve to give content to the term "natural rights"—so long as we agree to prioritize "the rights identified by [Rawls's] theory of justice" over those "defined by law and custom," as if Rawls's mere assertion of their priority made them natural (*Theory*, 442n).

12. Rawls sidesteps a major difficulty here by equating the capacity for a sense of justice with the "skill and capacity in applying the principles of justice and in marshaling arguments in particular cases" (*Theory*, 443), rather than with a disposition to act justly. If the latter (as common sense suggests) rather than the former, intellectual element, is the core of moral character, then holding as Rawls does that "the special advantages a person receives" for its exercise, such as being chosen for offices in which "the judicial virtues of impartiality and integrity" are especially needed, "are to be governed by the difference principle," it would follow that unusually unjust people deserve compensation from the just for their very lack of a sense of justice! Rawls buttresses that implication by asserting that the failure to actualize one's moral capacity "is the consequence of unjust and impoverished social circumstances, or fortuitous contingencies" (ibid.). Presumably he does not mean that those who are arrested for crimes deserve to be compensated for their misfortune in having a bad character by those who are fortunate enough to have just dispositions. But what else could it mean to apply the difference principle to such cases? Here we observe a further confusion resulting from Rawls's choice in chapter 5 (breaking sharply with Kant) to treat good character itself as an "unearned" natural asset.

13. This procedure is prefigured by Hobbes's reasoning for his ninth law of nature (*Leviathan* chap. 15). But Hobbes's deeper ground for accepting the principle of people's equality of right is a substantive one, as I note in the text that follows above.

By contrast to Rawls, as I have noted, the teachings of Hobbes and Locke, on which the doctrine of the Declaration is founded, provide a coherent argument for the fundamental natural equality of human beings. Hobbes's starting point is that men's roughly equal capacity to kill one another is more decisive politically than any inequalities of wisdom or skill among them. The primary need to distance ourselves as far as possible from the state of nature requires that governments accommodate the opinion that people tend to hold of their equal right to security, lest they otherwise use their collective force to overthrow any existing government. Without denying the existence of natural inequalities in various sorts of ability among human beings, Hobbes and Locke stress that there is no reliable correlation between natural inequalities in the capacity to rule and the actual political or conventional hierarchies that characterize human society.[14] Hence the most solid as well as legitimate foundation for government is the doctrine of equal rights.

What is at stake here is not merely a debate over the best theoretical foundation for the assertion of human equality. Rather, in the case of Hobbes, Locke, and the Declaration, the naturalness of equality in a particular sense generates a specific set of rights, with respect to which people must be regarded as equal and which it is the duty of just government to protect. No one may justly be governed without his consent, tacit (as measured by the security of his rights, according to Hobbes) or explicit (through representative institutions, as described by Locke). We are understood to have given up only that portion of our natural freedom that a sovereign must possess in order to protect our lives, properties, and our lawful liberty. By contrast, in the last pages of chapter 8, Rawls rejects the view that the equality to which we are "naturally" entitled is limited to such rights, or to an equality of respect "irrespective of [our] social position." Instead, he holds, no less "fundamental" is the right to an equality in the "distribution" of goods through which some individuals obtain "higher status or prestige" than others. Indeed, he reminds us that "taken by itself" his conception of fair opportunity would entail the abolition of the family, which inevitably "lead[s] to unequal chances between individuals." His acceptance of the family's legitimacy is so weak that he can say only that "within the theory of justice as a whole, there is much less urgency" about abolishing it, since the difference principle so moderates the effects of "the natural distribution of assets and the contingencies of social circumstances"

14. See Locke, *Two Treatises*, bk. 2, sec. 54; also Rousseau, *Discourse on the Sciences and Arts*, in *First and Second Discourses*, 3rd. par., 101–2.

that they "can more easily be accepted."[15] "We are more ready to dwell upon our good fortune," Rawls remarks, "now that these differences are made to work to our advantage, rather than to be downcast by how much better off we might have been had we had an equal chance . . . if only all social barriers had been removed." Hence Rawls believes that his conception of justice "seems more likely than its rivals to transform our perspective on the social world and to reconcile us to the dispositions of the natural order and the conditions of human life" (*Theory*, 447–48).

It is certainly wise to encourage people to appreciate their advantages in life rather than to wallow in self-pity and envy because others have achieved more. But Rawls should have weighed such considerations before deciding to develop his theory of justice, rather than near its completion. As things stand, his acknowledgment that when all is said and done, the persistence of the family is an apparently insurmountable obstacle to the full achievement of "fair equality of opportunity" (just as he previously acknowledged that we must settle for an equality of opportunity that operates only within classes, not among them) is reminiscent of Socrates' acknowledgment in the *Republic*, after he has called for the most far-reaching and often ridiculous sacrifices on behalf of the ostensible construction of a perfectly just city, that its purported justice is still imperfect, while the city itself may be unachievable.[16] (What price justice?)

But Rawls has proffered no evidence either that citizens of actual constitutional, liberal regimes like the United States cannot reconcile themselves to the conditions of the natural order right now—with or without the assistance of religious faith —or that his principles would better encourage such an outlook. To the contrary, whereas existing liberal institutions offer to all citizens the hope of advancement in life through their own endeavors, along with the respect that derives from the rights of equal citizenship, Rawls's difference principle can only embitter those who appear "less advantaged" at any given time about their lot, causing them always to doubt whether the inequalities that remain really benefit them, and convincing them that their situation is the consequence of bad luck or injustice rather than encouraging them to better their condition

---

15. As discussed in chapter 12 below, in *IPRR* (161–62, 169) Rawls extends the scope of justice to dictate a reformation of the family to equalize or compensate for the division of child care between parents, and denies the existence of any private sphere exempt from justice.

16. Plato *Republic*, 473a, 592a–b. For Socrates, the discovery of the impossibility of a perfectly just or "beautiful" city leads not to disgust with the human condition, but rather to the quest for *self*-perfection (591b–592b).

through their own efforts. As well, Rawls's teaching about the utter dependence of each person's self-esteem on how he is regarded by others, and his mandate that nobody's life plan is entitled to any more public esteem than devoting oneself to grass counting, can only weaken the sense of human dignity that justifies our claim to equal rights.

Chapter 9

The Just and the Good

I.

In chapter 9, "The Good of Justice," Rawls addresses the congruence of justice as fairness with goodness as rationality. Congruence means that a conception of justice not only harmonizes with each person's good but also contributes positively to it. Rawls contends that justice as fairness meets this standard because it (1) "allows for persons' autonomy and the objectivity of their judgments of right and justice"; (2) combines with "the ideal of social union" to mitigate "envy and spite" while maintaining the priority of liberty; and (3) supports "the unity of the self and enable[s] human beings to express their nature as free and equal moral persons" (*Theory,* 450).

It is noteworthy that at the outset Rawls describes his aim as to show that "the requisite match exists between the principles of justice that would be agreed to in the absence of information and the principles of rational choice that are not chosen at all" but are "applied with full knowledge" (*Theory,* 451). This formulation highlights the contrast between the apparent arbitrariness of the principles of justice, which are to be chosen as "we" wish, but on the basis of limited information, and the fact of the "rational" pursuit of one's own good, which is a given rather than something chosen and based on complete knowledge. It is all the harder to see how Rawls's artificially devised principles can somehow be "prior" to our actual good as real human beings.[1]

Rawls's initial approach to this difficulty in the present context is to emphasize that the members of a well-ordered society will acquire "moral attitudes" through a process of education that itself is regulated by the principles of justice. Nobody can object to such instruction, Rawls maintains, since in choosing principles of justice, the parties to the original position must be understood to have agreed to sanction it to make their agreement effective. Hence he infers that "no one's moral convictions are the result of coercive indoctrination" (*Theory*, 451–52).[2]

Again, Rawls's argument is circular. Rather than demonstrate any actual congruence between justice as fairness and the individual's good, Rawls simply asserts the possibility of molding people's beliefs so that they will see their good in terms of his view of justice. Of course, no sensible person doubts the need for children in any decent society to have their character shaped through a process of moral instruction that relies on means other than direct appeals to reason. In Rawls's case, however, the point seems to be to deter even adults from questioning, let alone challenging, the particular view of justice they have been "educated" to accept. Although Rawls assures us that moral instruction will be "as reasoned as the development of understanding permits" (*Theory*, 452), we have seen reason to doubt that the doctrine to be inculcated is itself rational. Since it contrasts with the liberal, Lockean doctrine of rights not only in lacking a genuine foundation in reason or nature but also in contradicting many of our commonsense

1. Cf. Schaar, "Reflections on Rawls' *Theory*," 161, regarding the oddity of Rawls's endeavor to give "what we chose in ignorance . . . priority over what we choose in knowledge." And see note 33 below.

2. In relying on "rational" moral education to induce the individual to subordinate his interest to justice, Rawls echoes Mill's call for "education and opinion" to so transform the individual's outlook that he will be "unable to conceive the possibility" of achieving happiness through "conduct opposed to the general good" (*Utilitarianism*, chap. 2, 21; cf. chap. 3, 33–34). Mill expected the individual's feeling of oneness with humanity "to become stronger . . . from the influences of advancing civilization," as suggested by August Comte's proposed "religion of humanity" (*Utilitarianism*, III, 38–41). But like Bentham, Mill never succeeds in grounding this self-identification with the common good in a manner consistent with the utilitarian principle itself. Thus he provides no proper substitute for older moral teachings that rooted concern with the common good in the elevation of the noble over the useful, in civic honor, or in divine sanctions. And his doctrine falls short as well of the more sober liberal teaching of *The Federalist*, which demands less of the individual and attempts to reconcile his interest with that of his country through institutional arrangements and an explicit dedication of the nation to the securing of individual rights. The problem is even greater for Rawls, given the unnaturalness of his demand that we treat our individual talents as a common asset.

moral beliefs (such as the deservedness of the fruits of people's own efforts, and the more general notion that rewards should somehow correspond to the individual's desert), it would be much harder to persuade anyone to accept it.

Once more, Rawls cites Kant for witness, albeit in an offhanded way, remarking that "following the Kantian interpretation of justice as fairness, we *can say* that by acting from these principles persons are acting autonomously" (*Theory*, 452 [emphasis added]). But whereas Kant's notion of autonomy depends on a complex metaphysical distinction between the noumenal (purely rational) and phenomenal (empirically sensed) realms of existence, all that Rawlsian autonomy means is that we transcend our natural preference for our own interest through the attainment of an ostensible "Archimedean point" that is hardly that in actuality. For Kant, we demonstrate our autonomy by obeying the moral law that each of us is capable of discerning without the need of an education directing us to adopt a particular interpretation of it; for Rawls we ostensibly attain autonomy by being guided to accept his idiosyncratic view of justice.[3]

The same problems characterize Rawls's claim (repeated from chapter 5) that his doctrine combines autonomy with "objectivity," the latter manifested in the way that the veil of ignorance enables us to choose principles of justice "unencumbered by the singularities" of our particular circumstances (*Theory*, 453). As we have seen, among those singularities are the distinct attributes that compose our natures. And the "knowledge" that Rawls allows to penetrate the veil predetermines the outcome of the choice.

As if to give the game away entirely, Rawls reminds us that the original position was designed to introduce "the greatest convergence of opinion" about justice. Part of the reason we were required to accept the veil was that "the contingencies of our different circumstances" might otherwise prevent our beliefs from "fall[ing] into line" (*Theory*, 453). But how can it be advantageous from a philosophic point of view to obscure the diversity of human opinions for the sake of consensus? What are the grounds of the "hope" Rawls expresses that simplifying political questions through devices like the veil will generate a "balance of justice" that "outweighs what may have been lost by ignoring . . . potentially relevant aspects of moral situations" (*Theory*, 454)?

---

3. Of course Kant stresses the need for moral education to accustom human beings to act in accordance with the moral law; see *Education*, introduction and pts. 5–6. But the *content* of the moral law or categorical imperative—essentially a secularized version of the Golden Rule—is itself a dictate of the reason inherent in all human beings (*Foundations of the Metaphysics of Morals*, pt. 1, 20–21 [Akad. ed. 403–4]). Cf. Joseph Knippenberg, "Moving Beyond Fear," 818.

By Rawls's account, the value of considering the world from the standpoint of the original position is that "the complexity of problems of justice is up to the persons" in that situation (rather than actual human beings in the real circumstances of life) to resolve. Consequently, "although ethical differences are bound to remain," that perspective permits "essential understandings to be reached." Without such a common perspective to narrow differences of opinion, Rawls believes, "reasoning and argument would be pointless and we would have no rational grounds for believing in the soundness of our convictions" (*Theory*, 454; recall the similar claim in chapter 1 [37] to the effect that without agreed on "weights" for competing ethical criteria, "the means of rational discussion have come to an end").

But how can these claims be true? How can the essential understandings that undergird political life be grounded in a hypothetical decision in which we are kept ignorant of the most critical sort of information and concerns of everyday life? Even assuming we wished to (and could) simulate that process, wouldn't the result amount to sweeping fundamental problems under the rug, only to have them recur in our daily lives without an adequate basis for addressing them? And how can Rawls explain the fact that human beings do customarily engage in reasoned discussion and debate about political and moral issues without any prior agreement on a theoretical framework such as he calls for, yet do not find such discussion to be "pointless"?[4]

This point bears emphasis because it shows that the germ of what Rawls will represent as the central innovation of his second book, *PL*—his stress on achieving consensus as the prime requisite for resolving the problem of justice, even at the cost of the pursuit of truth—was already present in *Theory*. In both works, Rawls professes to establish consensus by setting aside the concerns that underlie people's most deeply held opinions and consequent disagreements about justice, only to smuggle in resolutions to those disagreements, in the name of an ostensibly neutral process, that beg the important questions.

The dogmatism of Rawls's position reemerges in the sequel, where he elaborates his conception of moral autonomy. "From the standpoint of jus-

---

4. By contrast, in Plato's *Republic* (557c–d), Socrates represents democracy as the actual regime most conducive to philosophizing precisely because of the diversity of human types (and hence, presumably, opinions) that it generates. This is not to deny the need for some sort of constitutional consensus of the kind that has typically existed in the United States since its founding. But that consensus has never been held to eliminate debate on broad issues of justice as Rawls's theory ostensibly does. Cf. Zuckert, *Launching Liberalism*, 351–52, responding to Alasdair MacIntyre's comparable demand for a shared "conception of human good" as a precondition for "rationally founded moral rules."

tice as fairness," he explains, it is not true either that each person's "conscientious judgments . . . ought absolutely to be respected" or "that individuals are completely free to form their moral convictions." To assess the dictates of his conscience, each individual must "ascend" to the original position to determine whether he is seeking to impose conditions that would be rejected in that situation. Rather than respect beliefs contrary to the two principles, we should "respect" each person by constraining his behavior in accordance with those principles (*Theory*, 455–56). (Contrast the scrupulous respect Rawls ordained for practitioners of civil disobedience—illegal acts—in chapter 6, with his lack of respect for mere *beliefs* that contradict his principles.)

In fact, however, there is no reason to anticipate less disagreement about which judgments or policies would match the principles derived from the original position than there is in actual political life about the wisest and most just policies and actions. As I have noted, disputes about the proper extent of liberty can hardly be overcome by following Rawls's abstract recommendation to increase the scope of one liberty to the point just short of reducing another liberty to a greater extent. Ordaining that economic policies favor the least advantaged tells us nothing about how to identify the persons belonging to that category, how to weigh and balance different sorts of disadvantage, or how to alleviate them. Nor is any citizen likely to feel "respected" when his government tells him that his opinions lack value because they violate the principles he supposedly would have agreed to under abstract and hypothetical conditions that can have no interest for him in real life. The only gainers from Rawls's recommendation of substituting debate about decisions in the original position for debates over substantive issues of justice and policy are likely to be those skilled in the techniques of Rawlsian argumentation—that is, philosophy professors belonging to a particular school of thought. Such a mode of governance bears little resemblance to constitutional democracy as ordinarily conceived.

II.

The core of Rawls's ground for regarding justice as fairness as congruent with everyone's good in a well-ordered society is contained in the next section, "The Idea of Social Union." Here Rawls reiterates that despite the individualistic aspects of his doctrine, it views human beings as social creatures who share "final ends" and value their "common institutions and activities." Borrowing from the nineteenth-century German liberal theorist

Wilhelm von Humboldt (a source for Mill's notion of individuality in *On Liberty*), Rawls explains that it is only through social union that each person overcomes the limitations of his own capacities and opportunities so as to share in his fellows' "realized natural assets." This community extends over time, so that we profit from our predecessors' achievements and in turn develop them for our descendants (*Theory*, 458–60). When all citizens have "a shared final end and accepted ways of advancing it" that facilitate "public recognition" of everyone's attainments, we can say (as Socrates ironically maintains of the best city in Plato's *Republic* [462c–d]) that "all find satisfaction in the very same thing." To emphasize this point, Rawls states it three times within two pages (*Theory*, 461–62).

As previously noted, thinkers such as Edmund Burke have represented civilization as a partnership among generations.[5] The notion of political society as having a shared good that transcends individual interests can be said to characterize preliberal political philosophy as a whole, as well as liberal political thought as articulated by statesmen like Lincoln. (Consider President John Kennedy's celebrated call in his inaugural address for Americans to ask what they can do for their country, rather than the opposite.) Yet outside the realm of religious prophecy, no serious thinker ever promised such a unity of "satisfaction" among citizens as Rawls attributes to his well-ordered society.[6] (Isn't this unity more naturally to be approached in a harmonious marriage or the relation of close friends?)

5. Without mentioning Burke's view, Rawls in his later "Reply to Habermas" uncritically and inconsistently (in view of his ostensible concern for "justice between generations") cites Jefferson's contrary principle that "the earth belongs in usufruct to the living" only, as well as his recommendation of new constitutional conventions every twenty years, suggesting that adopting the Jeffersonian outlook might help address Habermas's concern for "reigniting the radical democratic embers in a just society" (*PL*, 408). For a critique of Jefferson's proposal, see Hamilton, Madison, and Jay, *The Federalist*, No. 49. Consider as well Mill's criticism of Bentham for underestimating the need of institutional continuity as a support to popular law-abidingness ("Remarks on Bentham's Philosophy," 113–14; also Rousseau, *Second Discourse*, Dedication, 82). Much of Mill's criticism of Bentham's failure to ground his philosophy in an understanding of human nature would apply to Rawls as well.

6. Despite the remarks cited in note 2, not even Mill demands the degree of social unity anticipated by Rawls. Nor does he maintain as Rawls does that such moral community can or should be nonjudgmental with regard to individual achievement and merit. As for Humboldt, one should note that unlike Rawls, he strenuously opposed the extension of government's concern to the citizen's "positive welfare" (aside from public education) as an interference with the development of individuality (*The Limits of State Action*, chap. 3).

Rawls's ideal social union also recalls the Kantian ideal of a "Kingdom of Ends"; but for Kant that realm is founded on people's obedience to the moral law, not on an empirical harmony among their particular ends. In other words, Kant doesn't claim that even in an ideal world the advancement of each person's specific aims, as distinguished

Remarkably, after having based his doctrine on the assumption that the only objective ("primary") goods are those for which we compete with others (wealth and power) or at least seek to enjoy without other people's interference (liberties), Rawls now justifies it on the basis of an abstract, communized conception of humanity in which the individual's identity collapses into the whole. In place of any natural wholeness that the individual might achieve through understanding—the reason Plato's Socrates represents philosophy as an essentially erotic activity—or at least through love, friendship, and family, as well as a meaningful public or private vocation, Rawls offers only an artificial "happiness," reducing the individual to a cog in the social machine, extending the division of labor from the factory floor to the whole of life.[7]

What is most distinctive about Rawls's notion of community—unlike Socrates' ostensibly just city in the *Republic*—is its nonjudgmental character. In accordance with the principle of "democracy in the assessment of one another's excellences," Rawls stresses that high scientific, artistic, cultural, or religious achievements "have no special merit from the standpoint of justice." It is better, he suggests, to understand social cooperation on the model of a game, in which each person's "zest and pleasure" presuppose a joint commitment to "fair play."[8] Only on such a foundation

---

from his obedience to the moral law, would always benefit his fellows (*Foundations of the Metaphysics of Morals*, pt. 3, 51–52, 57 [Akad. ed. 434–35, 438]). Nor (contrary to Rawls's claim [*Theory*, 459n]) does the second proposition of Kant's "Idea for a Universal History" strictly support Rawls's conception, since Kant is speaking only of the progressive perfection of human faculties over time.

Probably the most sweeping call for civic unity in the tradition of American political thought is John Winthrop's appeal, in his 1630 shipboard sermon on "Christian Charity," that the Puritan settlers "abridge ourselves of our superfluities, for the supply of others' necessities" and endeavor to "delight in each other, make others' conditions our own, rejoice together, mourn together, labor and suffer together." But the ground of this ideal of community (an exemplary "city upon a hill") is the Christians' communion with God, a promise of salvation that of course has no counterpart in Rawls's utopia. See Winthrop, "Christian Charity," 92–93. (I have modernized Winthrop's spelling and punctuation.)

7. Again, we are reminded of the ironic "best regime" in Plato's *Republic*, which eliminates the family in the name of the greatest civic unity, as well as subordinating philosophy to the city's service, thereby evincing Plato's view of the dangers of a fanatical pursuit of justice. Cf. Aristotle *Politics* 2.1–4; Mary Nichols, *Socrates and the Political Community*, chap. 3.

8. Rawls's game metaphor, which played a key role in the original development of his theory, is inapropos here for several reasons. First, although a game presupposes its participants' playing by the rules, their "final end" within the game is typically to win rather than ensure the maximum of fairness. Second, within a game, some actions (hitting a home run) are clearly ranked above others (striking out). Third, whereas the rules of a game are by definition artificial, the same cannot be said of the activities of

can a well-ordered society constitute "a social union of social unions" based on its members' sharing as their final end the maintenance of just institutions. Every individual is fitted neatly within his society, his "more private life . . . so to speak a plan within" society's overall plan. All appreciate "the collective activity of justice" as "the preeminent form of human flourishing" (*Theory*, 462–63; note that Rawls has proffered no evidence to support the latter judgment).

Even though the well-ordered society still includes a division of labor in the customary sense, Rawls promises that "the worst aspects of this division can be surmounted" so that "no one need be servilely dependent" and compelled to pursue "monotonous and routine occupations." More fundamentally, our opportunity to perform "willing and meaningful work within a just social union" overcomes any fragmentation resulting from that division (*Theory*, 461–64). As we have seen, however, Rawls offers no consideration of how the individual might attain a natural wholeness or completion in his own life, as opposed to deriving it from the overall society of which his own activities are merely a fragment.

Rawls's account of a just society as one that combines the greatest development of individuality, the abolition of all servile or monotonous labor, and the fullest degree of community is reminiscent, more than anything else, of the Marxian utopian vision of communist society. Although Rawls nowhere speaks of abolishing government, his assumptions about how agreement on justice eliminates major political controversies while people's development of their capacities engenders a total harmony among them effectively reduces government to a mere administrative organ, as envisioned by Marx and Engels.[9] Needless to say, Rawls has given no

---

society as a whole. Don't we inevitably think of some undertakings (such as the education of youth) as more serious than other, purely recreational ones? (Consider similarly Rawls's use of tourism as an illustration of fundamental life choices [*Theory*, 483], discussed below.)

9. Rawls elsewhere distinguishes his well-ordered society from Marx's communist society, governed by the precept "From each according to his abilities, to each according to his needs," only in presupposing that "the limitations of moderate scarcity" of resources still exist (*CP*, 252). But given Rawls's (Marxian) assumption that we each participate in one another's natures in a well-ordered society, it appears that disagreements over the distribution of goods will be so mild as hardly to resemble politics in any meaningful sense (cf. Young, *Reconsidering American Liberalism*, 274). Additionally, Rawls's espousal in *JF* (63–64, 159) of Mill's ideal of "a society in a just stationary state where (real) capital accumulation may cease" implies that any scarcity is ultimately to be overcome. Standing behind Marx, and in some respects even closer to Rawls's "social union of social unions," is the chiliastic vision held by various fanatical sects of the Middle Ages of an imminent earthly paradise of "total community, a society wholly unanimous in its beliefs and wholly free from inner conflicts": see Norman Cohn, *The Pursuit of the Millennium*, 308–12.

explanation of how merely agreeing to his principles can make the necessity for unattractive forms of labor disappear; this seems to be simply part of his wish list for an earthly utopia.[10] The deeper difficulty with his account of the just society as a union of social unions is that it abstracts from the existence of broad disagreements about ends, such that it misleadingly assumes that everyone else's development of his potentialities, or the fullest development of all kinds of particular unions, necessarily contributes to my happiness or well-being. It is obvious that, say, Hitler's or Saddam Hussein's full development of his potential for tyranny is contrary to the happiness of nearly all other human beings.[11] But it is equally doubtful that from the standpoint of a believing member of one religious faith, the fullest development of alternative religious possibilities is desirable—as distinguished from a unity of human belief that is grounded in the true religion. Moreover, if we take seriously Rawls's mandate of nonjudgmentalism with respect to artistic or scientific excellence, it would follow that the scientist is obliged to applaud the "advance" of astrology and alchemy and to acknowledge that these ostensible sciences are no less praiseworthy than mathematical physics; while "art" works such as "Piss Christ" must be accorded recognition as the equivalent of a Rembrandt portrait, lest the self-esteem of the "creator" of the former be weakened.

There is no need to work out further such consequences of Rawls's doctrine. The underlying point, again, is the impossibility of grounding an account of the good and just society on a wholly relativistic account of particular human ends. A genuine feeling of community that elevates human beings above petty self-interest derives precisely from the sort of shared commitment to a great, substantive, collective enterprise, or to the sense of helping to preserve a great national tradition, that is incompatible with Rawlsian relativism. (Such a perspective would also require renouncing Rawls's doctrine of primary goods.) The greatest critics of rationalistic liberalism—Rousseau, Burke, and Nietzsche—have charged it with

10. Rawls's fellow theorist Barry does offer a solution of sorts to this problem: government should simply outlaw the most monotonous, unpleasant, and dangerous jobs (*Liberal Theory*, 165).

11. More generally, as Schaar observes, it is impossible for all talents to be "developed equally in any given society," since each society will inevitably admire and reward some potentialities more than others ("Equality of Opportunity," 230). Of course, Rawls himself has stressed the need for particular conceptions of the good to be constrained by justice, thus ruling out tyranny as a way of life, and he later acknowledges that a just constitutional regime allows only some views of the good to flourish (*PL*, 197). But to the extent that he overcomes the conflict among human ends by excluding from the just society any ways of life that don't fit, his representation of that society as entailing a complementarity of ends reduces itself to tautology.

undermining the necessary sense of civic purposiveness and particularism or "local" attachment. On the other hand, liberalism's most profound‎ defenders, such as Tocqueville, have tried to show that the commitment of a nation to securing its citizens' equal rights is not incompatible with such civic dedication; indeed, requires it as a necessary support. But Tocqueville's substantive defense of liberalism demands that we make moral and cultural distinctions among different ways of life of a kind that Rawls prohibits. By contrast, Rawls has not shown that his well-ordered society offers any real possibility of human greatness or a truly human satisfaction. In fact, his account of an ideal social union is barren of empirical evidence of any kind.[12]

III.

This same defect is apparent in the next section of Rawls's argument, which aims to demonstrate that the well-ordered society will be free from envy—a problem from which Rawls had abstracted while describing the reasoning in the original position. After approvingly citing Kant's condemnation of envy as a misanthropic vice, Rawls departs from the teachings of Kant and every other respected previous moral philosopher and theologian by enunciating a novel doctrine of "excusable" envy. According to Rawls, even though envy as such is harmful to both the envious and the envied, "sometimes the circumstances evoking" it "are so compelling that . . . no one can reasonably be asked to overcome his rancorous feelings." Not only may a person's relative deficiency of primary goods "be so great as to wound his self-respect," a person can rightfully "resent being *made* envious" when "society" allows such great inequalities to exist. Hence, Rawls claims, "for those suffering this hurt, envious feelings are not irrational," since "the satisfaction of their rancor would make them better off" (*Theory*, 466–68 [emphasis added]).

Despite Rawls's initial condemnation of envy, the practical thrust of his argument is thus to encourage it, as, I have already suggested, the effect of the difference principle itself is. If people are taught that envy is "some-

12. In this respect Rawls's ideal of social union mirrors John Dewey's equally abstract account of the "great community" in *Public and Its Problems*, chap. 5. Contrast Aristotle's sober and realistic account of the means of fostering a genuine, if inevitably incomplete, community among citizens on the basis of a shared, substantive view of the good and the just derived from common critical reflection rather than from any overarching, transpolitical "theory" (Thomas W. Smith, "Aristotle on the Conditions for and Limits of the Common Good"; Yack, *Problems of a Political Animal*).

times" excusable and even rational, who will not judge that his own situation justifies such a feeling? In any society there will be inequalities of wealth, political power, social status, beauty, and brains that people could resent (or worse, have been encouraged to resent) if they have not been taught otherwise. Even in Rawls's just society, the more advantaged fare better than those less well endowed. But in addition, who can always resist resenting other people's particular successes, so that even a billionaire or a movie star may envy the greater accomplishments or just plain luck of a peer or nonpeer? Given Rawls's emphasis on the power of moral education to shape people's sense of justice, why doesn't he urge that human beings be reared and taught so far as possible to resist and overcome such ugly and harmful passions as envy, rather than offering justifications for it?[13]

Contrary to Rawls's contention that it is rational to feel envy whenever social or economic inequalities exceed a certain (unspecified) level, it is unlikely that it can ever be beneficial to experience, let alone try to satisfy, such a disposition. Lest we dismiss it as a merely personal vice, let us note how the potentially ruinous effects of teaching people that it is just to envy those who are better off (merely because they are better off, not because of any actual injury they have inflicted) and therefore to demand a greater share of the latter's possessions, are visible in the French and Russian revolutions and China's so-called Cultural Revolution (along with Islamic terrorism today).[14] Envy lay at the core of European anti-Semitism, as well as resentment (and mistreatment) directed against other industrious and hence relatively prosperous groups such as the Indians in East Africa and the ethnic Chinese in Malaya. It has been the source of bloody ethnic, racial, class, and political strife throughout history. Indeed, as a more insightful observer than Rawls—Tocqueville—famously observed, democratic institutions actually tend to increase envy, since the more people are encouraged to pursue equality as a goal, the more equal their conditions

---

13. By contrast, one of the central purposes of the ideal education Rousseau proposes in *Emile*, which takes its bearings by the actual human good, or happiness, is to liberate mankind from this passion (see, e.g., bk. 2, 92–3; bk. 4, 221, 223, 228–29, 235, 249, 284).

14. I emphasize that to condemn appeals to envy does not entail the illegitimacy of political movements or even revolutions aimed at overthrowing real oppression. But the mere fact that others have considerably more wealth than we do does not suffice to demonstrate that they have won it by denying us our legitimate rights. Nor does the fact that envy may sometimes fuel legitimate protest movements entail that the passion is itself "rational" or beneficial in its overall effects.

To reject the notion of "excusable envy" also doesn't mean that governments, in societies with relatively fixed hierarchies, may not sometimes need to take steps to moderate economic inequalities. Few respectable advocates of such policies, however, would ground them in the partial legitimation of envy as Rawls does.

become, and the more their particular socioeconomic positions fluctuate, the more irritating they find any inequalities that remain.[15]

Elsewhere, Tocqueville distinguishes two forms of the love of equality: a manly passion that encourages the individual to strive to rival or surpass the achievements of his better-situated fellows and a debased desire to pull others down to one's own level.[16] Rawls himself reminds us of Tocqueville when he distinguishes between "emulative envy," which "leads us to strive in socially beneficial ways" to achieve the goods that others have won, and envy in the blameworthy sense (*Theory*, 467). Unfortunately, neither Rawls's remarks on "excusable" envy nor his teaching as a whole do anything to promote the former rather than the latter.

Unlike Tocqueville, Rawls treats the problem of envy as an institutional rather than a moral one. The main reasons he doesn't expect his well-ordered society to be troubled by envy are as follows: (1) "In the public forum" all persons are treated as having equal rights; (2) since "the greater advantages of some" are conditioned on their "compensating" the less well-off, "no one supposes that those who have a larger share are more deserving from a moral point of view," hence "the less fortunate have no cause to consider themselves inferior," and "the disparities between themselves and others . . . should be easier for them to accept"; (3) the differences in people's situations in the well-ordered society "are *probably* less than have often prevailed," while "the plurality of associations" in such a society "tends to reduce . . . the painful visibility of variations in men's prospects," since "we tend to compare our circumstances with others in the same or in a similar group as ourselves"; (4) "In everyday life the natural duties are honored so that the more advantaged do not make an ostentatious display . . . calculated to demean the condition of those who have less"; and (5) "A well-ordered society *as much as any other* offers constructive alternatives to hostile outbreaks of envy" (*Theory*, 470–71 [emphasis added]).

Of these reasons, the first, the last two, and the second part of the third have no bearing on the alleged superiority of a society based on Rawls's principles to an existing constitutional democracy like the United States. The first part of the third one, concerning the range of inequalities, is bare assertion, ungrounded in any evidence (as is hinted by Rawls's hedging "probably"), and I have indicated in chapter 3 the reasons for doubting its truth. As for the second, I have suggested, Rawls's assertion is if anything a reversal of the truth. How could any sane member of the least-advantaged

15. Tocqueville, *Democracy in America*, vol. 1, pt. 2, chap. 5, 189; vol. 2, pt. 2, chap. 13, 513; vol. 2, pt. 4, chap. 3, 644–45.
16. Ibid., vol. 1, chap. 3, 52.

class esteem himself more as a consequence of knowing that the more able or industrious are compelled to work for his benefit simply because of his hopelessly inferior capacities and inability to provide sufficiently for himself? And how would believing that the advantages earned by others have no connection with desert make it easier to accept their legitimacy?

Perhaps most revealing is Rawls's assertion that the plurality of associations in a well-ordered society ought to reduce the painfulness of variations in people's life prospects. As already noted, the United States, even more than other liberal republics, has long been the home of such pluralism. If having a variety of associations, and the tendency to compare oneself most with one's peers, reduce the pain of inequality, don't these facts undermine the rationale for Rawls's difference principle: the alleged harm done to the psyches of the less advantaged by their cognizance of being less well-off?

Rawls misconceives self-esteem because he wishes to sever it from our having to do anything to merit our own esteem, let alone that of others. Similarly, in the concluding pages of this section, he offers a curious set of arguments intended to refute the claim "that the tendency to equality in modern social movements is the expression of envy." While Rawls asserts that this thesis presupposes that the sort of equality being demanded "is indeed unjust and bound in the end to make everyone including the less advantaged worse off," he previously suggested that even a justified movement of social reform might derive much of its energy and support from such unattractive passions. In any event, Rawls fails to refute the charge that his principles express envy: he simply asserts that the absence of envy is shown by the principles' "content" as well as by "the nature of the parties in the original position," who he assumes are unaffected by "rancor and spite" (*Theory*, 471–72).

Since the original position was designed to generate principles that "we" would find intuitively appealing, what is in question is not whether the hypothetical parties in that situation are envious (assuming it is even intelligible to ask that question), but whether the principles cater to sentiments of envy on the part of living human beings who Rawls hopes will adopt them. In this connection let us note that Rawls had described envy, just a few pages earlier, as a willingness to deprive those "whose situation is superior to ours . . . of their greater benefits even if it is necessary to give up something ourselves" to achieve that aim (*Theory*, 466). Formally, the difference principle expresses the opposite policy, since it allows others to earn greater benefits so long as the less advantaged also profit. But I submit that the spirit underlying that principle—I won't allow you to get ahead unless you give me a share of your gains—is not all that different. And since not even the most thoroughgoing application of the difference principle can prevent some people from enjoying greater success in love or greater physical health, thanks to their "unearned" genetic endowments (or plain luck), as well as (still) earning more money or status than others do, the principle and its rationale are likely to encourage a greater diffusion of envy rather than to moderate it. Instead of urging each individual in a liberal society to make the most of his situation and endowments and esteem himself on that basis, Rawls encourages anyone who considers himself less advantaged to focus attention on compelling others who have more to share the wealth. One need not be an economic libertarian like Nozick to detect a note of social blackmail or extortion in this outlook. And—to repeat—how can it truly enhance anyone's self-esteem?

IV.

In an oddly frank admission, Rawls concludes this section by remarking, "I believe, though *I have not shown,* that the principles of justice as fairness pass [the] test" of generating or harmonizing with psychological attitudes that support them (*Theory,* 474 [emphasis added]). He then completes his treatment of envy in the following section, "Grounds for the Priority of Liberty," by addressing the objection that even when people's basic material needs have been met so as to facilitate the prioritization of liberty over other goods, their concern for their relative economic status may persist, making them willing to undertake further sacrifices of liberty for the sake of increases in their wealth. Although Rawls does not mention him, this objection is reminiscent of Tocqueville's concern that modern egalitarianism would issue in an equality in servitude rather than in liberty precisely because of modern man's disposition to materialism, envy, and a petty estimation of his own capacities.[17] Tocqueville advocated a variety of remedies to ward off that danger, including decentralized administration, volunteerism, political associations, the encouragement of religious beliefs that give substance to the human soul, and limiting the scope of governmental regulation. By contrast, Rawls nowhere discusses administrative decentral-

17. Ibid., vol. 2, pt. 2, chap. 1; vol. 2, pt. 4, chap. 6. Rawls alludes to the argument that nonliberal societies such as feudal or caste ones "have other ways of affirming self-respect and of coping with envy and other disruptive inclinations," for instance confining people's comparisons to members of their own "caste or estate" (*Theory,* 479). He responds that such a system disregards "the general facts about society," including the malleability of political and social institutions. Yet only a few pages earlier, Rawls addressed the problem that envy would persist in his own well-ordered society by remarking that its members would chiefly compare their lot to that of others in the same social and economic class (*Theory,* 470–71).

ization or limiting the scope of governmental regulation (except over the "basic liberties"). Rather, he presents us with a vision of a unified society in which every individual's life plan is a subordinate element of his "social union." Additionally, Rawls denied that there was any intrinsic value to political activity, or any need for public encouragement of religion. Nonetheless, Rawls remains confident that liberty will be secure in his well-ordered society simply because its members "are not much affected by envy and jealousy," "do what seems best to them as judged by their own plan of life and those of their associates," and consequently "take little interest in their relative position as such" (*Theory*, 476–77).

Rawls is equally certain that everyone's social status will be secure in that society, thanks to "the public recognition of just institutions, together with the full and diverse internal life of the many free communities" citizens can join. Contrary to what I have shown is the actual likely effect of propagating the difference principle, Rawls explains that justice as fairness should "eliminate the significance of relative economic and social advantages" by relegating such concerns "to a subordinate place," in accordance with the priority of equal liberty (*Theory*, 477–78).[18]

Very late in developing his theory, Rawls acknowledges the possibility that this social equality cannot be fully achieved, so that people's sense of worth may still depend partly on their possession of offices or wealth. In that case, Rawls suggests, the index of primary goods in the original position can be adjusted "to allow for the effects of excusable envy"—meaning, apparently, that inequalities in social and economic goods may have to be limited even when they would otherwise benefit the least advantaged, simply to avoid generating such envy (*Theory*, 478–79). This is "an unwelcome complication" that Rawls hopes to avoid (*Theory*, 479); hence he does not elaborate it.

Reviewing the foregoing arguments, we find once again that they combine ungrounded assertions about the transformation in human perspectives that is to occur in a well-ordered society with premises that belie the foundation of Rawls's principles. It is likely that in a constitutional regime like the United States, which is dedicated to securing its inhabitants' equal rights, most citizens already feel the affirmation of their equal dignity that Rawls maintains can occur only in his utopia. As Irving Kristol has observed, preoccupation with the supposedly ruinous effects of economic inequality on people's self-esteem is far more characteristic of ambitious, secular intellectuals whose real grudge concerns the "bourgeois" character

18. Here again Rawls's assumption that focusing on redistributing wealth in the relatively short term will enable us ultimately to transcend materialistic considerations is reminiscent of Marx's doctrine.

of modern liberal society than it is of ordinary human beings who already find satisfaction in the blessings of friends, family, and religion, as well as enjoying the opportunity for advancement for themselves and their off-spring that a liberal regime provides more than any other political order.[19] It is Rawls with his difference principle who encourages indignation not only against supposed social constraints on individual advancement, but over a phenomenon that seems hardly to have troubled a single American outside Rawls's academic circle: the arbitrary "distribution" of people's natural talents and motivations.

Rawls's admission that when all is said and done, even a society based on his two principles may not be free from envy once again compels us to wonder about the value of his project, even aside from its many other difficulties. But instead of being driven to reconsider his account of justice, Rawls concludes this section on a note of radical historicism. In describing justice, he observes, "we must rely upon current knowledge," including the "scientific consensus," but must "concede that as established beliefs change . . . the principles of justice which it seems rational to acknowledge may likewise change." While Rawls cites the movement away from "the belief in a fixed natural order sanctioning a hierarchical society" as supposedly favoring his two principles (*Theory*, 480), we note that by his account, there is no such order sanctioning people's equal, inalienable rights, either. Contrary to Rawls, the mere fact that beliefs change over time does not establish that all political and moral, let alone scientific, beliefs are equally valid. We have traveled a long way here from the Declaration of Independence.[20] Again, there is much reason to doubt that Rawls has furnished a more secure foundation for liberty than Mill, let alone the Declaration.

19. Kristol, "About Equality"; cf. Lincoln, "Address to 166th Ohio Regiment," August 22, 1864, and Message to Congress in Special Session, July 4, 1861, *Collected Works of Abraham Lincoln*, 7:512, 4:437–38. Doubtless Rawls would respond that however valid Lincoln's views regarding the conduciveness of America's free institutions to the self-advancement of the common man may once have been, they were rendered outdated by the subsequent development of industrial capitalism with its "concentration" of wealth. But not only does Rawls offer no support for that claim, it is belied (as I have noted) by the continued mass immigration to this country and the statistical evidence of continuing socioeconomic mobility. (Far from being unfamiliar with industrial capitalism, Lincoln was a lawyer for large railroad corporations in the 1850s.)

20. Consider in this regard Alexander Stephens's claim that the Confederacy had improved on the Declaration by basing itself on the latest "scientific" consensus regarding the innate inferiority of black people ("Cornerstone Speech," 721–22).

Also suggestive of historicism is Rawls's remark in the introduction to *LHMP* (17–18) that the questions addressed by different philosophers are "shaped by the system of thought from within which they are asked," leaving it to "us to consider by contrast our own scheme of thought . . . from within which we now ask our questions" (cf. *LHMP*, 329 and Rawls's express agreement with the historicist view of R. G. Colling-

V.

Rawls returns to the relation between justice and the good in the follow-ing two sections, "Happiness and Dominant Ends" and "Hedonism as a Method of Choice." His aim in each case is to demonstrate the inferiority of "teleological" theories, which take their bearings by the primacy of the good, to his deontological one (*Theory*, 490–91).

Rawls explains "dominant-end" theories, which identify the human good as the maximization of some single end, as the result of seeking a method to guarantee a rational choice among alternative courses of life (*Theory*, 484). Contrary to Aristotle, Rawls denies that happiness itself can be the overall end of life, since the pursuit of happiness "as this is normally meant" seems to exclude the possibility of selfless devotion to "a righteous cause" or "furthering the well-being of others" (*Theory*, 482). Instead, Rawls defines happiness as the consequence of successfully "executing a rational plan of life already set out independently" (*Theory*, 484; recall, however, that Rawls has set out no substantive criteria for distinguishing "rational" from "irrational" plans). On the other hand, Rawls judges it "most implausible" and even "inhuman" to make one's dominant end "a personal or social objective such as the exercise of political power," the maximization of social status or wealth, or even (as Loyola maintained) personal salvation through service to God. Contrary to all such views, Rawls maintains that the human good "is heterogeneous because the aims of the self are heterogeneous." As he oddly puts it, "although to subordi-nate all our aims to one end does not strictly speaking violate the princi-ples of rational choice . . . it still strikes us as irrational or more likely as mad" to "disfigure" the self by compelling it to serve a single end (*Theory*, 485–86). (Why should it seem irrational if it conforms to Rawls's definition of rationality? And is it truly less rational to devote one's life to serving God than to make it one's chief occupation—balanced, no doubt, among

---

wood, xvi). The assumption that every thinker's outlook is constrained by his time and place may help explain Rawls's cavalier treatment of, or "creative" transformation of, the writings of such philosophers as Kant, Hobbes, and Aristotle, as well as his repre-sentation of utilitarianism and intuitionism (both relatively recent and nonsubstantive theories) as the only serious rivals to his doctrine.

In his Dewey Lectures, Rawls dismisses the likelihood that "the general beliefs ascribed to the parties in the original position" and consequently "the first principles of justice" will change as a "mere possibility," since it is hard to imagine "changes in the theory of human nature" that would refute the feasibility of its ideals "given what we know about the general nature of the world" ("Kantian Constructivism in Moral The-ory," *CP*, 352). As we have seen, however, Rawls's doctrine was not based on a realistic examination of human nature at all. On Rawls's historicism, see Rorty, "Priority of Democracy," 180–81, 186–92.

other pastimes—to count blades of grass? Finally, why should pursuing a single end "disfigure" the self by Rawls's account, given his claim that in the just society we each participate in one another's accomplishments, so that even the single-minded saint still somehow shares in the joys of grass counting as well?)

Rawls will elaborate his understanding of the self two sections later. At the present, however, it bears emphasis that Rawls gives no real argument against dominant-end views except to say that they strike him as inhuman. Rawls acknowledges that even those (such as Aquinas) who hold that human life should be governed by the single end of serving God do not mean we should ignore such other goods as health, honor, long life, friendship, and recreation, but rather that we should view such goods as ministerial to people's ultimate end (*Theory*, 485). It is not obvious why such an outlook is irrational.[21] (Indeed, didn't Rawls's demand that in the well-ordered society all citizens subordinate their particular plans to the final end of achieving just institutions amount to laying down a dominant end of his own?) Rawls's critique applies no less, we note, against Aristotle's view that the good life is ultimately directed at two peaks—moral and intellectual virtue—to which other goods such as recreation are instrumental. By contrast, Rawls represents as his model of how to pursue happiness "the example of planning a holiday." The best advice he can give is that if we want to visit Paris and Rome but don't have time to cover both, we should think through our reasons for preferring each one. In the end, we simply have to choose which we most prefer doing (*Theory*, 483).[22]

I doubt that many readers will find this counsel terribly helpful. More fundamentally, Rawls's example evinces a lack of seriousness on his part

21. In fact, Rawls reportedly described himself as "a monomaniac" about his own work (Rogers, "Portrait: John Rawls," 54; Rawls, *FTR*, 10).

On the compatibility of Thomistic Aristotelianism and its teaching "that rational human beings share a conception of how it is good and best for human beings to live" with the acceptance of the inevitable diversity in the specific ways that different individuals or peoples will pursue that good under varying circumstances, see Alasdair MacIntyre, review *Enlightenment's Wake*, 808.

22. Rawls's account of arbitrary choice as the ultimate ground of one's conception of the good constitutes a democratized and softened version of Max Weber's vision of the political world as guided by the uncompromising conflict of fundamental ideals: "Ultimate *Weltanschauungen* clash, world-views among which in the end one has to make a choice" ("Politics as a Vocation," 117). By softening Weber's value relativism, Rawls obscures its antiliberal implications. Although Rawls distinguishes Isaiah Berlin's position from Weber's on the ground that the latter, not the former, rests on "value skepticism and voluntarism" (*JF* 155n), it is Weber who sees more deeply into the "tragic" implications of the view that ultimate values are irreconcilable and incommensurable. See Eden, *Political Leadership*, chaps. 5–7; Strauss, *Natural Right and History*, chap. 2; Strauss, "Relativism."

about the human good.[23] In keeping with his relativistic standard, it just consists in the pursuit of idiosyncratic forms of entertainment tailored to one's preferences: different strokes for different folks.[24] The particular dilemma Rawls cites to illustrate the burden of decision is significant: having to choose between seeing "both the most famous church in Christendom and the most famous museum," Rawls would wish to visit a church to observe the monuments that others built to their faith, just as he would visit a museum "to study certain styles of art" (*Theory*, 483). His outlook exemplifies the emptiness that Nietzsche attributes to modern Europeans who think themselves "latecomers" on earth, regarding themselves as superior to previous generations because they can look on all religious beliefs, modes of art, and substantive philosophic teachings from a distance, comparatively and "scientifically," but actually inferior to their predecessors because no vision of beauty, of truth, or of God gives meaning to their own lives.[25] Rawls's ideal society exemplifies Tocqueville's fear that the unprecedented legal and social freedom enjoyed by modern democratic man could degenerate into a boring homogeneity bereft of any vision of greatness.[26] The profoundest critique of this outlook is Nietzsche's account of the "last man," who has lost his distinctive humanity because he has no serious goals to live for, pursuing trivial pleasures to while the time away before his peaceful death.[27] Doesn't Aristotle's distinction among work (necessary occupation), leisure (intrinsically choiceworthy activities befitting a free human being), and recreation, with recreation being instrumental to work, and work in turn a means to noble or choiceworthy activities, make infinitely more sense out of our lives, and correspond better to our commonsense understanding, than Rawls's touristic approach to life?[28] Doesn't admiration for those whose accom-

23. As noted by Bloom, "Justice," 659, and Barber, "Justifying Justice," 310. See also Gourevitch, "Rawls on Justice," 500–501.

24. Although such earlier liberal thinkers as Hobbes and Locke espoused a subjectivist view of the individual's positive good, as noted earlier, they did not seek to deter individuals from pursuing a "dominant end" so long as no one else's natural rights were violated as a consequence. Whereas they were aiming simply to secure political tolerance for a variety of ways of life, Rawls's subjectivism is more radical because of his demand that all pursuits receive equal "public esteem."

25. Nietzsche, *On the Advantage and Disadvantage of History for Life.*

26. Tocqueville, *Democracy in America*, vol. 2, pt. 1, chap. 12; vol. 2, pt. 2, chaps. 11, 17; vol. 2, pt. 3, chaps. 17, 19.

27. Nietzsche, *Thus Spoke Zarathustra*, in *The Portable Nietzsche*, prologue, 125–26; cf. Bloom, "Justice," 655, 662.

28. See Aristotle *Politics* 1133a30ff; *NE* 10.6–8. I emphasize that to describe a hierarchy of human activities as Aristotle does is not to deny that the good is heterogeneous. There is a big difference between saying that our good cannot consist entirely in a single activity such as contemplation, given our complex nature as rational animals

plishments are greatest move the rest of us to strive to make the best use of our own lives? (Recall Rawls's own favorable judgment of "emulative envy" earlier in the chapter—a pale reflection of noble emulation based on admiration rather than on envy.) Are all opinions about the good ultimately reducible as Rawls believes to mere preferences, so that all "rationality" means is figuring out the relative strength of your desires?[29]

Surely it takes considerable presumption on Rawls's part, or (otherwise put) a remarkable narrowness of view combined with a certain smugness, to dismiss the ways of life pursued or advocated by Aristotle, Loyola, and Aquinas (and by implication, Churchill and Beethoven) as irrational, proffering as the healthier alternative the life of the endless tourist.[30] In any event, Aristotle and Aquinas, who aimed to guide human beings toward their substantive good, did not put forth their views merely to provide a "method" of choice, as Rawls suggests.

Turning to hedonism, Rawls's chief criticism is once again that it "fails to define a reasonable dominant end" (*Theory*, 488). He pays no regard to the great classical (notably Lucretius) or modern (Hobbes and Locke) hedonists, but cites Wittgenstein and a variety of present-day scholars who deny that there is any "special experience" of pleasure to which all choice can be understood as ministerial (*Theory*, 489–90). Just as Rawls reduced Aristotle and Aquinas to methodologists, he disregards the substantive claims about the good made by serious philosophical hedonists (such as the Epicurean deprecation of public life in favor of private self-cultivation). Rawls, however, isn't interested in hedonism; his purpose is just to confirm that like other teleological doctrines, it is erroneous because it derives the right from the good. According to Rawls, "we should not attempt to give form

(*NE* 1154b20ff), and holding that all pursuits must be regarded as equally meritorious and constitutive of the human end. Cf. Galston, *Liberal Pluralism*, 31.

29. Here Rawls effectively agrees with the hedonistic/utilitarian view of Bentham, who famously claimed on that ground that pushpin is of equal value with poetry (*The Rationale of Reward*, pt. 3, chap. 1). But Bentham at least qualified that judgment by remarking that pushpin is an "innocent" enjoyment. Closer to Rawls's position, given his opposition to restricting what are thought to be degrading sexual practices, is Justice William O. Douglas's equation of the taste for masochism with that for Chopin (*Ginzburg v. United States*, 383 U.S. 463 [1966], at 489).

30. Rawls's judgment of the ways of life of history's great men as irrational recalls Hegel's comment on the scholar who explains away great individuals for sake of his own self-satisfaction at not having been one of them (*The Philosophy of History*, introduction, 32). Rorty acknowledges that Rawls's curt dismissal of the views of Nietzsche and Loyola "seems shockingly ethnocentric," but he defends it on the ground that human reason is incapable of transcending the outlook of "our historical situation" ("Priority of Democracy," 187–88). (Of course, Rorty thereby claims to transcend *his* historical situation by knowing the limits to reason's capacity.)

to our life by first looking to the good independently defined," since "it is not our aims that primarily reveal our nature but rather the principles that we would acknowledge to govern the manner in which they are to be pursued" (*Theory*, 489–91). He still offers no justification for this account of human nature.

As Rawls's demonstration of the goodness of justice approaches its culmination, the radically communal character of his claims is strikingly combined with a quasi-Nietzschean, though also neo-Kantian, doctrine of the self. "The self," Rawls explains, "is prior to the ends" it asserts (*Theory*, 491). Each person in a just society must "fashion his own unity" rather than act in accordance with a preexistent natural unity that he finds in himself. But he does so only within the "essential unity of the self [that is] already provided by the conception of right" (*Theory*, 493). Taken together, these remarks suggest that the doctrine of right or justice is a human construction, by which mankind imposes meaning on an otherwise arbitrary universe or, as Rawls puts it, gives "the self free reign" over the world's "contingencies and accidents" (*Theory*, 503).[31] But the self as Rawls conceives it is in essence indistinguishable from all other selves.

What little elaboration Rawls provides of these cryptic remarks is supplied in the next section, entitled "The Unity of the Self."

VI.

The indirect way in which Rawls introduces his account of the self's unity suggests that despite its seemingly momentous import, it is of only secondary significance to him. Rather than reflect on what it means to be a self or how the self is distinguished from its older counterpart, the soul, let alone elaborate how our selves or souls can be given a genuine unity, Rawls simply repeats his account of "moral personality" as embodying our capacities for a conception of the good and a sense of justice. He then asserts that each person's "unity . . . is manifest in the coherence of his plan." As we have seen, however, Rawls supplies no criterion of coherence—all pursuits are equally rational, and since there is no inherent value to deliberation itself, contradictory plans that reflect their maker's desire to change his mind are no less rational so long as he doesn't complain about the results. (And maybe complaining was part of his plan as well.)

31. In *PL* (89–129), Rawls expressly describes his doctrine as a form of "constructivism." A constructivist view was already implied in *Theory* by Rawls's notion that we "choose" rather than discover the principles of justice.

As Rawls reminds us, the aim of the parties to the original position was to "establish just and favorable conditions" for each person "to fashion his own unity" or "mode of life." But now he adds that since justice as fairness limits how we deliberate about our good, its constraints provide the self with its "unity," so that "in a well-ordered society this unity *is the same for all*," with each person's view of the good being "a subplan of the larger comprehensive plan that regulates the community as a social union of social unions" (*Theory*, 493 [emphasis added]). Thus Rawls gives a vast new scope to the enterprise of "community planning." As Rawls conceives the just social order, it is apparently impossible for human beings to form associations ("factions" in the language of *The Federalist*, No. 10) whose goals are antithetical to one another or to the common good. Since the aims of actual human beings often conflict, instead of devising political institutions to accommodate our desires while channeling them in more or less harmonious directions as the American founders did, Rawls opts to deconstruct our natures and then reconceive us into abstract selves that will fit neatly like Lego blocks into the broader, social whole. That's why Rawls's utopian society of artificial human beings, like Marx's utopia, has no need for politics.

Not only does the just society perfectly harmonize people's life plans, it also saves them the trouble of having to invent one:

> The many associations of varying sizes and aims being adjusted to one another by the public conception of justice simplify decision by offering definite ideals and forms of life that have been developed and tested by innumerable individuals, sometimes for generations. Thus in drawing up our plan of life we do not start de novo; we are not required to choose from countless possibilities without given structure or fixed contours. (*Theory*, 494)

What would appear to be problematic from the point of view of those who genuinely think in terms of fashioning their selves—the encouragement to choose an off-the-shelf model from among those our society offers[32]—constitutes a major superiority of justice as fairness over utilitarianism and other "dominant end" theories according to Rawls. The combination of "the constraints of right" with the availability of a ready-made supply of life plans designed to fit our society's overall plan is what makes

32. Consider, for instance, Mill, *On Liberty*, chap. 3, 153–57. Mill remarks that "he who lets the world . . . choose his plan of life for him, has no need of any other faculty than the ape-like one of imitation. He who chooses his plan for himself, employs all his faculties" (156).

"the indeterminacy of the conception of the good . . . much less trouble-some." In other words, there are fewer options to choose among once they are restricted by "the constraints of right." Besides, Rawls reminds us, within those constraints, "there need be no standard of correctness beyond that of deliberative rationality" (*Theory*, 494). That is, it doesn't really mat-ter what life plan you choose (so long as it is a just one), since all ways of life must be deemed equally meritorious anyhow.

Far from pursuing what might have seemed like the radically individu-alistic implications of his doctrine about the self as its own source of unity, Rawls reminds us that the "unanimity condition" for selecting his princi-ples of justice "is suited to express even the nature of a single self," since the veil of ignorance was instituted to ensure that everyone reasons iden-tically. Whereas utilitarianism imposes the difficult or impossible task of "maximiz[ing] the aggregate fulfillment" of the disparate plans that differ-ent individuals develop with "full information," in justice as fairness "all agree ahead of time upon the principles" that limit their claims. While nonconforming plans "must be revised," the result is our full participation in a community in which (as stated earlier) "the self is realized in the activ-ities of many selves" (*Theory*, 494–95). Thus the great advantage of justice as fairness over utilitarianism is that by closing off all sorts of life choices—through the veil and the resulting "constraints of right"—and then assur-ing us that the remaining choices we make within that framework are all equally acceptable, it alleviates the burden of social as well as individual choice. (Ignorance is bliss!)[33]

Again, we note how Rawls's passion for theoretical neatness is pursued at the expense of empirically considering what will actually serve the human good. But can anyone be persuaded that we would be better off if both government and the individual tried to make their most fundamental choices on a basis of ignorance, just to make it easier to arrive at pre-dictable and harmonious results? And isn't Rawls's fully planned society reminiscent of the inhuman homogeneity of Huxley's *Brave New World?* It is a world without conflict, but also without aspiration or nobility.

At last, in a manner that formally parallels Socrates' endeavor in book 9 of the *Republic*, Rawls directly addresses the question of whether acting justly "accords with the individual's good." Rawls emphasizes at the out-set that he is not addressing the egoist who is committed to pursuing "his

---

33. Contrast Aristotle's view, which corresponds more closely to our commonsense perspective, that while the human good is in principle determinate and hence know-able, it is justice that is indeterminate, since the balancing of different goods that it entails must vary with the circumstances of different regimes and with the outcome of political debate in them (see Yack, *Problems of a Political Animal*, 166–68).

own interests" above all; rather, he is speaking only of "the members of a well-ordered society" who already desire to be just and asking whether "this regulative sentiment is consistent with their good" (*Theory*, 497–98). Naturally, once he has excluded those who don't regard justice in his sense as conducive to their good, this isn't a very hard problem.[34] The case against injustice, Rawls explains, includes the "psychological costs" of having to deceive others; the difficulty of avoiding doing harm to those dear to oneself in a well-ordered society characterized by broad "ties of affection and fellow feeling"; and being deprived of the "great good" that comes from "participating in the life" of such a society. Positively, "acting justly is something we want to do as free and equal rational beings" so as "to express our nature as free moral persons" (*Theory*, 499–501).

Any persons who nonetheless find that "the affirmation of their sense of justice" is not beneficial for them may properly be threatened with penalties to make them comply with the rules of justice, Rawls holds, since they benefit from other people's observance of those rules. (He avoids considering whether some might doubt that obeying the difference principle, or the rule that government may not prohibit degrading or shameful religious or sexual practices, actually does benefit them or their fellow citizens.) Should just arrangements "not fully answer to their nature," Rawls responds, "their nature is their misfortune." In other words, we are tempted to say, if you're the kind of person for whom justice as fairness is good, then justice as fairness is good for you. But Rawls is confident that "granted a reasonable interpretation of human sociability," it will "seldom" be necessary to invoke "constraining arrangements to insure compliance" (*Theory*, 503–5).

It is hard to know what this confidence rests on. Rawls has not merely avoided trying to demonstrate the value of justice to the potentially unjust man (such as Glaucon in Plato's *Republic* or Callicles in the *Gorgias*), he has written off as irrelevant and unworthy of consideration the beliefs of all those who seek to live lives of heroism or piety for whom a society dedicated to the maximization and proper distribution of primary goods fur-

---

34. Rawls's student Paul Weithman reports that part 3 was Rawls's "favorite part of *Theory of Justice*," because it addressed "the most difficult question in moral philosophy: the question of why it is good to be just" ("John Rawls: A Remembrance," 9). But once one has excluded those "egoists" who aren't interested in being just in the first place, the problem's difficulty would appear to have vanished.

For a thoughtful account of how John Locke's teaching, by contrast, offers a plausible ground for individual responsibility (including respect for other people's rights), the desire to actualize our capacity as free and rational beings who appreciate the linkage between our own long-range interest and the good of our country, see Mark Blitz, *Duty Bound*, chap. 8. See also the references in note 11 to chapter 7 above; and Martin Diamond, *As Far as Republican Principles Will Permit*, chap. 21.

nishes rather unpromising terrain. Meanwhile, he effectively calls into question people's duty to live justly in existing societies through his near-misanthropic remark that "the often squalid behavior of others" as well as "the injustice of [existing] institutions" makes it "easier to endure" the psychological costs of living an unjust life (*Theory*, 499).[35] Here we observe how neo-Kantian idealism can tend in practice, paradoxically, to encourage neglect of one's duties to actual human beings and the society in which one lives—an outlook exemplified, for instance, by Henry David Thoreau, who in "Civil Disobedience" disparages his fellows for not living up to his standards and explains his own refusal to engage in lawful political action on behalf of justice by saying that he doesn't have the time to waste.[36]

Thus Rawls has not only failed in his aim of establishing the priority of the right to the good, he has provided an alibi for unjust behavior. Justice cannot truly be prior to the good, because of the fact—recognized by practically all philosophers (outside the Kantian tradition) and thoughtful statesmen—that human beings are primarily attached by nature to the pursuit of their good, and that they consequently establish political communities (as Aristotle observes) for the sake of living well. Justice is of necessity derivative from the good because its essence is the proper distribution of things—honors, offices, wealth—previously identified as good. The partial differences among various societies' views of justice ultimately reflect differing estimations of the relative rank of the things men hold good: honor, wealth, salvation, freedom, security, military glory.

What gives Kant's elevation of the just over the good (in the sense of individual self-interest) a degree of plausibility as well as nobility is that it does embody a view of the supreme human good: the claim that in acting in accordance with and for the sake of a moral law that is accessible to all rational beings, we transcend the merely animal condition and achieve a quasi-godlike status. To support this argument, Kant has no need of a veil of ignorance; rather, he appeals to the full use of human reason. As for

---

35. Contrast Rawls's denial in describing the duty of "toleration of the intolerant" that we can be released from that duty "whenever others are disposed to act unjustly" (*Theory*, 192). Curiously, Rawls seems more disposed to excuse unjust *behavior* as a response to what one perceives as other people's injustice than to allow any restrictions on the advocacy of doctrines that would encourage others to act unjustly (*Theory*, 187).

36. Thoreau, "Civil Disobedience," 224, 227, 229, and especially 237 (denying that he has "any right to be satisfied with men as they are" rather than according to his "requisitions and expectations of what they and I ought to be"). For the Kantian roots of Rawls's and Thoreau's misanthropy, consider the remark in "Theory and Practice" (pt. 3, 87) that we would be obliged to "hate or despise" the human race if we lacked grounds for confidence that it "will always progress and improve, so that the evils of the past and present will vanish in the future good."

Kant's political teaching, it is based on a liberal doctrine of equal rights that is similarly accessible to all and is designed to satisfy the legitimate aspirations of all human beings, rather than to serve the interests only of a favored class. By contrast, to erect an account of justice—and, ultimately, of the good—as Rawls does, on the basis of an artificially constructed notion of "personhood" that (by his acknowledgment) is historically relative, motivated chiefly by the desire to simplify or systematize our judgments, lacks the persuasiveness of either Kant's moral argument or the liberal natural-rights doctrine.

VII.

In the final section of *Theory* Rawls returns to the problem of how to justify a moral theory. Little need be said about these remarks other than that they confirm the narrowly academic character of his perspective. Acknowledging the limitation that he has tested his theory only against "the leading traditional theories" (actually, the only alternative theory to which he has given consistent attention is utilitarianism), Rawls says that he has done the best he can, and that he hopes to have indicated though "not proved" that "a finally adequate theory (if such exists) will look more like the contract view than any of the other doctrines we discussed" (*Theory*, 509). In fact, the essential limitation of Rawls's theory has been its failure to consider the substantive views of justice and the good held by real human beings and the actual context of political life in which those views are advanced and debated—to say nothing of the teachings of the Western philosophical tradition as a whole. Not only does Rawls remain oblivious to this problem, he concludes with the breathtaking claim that to join him in "see[ing] our place in society" from the perspective of the original position "is to see it *sub specie aeternitatis*" and to regard it "not only from all social but also from all temporal points of view" (*Theory*, 514). It is as if merely abstracting (as Rawls believes he has done) from our actual religious, political, and moral beliefs enables us to look upon the world as if we were gods. (And this, only a few pages after Rawls represented his doctrine as historically relative and then conceded that it builds on concepts that are far from "ethically neutral" or therefore free from possible bias, but he chose to "leave aside" that problem [*Theory*, 507].)

Rawls ends *Theory* with an uncharacteristically elegant turn of phrase to the effect that "purity of heart, if one could attain it, would be to see clearly and to act with grace and self-command from this point of view" (*Theory*, 514). But he has done nothing to justify that claim. If anything, such aspects of Rawls's teaching as his encouragement of envy, his deprecation of the obligation to law-abidingness in existing societies, and his implicit excuse for unjust conduct based on other people's allegedly "squalid behavior" are likely to have an opposite moral effect. Despite his closing line, Rawls is far from a moralist in any conventional sense, if we mean someone who encourages his audience toward right action in their daily lives. Unlike Kant, who sought to elevate humanity through a demanding morality of duty, Rawls has focused only on advancing a consensus on justice that would ostensibly right the world's wrongs through institutional improvement. Devoting oneself to advancing Rawlsian justice, unlike practicing justice as ordinarily understood, costs the agent no sacrifices. Representing oneself as a partisan of the less advantaged because one votes for political candidates who purport to favor their interests is a far cry from practicing genuine acts of charity.[37] In fact, although one would never know this from Rawls's writings, the United States, the world's preeminent "capitalist" nation, has a per capita rate of voluntary, charitable giving far exceeding that of other major developed countries.[38]

37. Undoubtedly, wealthy people who support political candidates promising programs of redistributive taxation believe they are making enormous sacrifices. How far this is genuinely the case, or how far it constitutes a pursuit of psychic "income" at the expense less of their own pocketbooks (given the availability of all sorts of tax shelters) than of their country's prosperity and the real opportunities it affords to the less advantaged, is a question calling for more detailed political, economic, and psychoanalytic inquiry than can be undertaken here. Consider Gregg Easterbrook's observation of the disappointment of American academics that most Americans don't resent the wealthy as they ought to (*Progress Paradox*, 156–57), and Daniel Henninger's reflections on how the growth of the entitlement state and its "bloodless charity from afar" beginning in the 1960s contributed to the erosion of the charitable impulse among our "elites" and the rise of self-absorption now decried by liberal (and conservative) social critics ("It Took 30 Years to Un-Learn Acts of Charity"). See also Lasch, *Revolt of the Elites*, 450n, on the depersonalization of moral obligation or ostensible compassion toward the poor, the burden of supporting which, when "exercised through the agency of the state . . . falls not on the professional and managerial class, but, disproportionately, on the lower-middle and working classes." For an illustration of Henninger's and Lasch's observations, see the June 20, 1999, column by the *New York Times Magazine*'s resident "Ethicist," Randy Cohen, "Uncharitable View," discouraging readers from donating to charity on the ground that providing for the needy is properly the job of government, not private individuals.

38. In 2002 the average American contributed $953 to charity, while averages in France, the Netherlands, and Japan were $380, $275, and $15, respectively (Worldwatch Institute, *Vital Signs 2002*, cited in Easterbrook, *Progress Paradox*, 131, 340). Consider also Easterbrook's well-founded observation of the disposition among America's social-intellectual elite "to denounce materialism in others while lusting for [material goods] ourselves" (145), a disposition comically portrayed in David Brooks's *Bobos in Paradise*. In 2003 Americans donated $241 billion to charity, or 2.2 percent of our gross domestic product—an amount "larger than the entire economies of most nations"

Although it is characteristic of the liberal tradition exemplified by Montesquieu and by the authors of *The Federalist* to rely on institutional devices more than religious or moral suasion to promote justice, such authors never claimed that institutional changes could engender the far-reaching transformation of human attitudes that Rawls anticipates from the adoption of his theory. In fact, through his disparagement of penal sanctions for criminal behavior and his disregard of such devices as federalism and administrative decentralization as means of promoting civic spirit, as well as his rejection of public encouragement of religion and legal enforcement of sexual morality, Rawls provides far less institutional support for virtue than the American founders did. And the American people's historical disposition to charity reflects both a religious heritage and a sense of personal responsibility that teachings like Rawls's can only weaken. Meantime, Rawls's doctrine of the autonomous self whose ultimate right is the freedom to alter its commitments tends to encourage the worst aspects of modern individualism, as conceived by Tocqueville. At a time when more serious and realistic observers were expressing concern about the erosion of America's "social capital"—this is, the disposition toward active concern with the welfare of one's community and country[39]—Rawls wrote as if all it took to build a harmonious and prospering community were a combination of economic redistribution, the freedom to live as one wished (within his specified limits), and fortification of everyone's self-esteem (merited or not).

Beyond the unlikelihood that his doctrine can provide a real basis for social unity, let alone elevate the situation of society's poorest members, Rawls's delusion that his political vision provides us with a godlike perspective is far from encouraging other important virtues (or elements of "purity of heart") such as moderation, tolerance, and a disposition toward self-questioning. He offers a purported recipe for achieving societal justice without any prescription for actually making human beings more just.[40] Rawls's admirers to the contrary notwithstanding, there is thus much reason to doubt that his teaching is morally edifying any more than it is philo-

---

(George Melloan, "'Tis the Season to Be Generous, Thoughtfully"). In 2004, according to the 2006 Index of Global Philanthropy issued by the Hudson Institute, besides U.S. governmental development aid of $19.7 billion, Americans privately donated at least $71 billion to the developing world ("American Generosity," *Wall Street Journal* editorial).

39. For a good brief summary of these concerns, see Jean Bethke Elshtain, *Democracy on Trial,* chap. 1. See also Michael Sandel, *Democracy's Discontent.*

40. Cf. Wiggins, "Neo-Aristotelian Reflections," 487, 509; Daniels, "Expensive Talk"; and note 22 to chapter 7 above.

sophically profound.[41] We are very far here from the genuinely elevated spirit of a Mother Teresa. One might rather call it "purity lite."

There is a marked contrast between the conventionality of Rawls's specific policy recommendations (such as public campaign financing and antitrust enforcement) and the Nietzschean, apocalyptic rhetoric by which he justifies them, such as the claim that they enable us to act *sub specie aeternitatis* and overcome the world's "arbitrariness," as if it were up to the present generation of human beings and its immediate successors to improve on the job that God somehow botched.[42] One wonders how far Rawls ever considered the implications of his project of compensating for the arbitrariness of nature or fortune: could even the fullest effort to alleviate the lot of the least advantaged (however defined) seriously mitigate the arbitrariness of the fate of individuals? Despite the relative mildness of most of his policy proposals (leaving aside his tentative speculations on eugenic policy, the possible abolition of the family, a lump-sum tax on natural assets, etc.), Rawls's endeavor to remake the world so as to overcome its arbitrariness exhibits the same dangerously utopian and potentially fanatical spirit that characterized the totalitarian ideologies that generated so much evil during the twentieth century.[43] The passions it evokes are not dissimilar from those now found among radical Islamists.

41. Weithman compares Rawls's mandate that our plans of life conform to the demands of justice to the Pauline commandment to love thy neighbor ("John Rawls," 8). But what kind of love is it to leave others free to pursue their idiosyncratic life plans, however foolish or self-destructive, while focusing attention on maximizing the wealth of the least advantaged, and even encouraging their envy, all the while purporting to deny that wealth-maximization should be one's goal? (Similarly, despite Weithman's describing Rawls as exemplifying the prophet Micah's command that we "love tenderly, walk humbly and live justly," I have tried to bring out the underlying presumption of Rawls's doctrine and even its tendency toward misanthropy. Interestingly, Weithman omits Micah's call to walk humbly "with our God," which offers a ground for humility that is lacking in Rawls's doctrine as it is in Kant's.)

42. It is in his assignment to humanity of a function formerly attributed to the biblical God, along with his elevation of justice over all other goods, that Rawls is most thoroughly "Kantian." But the history of German philosophy since Kant's attempted elevation of human will to a position of sovereignty over the world exhibits the deeply problematic consequences of that fateful move, consequences of which Rawls seems unaware. See Bernard Yack, *The Longing for Total Revolution*, especially 110–25 and chap. 8.

For this reason it is misleading to view *Theory*, as both defenders and critics sometimes do, as merely an apologia for the New Deal or the War on Poverty, along with the "neutrality" principle regarding religion enunciated by the Warren Court. For the latter interpretation of Rawls's neutrality principle, see Brian Barry, "How Not to Defend Liberal Institutions," 49–50.

43. Cf. Cohn, *Pursuit of the Millennium*, 182, on the aspiration of the medieval Brethren of the Free Spirit, a chiliastic sect, "to surpass the condition of humanity and to become God."

Since this most deeply problematic aspect of Rawls's thought has scarcely been noted in the scholarly literature some elaboration (drawing partly on his later writings) is in order here. My suggestion is that in contrast with the core tradition of American reform movements (beginning with the Revolution itself), Rawls's program suffers from a dangerous immoderation because it rejects the very notion that nature can be a ground of justice (and hence, at the same time, a limit to human willfulness in the name of justice). Without presupposing any sort of biblical faith, I submit that there is an elemental human wisdom in the acceptance of God's judgment of the goodness of His creation (Genesis 1:31) that contrasts with Rawls's determination to overcome its "arbitrariness." (Consider in particular the presumption that underlies Rawls's difference principle: the determination to regard human capacities as "a collective asset," even though this is not at all how we are equipped with them by nature—or by God.) Indeed, once one adopts the principle of compensating for nature's arbitrariness, it becomes hard to explain why we should stop at redressing "undeserved" natural inequalities among human beings, rather than compensating other animal species for nature's failure to supply them with reason or other distinctively human faculties.[44]

The apocalyptic outlook that Rawls's teaching encourages (however inadvertently), as a consequence of his determination to remake the world to accord with his intuitions, is most fully manifest in his remark in the last paragraph of his 1996 introduction to *PL:* "if a reasonably just society that subordinates power to its aims is not possible and people are largely amoral, if not incurably cynical and self-centered, one might ask with Kant whether it is worthwhile for human beings to live on the earth" (*PL*, lxii).[45]

44. Lest the reader underestimate the inventiveness of today's philosophy professors in this regard, one might consider Ingmar Persson's contention that "justice demands that humans and non-humans be so treated that the value of their lives (to them) be as equal as possible," and Martha Nussbaum's sketch of "a truly global" (i.e., interspecies) justice in her 2006 book (dedicated to Rawls's memory) *Frontiers of Justice.* (See Persson, "A Basis for [Interspecies] Equality," 191; Nussbaum, *Frontiers of Justice,* 405 and ch. 6, *passim*). Nussbaum attributes the dismissal of her "projects" for expanding the domain of justice as utopian to a cynicism born of the belief "that mutual advantage is the only cement for a liberal political culture" (414), that is, to the disposition of real human beings to ask (as other animals cannot) why they should be bound by rules that do not manifestly serve their well-being. Thus does professorial willfulness, masquerading as a commitment to justice, seek an ever-more-comprehensive empire over the human community.

45. In fact, the remark Rawls cites from Kant (*Theory,* lxiii n) says only that human existence would lose its value if "justice [*Gerechtigkeit*] perishes"; the context refers to the duty to enforce merited punishment against those who violate the criminal law (*Metaphysical Elements of Justice,* pt. 2, sec. 1, E1, 100 [Akad. ed. 6:332]; emphasis added). One can hardly equate the failure to approximate Rawls's utopian view of a just world order with the "perishing" of justice in Kant's (more elemental) sense.

Rawls poses this same question, this time regarding the response to the absence of a just world order, in the closing line of *LP,* cited in chapter 13 below.

Why does Rawls exclude the possibility envisioned by such sober liberal thinkers as Locke and the authors of *The Federalist*, as well as by Aristotle, that a reasonably just society is attainable even if most people are "largely amoral" or at least self-centered, so long as institutions are properly designed to channel their interests in ways that promote the public good— and institutional design is supplemented by familial religious and moral instruction?[46] Would it not make more sense for an advocate of justice to try to adapt political institutions to human nature to achieve that end, rather than demand that human beings be remade to fit one's vision of how they ought to be?

The curious or perverse sort of practical judgment that Rawls's apocalyptic or millenarian outlook may in turn generate is visible in his astonishing suggestion in *JF* that the contemporary United States may be no more democratic than "Germany between 1870 and 1945"—that is, including the Nazi period—and his reference in *LP* to the American government as only an *"allegedly* constitutional democratic regime" (*JF,* 101n; *LP,* 53 [emphasis added]). Such remarks certainly render Rawls liable to the charge of ingratitude. Other instances of this ingratitude can be seen in his periodic denunciations of what he represents as present-day America's "grave injustices," such as the lack of public campaign financing, the existence of "a widely disparate distribution of income and wealth," and the failure to provide "important constitutional essentials such as health care for many who are uninsured" (*PL,* 407). What is at issue here is not the validity of Rawls's positions on these issues, but whether even a sober-minded critic who shares his policy views can justify regarding the problems Rawls cites as injustices so fundamental as to erase the enormous difference between the justness of America and that of most other political regimes, past or present.

It seems evident that even if the United States instituted universal public campaign financing and complete government-financed health care, Rawls would have found other reasons for denying her the claim to justice: amid the ivied walls that overlook the Charles River, and elsewhere, such postures of moral superiority are typically far better received than parochial applause for one's country and its political regime. Hence Rawls maintains in *PL* that not only the U.S. but every society "contains grave injustices," or

46. The contrast between Rawls's approach and that of "classical theorists of the American polity" such as Madison is noted by Kukathas and Pettit, *Rawls,* 126, 137. Cf. Montesquieu, *Spirit of the Laws,* bk. 20, chap. 20, 389–90: "Happily, men are in a situation such that, though their passions inspire in them the thought of being wicked, they nevertheless have an interest in not being so." In book 21, where he makes this observation, Montesquieu shows how institutions that promote commerce and encourage the peaceful pursuit of economic gain help overcome people's cruel and vindictive passions. See also Mansfield, "Party Government," 944–45, as well as Aristotle *Politics* 4.1.

at least that "we may assume that every society is more or less unjust—usually gravely so" (*PL*, 398–401).[47] Such blanket judgments do not so much excuse Rawls's ingratitude as deepen it, by effectively putting the U.S. and other constitutional republics on the same moral level as the worst of regimes. This is the way in which despots once used the Christian doctrine of original sin, as Machiavelli and Montaigne observed, to excuse their own vices. It was also the characteristic device of Western apologists for Communist tyranny (who claimed that communism provided "social and economic rights" that counterbalanced the lack of personal or political freedoms).[48]

Rawls's lack of appreciation for the constitutional democracy he had the good fortune to inhabit is as I have noted the obverse of his abstract ideal-

---

47. Such an outlook is hardly peculiar, of course, to Rawls and other scholars of analytic philosophy. Witness the recent judgment by the prominent political sociologist Charles Tilly that the U.S. is a "deeply flawed democracy," and that "no European national regime, past or present" has been truly democratic, since in all such regimes some people have more political influence than others (*Contention and Democracy in Europe, 1650–2000*, ix). A prominent British-born fan of Rawls's work, Columbia University law professor Jeremy Waldron, applauds what he calls the "healthy lack of moderation [*sic*] in the way Rawls presented" his "idea of a well-ordered society," adding that "the American impulse to think and talk in terms of freedom and equality for all . . . is honoured most often in the breach, and . . . principles of rights, toleration and opportunity for all remain a cruel mockery for millions of US citizens." (Waldron, one might say, practices what he praises.) Waldron is particularly concerned to refute the accusation that Rawls was "an apologist for American institutions," on account of "Rawls's reputation as a liberal and . . . liberalism's reputation as an apologia for capitalist democracy," whereas Rawls actually offered "an apology at most for the American impulse to think and talk in terms of freedom and equality for all," while his "idea of a well-ordered society is a reproach" to his country's institutions for "perhaps perfidiously" failing to live up to such claims ("The Plight of the Poor," 5). (Of course not everyone shares Waldron's opinion: see, for instance, Neil MacFarquhar, "Pakistanis Find U.S. an Easier Fit than Britain," reporting that Pakistani immigrants to America are "far better off economically and more assimilated culturally than their counterparts in Britain," owing in part to "the United States' historical ideal of being a melting-pot meritocracy.")

In his written response to a 1973 American Political Science Association panel on *Theory*, Rawls was likewise at pains to defend himself against Brian Barry's charge that he believed the United States to be a just or "nearly just" society. To the contrary, he found it "very difficult to see how anyone who has lived in this country for the past decade or so could think" such a thing ("Comments," 6). (This was the decade that had witnessed the enactment of the 1964 and 1965 Civil Rights acts, Medicare, and Lyndon Johnson's War on Poverty along with other aspects of his Great Society program.)

48. See Machiavelli, *The Prince*, chap. 18, 70 (on Pope Alexander as the most successful liar in history), and chap. 21, 88 (on Ferdinand's "pious cruelty"); Michel de Montaigne, *Essays*, bk. 2, chap. 2, 244–45; also bk. 3, chap. 9, 757–58 on the dangers of political utopianism. Following Rawls's approach, even the U.S. State Department, during the Carter administration, in its 1980 "Country Reports on Human Rights Practices" praised the Soviet Union for placing "considerable emphasis on economic and social rights" (cited in Tom Bethell, *The Noblest Triumph*, 178).

ism. At the conclusion of the 1996 introduction to *PL* he represents his account of an ideally just regime as the only alternative to a cynicism that would deny the possibility of "a just and well-ordered democratic society" (*PL*, lx). The more sensible alternative—that a society that by reasonable and historical standards is quite just and well-ordered already exists in America (along with other constitutional democracies), and that our duty as citizens is to maintain as well as try to improve it in moderate ways rather than denounce it because it doesn't fully conform to our particular policy preferences—seems not to have occurred to him. Instead, Rawls suggests that his determination "to consider how citizens need to be conceived" so as "to support a reasonably just society" helps explain the seemingly "abstract and unworldly character" of his writings. He saw no need to "apologize for that," surely not recognizing the dangers of his doctrinaire political utopianism (*PL*, lxii).

Far from providing an alternative to cynicism, Rawls's outlook ultimately encouraged it. Late in Rawls's life, one of his disciples, Joshua Cohen, reported, "His hopefulness has been shaken by the world. His feelings have soured," as the result of such things as the lack of limits on campaign contributions in America.[49] This was during the same era that much of the world was celebrating the fall of the Soviet empire, surely a far more significant development than campaign costs from the standpoint of justice and the welfare of humanity.[50] Similarly, according to Ben Rogers, in his last years Rawls moved further leftward, as he came "to despair of the capitalist welfare state, which acquiesced in a dramatic rise of social inequality in the 1980s and 90s."[51] This was the period in which America enjoyed an unprecedented economic boom that benefited all sectors of our society, beginning under Ronald Reagan and continuing through most of the Clinton years, one that helped attract millions of mostly poor immigrants to our shores. Meantime, even the Chinese government abandoned the socialist "experiment," endeavoring through economic liberalization to rival the successes of free economies in nations such as Taiwan and South Korea. In the latter two countries, as well as Spain, Portugal, and the former captive nations of central and eastern Europe, democratization triumphed as well. Picturing Rawls's gloom amidst this scene, one is reminded of Jonathan Swift's portrait of another utopian-turned-misanthrope, Captain Lemuel Gulliver.[52]

49. Rogers, "Portrait: John Rawls," 55.
50. Rawls's remarkable disregard of that world-historic event is noted by John Gray, "Can We Agree to Disagree?"
51. Rogers, "John Rawls."
52. See *Gulliver's Travels*, especially the prefatory "Letter from Capt. Gulliver to His Cousin Sympson" and bk. 4, chap. 12.

As an antidote to Rawlsian ingratitude, one might consider the reflections of a young journalist, Bret Stephens, upon visiting his grandfather's homeland in Moldova, considering what would have befallen his family had they not emigrated to America following the pogrom of 1903: "It was only because of the United States that they were saved."[53] The same is true of many millions of others, both those who came here and those who remained abroad but were rescued from totalitarian despotism and aggression thanks to America's free institutions and its people's sacrifices in defense of freedom. Shouldn't Rawls somewhere have acknowledged the vindication of Lincoln's vision of this country as freedom's "last best hope on earth"[54] instead of self-indulgently lambasting the alleged injustices of our constitutional democracy in comparison with an abstract and incoherent utopian vision?

53. Stephens, "Coming to America."
54. Annual Message to Congress, December 1, 1862, in *Collected Works of Abraham Lincoln*, 5:537. Consider Joshua Muravchik's account of the fate of Robert Dale Owen, the most distinguished of the five children of the eccentric British industrialist and founder of the failed utopian-socialist community of New Harmony, Indiana, Robert Owen (all of whom led accomplished and satisfying lives in America once they abandoned their father's socialist vision and took advantage of the real opportunities available to all in a land of lawful freedom): he "found the 'Land of Promise' not in New Harmony, but in America itself" (*Heaven on Earth*, 59).

CHAPTER 10

Political Liberalism I
Principles

Having developed his doctrine of justice as fairness over two decades, Rawls did not stand pat with it. Rather, almost immediately after *Theory* appeared, he undertook a series of clarifications and modifications in response to sympathetic critics. The most important shift in Rawls's representation of his theory first appeared in his 1974 presidential address to the American Philosophical Association, where he distinguished his enterprise of moral theory, understood as the description of "the substantive moral conceptions that people hold, or would hold, under suitably defined conditions," from "the problem of moral truth," which he proposed to "bracket" on the ground that the history of philosophy shows such a notion to be "problematical."[1] This, in effect, was Rawls's way of finessing the problem I identified in chapter 1: the cloudy identity of the "we" whose moral perceptions were to ground his theory, and the unlikelihood that merely assessing whether the theory generated consequences that "we" found intuitively persuasive would suffice to confirm its truth. As Rawls put it in a later essay, in arguing for justice as fairness he wished to "avoid . . . claims to universal truth or claims about the essential nature and identity of persons," even though he had revised his account of primary goods so that "it

---

1. "The Independence of Moral Theory," *CP,* 288. Contrast the claim in *Theory* (398) that justice as fairness rests on "true general beliefs."

clearly depends on a particular conception of persons."[2] (The key to this paradox, we shall observe, is that just as in *Theory* the conception of persons on which Rawls rests his doctrine is not an empirically grounded account of human nature, but in circular fashion is derived from what Rawls thinks are the moral entailments of a democratic theory of justice.) Rawls elaborated this approach in his 1980 Dewey Lectures, where he called it "Kantian constructivism."[3]

Rawls finally brought together a series of essays elaborating his new approach in his 1993 volume *Political Liberalism*. The book consists of three parts, each divided into a set of "lectures" (so termed to reflect the manner of their original presentation). Part 1 describes "the general philosophical background of political liberalism," while part 2 elaborates several of its main ideas: Rawls's conception of "overlapping consensus," the priority of justice over "ideas of the good," and "public reason" (*PL*, xiv). Part 3, "Institutional Framework," contains lectures on "the basic structure" of a just, liberal society and on "the basic liberties and their priority." In this chapter I consider the chief theoretical innovations of *PL*. Chapter 11 will

2. "Justice as Fairness: Political Not Metaphysical" (1985), *CP*, 388.

3. "Kantian Constructivism in Moral Theory," *CP*, 303–58. Subsequently Rawls disclaimed representing "Kantian constructivism" as Kant's own idea, explaining that he was using the adjective only by "analogy" ("Justice as Fairness: Political Not Metaphysical," *CP*, 389n). Thus the term has the same looseness as "Hobbes's thesis" and "the Aristotelian Principle." What we might term the constructivist aspect of Kant's thought is signified by his remark in the preface to the second edition of the *Critique of Pure Reason* (B xiii) that "reason has insight only into that which it produces after a plan of its own," and hence it must lay down "principles of judgment based on fixed laws" of its own devising, constraining nature" to answer reason's questions. But for Kant, these laws are demonstrated to derive from pure reason, common to all human beings, rather than following from an arbitrary and historically bound construct like Rawls's original position.

Rawls was apparently the first person to apply the term "constructivism" outside the realm of mathematics, from which he borrowed it (*PL*, 90–91n, 102n, 123), although he may have been following Dworkin's account of the Rawlsian theory as following a "constructive" rather than a "natural" or realist view of moral understanding (*Taking Rights Seriously*, 160–68). The term has since spread to disciplines ranging from international relations theory (where it signifies the belief that the world order is "socially constructed" rather than having any fixed, inherent characteristics) to pedagogy (signifying that knowledge is "constructed" rather than learned). So long as this sort of hypernominalism remains confined to academia rather than bumping up against reality, it can be expected to flourish (such doctrines do invite the query posed by economist Thomas Sowell in the title of one of his books: *Is Reality Optional*).

By contrast, the implausibility of constructing a persuasive political argument while abstaining from judgments of truth should be apparent. Consider, however, the assertion by William F. Harris II in *The Interpretable Constitution*, 14, that "'Truth' is an inapposite category in political theory." (Where, then, within the human sciences, is it appropriate?)

treat Rawls's application of his theory to a few specific political issues, followed by a more general contrast between Rawlsian liberalism and the political science of Aristotle, Locke, and Tocqueville.

I.

In accordance with the truth-in-advertising legislation that he favors (*PL*, 364), Rawls warns readers of *PL* at the outset that his conception of political liberalism may be different from what they expect (*PL*, 3). The task of political liberalism as Rawls conceives it is not to uncover the "true foundation" of a "comprehensive doctrine" for guiding political life but only to provide a conception of justice that citizens can share "as the basis of a reasoned, informed, and willing political agreement," because it is "as far as possible, independent of the opposing and conflicting philosophical and religious doctrines" they hold (*PL*, xviii, 9).

Rawls continues to represent justice as fairness, which he restates in slightly modified form in the opening section of *PL*, as the most appropriate democratic theory of justice.[4] But while he acknowledges the need for further revision of that doctrine (*PL*, xviii n), Rawls's chief objective in his second book is to answer what he seems now to regard as the prior, methodological question of how political philosophy might "find a shared basis for settling" such issues as the institutions best designed to secure "democratic liberty and equality" (*PL*, 8). In brief, his solution is to apply "the principle of toleration," previously employed to resolve the great theologico-political issues of early modernity, "to philosophy itself" (*PL*, 10).[5]

---

4. Actually, there are two restatements of the principles in *PL*, but since Rawls singles out the second in the revised edition of *Theory* (xii), it is presumably his final version. In this formulation the first principle guarantees "an equal right to a fully adequate scheme of equal basic liberties which is compatible with a similar scheme of liberties for all," while the order of the (a) and (b) clauses of the second principle (respectively the difference principle and the equal opportunity clause) is reversed, though the latter change seems inconsequential (*PL*, 291). Rawls made the first change to emphasize "that the scheme of basic liberties is not drawn up so as to maximize anything" (i.e., an undifferentiated "liberty") but to secure the conditions for actualizing people's "two moral powers" (*LP*, 19, 331–33). But neither change affects the fundamental substance or ground of the principles. In a slightly different formulation earlier in *PL* (5–6), the first principle expressly requires that the "fair value" of "the equal political liberties . . . be guaranteed," although that requirement is omitted from the later formulation. (In a note to the earlier formulation [*PL*, 5n] Rawls seems to treat them as equivalent, so presumably the "fair value" qualification is to be incorporated into the later statement.)

5. In his 1996 introduction Rawls acknowledges that the opening statement of *PL* (xxxix) fails to clearly explain the "philosophical problem" that concerns him (the possibility of a just society whose members hold conflicting but reasonable comprehensive

Rawls's new strategy originates in his recognition of what he thinks was a major weakness in his previous work: his enunciation of justice as fairness as "a comprehensive philosophical doctrine" to be endorsed by all citizens of a well-ordered society. The flaw in that assumption is that it overlooks the "pluralism of incompatible yet reasonable" religious, philosophical, and moral doctrines held by citizens in a modern democracy. To resolve the problem, Rawls now represents justice as fairness as a purely "political conception of justice," meaning that it is a "freestanding" view depending on "no specific metaphysical or epistemological doctrine," and consequently one that can be accepted by citizens who hold differing comprehensive beliefs (PL, xvi–xvii, 10–13).

The reader may wonder at this point whether the fact that adherents of various religious, philosophical, and moral doctrines already coexist peacefully in well-established constitutional democracies like the United States, almost all of them agreeing to submit conflicts over issues of legal right to orderly resolution by the political and judicial process, does not render the quest for a new theory to harmonize them superfluous. What need can there be for a new application of "the principle of toleration" to philosophy, since professors and adherents of all sorts of philosophical and pseudophilosophical doctrines in modern democracies already enjoy the greatest legal freedom to teach, believe, and advocate them?

In reality, Rawls's concern is not with toleration as usually understood but with the same quest for consensus on issues of justice that inspired Theory as well as his previous essays. Even though Rawls acknowledges the inevitability of deep disagreements over political and nonpolitical "values" in a liberal regime (PL, 44), he laments (echoing Theory) that "the course of democratic thought over the past two centuries" exhibits no agreement on how to arrange the institutions of a constitutional democracy so as to satisfy "the fair terms of cooperation" between free and equal citizens. As evidence of this lack, Rawls cites "the deeply contested ideas

---

doctrines) and seems to admit the possibility that such a society could be grounded in such rival philosophic doctrines as those of Kant and Mill, which might already "endorse a just democratic regime" for differing reasons. Hence he now stresses the problem of ensuring support for a just regime among people holding conflicting religious beliefs. It isn't clear how this explanation sits with Rawls's stress in the text on the need to apply the principle of toleration to philosophy. In the original book Rawls had acknowledged that modern constitutional regimes were no longer grounded in particular theological doctrines (PL, 10), leaving it obscure why we need a new theory to address the religious issue. His real concern, we shall see, is to guarantee the "wholehearted" (rather than merely pragmatic) endorsement of his vision of a neutral liberal state on the part of the religious, ensuring that they will ground their public arguments on purely secular, "public" reasoning.

about how the values of liberty and equality are best expressed in the basic rights and liberties of citizens," a disagreement that he believes reflects a conflict between the Lockean emphasis on personal rights and the rule of law and the Rousseauean view, "which gives greater weight to . . . equal political liberties and the values of public life" (*PL*, 4–5). The result, Rawls maintains, is an "impasse in our recent political history" over how "basic social institutions" should be organized to respect citizens' liberty and equality (*PL*, 300; see also 338, 368). He cites no actual political controversy, however, to illustrate this supposed impasse.[6]

As in *Theory*, Rawls in *PL* continues to regard the existence of disagreement over fundamental issues of justice as proof that present-day constitutional democracies are not "well-ordered" (*PL*, 4–5, 35–36; *Theory*, 5). His proposed method of resolving them is also largely the same as in the earlier book: first to "collect such settled convictions" or "attitudes" of his democratic contemporaries on particular issues as the belief that slavery and religious persecution are wrong, and then "organize the basic ideas and principles implicit in these convictions into a coherent political conception of justice." By doing so he aspires to "adjudicate between" the Lockean and Rousseauean traditions. The test of an acceptable political conception of justice is that it "accord[s] with our considered convictions,

---

6. Nor does Rawls cite any earlier period in American history as exhibiting a greater degree of the consensus he now finds lacking. In *Theory*, Rawls's only solution to disagreements over the relative weight to be assigned to personal and political liberties was the formalistic one of adjusting the extent of each freedom to maximize the total sum of liberty. The solution he proposes in its place in *PL* (333)—that instead of maximizing liberty, we "adjust the basic liberties" to accommodate the exercise of people's "moral powers"—is no less formalistic. (On Rawls's ultimate retreat from the claim that his theory will generate consensus, see chapter 12 below.)

In his Dewey Lectures, Rawls acknowledged the artificiality and historical inaccuracy of his contrast between Locke and Rousseau, but he judged it nonetheless useful "to fix ideas and . . . see that a mere splitting of the difference between these two traditions . . . would be unsatisfactory" (*CP*, 307). But if the distinction is inaccurate, how could Rawls know that there was any "impasse" between the two traditions at all?

In fact, Rawls exaggerates the differences between Locke and Rousseau, both by downplaying the centrality of Locke's concern with political liberty and by underestimating Rousseau's concern for the "basic rights of the person and of property, and the rule of law" (*PL*, 4–5). See Rousseau, *Social Contract*, bk. 2, chap. 4, 62–64 (concerning the necessary generality of laws); bk. 3, chap. 9, 95 (on "the end of the political association" as "the preservation and prosperity of its members"); and especially bk. 4, chap. 8, 130n (agreeing with the Marquis d'Argenson's Millian maxim that the individual should be left "perfectly free with regard to everything that does not harm others"). On Locke, see Robert Faulkner, "The First Liberal Democrat." On the other hand, Rawls seems unaware of the more fundamental issue between Rousseau and his liberal predecessors, which concerns the conditions of human happiness. For an overview of that issue, see Allan Bloom, *The Closing of the American Mind*, 157–72.

at all levels of generality, on due reflection," or in what Rawls had described in *Theory* as reflective equilibrium (*PL*, 5, 8, 95).

It is in view of this aspiration that Rawls's proposal for extending "the principle of toleration" to philosophy must be understood. By "toleration," Rawls does not merely mean legal freedom for various doctrines to be promulgated or accepted. Nor does he literally mean only, as he puts it later, "to leave to citizens themselves to settle the questions of religion, philosophy, and morals in accordance with views they freely affirm" (*PL*, 154), since it is obvious that citizens of constitutional democracies like the United States already enjoy this freedom to the fullest extent. Rather, what Rawls means by toleration is the detachment of government and law from any conception of the good that is rooted in a comprehensive doctrine not shared by all citizens as such (*PL*, 10, 190, 192–94, 179–80, 209). This detachment is not, Rawls emphasizes, the consequence of a mere compromise or "modus vivendi," resulting from the inability of groups holding some particular view of the good to win sufficient electoral support to secure its enforcement by government (*PL*, 145–48, 208, 249). Instead, it reflects the fundamental principle previously asserted in *Theory*, the priority of right to conceptions of the good—only Rawls now reinterprets that principle as a specifically "political" ideal based on the notion of equal citizenship.

As in *Theory*, the principles of justice limit the ways of life that citizens may pursue: any claims to pursue ends that violate those limits "have no weight" (*PL*, 147, 174, 209). But in addition, Rawls would now limit the sorts of argument that citizens may advance to promote their political agendas, and even their motives for voting (*PL*, 214–19, 224–25). For the sake of achieving a morally based political consensus centered on the principle of toleration as Rawls understands it, citizens must agree to pursue only "admissible ideas of the good"—that is, those that "respect the limits of, and serve a role within, the political conception of justice" (*PL*, 176); "the priority of right gives the principles of justice a strict precedence in citizens' deliberations and limits their freedom to advance certain ways of life" (*PL*, 209).[7]

II.

The paradox that, in the name of toleration, Rawls continues not only to enunciate potentially severe restrictions on the conceptions of the good that human beings may pursue, but aims to constrain the sort of reasoning that

7. On the questionableness of Rawls's extension of restraints on the public use of theological arguments in a liberal regime to moral doctrines as well, see Galston, *Liberal Pluralism*, 45.

citizens may use to advance their goals in the public sphere, can be better understood in the light of several concepts that he introduces in the first few chapters of *PL*. First, there is his distinction between "the reasonable and the rational," which he believes is familiar from everyday discourse. As in *Theory*, Rawls represents rationality as a purely instrumental or calculating faculty that is used to determine the most efficient means to a person's ends or to balance his "final ends by their significance for [his] plan of life as a whole"; it is consistent even with a near-"psychopathic" disposition. Reasonableness, on the other hand, Rawls explains, is a quality that disposes people "to propose principles and standards as fair terms of cooperation and to abide by them willingly," so long as others do likewise. It also entails a willingness to recognize "the burdens of judgment," that is, the variety of factors that make it unlikely that "conscientious persons with full powers of reason . . . will all arrive at the same conclusion" on a controverted issue "even after free discussion." Reasonable individuals nonetheless wish for a world in which people freely cooperate on mutually acceptable terms. Rationality and reasonableness are independent but "complementary" ideas, in that the former quality leads people to pursue ends of their own that they seek (in a just society) "to advance by fair cooperation," while the latter provides them with a sense of justice and disposes them to acknowledge the validity of other people's claims (*PL*, 48–52, 58).

Rawls's account of reasonableness again manifests the linkage between his approach and that of the social-contract philosophers of early modernity, particularly Hobbes, whose statement of the "laws of nature" underlying the foundation of civil society is mirrored in some of Rawls's language.[8] But whereas Hobbes understood conformity with his laws of nature to be a dictate of reason, simply, inasmuch as the establishment of a stable, law-governed society is manifestly in the interest of all individuals, so that he found no need for supplementing rationality with a separate faculty of "reasonableness," in Rawls's revised version of his doctrine the reasonable and the rational constitute "two distinct and independent basic ideas," each reflecting one of the two "moral powers" with which human beings are endowed. Breaking with his own previous account of the theory of justice in terms of rational-choice theory, Rawls now disclaims any intention of deriving the reasonable from the rational (*PL*, 51–52, 53n). He believes that "only as a result of philosophy, or a subject in which the rational has a large place" such as economics, "would anyone think it necessary to derive the reasonable from the rational"—that is, try to show that it is in one's interest to be just. Hence Rawls denies that "the moral skeptic" can be or needs to be answered by reason (*PL*, 52). (Others might call Rawls's policy preaching to the choir.)

8. See the second, third, fifth, eighth, and ninth laws, in Hobbes, *Leviathan*, chap. 15.

Rawls's retreat from attempting to ground his doctrine in rational-choice theory does not represent a change in his substantive view of justice, but apparently exhibits his recognition of an inconsistency in the original framework of *Theory*. Whereas in the earlier work Rawls depicted the parties to the original position as simply seeking the best deal they could get for the persons they represented in terms of primary goods, in *PL* he stresses that the parties also aim to secure our "higher-order interests . . . in developing and exercising our two moral powers" of "further[ing] our determinate conception of the good, whatever it is" and of acting justly (*PL*, 106, 180). Given Rawls's emphasis on the independence of the reasonable from the rational as he defines them, his distinction between the theory of justice and the theory of rational choice reflects the fact that advancing persons' power to act justly could not be described as the consequence of a strictly "rational" decision in the narrow, economic sense. (Of course, even in part 3 of *Theory*, Rawls had disclaimed any hope that his account of the goodness of justice would persuade a moral skeptic or "egoist.") By representing primary goods as chosen for the sake of advancing people's moral powers rather than merely to satisfy their material interests, Rawls believes he has demonstrated that justice as fairness reflects our "rational autonomy" (*PL*, 76).[9]

9. In "Kantian Constructivism in Moral Theory" Rawls argued that this move renders his doctrine immune to Schopenhauer's criticism of Kant's categorical imperative as "a disguised form of heteronomy" (i.e., subjection to the natural world as distinguished from pure reason), since it required people "to test maxims in the light of their general consequences for our natural inclinations and needs." By contrast, Rawls maintains, since the interests that guide the parties in the original position "specify their needs as moral persons, the parties' aims are not egoistic but entirely fitting and proper"; indeed, he seems to say, as moral persons, the parties are free from "the limitations of our finite nature" that "we should like to overcome" (*CP*, 318–19). But the move is merely verbal, since the primary goods that the parties seek to maximize ("powers," "liberties," "income and wealth," etc.) must have some relation to natural human needs, and cannot effectually be limited in their use to purely "moral" ends. Rawls is driven to ever more extreme levels of abstraction in an attempt to maintain the priority of justice to the human good, and to avoid acceding to critics' observation that his account of primary goods encourages materialism and individualism.

The relation of Rawls's doctrine to Kant's in *PL* (169, 199) is even more convoluted than it was in *Theory*: Rawls now represents his doctrine as a "political" view that "requires far less" than Kant's "metaphysical" one, but nonetheless asserts that it "can . . . be derived" from the Kantian view as well as from other comprehensive doctrines. Moreover, Rawls describes his political conception of justice as "itself a moral conception" that "is affirmed on moral grounds" (*PL*, 147). Whether a merely "political" conception of justice severed from the metaphysical foundation Kant provided can nonetheless justify such moral allegiance as Rawls claims for it, such that "political values normally outweigh whatever nonpolitical values conflict with them" (*PL*, 146), is highly doubtful, since Rawls must consequently renounce the idea of autonomy that underlies Kant's subordination of the good to the just (*PL*, 98). Rawls's remarkable

III.

If the express distinction between the theory of justice and rational choice theory mitigates one problem in Rawls's doctrine, however, it highlights a deeper difficulty that we have repeatedly confronted: why should real human beings care about what moral principles a group of hypothetical individuals, their judgment clouded by a veil of ignorance, might adopt? For the original social-contract philosophers, as I have observed, the reason to interest oneself in the character of a prepolitical state of nature and the motives that would induce its inhabitants to limit their natural freedom by agreeing to institute government was obvious. Because the state of nature exhibits the most fixed and fundamental human traits, freed from the concealment of conventional law and custom, it provides us with an objective basis for determining the foundation and purpose of government from the standpoint of our own deepest needs, and consequently with a standard for judging the legitimacy of actual regimes. But the reason for taking an interest in Rawls's original position is far less evident, since the parties to it are not only "both hypothetical and nonhistorical," as Rawls reminds us (*PL,* 24), but also, as I have noted, literally nonhuman (lacking particular desires or interests of their own, and ignorant even of the defining characteristics of their "constituents").[10]

Although Rawls mentions Michael Sandel's criticism on this last point, his response does little more than repeat the circularity of his previous argument, if anything further obscuring the significance of the original position. "Fairness" dictates according to Rawls that we avoid imposing a view of justice on others that favors "a particular religious, philosophical, or moral comprehensive doctrine with its associated conception of the good." The original position is simply "a device of representation" designed to facilitate "public reflection and self-clarification," helping us to see clearly "what justice requires when society is conceived as a scheme of cooperation between free and equal citizens." Rawls still hopes that by promoting greater coherence among our judgments, consideration of the original position will supply a "deeper self-understanding" by which "we can attain wider agreement." Yet in response to Sandel's charge that his

---

offhandedness about the issue is signified by his willingness to accept Kant's account of the origins of "the principles of practical reason . . . *if* we insist on saying they originate *anywhere*" (*PL,* 100 [emphasis added]; cf. note 14 *infra*).

10. Moreover, as will be discussed below, in *PL* (288) Rawls specifically denies any use in his version of contract theory for the sort of contrast drawn by Hobbes and Locke "between the situation of individuals in the state of nature and their situation in society" to judge a regime's legitimacy.

description of the original position "presuppose[s] a particular [question-able] metaphysical conception of the person" that makes the self prior to its "final ends and attachments" (so that one can achieve an impartial standpoint vis-à-vis one's conception of the good no less than toward one's particular social position), Rawls remarks that when "we simulate being in the original position, our reasoning no more commits us to a par-ticular metaphysical doctrine about . . . the self than our acting a part in a play, say of Macbeth or Lady Macbeth, commits us to thinking that we are really a king or a queen engaged in a desperate struggle for political power": it is simply a form of "role playing" (PL, 24–27).

This analogy hardly fortifies Rawls's position. Although nobody thinks that playing a villain on stage commits one to a life of iniquity, doesn't using the ostensible reasoning of a group of hypothetical individuals to determine the meaning of justice entail in some sense adopting the defin-ing characteristics of those representatives that lead to their particular choice? If the parties to the original position are highly inaccurate repre-sentations of our selves, how can their reasoning contribute to our own "self-clarification"?[11]

IV.

Unsatisfactory though Rawls's response to Sandel is, it exhibits what he describes as one of the central innovations in PL: his account of justice as fairness as a "freestanding" view that relies for support on an "overlap-ping consensus" of various comprehensive doctrines (PL, xxi, 10, 12, 97). This move, prefigured in Theory (387–88) as well as in Rawls's 1985 article "Justice as Fairness: Political Not Metaphysical," serves several purposes. First, it is designed to enhance the "stability" of justice as fairness, in the sense of its capacity to win acceptance and support among a modern dem-ocratic people. Second, it is aimed at fending off what critics such as Sandel charge are the dubious metaphysical assumptions of the Rawlsian

11. Rawls himself acknowledges that merely to deny that his theory presupposes "a metaphysical doctrine of the person" is insufficient, "for despite one's intent [such doc-trines] may still be involved." As with many such problems, his response to the need to rebut such claims "in detail" is that he cannot do so "here" (PL, 29). But his subsequent account of citizens' viewing themselves "as independent from and not identified with" any particular conception of the good or "scheme of final ends" and as "self-authenti-cating sources of valid claims" appears to entail precisely the "metaphysical" problems noted by Sandel, however Rawls may qualify these remarks in PL by saying that they concern only citizens' "political" identity (PL, 30–33). Recall as well Rawls's represen-tation of the self in part 3 of Theory (491) as "prior to the ends" it pursues.

doctrine, simply by denying that the doctrine rests on any such assumptions. Third, Rawls seems to understand it as a substantive dictate of political liberalism.[12]

As noted, in describing his conception of justice as freestanding, Rawls means that it is independent of any particular comprehensive doctrine and hence should be acceptable to citizens holding a wide variety of such doctrines. But even though justice as fairness is a limited rather than a comprehensive doctrine, its efficacy as a means of resolving political controversies requires "that the comprehensive philosophical and moral views we are wont to use in debating fundamental political issues should give way" to it in public life (*PL*, 10). Rawls's response to the question of why citizens deeply attached to particular moral views founded in religious or philosophical beliefs should agree to subordinate them in civic affairs to a freestanding view that claims no such support is twofold. First, he asserts that political "values . . . are very great values and hence not easily overridden," since they "govern the basic framework of social life—the very groundwork of our existence" and "express . . . the liberal political ideal" that political power should be exercised "only in ways that all citizens can reasonably be expected to endorse in the light of their common human reason." (Rawls apparently doesn't consider that a pious human being might hold that divine law rather than "social life" provides the ground of his existence.) Second, he asserts "that the history of religion and philosophy shows that there are many reasonable ways in which the wider realm of values can be understood" so as to make it compatible with a political conception of justice. The "plurality of not unreasonable comprehensive doctrines" facilitates an overlapping consensus among them, in which citizens each find reasons within their respective doctrines for supporting the political conception (*PL*, 139–40).

To promote such accommodation, Rawls is at pains throughout *PL* to sever justice as fairness from the acceptance of particular views on a wide variety of issues; one of the recurrent phrases in the book is that Rawls's doctrine "neither assert[s] nor den[ies]" a specific claim, or words to that effect (*PL*, 95, 113, 126–27, 150, 235).[13] Among the issues on which Rawls

12. In *Theory* (340) Rawls introduced the notion of overlapping consensus in the context of elaborating the practicability of his doctrine of civil disobedience. In *PL* Rawls bases his account of justice on that notion rather than initially aiming at a deeper consensus; the move thus represents a kind of strategic retreat.

13. As Rawls explains in his 1998 *Commonweal* interview, his policy in *PL* is to avoid "discussing anything . . . that will put me at odds with any theologian, or any philosopher" (*CP*, 621–22). This is a tall order.

In the "Reply to [Jürgen] Habermas" appended to the 1996 edition of *PL* (380), Rawls engages in a kind of modesty competition with his German counterpart: whereas

takes an agnostic stand for the sake of promoting consensus, undoubtedly the most remarkable, at least to those not schooled in contemporary philosophy, is that of the truth of moral judgments. In the third lecture Rawls represents his account of justice as a form of "political constructivism," as distinguished from "moral realism." Whereas the latter doctrine regards correct moral principles and judgments as describing "an independent order of moral values" knowable to reason, political constructivism maintains "that the principles of political justice . . . may be represented as a procedure of construction" like that which takes place in Rawls's original position. Whether they "may be represented" in this way, we observe, hardly demonstrates the value or the adequacy of such a representation. But in order to encourage consensus among adherents of differing comprehensive doctrines, Rawls explains, political constructivism ingeniously "does without the concept of truth," substituting for it "an idea of the reasonable." This does not mean, to be sure, that the constructivist conception of political liberalism denies that the truth of moral judgments can be rationally assessed, "since constructivism tries to avoid opposing any comprehensive doctrine," including moral realism. Rather, "it claims only that its procedure represents an order of political values proceeding from . . . the principles of practical reason, in union with conceptions of society and person," and that "this represented order is the most appropriate one for a democratic society marked by the fact of reasonable pluralism" (PL, 91–95).

But what can it mean to advance a particular conception of justice for popular acceptance without asserting its truth? Rawls answers this question by referring back to the notion of reflective equilibrium. Even though "the political constructivist regards a judgment as correct because it issues from the reasonable and rational procedure of construction," Rawls grants that a given procedure for selecting principles of justice may in particular cases yield unacceptable judgments. But the remedy, as explained in *Theory*, is simply to alter the procedure so that it generates the desired results. Because the process of constructing the proper procedure entails "using our reason to describe itself, and reason is not transparent to itself . . . the struggle for reflective equilibrium continues indefinitely" (PL, 96–97).

Habermas "sees his view as more modest than [Rawls's], since it is purportedly [only] a procedural doctrine that leaves questions of substance to be decided by . . . real and live participants," Rawls insists that it is his own view that "is more modest" because "it aims to be solely a political conception and not a comprehensive one." Amy Gutmann believes that Rawls's modesty in not claiming universal validity for his principles makes him "in this respect" the "wisest of the grand philosophers" ("The Central Role," 20).

Let us try to clarify this rather convoluted account. On the one hand, Rawls has borrowed his language about practical reason as the faculty by which we "produce" moral concepts—as distinguished from theoretical reason, which seeks knowledge of actual, given objects—from Kant (*PL*, 93). Yet, as in *Theory*, Rawls acts as if he can borrow whatever Kantian terminology suits him without endeavoring to demonstrate the harmony of his doctrine with the metaphysical foundations of Kant's position. (Indeed, he expressly denies the suitability of Kant's conception of human autonomy as a foundation for political liberalism precisely because Kant's position is a comprehensive one with which not everyone can be expected to agree [*PL*, 99–100; 37].[14]) On the other hand, not only does Rawls's account of the constructivist procedure as already quoted rely on the terms "correct" and "correctly," the difference in meaning of which from "truth" is obscure; in a parenthetic qualifying phrase, Rawls adds that a "rational procedure of construction" must "rel[y] on true information" (*PL*, 96). Not surprisingly, it thus appears impossible for Rawls to live up to his promise of dispensing with "the concept of truth." (Rawls presumably means to distinguish the correctness of a model of practical reason from a judgment of truth by saying that the former term simply refers to the capacity of a given model to generate judgments that "we" find acceptable. But this begs the question of why we find them acceptable: don't we inevitably suppose that our judgments embody true beliefs?)[15] How could one hope to persuade other people to accept a political teaching or proposed set of political procedures while denying that their foundations are any truer than the alternatives?

It is one thing, however, to recognize the inevitability of judgments of truth, and another to demonstrate that a given doctrine meets that criterion. Despite Rawls's emphasis on the need for reflection as the prerequisite for arriving at an adequate account of justice, nowhere in *PL*, any more than in *Theory*, does he provide much explanation of what one is to reflect *on* in pursuit of equilibrium,[16] or why we should regard any particular

14. Of course Rawls observes that the Kantian "can endorse political constructivism as far as it goes": like a political candidate following the big-tent approach, he is eager to solicit "endorsement[s]" for his doctrine from all respectable sources (*PL*, 100; cf. 211n [last sentence]). On the incoherence resulting from the post-*Theory* Rawls's selective use of Kant, see William Galston, *Liberal Purposes*, 134–39, 146–55, 158–62.

15. Cf. Galston, *Liberal Purposes*, 155–58. For a persuasive argument by a progressive liberal that liberalism presupposes moral realism, see Sotirios A. Barber, *Welfare and the Constitution*, 77–79, 86–91. Rawls pays lip service to Isaiah Berlin's view, as he interprets it, that "the realm of values is objective" even though some values must be sacrificed to fit within a given social world (*PL*, 197n); but Rawls's own doctrine of goodness as rationality as seen in *Theory* is more thoroughly relativistic than Berlin's.

16. Cf. Sandel, *Liberalism and the Limits of Justice*, 152–74, 180.

equilibrium as sufficiently stable to ground fundamental moral or political principles. If "the struggle for reflective equilibrium continues indefinitely," what security after all do Rawls's principles provide for what are treated in the Declaration of Independence as inalienable human rights, grounded in "the laws of nature and of nature's God"? (The tinge of historicism in the last chapter of *Theory* will be repeated in *IPRR*, as I note in chapter 12.)

The shakiness of the ground on which Rawls would rest the case for liberty is exhibited in his explanation of how political contructivism accounts for the wrongness of slavery. After denying that that judgment requires any grounding at all, he explains that while we may accept such judgments *"provisionally, though with confidence,"* "a fully philosophical political conception" requires that they be "coherently connected together by concepts and principles acceptable to us on due reflection." In addition, "constructivism thinks it illuminating to say about slavery that it violates principles that would be agreed to in the original position by the representatives of persons as free and equal" (*PL*, 124 [emphasis added]). Leaving aside our puzzlement as to how a doctrine could "think" anything, we wonder what it adds to the judgment that slavery is wrong to say that our artificial "representatives" would agree. We also wonder how further reflection will deepen our understanding of the wrongness of slavery, if such reflection is to dispense with judgments of truth. And doesn't that "provisionally" make the security of our right to freedom just a bit shaky, as if we cannot entirely depend on our representatives (or more precisely, philosophy professors who interpret their judgments) not to sacrifice it for the sake of some as yet undeveloped theory?

The reason for Rawls's endeavor to replace the Declaration's unequivocal derivation of our right to freedom from nature, and the Lockean reasoning on which that claim is founded, is not only that he doesn't believe nature can be a ground of rights (rather than a source of "arbitrariness" to be overcome by human will), but that he finds the Declaration's substantive doctrine unsatisfactory. In the 1996 introduction to *PL*, Rawls endorses the complaint of "Hegel, Marxist, and socialist writers" that the liberties guaranteed by the Declaration "taken alone are . . . purely formal" and amount to at best "an impoverished form of liberalism"(*PL*, lviii). But rather than enriching liberalism, it would be more accurate to say that Rawls was now joining Marx in *rejecting* liberalism and its prioritization of liberty in favor of socialism. Despite his continued professions of liberalism and of adherence to "our" considered convictions of justice, by 1996 Rawls was explicitly attempting to replace American constitutional liberalism with a Marxian subordination of the individual to the supposed interests of "society"—a move already anticipated by his "threshold" for limiting the priority of liberty in *Theory*.[17] Indeed, in *PL*, going beyond his qualifications to the priority of liberty in *Theory*, Rawls explains, in response to the suggestion of a Marxist critic, that it "must be assumed" that the first principle of justice guaranteeing "equal basic rights and liberties" is "preceded by a lexically *prior* principle requiring that citizens' basic needs be met," thereby elaborating the previous excuses he (inadvertently?) offered to the world's despots for denying their subjects the most essential human rights (*PL*, 7, 7n [emphasis added]; see also *JF*, 44n). (Isn't freedom from arbitrary confiscation, imprisonment, torture, and execution at least as basic a need as a balanced diet?[18]) In continuing to hold that his difference principle "underwrites the worth" of the "basic" rights and liberties (*PL*, 6), Rawls again implies that those freedoms would be without adequate worth to merit support in the absence of redistributionist economic policies. And he continues to ignore the link between the economic freedoms he consigns to secondary status and the other liberties he purports to secure.[19]

17. Rawls believes that Marx "greatly values" political liberty, citing his *On the Jewish Question* (*JF*, 177n). In fact, in that virulently anti-Semitic work, no less than in his later writings, Marx anticipates the ultimate obliteration of the political, as well as of "the so-called rights of man," as exemplified by the guarantees of religious freedom contained in American state constitutions as well as the French Declaration of the Rights of Man and Citizen, through the actualization of man's supposed "real" nature as a "species being." He praises *"political* emancipation" only as a temporary means to that end. Contrary to Rawls's ostensible belief in the "inviolability" of each individual, the Marxian work he draws on for support denies any meaning to "the rights of man" because they treat each individual "as a self-sufficient monad"; instead of upholding "egoistic" individual rights in the 1791 declaration, Marx maintains, the French revolutionary authorities should have "punished" egoism "as a crime." See Tucker, ed., *The Marx-Engels Reader*, 40–43, 51 (emphasis in original); also note Rawls's concern to fend off the charge that his purported variant of liberalism is "arbitrarily biased" in favor of "individualism," i.e., the elevation of individual rights over the supposed interest of society (*PL*, 190).

18. Rawls's source for his new qualification (R. G. Peffer, *Marxism, Morality, and Social Justice*) explicitly ordains, on the page Rawls cites (10), that such rights as "freedom of speech and assembly, liberty of conscience and freedom of thought, freedom of the person along with the right to hold (personal) property, and freedom from arbitrary arrest and seizure" must be subordinate to the securing to all of "a minimum level of material well-being."

19. In fact, as a report on the AIDS epidemic in China suggests, both Rawls and his source (Peffer) may have the relationship between some measure of political freedom and material well-being backwards:

> The AIDS epidemic in Henan, which local officials have tried to cover up and have done little to relieve, is only the latest of many indications that [the] distinction between freedom from hunger and political freedom—especially the freedom to tell the truth when officials lie—is too glib. For it has long been clear that

Contrary to Rawls, there was good reason for the authors of the Declaration, following Locke, to limit their specification of people's inherent, inalienable rights to what may be termed (following Isaiah Berlin's usage) "negative" liberties. Because the most fundamental reason for having a government is to protect each individual against being robbed, raped, enslaved, or murdered by other human beings, no regime that is unable to provide reasonable security against these dangers merits the name of a government—or has a claim on the individual's obedience—at all. And the provision of this sort of protection hardly depends on a supply of resources that aren't universally available. By contrast, to assert a right to such goods as a certain level of income, comfort, education, medical care, or leisure is to impose a claim that many governments will be unable to satisfy—by virtue of the scarcity of wealth in their societies—and about the adequacy of which opinions will always vary. Moreover, to assert an individual right to possess such goods is to lay an (inherently disputable) claim to be supplied with them at the expense of other citizens, who must be taxed to pay for them. Finally, such "positive" rights can hardly be said to inhere in human nature: while we have an innate inclination to resist assault, robbery, or enslavement that no authority may justly disregard, nobody can plausibly claim that others have deprived him of something that was inherently his simply by not giving a good to him.

To deny that people have a natural right to goods such as education or medical care is by no means to deny that governments ought to ensure that all citizens can enjoy these goods to an adequate degree, to the extent that it is within particular governments' capacity to do so. But to blur the line between inherent, natural rights and these other goods—as is done in the UN's Universal Declaration of Human Rights and the draft constitution

---

China's most widespread human rights violations . . . afflict the country's poor masses most of all, endangering their physical as well as political welfare, and that official silence about bitter truths undermines public faith in the political system itself.

(Erick Eckholm, "When Lies Kill.") Chinese state media similarly attempted "to hush up the detention of Jiang Yanyong, the doctor who became a national hero by blowing the whistle on Beijing's SARS coverup" in 2003 (Emily Parker, "China's 'Netizens'"). See, on the Arab world's "freedom deficit" as the chief cause of its underdevelopment, the report of the Arab Fund for Social and Economic Development, cited by Thomas Friedman, "Arabs at the Crossroads."

The independent authoritarian regimes that most successfully made a peaceful transition to constitutional republicanism during the post-World War II period (such as Spain, Portugal, Taiwan, and South Korea) were ones that had previously secured property rights, thereby generating economic prosperity—the opposite of Peffer's preferred scenario.

issued by the European Union in 2003—can only encourage cynicism about the doctrine of natural rights, as in Alasdair MacIntyre's comparison of rights to unicorns—that is, nonexistent entities.[20]

Two aspects of Rawls's argument in *PL* further threaten to weaken the support that Locke's doctrine supplies to liberty. First, contrary to Locke, Rawls denies the possibility of "contrast[ing] . . . the situation of individuals in the state of nature and their situation in society" to test a regime's legitimacy (*PL*, 278–79, 288). Second, Rawls alludes vaguely to the need for "suitable qualifications" to the right of emigration (*PL*, 277, 222; cf. *LP*, 74n). The link between these two points is perhaps indicated by Rawls's treatment of freedom of movement as an issue of "distributive justice" rather than one of the "basic rights and liberties" (even though he deems it a "constitutional essential" [*PL*, 228]) and is further suggested by his representation of the just society as a "closed" system (*PL*, 12, 67–68, 272n). Does he mean that citizens of his "just" regime might have to be deterred in some measure from appealing beyond it, not only in theory, but in practice (by emigrating) lest some of them judge that Rawls's principles leave them worse off than they would have been in a state of nature or in another existing society?[21]

For Rawls, political philosophy consists not in the quest for natural standards of right but rather in the use of "abstract conceptions" to which we can appeal "when our shared political understandings . . . break down" (*PL*, 44). But the example he chooses to illustrate that claim hardly inspires confidence. He invites us to "imagine Alexander Stephens [future vice

20. MacIntyre, *After Virtue*, 69–70; see Edward Rothstein, "Europe's Constitution: All Hail the Bureaucracy," on the contrast between the EU Constitution's grab-bag list of rights, which as "the language of interest groups . . . will end up guaranteeing the ruling bureaucracy its right to daily bread," and the natural rights enunciated in the Declaration of Independence. Although those natural rights require positive governmental action to secure them, which entails taxing the populace to finance such protections, Berlin's term "negative liberties" does capture what essentially distinguishes such rights from claims to be given other goods by government or other individuals, contrary to Sotirios Barber's denial of the distinction on the ground that all taxation is inherently redistributive (*Welfare and the Constitution*, 14–17). See, on the reasons for restricting the rights that government is constitutionally obliged to secure to the truly natural, negative rights, Robert Goldwin "Rights Versus Duties," 70–72. For a spirited defense of the natural-rights doctrine against Macintyre's critique, see Zuckert, *Launching Liberalism*, chap. 13.

21. In *JF* (94n) Rawls offers a noncontroversial illustration of necessary qualifications to the right of emigration: "those properly convicted of certain sufficiently serious crimes" may be prohibited from emigrating until they finish serving their sentences. But he appears to leave room for further restrictions by adding simply, "I shall not discuss these qualifications." In *LP* (74n) Rawls implies that the right to emigrate from a liberal society is *more* subject to "qualifications" than the right to emigrate from a nonliberal, hierarchical regime; cf. Seyla Benhabib, *The Rights of Others*, 85–86.

president of the Confederacy] rejecting Lincoln's appeal to the abstractions of natural right" and demanding that the North "respect the South's shared political understandings on the slavery question" (*PL*, 44–45). But far from appealing to abstractions in the letter to Stephens that Rawls cites (*PL*, 45n), Lincoln begins by pledging that his administration will not interfere with the institution of slavery in the states where it legally exists, and proceeds to identify "the only substantial difference" between North and South as concerning whether slavery "is *right* and ought to be extended" or "is *wrong* and ought to be restricted."[22] Although Lincoln's condemnation of slavery rested on his conviction that it violated the principles of natural right, there is nothing in those principles to rival the abstractness of Rawls's conceptions of the original position, the distinction between rationality and reasonableness, etc. Nor does Rawls explain how *he* would have answered Stephens, in view of his apparent renunciation of natural-rights philosophy as one of those comprehensive doctrines that "cannot be endorsed by citizens generally" or serve any longer, "if they ever could, . . . as the professed basis of society" (*PL*, 10).[23]

In *LP*, I note, Rawls will describe the issues that divided North and South in the Civil War as an "impasse" of a kind that philosophy cannot resolve, reflecting the fact that the two sides had "final ends that require[d] them to oppose one another without compromise" (*PL*, 123). But this seems a needless counsel of despair: instead of taking for granted the South's irrevocable commitment to its supposed "final end," wouldn't a Socratic philosopher or statesman have tried (as Lincoln did) to show the South that its support of slavery contradicted its own commitment to the right of self-government (the cause espoused by Jefferson Davis in Rawls's quotation in *LP*, 123n)? Isn't it likely that Lincoln's arguments actually did persuade thousands of waverers in the northern and border states (as well as observers in England tempted to intervene on the South's behalf) of the

---

22. *Collected Works of Abraham Lincoln*, 4:160 (emphasis in original).

As William Galston observes, it seems difficult to reconcile Rawls's claim to derive justice from a public consensus that dispenses with judgments of moral truth with the fact that the American political culture originates with a declaration of self-evident moral truths. Consider in this regard Rawls's curious counterpart to Lincoln's biblical remark that a house divided against itself cannot stand: "a society in which every one *affirms* a reasonable liberal doctrine . . . cannot long endure" (*PL*, 37–38n; emphasis added). Contrast James McPherson's account of the high degree of conscious commitment to liberal principles among Union soldiers during the Civil War: *What They Fought For, 1861–1865*, chap. 2. Can one imagine soldiers then or now battling instead on behalf of Rawls's "overlapping consensus"?

23. Galston, *Liberal Purposes*, 158; *Liberal Pluralism*, 40–41.

justice of the Union's cause? The relativistic character of Rawls's liberalism regarding "final ends" makes it a far less promising ground than Lincoln's natural-right position for a genuinely liberal consensus.

As in *Theory*, renouncing any attempt to derive an understanding of justice from human nature saves Rawls a good deal of work. Since he represents "the political philosophy of a constitutional regime" as "autonomous" from any "natural basis," Rawls contends, he "need not explain its role and content scientifically" (*PL*, 87–88). In a characteristically odd turn of phrase, he represents the "moral psychology of the person" that his theory presupposes as "philosophical not psychological," meaning that it is "drawn from the political conception of justice as fairness" rather than from "the science of human nature" (*PL*, 86). In other words, rather than examine human psychology empirically, we construct a psychology based on the way we would like people to behave! Although this again seems circular, and Rawls himself anticipates the objection that his account "is unscientific," he responds that "human nature and its natural psychology are permissive; they may limit the viable conceptions of persons and ideals of citizenship . . . but do not dictate the ones we must adopt" (*PL*, 87).

Instead of nature, Rawls proposes in *PL* to ground his liberal political theory in the "public culture" of a modern democratic society, which will provide a "shared fund of basic ideas" on which to draw (*PL*, 8, 13, 43, 67, 192). Rawls attributes enormous influence to the public culture, contending that each of us inevitably "affirm[s]" it "in large part" even if we "question, if not reject" much of it (*PL*, 222). And one of the reasons for accepting just social principles is that they enable us to participate fully in a public culture that "is always in large part the work of others" (*PL*, 322). Yet nowhere in *PL* (nor in his other writings) does Rawls engage in any serious attempt to explain what culture is, how one identifies the ideas that are central to it, or how it is shaped and sustained.

The importance of these issues may be indicated by the following considerations. First, there is a central paradox running throughout Rawls's project, in that he seeks to resolve a supposed impasse in the public political culture by articulating an account of justice derived from ideas that are already implicit in that culture. Yet if the existing culture is divided on major political issues, how can one expect to overcome the division by drawing what one takes to be "fundamental" principles from that same culture? Isn't the selection bound to be arbitrary? Second, while Rawls insists that the ideas out of which a political conception is built must be derived solely from the public political culture, not the "nonpublic" one (*PL*, 43, 220–21), he never explains how this distinction is to be maintained—that is, how one can ensure that what he identifies as political ideas have not already been "infected," so to speak, by nonpolitical ones.[24]

In practice, Rawls endeavors to avoid the issue by recalling that the veil of ignorance prevents the parties to the original position from favoring any particular comprehensive doctrine. But since the ultimate test of the entire procedure that takes place in that situation is, as Rawls acknowledges, "what we regard—here and now—as fair conditions" for "the terms of social cooperation," as well as that it yields a "conception of justice that we regard—here and now—as fair" (*PL*, 25–26), the dilemma remains: what assurance do we have that our judgments of justice are "removed from and not distorted by the particular features and circumstances of the all-encompassing background framework" we inhabit (*PL*, 23)—say, by our membership in the faculty of Harvard University? As I have argued previously, the fact that it is impossible for real human beings to reason under the veil—that is, somehow to forget our particular political, moral, and religious beliefs, as well as our personal attributes and social position—inevitably makes the pretense of calculating the decision that would be reached in the original position an exercise in self-delusion.

In the end, there is far less to Rawls's supposed innovation of overlapping consensus than he makes out. After all, *Theory* didn't offer anything approaching a "comprehensive doctrine" of life, in the sense that a religion or a moral code, a set of standards of cultural excellence, or a substantive philosophical view do. Instead, Rawls insisted that for the sake of expressing our essential "nature" as equal moral persons, we set all such beliefs aside in establishing a just and well-ordered society. Within the limits of that society, we were still free to pursue our own visions of our good (assuming that we didn't violate the restrictions of justice, for instance by demanding that the government ban degrading sexual practices, trying to gain primary goods without giving the less advantaged their share, or undermining some people's self-esteem by disparaging their vocation of, say, grass counting). Yet Rawls was emphatic that his argument for liberty of conscience in *Theory* (which he used as the model for explaining the implications of the first principle more generally) did "not rely on any special metaphysical or philosophical doctrine" and that "different arguments" could be used to support it (*Theory*, 188, 187).

Meanwhile, Rawls stresses in *PL* that the overlapping consensus he demands must be something more than a modus vivendi, but must be

---

24. Rawls's own readiness to alter religious doctrines to accommodate his political conception of justice is exemplified by his implicit rewriting of the Ten Commandments, continued from *Theory*, to legitimize what he calls "excusable envy" (284).

grounded on the priority of the right to the good. Thus for the sake of a Rawlsian moral principle we are supposed to give priority to a merely "political" conception of justice over our particular comprehensive doctrines, even though that conception isn't even grounded in a claim to truth. This sounds a lot like Rawls's original program of elevating his conception of justice over people's diverse views of the good, only, we are tempted to say, with a bit more hocus pocus or sleight of hand, making it slightly harder for people to realize that they are being asked to forego their own notions of the good for the one favored by Rawls and those who share his intuitions. The whole notion of grounding Rawls's doctrine on an overlapping consensus appears to constitute little more than an effort at rhetorical repackaging—one that further distances him from feeling the need to defend that doctrine on rational grounds. But its underlying yet unacknowledged partisanship remains.

In some advanced philosophical circles, indeed, Rawls's decision to dispense with any claim to truth for his doctrine has won him applause. Hence the "anti-foundationalist" theoretician Richard Rorty, for one, claims that Rawls "strengthen[ed] liberal institutions" by "free[ing] them" from "having to answer the question 'In what does the privileged status of freedom consist?'"[25] But to think we have saved ourselves from answering the question by refusing to pose it sounds like a philosophical version of whistling in the dark. (Recall Carl Becker's dilemma.)

For the reasons just given, I believe it is an error to interpret Rawls's renunciation of the claim to objective truth for his doctrine in *PL* as marking a major "turn" in his thought, as most commentators have maintained. Rather, as Rorty observes, that renunciation was already implicit in *Theory*.[26] Further casting doubt on the novelty of the renunciation in Rawls's own eyes is the fact that he first stated it explicitly only three years after the publication of *Theory* in his APA presidential address, without representing it as a departure from that book.[27] Having fudged the issue in *Theory* through his ambiguous use of the first-person plural, Rawls evidently found himself compelled to adopt a more explicitly historicist position by

25. Rorty, *Contingency, Irony, and Solidarity,* 57.

26. Rorty, "Priority of Democracy."

27. Despite having explained in the original introduction to *PL* (xviii–xix) that the decision to represent justice as fairness as a political rather than comprehensive doctrine compelled "many other changes" (i.e., the invention of such terms as overlapping consensus and public reason). Rawls acknowledges in his 1996 introduction that "not very much of the content" of his doctrine had to be changed. In fact, the only difference he now cites is that the political conception of justice developed in *PL* (xliii) exemplifies "political autonomy" rather than "moral autonomy"—which just means altering its rhetorical presentation. See also Berkowitz, "Ambiguities of Rawls's Influence," 123.

his incapacity to defend the truth of his claims about justice against crit-ics.[28] In sum, like his renunciation of a rational-choice account of the deci-sion in the original position, Rawls's explicit disclaimer of truth-claims for his doctrine is only a strategic retreat, but not one that strengthens his posi-tion. Rawls notably fails to appreciate how the historicist stance under-mines the representation of his principles in *Theory* as embodying a transcendental "Archimedean point."

V.

The remaining theoretical concept introduced in *PL* is "public reason." This term signifies that in a democratic society, citizens are to settle such critical issues as voting rights, religious toleration, the extent of equality of opportunity, and property rights by reference to "political values alone," that is, by relying on a "public conception of justice" as distinguished from beliefs or interests that are not universally shared (*PL*, 214, 216). The exer-cise of democratic political power imposes a duty of "civility" that requires citizens to justify their preferred policies "by the political values of public reason" (*PL*, 217). Not only would citizens violate that duty by voting on the basis of mere "preferences and interests," they would also be wrong to "vote what they see as right and true as their comprehensive convictions direct without taking into account public reasons" (*PL*, 219). The content of public reason, in turn, is provided by a political conception of justice (such as Rawls's two principles) that specifies people's "basic rights, liberties, and opportunities," gives them "priority" vis-à-vis "claims of the general good and of perfectionist values," and "affirms measures assuring all citizens adequate all-purpose means to make effective use of their basic liberties and opportunities" (*PL*, 223). As Rawls repeats, "in discussing constitu-tional essentials and matters of basic justice we are not to appeal to compre-hensive religious and philosophical doctrines—to what we as individuals or members of associations see as the whole truth," but must ground our reasoning on "the plain truths now widely accepted, or available, to citi-

28. Even Kukathas and Pettit, who claim to identify a two-stage evolution in Rawls's thought after *Theory*, observe that Rawls's first move, in response to critics such as Steven Lukes who pointed out the time-bound character of his doctrine as early as 1972, was to acknowledge that it was designed only to fit "modern liberal democratic polities"; they describe his focus as increasingly "parochial" (Kukathas and Pettit, *Rawls*, 122–23). Another aspect of the retreat in *PL* (228–29) is Rawls's denial that his difference principle is a "constitutional essential," allowing citizens of a just society the right to choose between it and other means of ensuring a "social minimum" to all citi-zens on the basis of the "political values of public reason."

zens generally" (*PL,* 224–25). (It is surprising to encounter the claim that constitutional issues can be resolved by reference to "plain truths," coming from an author who finds the very notion of truth too controversial to serve as a basis for moral reasoning.)

The "exemplar" of public reason according to Rawls is the Supreme Court, since in interpreting the Constitution the justices are obliged not to "invoke their own personal morality" or "religious or philosophical views," but to appeal only to "the political values they think belong to the most reasonable understanding of the public conception [of justice]," that is, the "values that they believe in good faith . . . that all citizens as reasonable and rational might reasonably be expected to endorse" (*PL,* 216, 236). When the Court "clearly and effectively interprets the constitution in a reasonable way," it "forces political discussion to take a principled form" rather than being merely "a contest for power and position" (*PL,* 237, 239).

As the foregoing summary will have made apparent, Rawls's account of public reason is simply an alternative formulation of his project of severing the ground of justice and, more specifically, of liberal constitutionalism from any particular comprehensive doctrine. As such, it exhibits many of the difficulties I have already identified in the project as a whole. First, while a constitution like the American one is designed to secure the fundamental rights of all citizens without regard to their particular religious beliefs, to try to completely separate our beliefs about what the Constitution requires, or about sound public policy, from our particular moral beliefs is neither possible nor desirable. (The notion that we can sever our political and moral beliefs is another variant of the myth of reasoning under a veil of ignorance. And who identifies the "plain truths . . . available to citizens generally"? Does anyone believe that Supreme Court justices somehow forget their personal moral views when deciding cases before them?) Second, Rawls's account of how public reason should operate—notably, his demand that voters set aside their particular "preferences and interests"—is so impractical and unworldly that its actual effect can only be to deepen the unjustified and uncivil self-righteousness of those who believe that they are actuated by "principles" while their opponents are motivated by selfishness or bias.[29] Third, Rawls's account of the ordinary political process as determined merely by the pursuit of "power and position" constitutes an unjust disparagement of democratic governance, by contrast with the ostensibly more principled and disinterested process

29. Contrast *The Federalist,* No. 10's realistic account of how the interplay between man's "reason and his self-love, his opinions and his passions," may generate a factional strife over principles that is potentially more dangerous than that caused by economic interest (46–47).

of government-by-judiciary. As I shall observe in the next chapter, this disparagement naturally leads Rawls to favor further restrictions on the democratic process, even as he applauds judicial efforts to read new rights, such as a "social minimum" (*PL*, 237n), into the Constitution, so long as the judges think citizens would endorse these efforts if they were "reasonable and rational." (That sounds a lot like the doctrine of "virtual" representation, roundly rejected by American colonists in 1776.)[30]

The final and most important point to note about Rawls's doctrine in *PL* is how unnecessary the project of severing liberalism from particular "comprehensive doctrines" is. Liberalism, as conceived by Locke, Montesquieu, and the American founders, never was a "comprehensive doctrine." By limiting the purpose of government to securing the conditions in which individuals may pursue happiness as they conceive it, American constitutional liberalism already provided the conditions for "overlapping consensus" among (tolerant) religious believers of differing faiths, rationalists, and individuals with varying conceptions of how to live.[31] But the natural-rights teaching of Locke and the Declaration provides a substantive ground for mutual toleration and respect for one another's rights, instead of leaving them suspended in an air of abstraction as Rawls does, and without the unrealistic (and intolerant) demand that religious believers exclude their faith from their public arguments.

The United States has never required its citizens to subscribe to the Lockean natural-rights doctrine or any other, so long as they conduct themselves in a law-abiding manner. Nonetheless, its survival as a free country presupposes that the vast majority of its citizens will come to accept and uphold the principles of the equal rights of all individuals, government by consent of the governed, and constitutionalism on which it rests. Despite occasional denunciations from so-called multiculturalists, radical libertarians, and other fringe groups, our Constitution has largely succeeded in drawing the continued adherence and support of the vast majority of both native-born citizens and immigrants. Much as we may disagree about particular religious, moral, or policy issues, we manage to get along and to participate in a constitutional political process in which everyone accepts that his particular group or sect will not be able to get everything it desires—much in the manner sketched in *The Federalist*, No. 10. (That document manifests the founders' full awareness of "the burdens

---

30. Cf. Harvey C. Mansfield, *The Spirit of Liberalism*, 100, and Deneen, *Democratic Faith*, 27–28.

31. On the "amalgam" of Lockean liberalism with the biblical tradition adopted by eighteenth-century Americans, largely following Locke's own intention, see Zuckert, *Launching Liberalism*, part 3; and Zuckert, *The Natural Rights Republic*, especially chap. 6.

of judgment"—that is, differences of judgment arising from varying opinions as well as diverse passions and interests—and their belief that the scheme of government they had devised could successfully channel and accommodate that diversity.) Any real threat to our regime of toleration today comes not from religious fanatics demanding the imposition of some specific doctrine on their fellow citizens but rather from militant secularists, driven by ideological principles like Rawls's, determined to wipe out any references to God in the public sphere, merely so that their sensibilities won't be offended.

Meantime, no serious statesman or thinker in the American constitutional tradition ever doubted the need for a liberal regime to inculcate the moral virtues, albeit largely in an indirect or noncoercive manner, and to encourage all individuals to strive for excellence—rather than pretend that it is no more rational and estimable to practice an honorable trade or profession than spend one's life counting blades of grass. To demand the universal acceptance of Rawlsian relativism about the good is truly illiberal.

What Rawls has done is worse than trying to reinvent the wheel: he aims to supplant the fully functioning set of wheels on which our Constitution rides with a postmodern set that aren't likely to take sober friends of liberty anywhere they want to go. When Rawls laments the absence of "reasonable" consensus among us, his real complaint is that Americans haven't agreed on the beliefs that *he* regards as reasonable.[32] Far from deriving his doctrine from "the public culture of a modern democratic society," as John Gray observes, Rawls has simply summarized the politically marginal perspective of "American East Coast liberals" and demanded in the name of justice that everyone else alter their beliefs to conform to it.[33] This demand is hardly a democratic one. Rawls's doctrine of public reason is neither public nor reasonable.

32. Cf. Anderson, "Antipolitical Philosophy," 47.
33. Gray, "Can We Agree to Disagree?"

CHAPTER II

Political Liberalism II
Applications

I.

Rawls's inability to achieve his professed goal of an "impartial" treatment of particular comprehensive doctrines (*PL*, xxi, xxx) is manifest in the handful of passages in *PL* that address concrete political issues of the present era. To illustrate how public reason is compatible with all reasonable doctrines (*PL*, 243), Rawls first cites the abortion debate. After proposing to consider the issue in light of the "political values" of "respect for human life, the ordered reproduction of political society," and women's equality, he simply asserts that "any reasonable balance" among them will authorize "a duly qualified right" to abortion during the first trimester, since "at this early stage of pregnancy the political value of the equality of women is overriding." While leaving open the extent of that right beyond the first three months, and without specifying any qualifications, Rawls concludes that any doctrine that prohibits abortion in the first trimester is not only "unreasonable" but "may also be cruel and oppressive; for example, if it denied the right altogether except in the cases of rape and incest" (*PL*, 243–44n). One needn't take sides on the abortion issue to doubt that Rawls's ex cathedra pronouncements somehow offer a deeper basis for resolving it.[1]

1. In *IPRR* (169) Rawls will explain that the abortion mandate was only his "opinion . . . not an argument"; but in the same essay he extends the scope of justice, as I have

A second illustration Rawls provides of the policy implications of his principles concerns advertising. He distinguishes informational advertising concerning prices and product features, which should be encouraged, from "market-strategic advertising," which "is found in imperfect and oligopolistic markets dominated by a relatively few firms." Since such advertising, which leaves consumers "unable to distinguish" among products "except by rather superficial and unimportant properties," is "socially wasteful," Rawls holds that a well-ordered society should limit it through taxes or government-sponsored agreements among firms, thereby releasing the funds "for investment or other useful social ends" (*PL*, 364–65).

This proposal exhibits a considerable economic as well as political naiveté. As a good economics textbook will explain, "market-strategic" advertising—aside from financing goods that many (depending partly on gender) regard as socially useful such as TV soaps and football broadcasts—is an inseparable part of the process of market competition; it contributes to economies of scale in the sale of products, ranging from beer to detergents to automobiles, that bring prices down. From Rawls's perspective, of course, it's unfortunate that so many Americans tolerate or even enjoy commercials focused on such less-than-burning issues as "Tastes Great vs. Less Filling," when they should be reading *Consumer Reports* before buying a Volvo. But can anyone believe that a government agency authorized to distinguish more and less "socially useful" advertising would be other than an enormous political boondoggle and administrative nightmare? (Why not extend its mandate to ban *products* it considers "socially wasteful"?) And are such intrusive regulations really a mandate of justice?

For Rawls, restrictions of "merely" commercial speech are allowable because the right to such speech is "not inalienable" (*PL*, 365). But while he follows a line of Supreme Court precedents that grant greater protection to political speech than commercial communication, nothing in the constitutional text authorizes this distinction, and its legitimacy is dubious. (Might not a coalition of corporate advertisers and tuition-paying parents demand with equal plausibility that government restrict the publication of philosophy textbooks that lack demonstrable social utility, on the ground that financing them only raises college costs while encouraging unjustified disparagement of America's free economy?)

---

noted, to dictate such policies as correcting women's "unjust share" of child rearing. This judgment appears no less ex cathedra.

II.

In fact, inadvertently confirming what I have argued is the inherent link between economic and political freedom, Rawls's major illustration of the policy implications of his doctrine of public reason—its treatment of political speech—shows a lamentable willingness to constrain political debate that parallels his eagerness to restrict commercial advertising. Curiously (but in a way that mirrors recent academic fashions), Rawls wishes to buttress the legal protection of speech aimed at the violent overthrow of democratic institutions, while mandating severe limitations on the capacity of political candidates as well as private organizations and individuals to advance political views that respect our Constitution and laws.

Rawls's treatment of "ordinary" political advocacy in *PL* has two parts: a brief proposal for public financing of campaign expenditures (citing his somewhat longer discussion in *Theory*, chapter 4) and a demand for limits on private campaign contributions, including a criticism of the Supreme Court's opinion in *Buckley v. Valeo* (1976) that held unconstitutional various limits imposed by the Election Act Amendment of 1974 (*PL*, 235n, 356–63). (The Court moved closer to satisfying Rawls's wishes in its constitutionally dubious 5–4 decision in *McConnell v. FEC* [2003], upholding the so-called Bipartisan Campaign Reform Act that not only restricted donations to political parties but prohibited private organizations and individuals from sponsoring "issue" ads in the weeks immediately preceding an election.) Both arguments are set forth in the name of the "fair value" clause of Rawls's first principle ordaining that all citizens have "a fair opportunity to hold public office and to influence the outcome of political decisions" (*PL*, 5, 327). While acknowledging that a detailed account of the arrangements needed for this end is "beyond the scope of a philosophical doctrine" (*PL*, 327), Rawls focuses on the campaign finance issue to demonstrate that the liberties secured by his scheme are "not merely formal" (*PL*, 324, 328).[2]

Rawls explains the need for public campaign financing and limits on private contributions by representing the political process as a "public facility" that has "limited space," enabling wealthier individuals to "combine together and exclude those who have less" in the absence of such "guarantee[s]," even with the limitations on social and economic inequalities mandated by the difference principle (*PL*, 328). Despite holding it to

2. In his 1996 introduction (*PL*, lvii–lviii) Rawls describes public campaign financing as a mandate of any "reasonable" form of liberalism so as to prevent "excessive inequalities," terming this "an application of common sense sociology." Because he thinks it a dictate of common sense, Rawls sees no need to support the claim with evidence.

be one of "fixed points" of our judgment that "the advocacy of revolution-ary and subversive doctrines is fully protected" by a just constitution (*PL*, 342), Rawls is far less of a First Amendment absolutist when it comes to restricting campaign contributions; he is confident that "the prohibition of large contributions from private persons or corporations is not an undue burden . . . on wealthy persons and groups," and thus not an infringement on anyone's constitutionally protected rights of political advocacy. Hence he finds "profoundly dismaying" the Court's 1976 limitation of congres-sional efforts "to establish the fair value of the political liberties," espe-cially in view of the Court's dictum in one of its reapportionment decisions that the Constitution ordains that each citizen have "an equally effective voice in the election" of legislative representatives (*PL*, 358–61; citing *Reynolds v. Sims* [1964]). He seems particularly incensed by the Court's judgment in *Buckley* that "the concept that the government may restrict the speech of some elements in our society in order to enhance the relative voice of others is wholly foreign to the First Amendment" (*PL*, 360).[3]

Here again, it is unnecessary to take sides on the issue to recognize that Rawls's partisan slip (as well as the limitedness of his empirical under-standing of American politics) is showing. To begin with, Rawls offers no support for his account of the political process as having "limited space," and I know of no way it could be documented. In a country that allows a broad freedom of political speech, nobody is compelled to listen to one speaker rather than another, and rich individuals can spend billions to advance their views and even their own political candidacies while having little to show for it if voters don't find their message sufficiently attractive. (Remember Ross Perot.) There is, indeed, considerable evidence that the contemporary mass media as a whole have a strongly left-leaning political bias, but this is hardly the problem that concerns Rawls, and no one main-tains that governmental regulations would cure it.[4] In fact, our existing system, as enhanced by recent technological developments, offers the best remedy: a widening of alternative news and opinion outlets through cable television and the Internet. (Witness the exposure by bloggers of the forged memoranda on George Bush's military service trumpeted by CBS newsman Dan Rather during the 2004 campaign.)

3. Even in *McConnell* the Court reiterated this principle (*McConnell v. FEC*, 540 U.S., Chief Justice William Rehnquist speaking for the Court [slip opin. 6]).

4. See, e.g., Bernard Goldberg, *Bias*; William McGowan, *Coloring the News*; S. Robert Lichter, Stanley Rothman, and Linda S. Lichter, *The Media Elite*, 13–19, 25–51. In 2004 politically galvanized Hollywood producers and scriptwriters used their positions to insert anti-Bush messages into their weekly television shows (Jim Rutenberg, "TV Shows Take on Bush, and Pull Few Punches").

With considerable justification, legislative campaign finance restrictions have been dubbed "incumbent protection acts," since they weaken the capacity of electoral challengers to overcome the advantages of incumbency (notably name recognition, publicity, and the capacity to dispense "pork" strategically). But such restrictions have a further effect as well: they heighten the relative influence of the ostensibly nonpartisan sources of political information (TV, radio, and newspapers) and also of certain voter groups (union members, college students, and senior citizens), who can afford to donate large amounts of nonfinancial contributions (i.e., time) to electioneering, donations that Congress is unlikely to restrict, and who typically favor policies of increased government spending and taxation at other citizens' expense.[5] Meanwhile, unless Congress takes a step that not even Rawls advocated—completely prohibiting wealthy individuals or nonprofit advocacy organizations from sponsoring "issue" ads—these unaccountable groups and individuals will gain influence at the expense of established political parties, weakening the moderating effect that the major parties typically have on the formulation of political demands.[6] (Such groups did proliferate in 2004 in the wake of the 2003 act.) In other words, as noted in chapter 4, there is no way of equalizing the political clout of all individuals: even if the CEO of General Electric is disallowed from using his wealth to support candidates and policies he favors, TV anchormen, Rush Limbaugh, the editors of the *New York Times*, filmmakers like Michael Moore, and professors like Rawls will still have considerably more influence than the average person. Nor is there reason to think that the voices of academics or media personalities are any less prone to bias than those of corporate tycoons.[7]

5. See, on this last point, Ralph Winter, *Campaign Financing and Political Freedom;* and, more generally, Bradley A. Smith, *Unfree Speech.*

6. On George Soros's donation of millions to lobby groups that helped bring about passage of the 2002 act, thus enhancing his own influence relative to that of contributors to political parties, see "The Soros Agenda," *Wall Street Journal* editorial. Subsequently Soros became the major financier of Moveon.org, an "independent" organization dedicated to the defeat of President Bush and free of legal restrictions on the donations it could accept. See Byron York, *The Vast Left-Wing Conspiracy,* chap. 2.

7. In fact, there is more cause to distrust the enhanced influence of college student volunteers on the political process, given their tendency to favor simplistic solutions to domestic and international problems. The "swarm" of such supporters who fueled Howard Dean's campaign for the Democratic presidential nomination in 2003–2004 were described in the *New York Times* as "young, at loose ends, and searching for a cause—or anyway, looking to connect with some cool new friends" (Samantha M. Shapiro, "The Dean Swarm" [quotation from cover page]). Consider also the concerns expressed by Frank Knight about opinion leadership in democratic politics, cited in note 17 to chapter 4 above.

Rawls's real concern, it is apparent, is not that there isn't presently enough space for disseminating political information, but that the space (without congressional restrictions of the sort he favored) is *unlimited*: wealthy donors to political parties may be getting out too much of the "wrong" information to voters, who should be receiving guidance instead from mainstream media, self-styled public-interest lobbies, and ideally, public broadcasting stations. This interpretation of Rawls's intention is confirmed by his dictum that any "ideas of the good" used in political debate "must be tailored to meet the restrictions imposed by the political conception of justice and *fit into the space it allows*" (*PL*, 203 [emphasis added]. In other words, it is Rawls's doctrine, not the existing political forum, that would limit political debate. His conception of political liberalism mandates that people be precluded from even making political arguments that derive from their religious views. (And if the combination of restrictions on private campaign donations with those government-subsidized discussion groups he advocated in *Theory* doesn't suffice to get voters to see the light and favor just policies as Rawls conceives them, maybe participation in the discussions will have to be made mandatory, just as voting is in some democracies.) Rawls has an uncanny capacity to represent restrictions on freedom as if they enhanced it.

Aside from his cavalier dismissal of the notion that the right of political advocacy applies no less to wealthy individuals than to poor ones, the most noteworthy aspect of Rawls's treatment of this issue is its disregard of the central substantive problem addressed by the American founders: how to frame constitutional democracy so as to secure the rights of minorities (including the rich) against tyrannical political majorities. The need for specific protection for the wealthy in a democratic regime arises from a fact already noted by Aristotle: since there are inevitably fewer rich people than poor ones (or, in modern commercial republics, fewer rich individuals than members of the lower and middle classes combined), any regime based purely on the majoritarian principle, without any structural or informal means of moderating it, while formally treating all citizens alike, will in practice consistently favor the short-term interests of the poorer multitude at the expense of the wealthy minority, ultimately undermining any ground for attachment to the regime on the part of the latter.[8] Meantime, such policies will certainly weaken the incentives for the rich (and, more important, those who aspire to become rich) to work, save, and invest, activities that benefit those they employ and increase public revenues along with the gross national product.

8. Aristotle *Politics* 3.7, 10; 4.4, 1291b29–1291a38; 5.5, 1304b20–1305a27; 5.9, 1309b35–1310a6.

By contrast, Rawls implicitly dismisses the founders' and Aristotle's concerns elsewhere in *PL* in describing the role of the supreme court in a constitutional democracy: "by applying public reason the court is to prevent" the erosion of the "higher law" that expresses the people's will "from being eroded by the legislation of transient majorities, *or more likely* by organized and well-situated narrow interests skilled at getting their way" (*PL*, 231, 233 [emphasis added]). In reality, the Court's record of defending broad public interests against special-interest legislation aimed at reducing competition, or the rights of ordinary property owners against governmental schemes of "agricultural adjustment" or "urban development," has been notoriously weak ever since it withdrew from effectual scrutiny of economic legislation under pressure from Franklin Roosevelt's New Deal coalition.[9] Instead, over recent decades, federal courts have provided a venue in which so-called public-interest lobbies can thwart the people's deliberate will as expressed through the political branches, at the cost of coherent public policy and, often, the public good.[10] As noted, such lobbies will only gain in relative influence the more that the countervailing power of businesses to contribute to political campaigns is restricted.

Rawls doesn't explain how he would improve our courts' performance in these regards. Instead, extending the claims made in *Theory*, he contends that in the absence of the second principle of justice designed to limit social and economic inequalities (which principle has not, thus far, been incorporated into the Constitution), the effectual exclusion of the less advantaged from the political process "is a foregone conclusion" (*PL*, 328). As I have observed, such claims are belied by all sorts of American legislation that go against at least the short-term or class interests of wealthy individuals and corporations.[11] And Rawls has never demonstrated that such economic inequalities as currently exist in the U.S. violate the difference principle. But as in *Theory*,

9. See, e.g., *Wickard v. Filburn*, 317 U.S. 111 (1942); *Williamson v. Lee Optical Co.*, 348 U.S. 483 (1955); *Kelo v. City of New London* (2005); Schrock, "The Liberal Court."

10. See Jeremy Rabkin, *Judicial Compulsions*.

11. Contrast the study by Janet Grenzke, "PACs and the Congressional Supermarket," which concludes from an analysis of contributions from 120 political action committees affiliated with ten large interest groups that such contributions "generally do not maintain or change House members' voting patterns" (19).

The manner in which purely electoral concerns outweigh financial ones was illustrated by the Bush administration's 2002 accession to demands for increased steel tariffs, contrary to its "official" free-trade policy, while it had ignored calls from the Enron Corporation for assistance despite having received large campaign contributions from company officials. As an astute observer noted, whereas Republicans needed to pick up votes in the steel-producing states, where the parties were closely balanced, they hardly needed more in Texas (where Enron was headquartered) (Virginia Postrel, "Why Bush Stiffed Enron").

he does not permit his recognition that such issues lie beyond his scope to prevent him from repeatedly issuing obiter dicta proclaiming the existence of various defects in American democracy as presently constituted.

This particular bee, I pause to note, remains in Rawls's bonnet to the end. In *LP*, his rhetoric is even less restrained: he warns against allowing government to be "directed by . . . large concentrations of private economic and corporate power veiled from public knowledge and almost entirely free from accountability" and charges that under the existing American political system "congressional legislation is in effect written by lobbyists, and Congress becomes a bargaining chamber in which laws are bought and sold" (*PL*, 24).[12]

It is troubling to note how Rawls's disparagement of American popular government as a front for domination by the special interests echoes the imprecations against the Weimar Republic issued by proto-Nazi theorist Carl Schmitt in a work Rawls himself cites to illustrate the sources of that regime's delegitimation (*PL*, lxi–lxii). It also resembles the rhetoric of the right-wing, self-styled populist Pat Buchanan, who has remarked (apropos of the government's failure to institute stricter restrictions on immigration) that "we have a virtual democracy and not a real one."[13]

But Rawls himself is neither a majoritarian democrat nor a constitutionalist in any proper sense. It is significant that in the sentence quoted above, Rawls ambiguously refers to the Supreme Court's role as upholding the "higher law" that expresses the people's will against the demands of transient majorities or influential special interests. Rather than hold that the Constitution itself embodies and reflects the people's sovereign will, as a result of the ratification process (as argued in *The Federalist*, No. 78), so that it is the duty of the courts to uphold constitutional limitations on government (which presupposes that the Constitution has a broad, fixed meaning), Rawls proceeds to define a democratic constitution as "a principled expression in higher law of the political ideal of a people to govern itself in a certain way," which he equates with his doctrine of "public reason," of which the Court is to be the exemplar (*PL*, 232, 235). Far from espousing a jurisprudence of original intent or natural right, as Paul Carrese observes, Rawls favors an activist, "judicialized liberalism" rooted in Holmesean pragmatism.[14] Rawls specifically holds that a just constitution should be

12. See also the denunciations of American democracy and "welfare-state capitalism," respectively, in *JF*, 101n, 135–40.

13. See Carl Schmitt, *The Crisis of Parliamentary Democracy*, 49–50; Patrick Buchanan, interview with Chris Matthews.

14. Carrese, *Cloaking of Power*, 258. On the inappropriateness of the term *higher law* to denote America's fundamental law, see James Stoner, *Common Law and Liberal Theory*, 224.

founded "in the first instance" not on the doctrine of natural rights but on his preferred "conceptions of the person and of social cooperation" (*PL*, 339). It is hard to imagine a more open-ended conception of judicial review.[15]

In one respect Rawls seems to qualify his support for unfettered judicial activism by restating Lincoln's view that "in a constitutional government the ultimate power cannot be left to the legislature or even to a supreme court," but rather "is held by the three branches" of government "in a duly specified relation with one another with each responsible to the people" (*PL*, 232). Unfortunately, Rawls's subsequent account of constitutional interpretation as properly guided by "no other values than the political" ones in his sense, treating "the ideals and virtues of morality generally" along with "people's religious or philosophical views" as irrelevant (*PL*, 235–36), again severely circumscribes the people's right to self-government.[16]

Additionally, even if all the restrictions he favors on the democratic political process were adopted, Rawls remains uncertain whether the very existence of private ownership of the means of production is compatible with justice. While acknowledging the need "to keep political parties independent . . . of government control" in what he again (perhaps oxymoronically) calls "a liberal socialist regime" (*PL*, 328), Rawls remains agnostic on the relative merits of free-enterprise and socialist economic systems (*PL*, 7–8n, 298, 338–39) and still relegates economic issues to the second principle of justice, which treats liberties that "are less significant in a well-ordered society than the basic liberties secured by the first" (*PL*, 368), or to the legislative stage, which stands even lower in the hierarchy of just decision making (*PL*, 338). Rawls curiously disregards the American Constitution in holding that a constitution that provides no specific security for private property or economic freedom, as distinguished from his preferred "basic liberties," "conforms to the traditional idea of democratic govern-

15. In this context (*PL*, 339n) Rawls cites Frank Michelman's essay on *Theory* as a mandate for "constitutional welfare rights," indicating the direction he wants the courts to go with this extraordinary discretion: creating new "rights" that the public is too shortsighted or selfish to support through the political process.

On the detrimental effects for coherent policy and public legitimacy of the collaboration between left-liberal intellectuals and the courts in shaping welfare policy so as to circumvent the legislative process before 1996, effects that Rawls's and Michelman's approach would exacerbate, see Teles, *Whose Welfare?* especially chap. 6.

16. Contrast Justice Douglas's majority opinion in *Zorach v. Clauson* (1952), observing that Americans "are a religious people whose institutions presuppose a Supreme Being" (346 U.S. 306 at 313). Although the latter claim would no longer be accepted by most judges or academics, it remains valid as an expression of the belief of many Americans, thus inviting us anew to question the breadth or representativeness of Rawls's ostensible "reasonable consensus."

ment" (*PL*, 339). In fact, he is now somewhat apologetic about not revising his two principles to "*require* a socialist form of economic organization," stressing that "the difficulty here is not with socialism as such," but with its inclusion in "the first principles of political justice," which set out "fundamental values in terms of which," depending on a country's "tradition and circumstances . . . one can consider whether socialism in some form is justified" (*PL*, 7–8n [emphasis added]).[17] Reminding us of the alleged political impasse that his account of justice was supposed to resolve, Rawls opines that since "philosophical argument alone is most unlikely to convince either side" on the issue of free enterprise versus socialism, "it seems more fruitful to look for bases of agreement implicit in the public culture of a democratic society." In this regard he concludes that even though the conceptions he propounds in *PL* "are obscure" and can be "formulated in various ways," the two principles at least provide "a possible common court of appeal for settling the question of property . . . in the light of current and foreseeable social circumstances" (*PL*, 338–39). To the contrary, the fate of the Soviet empire would seem to have fully vindicated, for those who still needed proof, the choice made by the American founders, and supported by every subsequent generation of Americans, on this question. What new light could Rawls's "court" shed on it?

III.

I now turn to the other component of Rawls's treatment of political speech: his account of the "central problem" that arises once it is agreed "that all general discussion of doctrine as well as of the justice of the basic structure and its policies is fully protected," the issue of "subversive advocacy." At the outset Rawls plausibly remarks that freedom of speech, by providing an outlet for the expression of popular grievances, can provide "an alternative to revolution" (*PL*, 344). He then proceeds to denounce the Supreme Court's past use of "the so-called clear and present danger rule" to determine the "point at which political speech becomes so closely connected with the use of force that it may be properly restricted" (*PL*, 344,

---

17. Remarkably, the book Rawls approvingly cites for this proposed revision (Peffer, *Marxism, Morality, and Social Justice*) was published at the very time the Soviet empire was falling. The author denies that Stalin's policies had any connection with Marxism and suggests that "capitalism" rather than communism was "the primary cause of human-rights violations" worldwide (446–47). As noted previously, in *JF* (178) Rawls himself leans toward Marx's view "that no regime with private property in the means of production" can be just.

348). For Rawls, that point is reached only amidst "a constitutional crisis of the requisite kind," as distinguished from "an emergency in which there is a present or foreseeable threat of serious injury . . . or even of the destruction of the state." (Not even the threat of our government's imminent destruction can justify limiting revolutionary advocacy.)

The reader may be curious to learn what would constitute "a constitutional crisis of the requisite kind" to justify restrictions on political speech. Unfortunately, as is often the case, Rawls "cannot go into a systematic explanation"; like Supreme Court justice Potter Stewart, who said of pornography that he knew it when he saw it, Rawls is still confident that "often we can tell when [the distinction] applies" (PL, 356). He goes on to argue that "a number of historical cases" demonstrate that "free democratic political institutions have operated effectively to take the necessary measures in serious emergencies without restricting free political speech; and . . . where such restrictions have been imposed they were unnecessary and made no contribution whatever to meeting the emergency" (PL, 354). He does not, however, cite any instances to illustrate this claim. Since there has "never in our history . . . been a time when free political speech, and in particular subversive advocacy, could [legitimately] be restricted or suppressed," Rawls concludes that that right "in a well-governed democratic society under reasonably favorable conditions" is effectively "absolute" (PL, 355).[18] As with his remarks about the supposed domination of the democratic political process by the rich, Rawls provides no evidence to support these sweeping assertions, which would seem to be belied by the historical record (such as Lincoln's judgment of the necessity of restrictions on political speech during the Civil War, a period Rawls cites to show that not even our most serious national crisis was sufficiently grave to justify such restrictions [PL, 355]).[19]

18. It is a bit surprising to find Rawls implying here that the United States is a reasonably "well-governed" and democratic society, in view of his repeated denunciations of the supposedly grave injustices from which we suffer, his representation of the U.S. as a merely "alleged" constitutional democracy in LP, and his comparison of this country to the Germany of 1870–1945 in JF. Or does he mean only that if even an undemocratic and badly governed country like the U.S. can survive any shocks from seditious speech, a truly just and democratic one would be more secure still?

19. To demonstrate that restrictions on political speech have never been necessary in this country, Rawls rhetorically asks, "Wasn't it dangerous to hold free elections in 1862–64 in the midst of a civil war?" (PL, 355). As elsewhere, Rawls here adopts an all-or-nothing approach to questions of liberty that leads him to overlook the difference between the fundamental character of regular elections in a constitutional democracy and particular, temporary restrictions on political advocacy or other liberties. Contrast Lincoln, "Message to Congress in Special Session," and letter "to Erastus Corning and Others," June 12, 1863, Collected Works of Abraham Lincoln, 4:429–30, 5:260–69. See also John Herman Randall, Constitutional Problems Under Lincoln, especially chap. 19.

Rawls's confidence that no restraints on subversive advocacy are ever needed in a "moderately well-governed regime" rests not on empirical or historical analysis but only on a dogmatic assumption that "if free political speech is guaranteed . . . serious grievances do not go unrecognized or suddenly become highly dangerous," but rather are "taken into account." (He does not explain why such grievances would go unheard in a democracy in the absence of the threat of revolutionary violence.) Given people's "natural political virtue," Rawls believes, "the basic institutions of a moderately well-governed democratic society are not so fragile as to be brought down by subversive advocacy alone"; whereas in a truly "well-ordered society . . . by definition the problem does not arise." (He maintains, characteristically, that the resolution of such issues depends not on empirical observation but on "a theory of how democratic institutions are likely to work" [PL, 347]. Note the question-begging character of that "alone.") Hence Rawls renounces the Hobbesian view "of the very great fragility and instability of political arrangements," which supposes that "even in a democratic regime . . . volatile and destructive social forces may be set going by revolutionary speech." Rather, "to repress subversive advocacy" may cause the government to ignore the "warning" of "an impending crisis rooted in the perception of significant groups" that the existing political and social system is unjust (PL, 346–48).

In view of these remarks, one might wonder (for instance) what advice Rawls would have given the fragile but liberal-democratic regime of Weimar Germany on how to deal with Nazi and Communist rabble-rousers during the 1920s and early 1930s. As in his civil-disobedience doctrine, he seems unable to conceive that "significant," well-organized groups may seek to overthrow a decent government on the basis of fundamentally *unjust* claims. (This despite Rawls's earlier observation of the likelihood "under many historical conditions" that a reasonable consensus will be overwhelmed "by unreasonable and even irrational [and sometimes mad] comprehensive doctrines" [PL, 126].) In his 1996 preface to PL Rawls attributes the fall of the Weimar Republic to the fact that "none of the traditional elites of Germany supported its constitution" or "believed a decent parliamentary regime was possible," but he does not address the causes of that alienation of support, notably the government's impotence in dealing with violent extremists on the Left or Right. Instead of concerning himself with such practical issues, Rawls explains the lack of support for the Weimar government, in circular fashion, as a consequence of people's "tak[ing] for granted . . . that a just and well-ordered democratic society is impossible," an assumption that he suggests could have been combated if only theories like his own had circulated so as to "shape the underlying attitudes of the public culture" (*PL*, lxi). This doesn't take us very far. Would Rawls have sought to engender an "overlapping consensus" among Nazis, Communists, and democrats by assuring all parties that there was no need to subscribe to a particular set of truths as the foundation of just government? (Recall his judgment that the less radical split that led to the American Civil War was unresolvable.)

Whether or not Weimar's fall was inevitable, as Rawls maintains, citing Schmitt (*PL*, lxii n), there was certainly nothing inevitable about the regime that succeeded it. But Rawls's free-speech doctrine would only have handcuffed a government trying to prevent the rise to power of a movement such as Nazism. A reading of Thucydides, or a viewing of "Cabaret," might call into question Rawls's confidence that democratic institutions can never be overthrown largely as the result of "mere" political advocacy.[20] (If Rawls's answer is that his advice holds only for "well-ordered" regimes that are not seriously threatened by subversion, his argument that they cannot be overthrown by subversive advocacy is circular.[21])

In other passages of *PL*, Rawls himself acknowledges the historical rarity of "just cooperation among free and equal citizens" (*PL*, 4), observes that a publicly "shared sense of justice . . . is the result of time and cultiva-

20. In this connection Rawls's exaggerated contrast between Hobbes and Locke (*PL*, 347) overlooks the fact that (as I have noted) for Locke, what deters the people from lightly exercising their right of resistance is not any "natural political virtue" he assumes they possess, but the fact that if a grievance is not widely enough shared to induce a large multitude of the population to rebel, the rebellion is likely to fail and its instigators severely punished. Note also Locke's Hobbesian reservation to the sovereign of the authority to forbid the teaching of opinions that are "contrary to human society," including atheism (*A Letter Concerning Toleration*, 50–52). Rawls apparently borrows his attribution of a doctrine of "natural political virtue" to Locke from Peter Laslett, who fabricates it for the sake of a "sympathetic" reading that he admits is not entirely consistent with the text: see Locke, *Two Treatises*, editor's introduction, 109–16.

21. In fact, the U.S. has prosecuted subversive advocacy only in times of war or in the face of revolutionary agitation or espionage sponsored by foreign governments: France in the 1790s, the Soviet Union in the 1950s. But even though Rawls allows, following the Supreme Court's 1969 *Brandenburg* decision, that subversive speech may be punished "when it is both directed to inciting imminent and unlawful use of force and likely to achieve this result" [*PL*, 348], which sounds a lot like the "clear and present danger" test he rejects, it isn't clear how far his doctrine would allow American authorities to restrict the open advocacy by Islamic "fundamentalists" of violent jihad and suicide bombings against Western polities, such as has become widespread in Europe in recent years, and which may have led to the 2005 London subway bombings and the 2006 airline plot, as well as having previously inspired the shoe-bomber Richard Reid. See Patrick E. Tyler and Don Van Natta Jr., "Militants in Europe Openly Call for Jihad and the Rule of Islam"; Andrew McCarthy, "Free Speech for Terrorists?"; Melanie Phillips, *Londonistan*, chap. 1.

tion, easier to destroy than to build up" (*PL*, 316), and warns that "frequent controversy over the structure of government . . . raises the stakes of politics and may lead to distrust and turmoil that undermines constitutional government" (*PL*, 228). It is regrettable that Rawls neglects to consider these points when formulating his free-speech doctrine.

To point out the deficiencies of Rawls's rationale for an effectively unlimited right of seditious speech is not to argue for any particular alternative judicial formulation limiting that right; it is simply to indicate the imprudence of putting such a privilege on the same constitutional footing as the essential right of citizens in a constitutional democracy to advocate peaceful changes in the law or Constitution that are compatible with the overall principles of such a regime.[22] But Rawls's unreflective confidence regarding the inherent capacity of democratic institutions to preserve themselves against domestic challenges points to one of the more glaring deficiencies in *PL* (as in *Theory*): the author's failure to consider substantively the means by which liberal-democratic regimes can be perpetuated. It is in this connection that the defect of Rawls's procedure of deriving a "political" conception of justice from ideas that he represents as implicit in the public culture, and then holding up the resultant conception as a standard that actual institutions must meet to be deemed just, can be seen most fully. In contrast to the great tradition of Western political philosophy from Plato on, and to the tradition of liberal statesmanship exemplified by the American founders and individuals such as Lincoln and Churchill, Rawls puts the political cart before the horse. He never considers how the United States and other modern, liberal republics acquired the particular civic culture they enjoy; what the roots of that culture are; or what elements might be responsible for its broad coherence.[23] It is as if after finding the shards of an ancient vase, an archeologist thought it his task to piece them together in any manner that pleased him, without regard to the vase's original design or what it would take to restore its functionality. Just as Rawls's doctrine of civil disobedience took for granted a widespread disposition toward law-abidingness that it did nothing to encourage, Rawls presupposes the existence of a liberal political culture without considering its origin or appreciating its potential

22. For an excellent treatment of this issue, see Harry V. Jaffa, "On the Nature of Civil and Religious Liberty"; also Walter Berns, *The First Amendment and the Future of American Democracy*, especially 169–85.

23. Hence despite the revisions Rawls made to his abstract and ahistorical account of how people might be induced to alter their "wider doctrines" to accommodate his "political conception" (*PL*, 160) in response to Kurt Baier's criticisms of an earlier version, Baier's judgment of it as "armchair sociology" remains valid (Baier, "Justice and the Aims of Political Philosophy," 783).

fragility, thinking that it can be reconfigured to fit his demands without weakening people's attachment.[24]

IV.

Fortunately, more than two centuries since the founding, America's constitutional-liberal political culture is far from a broken vase, and the documents outlining its essential principles, along with the philosophical writings containing the reasoning underlying them, are still accessible to us. Although Rawls scarcely acknowledges this fact, it is not accidental that he should find the principles of liberty and equality to be at the core of our tradition: they are there largely because Locke and his philosophic and political successors put them there, and because in their Lockean formulation (as developed by the American founders) those principles apparently answer sufficiently to fundamental human needs to facilitate the prosperity of a regime built on them like the United States.

Part of the genius of the Lockean natural-right teaching, however, is that it does not ordain either the acceptance of a specific formula for resolving particular civic issues (leaving them to be settled by representative institutions in the light of changing circumstances and popular wishes) or full agreement on the theoretical grounds of men's inalienable rights (hence providing, as I noted in chapter 10, a genuine basis for "overlapping consensus" such as Rawls aspires to but fails to deliver through his doctrine).[25] Neither the American public culture nor any other was founded de novo; hence our beliefs and mores reflected from the outset an only partly coherent blending of the British political and legal traditions, biblical religion, the classical philosophical and literary heritage, and Americans' own experiences in self-government before 1776 with the teachings of modern, liberal political philosophy enunciated by Locke and Montesquieu. But those philosophers had designed their teachings to outwardly harmonize with, while gradually liberalizing, the moral and cultural heritage of their respective countries.[26]

24. Cf. Galston's observation of how Rawls's representation of liberalism as a "freestanding" view reflects the illusion that the legitimacy of existing political institutions can be taken for granted, without reference to the more fundamental doctrines from which they derive (*Liberal Pluralism*, 40–41).

25. On the flexibility of Lockean principles in this regard, see Zuckert, *Launching Liberalism*, 21, 361–63; similarly (with respect to Hobbesean liberalism), Gray, "Can We Agree to Disagree?"

26. For Locke's endeavor to harmonize Christian belief with his philosophic teaching, see his *On the Reasonableness of Christianity*; Sanford Kessler, "John Locke's Legacy of Religious Freedom"; and Zuckert, *Launching Liberalism*, 147–68, 361–62. On Montesquieu, see Thomas Pangle, *Montesquieu's Philosophy of Liberation*.

Regarding Rawls's project of supplying a basis for consensus derived from his artificial conception of human beings as "equal moral persons," we might repeat Montesquieu's judgment of James Harrington's political scheme: "he built Chalcedon with the coast of Byzantium before his eyes"; that is, he ignored the great liberal good that was already present in his country in pursuit of an abstract ideal.[27] By contrast with Locke's liberalism, Rawls's theory is too specific (and partisan) where it ought to leave more room for prudential judgment (e.g., regarding the toleration of subversive speech or of degrading sexual activity, or the legitimacy of public financing of "high" culture) and too general where it ought to be more specific (notably, regarding the choice between socialism and free enterprise). The very development of the American welfare state over the past century indicates that our constitutional-democratic institutions were conceived with sufficient breadth and openness to allow government, in response to popular demands, to vastly increase the scope of its social-welfare spending, without the need of anything like Rawls's difference principle to guarantee it. (Although, beginning with the New Deal, presidents and Congresses have frequently disregarded constitutional limitations on the scope of federal domestic powers, with effects on our political culture that are lamentable from a Tocquevillean perspective, our fundamental constitutional consensus has led even those who oppose these extensions to accept their legitimacy—in contrast with continued widespread challenges to constitutional inventions imposed on the people by unaccountable judges.)

Rawls rightly senses that a constitutional regime cannot be held together merely by a modus vivendi among adherents of rival doctrines. But the thin gruel of his "political conception of justice" (to say nothing of his abstract, apolitical account of moral education in *Theory*) could hardly supply the needed civic cement. Locke's *Thoughts Concerning Education* as well as the writings of a number of American founders exhibit a thoughtfulness about civic education that has no counterpart in Rawls's writings.[28] It is the shared attitudes that Tocqueville called *moeurs,* along with the substantive principles of the Declaration, rather than artificial formulas like Rawls's "public reason," that normally prevent policy disagreements in the U.S. from becoming unbridgeable impasses. By contrast, reflecting his putatively cosmopolitan ("Archimedean") outlook, Rawls offers no account

27. Montesquieu, *Spirit of the Laws,* bk. 6, chap. 6 (last sentence). (Harrington's scheme was in fact far less utopian than Rawls's.)

28. See Tarcov, *Locke's Education;* Zuckert, *Launching Liberalism,* 361–62; Frederick Rudolph, ed., *Essays on Education in the Early Republic;* Thomas Pangle and Lorraine Pangle, *The Learning of Liberty;* Galston, *Liberal Purposes,* chap. 11. On the deficiency of Rawls's abstract approach to political culture, cf. Richard John Neuhaus, *The Naked Public Square,* 152, 257–58.

of the nation-state or the patriotic virtues. Rawls's account of liberalism presupposes for its success that people's lives will be molded by morally and politically healthy comprehensive views, yet does nothing to encourage such views, implicitly relying instead on a cultural "invisible hand" (as it were) that is far less reliable than the economic one.[29] Again, the fundamental defect of Rawls's notion of "political" philosophy is that it is so unpolitical.

Given the natural flux of human affairs, especially in the modern era of commerce, technology, and the global interchange of ideas, no political regime can prosper over the long run simply as the result of the soundness of its originating principles. As Locke and his successors recognized, the partisan of liberalism cannot afford to take for granted the existence of a public culture that supports it. Rather, philosophers, poets, and statesmen who are in a position to shape popular beliefs require both a continuing understanding of liberal principles and a reflective consideration of how those principles apply in changing circumstances if they are to exercise their influence responsibly. Since a liberal regime has only limited resources with which to shape people's beliefs and mores, the survival and continued prosperity of such a regime depend on the combined efforts of statesmen and thoughtful private individuals to supply the kind of civic education that the overall *politeia* or regime of preliberal polities once aspired to provide.[30] The success of the American polity since its founding

29. Revealingly, in his *Commonweal* interview, Rawls responds to the suggestion that his conception of individual dignity derives from a biblical view of human sacredness as if pleading the Fifth—"I don't have to deny that" (*CP,* 621). With his antifoundationalist approach, he sees no need to consider the ground of human dignity and therefore no need for a persuasive response to nihilism.

On the neglect by contemporary liberal theorists like Rawls and Dworkin of the moral foundations of public-regardingness in a liberal society, see Clor, *Public Morality,* 71–76, 148–74; Berkowitz, *Virtue and the Making of Modern Liberalism,* 22–34.

30. It is curious that Rawls should claim that "the problem of stability has played very little role in the history of moral philosophy" (*PL,* xix), even granting that his reading may have been limited to such "writers we usually study" as Hume and Kant (*PL,* xxix). In fact, his reading of Hume and Kant on that issue is highly dubious: he attributes to both thinkers (without textual citation except for a single secondary source) the view that human beings "have in our nature sufficient motives to lead us to act as we ought without the need of external sanctions" (*PL,* xxix) (contrast Hume, *Treatise of Human Nature,* bk. 3, pt. 2, chap. 7, and "Of the Origin of Government," in *Essays Moral, Political, and Literary,* 37–41). Although Kant articulates an intrinsic motive for acting from duty (the attainment of rational freedom) and represents as an ideal a state in which punishment would no longer be needed (*Critique of Pure Reason,* B373), he never denies the need for sanctions to enforce just conduct in the actual world (see *Lectures on Ethics,* 55–57; *Education,* pt. 5, 82–83; "Idea for a Universal History with a Cosmopolitian Purpose," in *Political Writings,* 6th thesis; *Metaphysical Elements of Justice,* I, sec. 42, [Akad. ed. 307]).

has reflected not only the wise design of its institutions but the efforts of a series of great civic teachers both public (notably, Lincoln) and private.[31]

As I observed in the introduction, despite the work of our wisest civic teachers, American political culture has experienced a certain decay since the late nineteenth century as the founders' principles came to be obscured under the influence of historicism and pragmatism. No matter how great the efforts of prudent statesmen and thinkers to mold it, the culture of a liberal regime is never simply controllable by them. Over time, and especially since the advent of the electronic media, the popular habits and mores of people in the United States and in other modern democracies have been shaped by a multitude of sources, the majority of which cannot be said to have the elevation of people's moral character as their primary goal, or to embody serious reflection on the sorts of virtue required either for individual happiness or collective well-being. To a degree, this openness to all sorts of random influences is part of the price we pay for enjoying the liberty to pursue more noble sorts of endeavor; but at the least, it is a problem requiring consideration by anyone concerned with the perpetuation of liberal democracy.[32]

In view of the multitudinous sources of American political culture, it is not surprising that it should contain numerous partly inconsistent strands, of which the Lockean and Rousseauean elements cited by Rawls are but two. (Much more powerful and problematic today, though never addressed by Rawls, is the postmodern, anti-Enlightenment, and antiliberal impulse ultimately derivative from Nietzsche and Heidegger—an impulse that underlies Rawls's own doctrine of the "self" and his wish to avoid grounding political life in consideration of the truth.[33]) Nor can there possibly exist a clear division between political and nonpolitical elements of the common culture, such as Rawls's political conception of justice presupposes. In fact, as we have seen, Rawls's account of justice is far from the impartial adjudicator between contending traditions, "neutral" in its

31. On the role of American novelists in shaping popular political mores, see Catherine H. Zuckert, *Natural Right and the American Imagination*.

32. For an excellent summary of the problem alluded to here, see Cropsey, "The United States as Regime and the Sources of the American Way of Life," in *Political Philosophy*, 1–15. On the problem posed for representative government by the modern mass media, see Mansfield, "The Media World and Constitutional Democracy," in *America's Constitutional Soul*, 163–76.

33. Rawls's attempt to make his political doctrine independent of "metaphysical" or natural foundations parallels Jacques Derrida's endeavor to purge Martin Heidegger's thought of remaining "ontological" elements. On the problematic implications of Derrida's project for liberalism, see Luc Ferry and Alain Renaut, *French Philosophy of the Sixties*, chap 4.

"aim" if not its procedure (*PL*, 5, 193–94), that he claims.[34] Rather, in *PL* no less than in *Theory*, Rawls has summarized in a peculiarly abstract form some tenets of the political ideology that seems most congenial to members of the American academic and intellectual class of recent decades. (There is a curious naiveté in Rawls's attributing an impartiality of aim to his position in *PL* shortly after accepting, in the 1987 preface to the French edition of *Theory*, the designation "left-liberal" for his broader doctrine [*CP*, 415–16]: did he never wonder how a purportedly impartial adjudicative principle just happened to generate left-liberal consequences that all reasonable human beings should accept?)

Had Rawls looked beyond the narrow confines of his academic environment, he might have noticed that the greatest danger to the perpetuation of the broad American cultural and political consensus today arises from a development originating in academia itself: the multicultural movement, which at its extreme challenges the "privileging" of liberal principles of natural right, to say nothing of a collective national identity. A year before the publication of *PL*, this movement's threat to the American liberal consensus had already prompted a prominent liberal historian to warn against "the disuniting of America."[35] But Rawls had nothing to say on the subject.

As I have shown, Rawls's real concern is not Americans' lack of consensus, but their failure to adopt a consensus supporting his favored left-liberal policies. In this regard it is noteworthy that Rawls selected the abortion issue to highlight the practical implications of "public reason," suggesting that any "reasonable" view must accept the principle of *Roe v. Wade*. In fact, that decision exemplified the same approach as Rawls's ostensible pursuit of consensus—reading the justices' own partisan convictions into the Constitution without any textual foundation, in the hope thereby of removing the issue from the sphere of political debate, just as

34. Again, see *JF* (154) for Rawls's retraction of the claim to neutrality, prefigured in *Theory* (507). On Rawls's use of the pretense of metaphysical neutrality to justify partisan judgments without actually defending them, cf. Peter Berkowitz, "John Rawls and the Liberal Faith," 66–67.

35. Arthur M. Schlesinger, *The Disuniting of America*. For a more recent warning by a distinguished political scientist, see Samuel Huntington, *Who Are We?* On the tension between contemporary multiculturalism and the principles of natural right as well as philosophy, see Allan Bloom, "Western Civ," in *Giants and Dwarfs*, 13–31, and the essays by Walter Berns, Wilson Carey McWilliams, James Ceaser, Marc Plattner, and Lorraine Pangle in Arthur Melzer, Jerry Weinberger, and M. Richard Zinman, eds., *Multiculturalism and American Democracy*. See also Gray, *Enlightenment's Wake*, 23–25. In "Can We Agree to Disagree?" Gray cites Rawls's disregard of recent political conflicts worldwide over issues of religious, ethnic, and national identity to illustrate the "political irrelevance" of his version of liberalism.

Rawls endeavors to put religious and moral challenges to his "reasonable" consensus "off the agenda" (*PL*, 151–52, 161). The abortion controversy is one of several, as William Galston observes (the others including church-state relations and pornography), in which the Court has sharpened the political conflict between liberals and "fundamentalists" by "emphasiz-[ing] the requirement of state neutrality in areas previously seen as the legitimate arena for collective moral judgment," threatening the possibility of reasonable consensus by pushing libertarian and egalitarian principles to a doctrinaire extreme.[36] In the recent words of a federal appellate judge, lamenting his colleagues' ruling that voluntary dinner prayers at Virginia Military Institute violated the First Amendment's establishment clause, "When courts push too insistently at shared understandings and accommo-dations—reached over time and given meaning through the customs and rituals of observance—they risk inflaming the sorts of religious passion that the establishment clause was designed to prevent."[37]

V.

If it is impossible to reduce the American political culture (or that of any regime) to a simply coherent set of underlying principles, I suggest, the political philosopher who is genuinely concerned to promote a just and rea-sonable political consensus should follow a very different approach from Rawls's. The classical and modern models most clearly relevant to our sit-uation are those of Aristotle and Tocqueville, respectively. In the *Politics*, Aristotle devotes much of his attention to showing how the variety of imperfect political regimes that typically exist may be improved by making them more moderate—that is, making democracies less simply democratic by providing some political representation and civic security to the rich, and conversely making oligarchies less oligarchic by admitting an element of democracy. The practical ideal, difficult of attainment, is a polity or mixed regime, embodying a blending of democracy and oligarchy, and

36. Galston, *Liberal Purposes*, 269. Other issues on which recent Courts have inflamed partisan controversy by reading a questionable ideological agenda into the Constitu-tion include gender differences and school busing, while in such areas as the death penalty and the exclusionary rule they have obviously endeavored to circumvent the ordinary political process through "creative" readings of the constitutional text. For a critique of the Court's judicialization of political issues at the expense of republican self-government, ostensibly in the name of "rationality," see Robert F. Nagel, "Is 'Ratio-nality Review' Rational?"

37. J. Harvie Wilkinson III, cited in Stuart Taylor, "The Court's Gone Too Far in Purg-ing Religion from the Square," 2604.

thus securing the support of the two major political classes (rich and poor). Even the worst of regimes, tyranny, might be improved by persuading the tyrant that it is in his long-range interest to act more lawfully and justly. Aristotle's procedure is almost the opposite of Rawls's (as well as that of organizations such as the American Civil Liberties Union or, on occasion, the Christian Coalition). Instead of trying to push one partisan principle to its extreme, Aristotle endeavors to moderate it so as to secure a broad consensus that can serve as the foundation of law and therefore of (an inevitably imperfect) justice.[38] The American Constitution, whose creators endeavored (in the words of the authors of the *The Federalist*) to provide "a republican remedy" for the diseases to which republican government is prone, may be understood as a modern application of Aristotle's practice.[39]

Tocqueville is exemplary for our case because he sees in American political life precisely the sort of theoretical "incoherence" that dissatisfied his more ideological European intellectual contemporaries on both the Left and Right, much as it distresses Rawls, yet views this as one of our practical strengths. While Tocqueville's attachment to the principles of republicanism and equal rights is undeniable, he emphasizes (as noted in chapter 8) that the egalitarian principle by itself is no guarantee of liberty, since it is no less compatible with an equality of servitude than with the equality of freedom. He attributes the remarkable blend of freedom and law-abidingness, economic enterprise and civic-mindedness that he finds in America in large measure to the perpetuation in this country, alongside the universal principles of political right articulated in the Declaration of Independence, of more traditional elements of our civic and social life that derive from sources other than Enlightenment rationalism: moderate religious piety, a differentiated family structure, and an "inefficient" but invigorating system of decentralized administration, or local self-government.[40]

---

38. For Aristotle's guiding principle, see *Politics* 1309b18–1310a11, 1320a1–16. For an excellent exposition of Aristotle's procedure in the *Politics*, see Mary P. Nichols, *Citizens and Statesmen*. For an account of his treatment of ethical issues that emphasizes its harmony with the principles of modern liberal democracy, see Stephen G. Salkever, *Finding the Mean*.

39. See Hamilton, Madison, and Jay, *The Federalist*, No. 10, 52. On the sense in which American constitutional democracy is properly understood as a mixed regime requiring a practical harmony between "liberals" and "democrats," see Mansfield, *Spirit of Liberalism*, chap. 1.

40. Tocqueville, *Democracy in America*, vol. 1, pt. 1, chap. 2, 42–44; vol. 1, pt. 2, chap. 9, 274–82; vol. 2, pt. 1, chap. 5; vol. 2, pt. 2, chap. 4; vol. 2, pt. 3, chaps. 9–12. The intent of Tocqueville's political teaching in *Democracy* and its relation to the ideological battles then being waged in continental Europe are cogently articulated by Ceaser in *Liberal Democracy and Political Science*, chap. 7.

VI.

The examples of Aristotle and Tocqueville show us how a political philosopher might promote a political consensus that is truly reasonable, as Rawls aspires but fails to do in *PL*. A genuinely reasonable consensus presupposes, even in a liberal regime founded on the principle of limited government, that the political process is open to the variety of reasonable claims that people make. In assisting the attainment of such consensus, the political philosopher aims to encourage a practical harmony among people's claims rather than demanding that they be transformed to achieve some artificial unity.[41] But while that endeavor exemplifies the "political" function of philosophy, it does not comprehend the *goal* of political philosophy, which entails (Rawls to the contrary notwithstanding) the pursuit of truth about political life. That there is potentially a tension between these aims—as epitomized, at the extreme, by the fate of Socrates—cannot mean that the quest for truth should be abandoned, which would mean sacrificing the highest human potentiality for the sake of other goods to which political life is more immediately instrumental.[42]

In this regard, *PL* is noteworthy not only for Rawls's proposal to dispense with the concept of truth, but also for his aspiration to make "political philosophy possible, independent of other parts of philosophy, especially from philosophy's long-standing problems and controversies," so as to facilitate "an overlapping consensus of reasonable doctrines" while encouraging "reasonable faith in the possibility of a just constitutional regime" (*PL*, 171–72). In effect, Rawls is willing to set aside the very

---

In his 1998 *Commonweal* interview as well as in *JF*, Rawls himself cites Tocqueville to show that religion can flourish in America precisely because of the separation of church and state (*CP*, 620–21; *JF*, 167). But neither in historical practice (until Supreme Court decisions beginning in the 1960s) nor in Tocqueville's account did Americans maintain strict governmental neutrality between religion and atheism (as a requirement that the political regime be strictly impartial among rival comprehensive doctrines would seem to demand). Nor, of course, has there ever been a rule that people are forbidden to make religious arguments in the public sphere on issues of public policy.

Rawls further defends himself against the charge that he provides "a veiled argument for secularism" by maintaining that a secularist might equally maintain that he gives "a veiled argument for religion" (*CP*, 619–20)—though it is hard to imagine what more a committed secularist could demand of Rawls, short of requiring government dissemination of antireligious propaganda. Then again, in the *Commonweal* interview Rawls acknowledges that his own "experience of religion suggests that very few people are actually religious in more than a conventional sense" anyway (*CP*, 616).

41. For Aristotle's critique of an early endeavor at the theoretical simplification of politics, see *Politics* 2.8.

42. Cf. Aristotle *NE* 1145a8–13 (on the relation between philosophy and practical wisdom), 10.7–8.

question of the relation of justice to the order of nature for the sake of securing people's agreement on a particular view of it. Although he claims that "connect[ing] the role of a political conception to the fact of reasonable pluralism" refutes the objection that political liberalism as he conceives it "is skeptical of religious, philosophical, and moral truth, or indifferent to their values" (*PL*, 172), the purported refutation is made doubtful by Rawls's dogmatic assertion that "the question the dominant tradition [of political philosophy] has tried to answer"—that of the "one reasonable and rational conception of the good"—"has no answer: no comprehensive doctrine is appropriate as a political conception for a constitutional regime" (*PL*, 135). Rawls has surely discovered no facts about the good, or about the diversity of human opinions concerning it, that were unknown to Plato or Aristotle, let alone Locke.[43] In fact, it is doubtful that Plato, Aristotle, and their philosophic successors did claim to identify "one reasonable and rational conception of the good," as Rawls contends, let alone that they thought a single "comprehensive doctrine" could serve as the foundation for a constitutional regime.[44] But neither did they think that a regime could be demonstrated to be just, as Rawls endeavors to do, without showing that it is conducive to the substantive human good or goods toward which our nature impels us, or that its stability could be established in the absence of some degree of substantive agreement among citizens on the elements of a good life. And it is an enormous, question-begging leap from observing that a constitutional, liberal regime cannot require all citizens to agree on a specific comprehensive doctrine to the inference that it can do without any agreement on a substantive understanding of the good (such as the doctrine of natural rights), one that entails a broad understanding of the kind of ways of life that ought to be encouraged. As a result of Rawls's exclusion of substantive consideration of the good, his entire demonstration of the "completeness" of justice as fairness and the goodness of a society constituted in accordance with it in his lecture on "Priority of Right and Ideas of

43. On the diversity and variation of good things, and of opinions about noble and just actions, such that the latter might appear to be entirely conventional, see Aristotle *NE* 1094b15–20. (Contrast the unsupported claim of Rawls's admirer Daniel Dombrowski that "Rawls is much more aware than Aristotle of the indeterminacy involved in deciding among the many aims that human beings typically have" [*Rawls and Religion*, 57].) Consider also the variety of characters and their associated conceptions of the good portrayed in Plato's dialogues.

44. Consider in this connection Stauffer, *Plato's Introduction*, 10–12; Galston, *Liberal Pluralism*, 31–32; also Martha Nussbaum's discussion of Aristotle's "thick" but intentionally "vague" account of the good, in "Aristotelian Social Democracy," 62ff; and Harvey C. Mansfield, "Good and Happy." And consider Aristotle's enumeration of the elements of happiness in *Rhetoric* 1.5.

the Good" (*PL*, 173–211) is (like the account of the good in part 3 of *Theory*) purely formal, as is signified by its concluding sentence, which states that "the constraints [of justice] do not refer to, *although they limit*, the substantive content of comprehensive conceptions of the good" (*PL*, 211 [emphasis added]).

Not once but three times in *PL*, Rawls attempts to deter people from seeking to impose their conception of the good on their fellow citizens by observing that "those who insist, when fundamental political questions are at stake, on what they take as true but others do not, seem to others simply to insist on their own beliefs when they have the political power to do so" (*PL*, 61; cf. 127–28, 247); the near circularity of this argument apparently does not dissuade him from thinking it highly persuasive. Although Rawls's endeavor to promote consensus by bracketing the problem of the good was prefigured by Hobbes's and Locke's denials of the existence of a summum bonum and their elevation of the principle of consent over that of wisdom,[45] both thinkers surely do represent their doctrines as accounts of what is by nature good for human beings (or of how to avoid what is naturally bad for them), in the sense that they are rooted in the most fundamental human desires and aversions; and they argue explicitly against the alternative views presented by their philosophic and theological predecessors.[46] Hence the writings of these philosophic founders of liberalism belie Rawls's claim that "historically one common theme of liberal thought is that the state must not favor any comprehensive doctrines and their associated conception of the good" (*PL*, 190).[47]

Later in *PL*, just as in *Theory*, after having denied the need for substantive consideration of the human good while constructing his account of justice, Rawls tries to slip a conception of the good in by the backdoor, ex post facto, to buttress his claims for the "stability" of justice as fairness. The conception (elaborating a two-page discussion in the "Priority of Right" lecture [*PL*, 202–4]) emerges in an account of three grounds that would prompt the parties to the original position "to adopt principles securing the basic liberties and assign them priority." Each of these grounds is simply a restatement of what Rawls had asserted in *Theory*. The first argument asserts "the great advantage to everyone's conception of the good," whatever it may be, "of a just and stable scheme of cooperation"

45. See, on the latter point, Strauss, *Natural Right and History*, 185–86.

46. See, e.g., Hobbes, *Leviathan*, chap. 46, "Of Darkness from Vain Philosophy."

47. Cf. Galston, *Liberal Purposes*, chap. 4; see also Orwin and Stoner, "Neoconstitutionalism?" 469–70, on the "complex structure of values underlying" the American regime, as expressed in the Preamble to the Constitution, including "an ideal of public spiritedness and republicanism" that is given short shrift by Rawls.

such as Rawls's principles facilitate. The scheme embodied by these principles is said to be stable because it "enjoin[s] the basic liberties directly" rather than making them "depend on the greatest net balance of social interests" or "values." The second ground is that the two principles best support people's self-respect, which is "rooted in our self-confidence as a fully cooperating member of society capable of pursuing a worthwhile conception of the good over a complete life." As in *Theory*, Rawls holds such confidence to derive from the respect others display for us by "publicly affirming the basic liberties." The third ground embodies the conception introduced in *Theory* of a well-ordered society as "a social union of social unions." Just as the members of an orchestra achieve a greater good by participating in it, a well-ordered society is such a union "once [the] diverse kinds of human activities are made suitably complementary and . . . properly coordinated" with another (*PL*, 316–21; cf. *Theory*, 459n).

The qualifying clause last quoted exhibits the circularity of this entire argument. As we have repeatedly seen, by making his conception of justice prior to the good, Rawls excludes from consideration or acceptance into a just society all views of the good that are incompatible with it. The consequence is not merely the rejection of regimes based on the enforcement of particular religious visions or on such nonliberal goals as military glory and conquest, but the prohibition of governmental regulations designed to preserve moral decency, to encourage civic virtue, or to express public support for religion as such, which until recently have characterized liberal regimes like the United States no less than nonliberal ones: as Rawls explains in *PL*, "the government can no more act . . . to advance human excellence, or the values of perfection . . . than it can act to advance Catholicism or Protestantism" (*PL*, 179–80). Satisfying as such a vision may be to partisan organizations such as the ACLU, it can hardly be said to support a wide variety of conceptions of the good.[48]

Similarly, Rawls's assurance that his conception of justice supports everyone's self-respect is likely to prove persuasive, I have suggested, only

48. Consider Rawls's account in *PL* of how he identified the primary goods to be allocated in accordance with his principles: this question "is not decided by asking what general means are essential for achieving the final ends which a comprehensive empirical or historical survey might show that people usually or normally have in common. There may be few if any such ends; and those there are may not serve the purposes of a conception of justice. . . . While the determination of primary goods invokes a knowledge of the general circumstances and requirements of social life, it does so only in the light of a conception of the person *given in advance*" (308 [emphasis added]). Apparently Rawls thought his artificial "conception of the person" so attractive that actual human beings would revise their aims and desires just to fit it.

For Rawls's partial retraction in *IPRR* of the mandate of religious neutrality, with reference to issues such as school prayer, see chapter 12 below.

to people whose expectations of respect are on a par with Rodney Danger-field's. Since the first principle treats people's life plans as worthwhile only in the sense that everyone whose plan meets Rawls's criteria of justice has the right to pursue it, "self-respect" means here merely that nobody's way of life is publicly regarded as inferior to anyone else's. Hence Rawls again ordains that people "are not to be criticized" for failing to think through their aspirations, since "in the liberal view there is no political or social evaluation of conceptions of the good within the limits permitted by justice" (*PL*, 314). As we have seen, in *Theory* Rawls carried this thought to the extreme of holding that the "plan" of devoting oneself to grass counting must be deemed no less worthy of social respect than any other. What sane person would be comforted by knowing that his achievements are regarded as just as worthwhile as that of someone who had counted the greatest number of blades of grass?

In this connection, we note the circularity of Rawls's earlier assertion that "if a political conception of justice is mutually recognized by reasonable and rational citizens who affirm the reasonable comprehensive doctrines in an overlapping consensus . . . this fact itself confirms that its free basic institutions allow sufficient space for ways of life worthy of citizens' devoted allegiance" (*PL*, 210). Since Rawls had specified that ideas of the good must be "tailored to meet the restrictions imposed by the political conception of justice" (*PL*, 203), it follows necessarily that citizens of a just society as he defines it will find the conception acceptable; but this demonstrates nothing about the substantive worth of the ways of life they are allowed to pursue.

Elsewhere, Rawls acknowledges in response to William Galston that it is not only "unworthy forms of life" that would "lose out" in his "just constitutional regime" and agrees with Isaiah Berlin's point that "there is no social world without loss" (*PL*, 197–98). But Rawls's response to the objection that his theory allows insufficient space for worthy ways of life only deepens the problem: he maintains that "there is no criterion for what counts as sufficient space except that of a reasonable and defensible political conception of justice" such as he claims to have provided. This defense is also circular: Rawls is saying that his conception of justice simply doesn't allow us to ask whether it leaves sufficient scope for worthy ways of life. A serious consideration of the elements of a good life would offer such a criterion, even if it obstructed Rawls's demand that the good be subordinated to the just as he conceives it. (If living in any society, even a perfectly just one by Rawls's standards, entails compromising or sacrificing some people's legitimate ideals and aspirations, how can justice itself merit the "uncompromising" status that Rawls attributes to it in *Theory?*)

No less circular is Rawls's account of people's "moral power" of choosing a "rational" conception of the good, given his failure to provide any substantive distinction between rational and irrational conceptions, and his acknowledgment that rationality in his sense is compatible with being "psychopathic" (PL, 51). And the dismissal of "moral skeptic[s]" as not even needing to be answered by demonstrating how justice in Rawls's sense is compatible with their good (PL, 52) similarly circumscribes the range of views that must be considered, but thereby further limits the relevance of Rawls's argument to the real issues and possibilities of political life.[49]

Reconsidering, finally, Rawls's conception of society as a "social union of social unions," the orchestra analogy disregards the fact that an orchestra has a specific goal to which all members must contribute if they wish to remain in it and enjoy the resultant benefits. No one whose aim (or competence) is limited to playing out of tune, let alone counting blades of grass, can be expected thereby to earn the other players' respect or even their tolerance. On the political stage, analogously, people can be said to "share" in one another's "resources" (as asserted in a passage Rawls quotes anew from Humboldt [PL, 321]) only to the degree that their resources contribute to a common, substantive aim. As I suggested in chapter 9, the life of a pious man is not typically "enlarged" (PL, 323), at least from his point of view, by the efforts of militant atheists. Advocates of free enterprise do not find their society enhanced by the votes of socialists as such (however well members of the two groups may cooperate in nonpolitical endeavors). And how would one demonstrate to Socrates (who by his testimony abstained from political affairs to the extent feasible) that the "democratic society" of Athens embodied "a far more comprehensive good" than the pursuit of philosophy in which he engaged with his friends?[50]

VII.

Let us return, then, from Rawls's imaginary "social union of social unions" to the real, only partly united, but surely liberal American political regime as it exists. Despite the sometimes heated rivalry of advocates of alternative political, economic, and moral agendas, the vast majority of Americans continue to respect the Constitution and laws to which they owe their liberty and prosperity. Attempts to overcome or circumvent this

49. Cf. Galston, *Liberal Purposes*, 88.
50. See Plato *Apology of Socrates* 31d–32a. Consider in this connection Rawls's denial that there is any "such thing as private reason," in contrast with "public and social reason" (PL, 220n).

diversity by imposing a theoretical perspective on which all citizens are to ground their political demands—whether it is Rawls's doctrine or, say, the libertarian alternative propounded by his Harvard colleague Nozick—are unlikely to improve our situation.[51]

In his use of the term "political philosophy," Rawls correctly discerns that it doesn't mean only philosophizing about politics, but entails philosophizing in a politic manner. In its original sense, this meant pursuing truth in a way that takes account of the political effects of the public presentation of philosophy, in a way that the mature, Platonic Socrates did but the Aristophanic or "pre-Socratic" one and his predecessors did not. By contrast, in his practice of what he calls political philosophizing, Rawls proves to be neither politic nor philosophical. Whereas Aristotle and Locke, for instance, along with the American political tradition itself, teach us to appreciate vigorous but nonviolent political debate as a way of asserting our spirited claim to self-rule while potentially inducing us to transcend our unreflective biases, Rawls persistently treats such controversies as problems or "impasses" calling for an academic theorist to settle them by ruling various claims out of bounds.[52] In contrast not only with the substantive tradition of liberal political philosophy but also with that of common-law jurisprudence, Rawls severely constrains the scope of empirical political and legal reasoning whereby the principles of individual liberty are harmonized with the necessity of democratic political consent and the requirements of statesmanship.[53] As well, his attempt (along with Ronald Dworkin's) to replace the natural-rights teaching of the Declaration, with

51. On the deficiencies of the abstract and apolitical perspective that Nozick shares with Rawls, see Orwin and Stoner, "Neoconstitutionalism?" 459–63, 467–69; and my essay "Libertarianism and Political Philosophy."

52. Consider the observations on this point by Kukathas and Pettit, *Rawls,* 148–50. Rawls's late account of political philosophy as "forging a stable practical agreement among various comprehensive doctrines," they remark, would "eliminate political philosophy," since Rawls's primary concern is now to "end political argument by taking the most fundamental disputes 'off the political agenda'" (149). My reading differs from theirs in that, as noted in the preceding chapter, I believe the emphasis on consensus over truth was already the guiding principle of *Theory.*

53. On the use of Rawls's "political conception of justice" and his notion of overlapping consensus by defenders of the Supreme Court's continued adherence to its abortion-rights doctrine, see Paul O. Carrese, "Judicial Statesmanship, the Jurisprudence of Individualism, and Tocqueville's Common Law Spirit," 470n, 477. The influence of Rawls's doctrine of overlapping consensus derived from the "public political culture" that removes controversial issues from the political agenda may also underlie Chief Justice Rehnquist's opinion in *Dickerson v. United States* (538 U.S. 428 [2000], 443) denying Congress's power to overturn the Court's previous *Miranda* decision on the ground that so-called Miranda warnings to criminal suspects, even if ungrounded in the Constitution, "have become part of our national culture."

its entailment of limited government (hence limiting the scope of political controversy), with a fuzzy doctrine of rights based merely on his private opinions (along with those of his academic peers) threatens to undermine the constitutional consensus that exists in America, restoring, as Fred Baumann observes, the sort of political chaos from which the originators of modern natural-rights philosophy endeavored to rescue us.[54] To the extent that abstract theories like Rawls's are smuggled into our Constitution by judges under the guise of constitutional interpretation, as Rawls encourages them to do (*PL*, 368), they threaten not only self-government but the very civic concord he purports to promote.[55]

54. Baumann, "Affirmative Action," 84–85.

55. In *PL* (360) Rawls suggests that judges use his treatment of freedom of speech as a "guiding framework," while he writes as if his notion that the speech of some should be constrained so as to give that of others its "fair value" were already part of the Constitution (*PL*, 360). Then again, the passage Rawls quotes from *Reynolds v. Sims* regarding citizens' right to an "equally effective" political "voice" demonstrates how federal judges were already capable of distorting the Constitution through careless language well before Rawls's first book was published (*PL*, 361).

CHAPTER 12

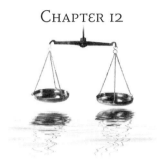

"The Idea of Public Reason Revisited"

I.

Rawls presents his final account of public reason in his essay "The Idea of Public Reason Revisited" (originally published in 1997). Here he distinguishes among (1) "political discussions of fundamental questions" in "the public political forum," including the discourse of judges, government officials, political candidates, and party managers; (2) "the background culture" of civil society, consisting of the "internal life" of private associations within it, to which the limitations of public reason do not apply; and (3) "the *ideal* of public reason," which is realized as government officials and candidates act on the basis of public reason and explain their political positions "in terms of the political conception of justice they regard as the most reasonable." Citizens, in turn, must "think of themselves as if they were legislators" and consider "what statutes . . . they would think it most reasonable to enact" on the basis of public reason, while "repudiat[ing] government officials and candidates who violate" it (*IPRR,* 133–35 [Rawls's emphasis]).

We exercise political power properly according to Rawls "only when we sincerely believe that the reasons we would offer for our political actions—were we to state them as government officials—are sufficient, and we also reasonably think that other citizens might also reasonably accept those reasons" (*IPRR*, 137). (Merely repeating these formulas can become rather confusing.) For instance, to justify depriving some citizens of their religious liberty we must be able to supply reasons that "we might reasonably expect that they as free and equal citizens might reasonably also accept" (*IPRR*, 138). (One wonders how far this sincerity requirement will console those whose liberties are abridged.)

Rawls proceeds to offer a brief account of how a "well-ordered constitutional democracy" in his sense can also be understood as a "deliberative democracy." The latter is a term invented by a school of American political theorists led by Rawls's student Joshua Cohen, along with Amy Gutmann and Dennis Thompson, to describe a form of liberalism that (as Rawls summarizes it) "limits the reasons citizens may give in supporting their political opinions to reasons consistent with their seeing other citizens as equals" (*IPRR*, 139n). In other words, the emphasis is not on fostering open-minded deliberation about public issues but rather on limiting debate (in accordance with Rawls's doctrine of public reason), so as to foreclose appeals to considerations of religion or human excellence on which not all citizens can be expected to agree, and also on (ostensibly) equalizing the influence of citizens who possess different amounts of wealth.[1] Hence one of the two key requisites of deliberative democracy in Rawls's account, besides "an idea of public reason" itself, is the establishment of public campaign financing and the provision of "public occasions of orderly and serious discussion" of government policy to facilitate public deliberation and free it from "the curse of money" (a term Rawls borrows from Ronald Dworkin). Liberation from that curse is in turn required for the other element of deliberative democracy: "widespread education in the basic aspects of constitutional democratic government for all citizens" that would enable "farsighted political leaders . . . to make sound changes and reforms." Unfortunately, "as things are," Rawls laments that (for instance) "sensible proposals for what should be done regarding the

1. In the seminal article that Rawls cites (*IPRR*, 139n), Cohen not only reiterates Rawls's demand for public financing of citizen deliberations, as well as of political campaigns, and the "redress" of "inequalities of wealth," as conditions of true "deliberation," but also stresses that the individual "preferences" on which citizens' deliberations should be based are to be "formed and defined in the first place" by the deliberative institutions themselves. In other words, just as in Rawls's own prescriptions, once the conditions for Cohen's vision of deliberative democracy (which is partly inspired by Habermas's notion of "neutral" political discourse) are achieved, there will be little left to deliberate about ("Deliberation and Democratic Legitimacy," 27–32, 31n12).

For a trenchant critique of the "deliberative democracy" doctrine, see Deneen, *Democratic Faith*, 21–29; also Stephen Salkever, "The Deliberative Model of Democracy and Aristotle's Ethics of Natural Questions."

alleged coming crisis in Social Security," such as increasing the retirement age and "rais[ing] taxes now," have been rejected only because of the corrupting effect of money on "the great game of politics" (*IPRR*, 139–40 [emphasis added]). (That polls haven't detected a groundswell of public opinion calling for taxes to be raised presumably reflects the ability of the rich to conceal the need for this solution, or its attractiveness, from the people. Almost by definition, it appears, the test of an adequate civic education in Rawls's sense is that it would engender public support for the policies he happens to favor.)[2]

Rawls believes the pursuit of campaign donations has also prevented the American government from adequately supporting international institutions such as the United Nations, "foreign aid properly spent," and "human rights at home and abroad" (*IPRR*, 140). He offers no documentation for any of these assertions, apparently regarding them as self-evident. (In fact, it is hard to think of any major corporate lobbies whose interests induce them to work against foreign aid or internationalism; foreign aid and increased subsidies to the UN are typically a hard sell to the public at large, largely on account of often-justified skepticism about their efficacy.) As in *PL*, we cannot avoid noticing the contrast between Rawls's professions of impartiality, openness to diverse views, and pursuit of reasonable consensus and the dogmatism of his actual treatment of political issues.

Turning to the content of public reason, Rawls explains that it is supplied by a "family" of liberal conceptions of justice, of which justice as fairness is but one. While repeating his mandate that all such conceptions give priority to "basic rights, liberties, and opportunities" over "the general good and perfectionist values," and ensure all citizens "adequate all-purpose means to make effective use of their freedoms," Rawls insists that his version of political liberalism "does not try to fix public reason once

2. For his source on the Social Security issue Rawls cites a single review by the left-leaning *New York Times* columnist Paul Krugman of two books on the subject, including one entitled *The AARP: America's Most Powerful Lobby and the Clash of Generations*. As that title suggests, the electoral power of the AARP derives mostly not from money—its dues are nominal—but from its success in persuading Congress of the number of votes it commands. Doubtless AARP's outlook is often lamentably selfish and short-sighted, exemplifying one of the negative side effects of government entitlement programs. But Rawls's real quarrel, as the AARP example shows, is not with "the power of money" but with the power of democracy. In fact, as noted in chapter 11 above, restrictions on campaign contributions of the sort Rawls advocates would only increase the electoral influence of groups such as AARP, whose members have plenty of time to write letters and donate in-kind services to favored candidates.

Needless to say, Rawls makes no mention of another major proposal for "fixing" Social Security over the long term: partial or complete privatization. (It comes from the wrong end of the political spectrum.)

and for all in the form of one favored political conception of justice." Although he believes (with a hint of paternal pride) that justice as fairness "has a certain special place" among such conceptions, Rawls is at pains to explain that "political liberalism also admits [Jürgen] Habermas's discourse conception of democracy . . . as well as Catholic views of the common good and solidarity when they are expressed in terms of political values"—that is, not grounded in faith. However, public reason is not "secular reason" either, according to Rawls, because he has defined secular reason as "reasoning in terms of comprehensive nonreligious doctrines," and political liberalism doesn't rest on any particular comprehensive doctrine at all (*IPRR*, 141–43). In fact, contrary to one critic, Jeremy Waldron, Rawls insists that political liberalism remains open to "new and changing conceptions of political justice," though he does not explain what sort of changes would be allowed, and it is difficult to imagine what they might be (*IPRR*, 143).[3]

Rawls next endeavors to explain how religious believers can wholeheartedly "endorse" the "political ideals and values" of a democratic society rather than "simply acquiesce in the balance of political and social forces . . . even when their comprehensive doctrines . . . may decline" under it (*IPRR*, 149). To achieve this goal believers must be brought to understand that "there is no other way fairly to ensure" their religious freedom than to endorse the principle of toleration (*IPRR*, 151). This point seems unexceptionable because it is tautological, though it begs the question of the proper criterion of fairness. Why should a religious believer think that "fairness" to other religions or nonreligious beliefs, in the sense of giving them an equal chance to triumph, trumps fairness in the sense of obeying God's will? Wouldn't it be easier to persuade the religious to accept a broad range of toleration if we didn't require government to adopt a policy of strict neutrality between religion and secularism, to say nothing of tolerating all consensual sexual practices, however abhorrent they seem? And may not broad toleration, in a society where many people remain ardently religious, depend critically as well on a "balance of political and social forces," hence *The Federalist*'s recommendation of encouraging a multiplicity of religious sects as the best security for religious liberty?[4] A strategy of trying to satisfy

3. In the 1996 preface to *PL* (liii) Rawls similarly affirms that "the content of public reason is not fixed," but remains open to the demands of "new groups with different political problems." Recall as well the tinge of historicism in part 3 of *Theory*, and Rawls's lack of recognition of how such doctrines undermine the status he wants to give to justice. In his late writings, Rawls shows himself so eager to placate critics by assuring them that his doctrine can accommodate their concerns that it becomes increasingly difficult to locate any fixed content in it at all.

4. Hamilton, Madison, and Jay, *The Federalist*, No. 10, 52; No. 51, 292.

the reasonable claims of the religious to a morally decent civic environment surely seems more promising than Rawls's suggestion that we reinterpret each sect's religious doctrine for them (as he did in chapter 4 of *Theory*) to "show them that *despite what they might think,* they can still endorse a reasonable political conception of justice" (*IPRR,* 152; emphasis added).

Later in *IPRR,* I shall observe, Rawls actually bends in the direction of accommodating religious concerns by allowing the possibility that school prayer could be acceptable to public reason so long as the arguments for it derive from its secular benefits. But he never integrates this concession into his interpretation of religious liberty as requiring strict state neutrality among alternative "comprehensive doctrines" in *PL.* Nor does he ever withdraw his prohibition on government enforcement of sexual morality.

In this connection, we must acknowledge the particular urgency today of encouraging a moderate if not liberal interpretation of Islam, as one contemporary Muslim scholar Rawls cites tried to do (*IPRR,* 151n). But in this quest, it is vital to appreciate that part of the appeal of Islamic fundamentalism and its rejection of, and hatred toward, Western ways in recent decades originates in the perceived identification of contemporary liberalism with sexual libertinism. While Islamic fundamentalists have much to answer for in their own treatment of women, it must be acknowledged that the weakening of traditional family values in America, the spread of pornography, and the growing insistence on strict governmental neutrality between religion and atheism has tended to weaken the respectability of the American way of life among traditional believers of various faiths. As the distinguished Islamicist Bernard Lewis observes, "the most powerful accusation of all" against America in the contemporary Muslim world "is the degeneracy and debauchery of the American way of life, and the threat that it offers to Islam."[5]

II.

In the next section, Rawls elaborates his account of public political culture by holding that "reasonable comprehensive doctrines . . . may be introduced in public political discussion at any time, provided that in due course proper political reasons" are supplied that suffice to support the same policies; he calls this "the proviso" (*IPRR,* 153).[6] For instance,

5. Lewis, *The Crisis of Islam,* 81.
6. "The proviso" and several other elements of Rawls's argument in *IPRR* were first laid out in his introduction to the 1996 edition of *PL* (see li–lii).

though the abolitionists and the leaders of the civil rights movement "emphasized the religious roots of their doctrines," their doctrines are acceptable because they also "supported basic constitutional values" (as Rawls judges) (*IPRR*, 154–55). Rawls does not consider whether either movement would have enjoyed the force it did if its members had been educated to believe that their religious concerns were essentially irrelevant to what was constitutionally desirable. Nor does he acknowledge the fundamentally anticonstitutional character of radical abolitionism, as expressed in the slogan "No Union with Slaveholders!" and in John Brown's raid.[7]

Turning to the family, Rawls is apologetic for not having made sufficiently clear in *Theory* that a "liberal conception of justice . . . implied equal justice for women" and hedgingly judges that a political conception of justice requires "no particular form of the family (monogamous, heterosexual, or otherwise)," so long as it is arranged to provide childrearing "effectively" (*IPRR*, 156–57).[8] Although (for reasons he does not spell out) "we wouldn't want political principles of justice . . . to apply directly to the internal life of the family," Rawls emphasizes that those principles "still put essential restrictions" on it as on "all other associations." "If the so-called private sphere is alleged to be a space exempt from justice, then there is no such thing." Acknowledging the possibility "that the family itself is the linchpin of gender injustice," Rawls still believes it may be necessary to "allow for some traditional gendered division of labor within families . . . provided it is fully voluntary and does not result from or lead to injustice." Nonetheless, he denounces ("on behalf of children"!) the "historic injustice" of women's "unjust share of the task of raising, nurturing, and caring for their children" and mandates that steps "be taken either to equalize their share, or to compensate them for it" (*IPRR*, 159–61).[9]

7. As will be noted subsequently, Rawls is less charitable in his judgment of those who forcibly block abortion clinics, not only inspired by their religious beliefs, but also provoked by what they regard as unconstitutional Supreme Court decisions striking down laws limiting abortion.

8. In *JF* (163n) Rawls elaborates that justice as fairness admits "gay and lesbian rights" so long as they "are consistent with orderly family life and the education of children," again begging the question of whether they are so in fact. Cf. Galston, *Liberal Purposes*, 282–86, on the need to "resist the easy relativism of the proposition that different family structures represent nothing more than 'alternative life-styles'"; also Philips, "What about the Overclass?"

9. In *JF* (167) Rawls applauds Susan Okin's suggestion for generating a "critique of the family and gender-structured social institutions" by specifying that the parties in the original position "do not know their sex." Of course this will make them even less human, but once having denied the parties so much other knowledge, there seems no reason not to take this further step. One wonders why Rawls didn't go on to add such factors as sexual orientation, handicapped status, or degree of physical attractiveness to the personal attributes of which knowledge is to be excluded. Doesn't the process amount to "interest-group liberalism," as Schaar remarks ("Reflections on Rawls' *Theory*," 162)?

It is characteristic of Rawls's perspective that at a time when observers from various shades on the political spectrum had come to recognize a national crisis in childrearing, owing to the monumental growth in the U.S. of births to unwed mothers, with all the resultant troubles afflicting children's moral and intellectual development, he was chiefly concerned about whether the family should be allowed to remain in something resembling its traditional form.[10] When push comes to shove, Rawls displays remarkably little substantive concern for those purported objects of his solicitude in *Theory*, the "least advantaged." (As political scientist Joel Schwartz observes, "it is hard to imagine that much can be done to improve the social mobility of impoverished Americans so long as so many of them continue to produce children out of wedlock.")[11] Meanwhile, Rawls's account of the family as such is strikingly negative: he asserts elsewhere that the difference principle is necessary to enable the less advantaged to "accept more easily the constraints the family and other social conditions impose" (*JF*, 163), as if poor people would otherwise find the family a burden rather than a joy. This displacement of the erotic in favor of the (ostensibly) just again reminds us of Socrates' *reductio ad absurdum* of the pursuit of perfect justice in Plato's *Republic*.[12] At the same time, Rawls's emphasis on the need to minimize differences in gender roles is animated not by the concern to subordinate the private to the public, as in the *Republic*, but by the wish to equalize the "constraints" on individuals' pursuing their respective interests, thus highlighting anew his individualism.[13]

10. Recall also Rawls's elevation of the freedom to "revise our final ends" as the most important liberty in chapter 3 of *Theory*—a self-centered outlook that contributes to undermining the institution of marriage as a lifelong commitment today. As of 2003, 35 percent of all births in the U.S. were to unmarried women; for African-Americans, the figure was 68 percent (Charles Murray, "The Hallmark of the Underclass"). The link between growing up in a single-parent family and poor educational achievement is widely documented, as noted by George Will, "'Fixing' Education." See also Sawhill, "Behavioral Aspects of Poverty," 87–92. On the link between the rise in unwed motherhood and the increase in violent crime in Britain—an increase that arguably was prevented in America only by a large rise in imprisonment—see Charles Murray, "The British Underclass: Ten Years Later," 31–35.

11. Schwartz, "Growing Pains," 39.

12. See especially book 5, wherein gender differences and the family itself are suppressed in the name of the ostensible production of the best possible "guardians." Socrates even proposes a comprehensive solution to the day-care problem (460c–d).

13. Here a contrast with Tocqueville's account of the American family would be instructive: while implicitly conceding that women typically make greater sacrifices to maintain the democratic family than men do, he suggests that the household created by women constitutes a needed refuge from the competitive individualism of bourgeois society. Rawls's "just" family, characterized by continual attentiveness to how the division of labor is arranged and whether women receive their proper compensation, seems less likely to offer such refuge. See Tocqueville, *Democracy in America*, vol. 2,

III.

Little need be said about the last two sections of *IPRR*, in which Rawls defends his doctrine against various objections. Here, his strategy is largely to back off from claiming to derive particular substantive conclusions from it. Hence in response to the charge that public reason "mistakenly tries to settle political questions in advance," Rawls indicates that even when it comes to an issue like school prayer, public reason doesn't prohibit it: it just requires that satisfactory "public" reasons be given to the effect that by promoting religion, government, as Patrick Henry maintained, supports civic morality and tranquility (*IPRR*, 164–65). But if public reason is compatible even with Henry's proposal for mandatory taxation of Virginia citizens to support clergy of their respective faiths—which occasioned James Madison's celebrated "Memorial and Remonstrance" in opposition—it is hard to see what substance that notion adds to our political debates at all. (Most advocates of school prayer and other public support of religion today advance secular as well as religious reasons for their position.)

Similarly, Rawls now describes his assertion of the right to first-trimester abortions in *PL* as merely his "opinion"; public reason would provide a resolution for the abortion controversy only if it supplied "a reasonable argument . . . for the right to abortion but there is no equally reasonable balance, or ordering, of the political values in public reason that argues for the denial of that right" (*IPRR*, 169n).[14] In other words, if good public reasons can be given to uphold legalized abortion that outweigh the reasons against it, then public reason favors legalized abortion. Besides, Rawls adds, even if abortion opponents lose the public debate, "they need not themselves exercise the right to abortion" (*IPRR*, 170). (That is, they will not be required to abort their fetuses.) Hence he urges them (in a tone rather different from that of his account of civil disobedience and conscientious refusal in *Theory*) not to resort to forcible resistance, which would be "unreasonable" (*IPRR*, 170).[15]

---

pt. 3, chap. 10, 566–67; vol. 2, pt. 3, chap. 12; Dorothea Israel Wolfson, "Tocqueville on Liberalism's Liberation of Women," 203–7. Cf. Berkowitz, *Virtue and the Making of Modern Liberalism*, 185–86.

14. On the other hand, as previously noted, in 1997 Rawls signed the so-called Philosophers' Brief urging the Supreme Court to create a constitutional right to physician-assisted suicide (*CP*, 617–18). Why did Rawls now hold that physician-assisted suicide is a constitutional principle rooted in public reason but abortion rights are not? The decision seems an arbitrary or ad hoc one on which his answers might vary from day to day.

15. In an odd shorthand Rawls even calls abortion (not just abortion rights) a near-"Constitutional essential" (*JF*, 117).

In the end, Rawls concedes not knowing "how to prove that public reason is not too restrictive, or whether its forms are properly described"; he even suspects "it cannot be done." But this "is not a serious problem" if, as Rawls believes, "the large majority of cases fit" its framework (*IPRR*, 175). The real issue, of course, is not whether the doctrine of public reason can be stretched to fit all cases, but whether it provides us with any assistance that a constitutional liberal order did not already supply—and far less dogmatically or verbosely. After all, the United States has been largely free of serious religious strife since well before the Revolution, and the religious problem has long since been solved (largely as the consequence of the "Enlightenment Liberalism" that Rawls disparages [*IPRR*, 176]) in most European nations as well, at least until the recent rise of Islamism there. And if the spread of religious fanaticism in the Islamic world can't be overcome by encouraging constitutional government, economic growth, and Enlightenment rationalism, the job surely won't be done by teaching Muslim clerics the "idea of public reason."

The recent growth in political participation among Christian fundamentalists in the U.S. was the not the result of some newfound ambition to impose a theocratic regime on their fellow citizens. Rather, it was a reaction against the endeavor, led by the Supreme Court, to impose a way of life favored by cosmopolitan intellectuals on the entire country.[16] Our Constitution expressly forbids the establishment of a national church, and throughout our history this country has displayed a history of religious toleration that, while not free from blemish, is unrivaled in the history of any other great nation. Is there any need, then, to instruct citizens to be careful, when reasoning about public affairs, to distinguish their "public" reasons for advocating a certain policy from those that derive from their "comprehensive doctrine" (assuming that they know what these terms mean)? Is it even possible to sever one's beliefs about what is best for one's country as a liberal regime from one's beliefs about what is morally best, or best in the eyes of God—any more than one can imagine the reasoning of those parties to the original position who were supposed to defend their religious convictions without knowing what they were or that they had any?

---

16. See Galston, *Liberal Purposes*, 267–73. The quest to make America's backwaters safe for her cosmopolitan intellectuals mirrors the one that Rousseau forcefully challenged some 250 years ago, on behalf of popular mores, especially in his *Letter to M. D'Alembert on the Theater* and *Discourse on the Sciences and Arts*. By highlighting the tension between intellectual cosmopolitanism and the moral virtues that support republicanism, Rousseau, like his successor Tocqueville, helps equip the friends of constitutional republicanism today to diagnose its needs and devise ways of meeting them in a way that Rawls's abstract liberalism does not.

It is somewhat embarrassing to observe how Rawls, in his last years, endeavored mightily to show that he had kept up with the times: that his doctrine, conceived in the wake of postwar liberalism, the civil rights movement, and the Vietnam protests, could accommodate the shibboleths of the 1990s, such as feminism, gay rights, abortion rights, and (in *LP*) the critique of globalization. (Hence in the 1996 introduction to *PL* [liii] he invites the consideration of new "political conceptions" of justice based on concerns regarding "ethnicity, gender, and race.") From the beginning of his career, in "Decision Procedure," to its end, Rawls possessed a remarkable faith that framing issues of political principle with the right technical terminology and devices—the original position, goodness as rationality, the social union of social unions, overlapping consensus, public reason—could somehow improve our civic life in a way that surpassed what America's greatest statesmen and political thinkers, and the liberal philosophers who guided the founders, had managed to accomplish. And just coincidentally, as it were, his procedures issued in consequences that the habitués of Rawls's academic milieu favored all along.

At the same time, in his last writings, Rawls considerably retreated (without acknowledging the fact) from his earlier aspiration to promote consensus on fundamental issues through the adoption of his principles. In the 1996 introduction to *PL*, Rawls acknowledges that his ideal of public reason "does not often lead to general agreement of views" (*PL*, lvii), making it questionable how far it will enable us to overcome "impasses" in our politics as he originally promised. Apparently sensing that he has given away too much, Rawls then rewords this statement in *IPRR* to read that "political liberalism does not hold that the ideal of public reason should *always* lead to a general agreement of views, nor is it a fault that it does not" (*IPRR*, 170; emphasis added). But this verbal change hardly solves the problem.

In another explanation, Rawls holds that once we agree on principles of justice like his, while differences arising from people's conflicting comprehensive doctrines and from "the burdens of judgment" will remain, we can (a) be "reconcile[d] to" conflicts arising from differences in "status, class position, and occupation, . . . ethnicity, gender, and race"; (b) discover that such conflicts "no longer arise, or arise so forcefully"; or (c) find that "these sources of conflict can be largely removed" (*PL*, lx). Nowhere does Rawls demonstrate that Americans are currently unable to reconcile their differences peacefully without needing to reinterpret their beliefs to accord with his concept of public reason. Nor does he explain how his doctrine would mitigate such differences as currently exist, or that eliminating them is either possible or desirable, contrary to the argument of *The Feder-*

alist, No. 10. Meanwhile, he retains the unrealistic notion that human identities can somehow be carved up among people's personal attributes and interests, their beliefs, and their judgments, so that the causes of human conflict can be practically eliminated even as fundamental differences of belief and judgment remain.[17]

In fact, however, Rawls's theory, aside from its barely disguised partisanship, offers only specious solutions to imaginary problems. Just as Rawls warned in *Theory* that our rights were threatened by utilitarianism (a threat unnoticed outside the academy) unless we adopted his principles, in *PL* he alerted us to a nonexistent political impasse between partisans of Locke and Rousseau to justify the renunciation of the doctrine of natural rights and the moral neutralization of our Constitution in the name of public reason. And even though Rawls could offer no evidence that existing economic inequalities in the United States violate his difference principle—that is, there is no way of showing that our social and economic structure doesn't tend as a whole to elevate the living standards and opportunities of the less advantaged to the greatest extent—he used that principle as an excuse for repeatedly denouncing this country's supposed injustices in ways that pleased his academic peers.

Rather than promote justice or civic harmony, Rawls's theory, I have tried to demonstrate, is dangerously misleading in encouraging the reduction of complex political issues to simplistic moral battles between the just and the unjust; promoting self-satisfaction on the part of left-liberal political partisans at the expense of genuinely shared national deliberation; and disparaging the American Constitution itself. In these regards, as well as in its effect on philosophy (as discussed in the preceding chapter), Rawls's legacy is not an edifying one. I believe that it represents a dead end, not only from the perspective of those who reject many of Rawls's favored policies, but also from that of thoughtful liberals who wish genuinely to persuade their fellow citizens while retaining a constitutional framework that makes common deliberation and genuine tolerance possible. After

17. Rawls's continued faith that merely framing his doctrine in the right way would transform political life for the better—thereby qualifying him to be our teacher and guide—is exemplified by the manner in which he originally introduced "the proviso" in the 1996 preface to *PL* (li): "I *now believe* [in the desirability of the proviso], and *hereby I revise*" the previous text of *PL* in that regard [emphasis added]. How often has such language been heard outside the courts of kings, popes, and (in recent decades) activist judges? (On the following page, Rawls mentions that his new doctrine is now "more permissive"—as if he has granted his subjects an indulgence—and even indicates the need to resolve on which day—the same as the one on which arguments based on comprehensive doctrines are made, or "some later day"—they must be supplemented by "public" reasons [*PL*, lii n.].)

surveying Rawls's last treatise, which applies his theory to international morality, I shall return to the problem of his legacy in my conclusion.

Postscript

I write these words at a time when the world is reeling from the latest outbreak of rioting and violence unleashed by Islamist demagogues, ostensibly on account of the publication by a Danish newspaper of a series of cartoons satirizing Islamist terror and intolerance. While the Danish government displayed admirable steadfastness in the wake of ensuing threats against it, many European leaders and intellectuals, as well as much of the "prestige" media in America, exhibited a lamentable spinelessness. Two of the four major American television networks, and all the leading American newspapers, refused to display the cartoons, despite their vaunted commitment to free speech and their normal readiness to publicize "art" works that are specifically designed to insult the religious beliefs of Christians or express contempt for the American flag.[18]

In this connection, it is interesting to note the apologia for the Continental version of "universalist" liberalism, as distinguished from the supposedly narrow and "fundamentalist" response of representative Americans to Islamist terror, offered by one of Europe's most influential political theorists, and Rawls's leading Continental admirer, Habermas. In a 2003 column in *Le Monde*, Habermas argued that promoting democracy in the contemporary world requires "step[ping] outside of one's one viewpoint in order to put it into relationship with the viewpoints adopted by another, which are to be regarded as equal."[19] This amounts to the same mandate as Rawls's insistence that in the name of justice we "see the situation of others . . . from the perspective of their conception of the good" (*Theory*, 297).

Habermas's extension of Rawlsian relativism regarding the good to the global "community" naturally invited its own radicalization. It was thus only a small step further when a prominent exponent of foundationless liberalism, posing as one of liberalism's critics—Stanley Fish—praised the actions of "Muslim protestors" over the objections of liberal editors who criticized their intolerance, pointing out that mere liberal "respect" for other people's religious beliefs "doesn't cost you anything . . . and is in fact a form of condescension," while Islamists, unlike liberals, believe that some

18. See David Lewis Schaefer, "The State Department as Cultural Critic."
19. Habermas, "Révolutionnaires," *Le Monde*, May 3, 2003, cited by James W. Ceaser in "Faith in Democracy."

ideas are "worth fighting over."[20] It may be a more or less accurate depiction of today's self-styled liberals to say that they don't believe in fighting even for their own cause. But can anyone recognize in this portrait the liberalism of Jefferson, Hamilton, or Lincoln, of FDR or John F. Kennedy?

The Islamist crisis of our time has brought into even sharper relief the insufficiency of the neutralist liberalism advocated by Rawls, Nozick, and their fellows in the American academy—along with their European counterparts like Habermas. In the midst of that crisis, however, we were informed by a prominent professor of political theory, "democratic theorists" maintain that Rawls's conception of public reason, which justifies public policies in terms independent of natural right or other "contested foundational ideas," constitutes the "most stable basis" for political life.[21] This conception of stability is, I have shown, a purely abstract one. Instead of responding to the real challenges to the survival of liberal constitutionalism, it focuses on somehow severing our political opinions from our moral and religious beliefs, including the doctrine of natural rights, as if the security of our polity depended chiefly on convincing Americans that our fundamental principles have no substantive, transhistorical ground at all. Despite all sorts of terminological changes, today's liberal political theory thus retains its vain hope from the mid-twentieth century that liberal tolerance can best be defended by asserting the relativity of all "values." Amid the present world crisis, one might term this a policy of unilateral moral disarmament.

Those seeking guidance for the perpetuation of liberal politics, as I shall argue in the conclusion, will do better to return to the wellsprings of authentic liberal thought in the writings of Locke, Montesquieu, Tocqueville, and the American founders. Their liberalism is not only grounded in a rational account of human nature, as Rawls's is not; it enlists the spiritedness and pride in self-government, as well as the moderate religious and moral beliefs, of an enlightened people in the defense of liberty, in a manner that neutralist liberalism can never do.

20. See Fish, "Our Faith in Letting It All Hang Out," *New York Times,* February 12, 2006, sec. 4, 15.

21. Nancy Rosenblum, "Replacing Foundations with Staging," 133–35. For a more serious appreciation of the issues posed for political theory by Islamism, see J. Judd Owen, "The Task of Liberal Theory after September 11."

CHAPTER 13

The Law of Peoples

I.

Rawls's last and shortest programmatic treatise, *The Law of Peoples*, enunciates a "political conception" of justice for international law and practice. Rawls derives the law of peoples from "a liberal idea of justice similar to, but more general than," justice as fairness (*LP*, 3).

Rawls's approach to international justice is inspired by Kant's account of a pacific federation of states in *Perpetual Peace* (*LP*, 10), which influenced Woodrow Wilson and the formation of the League of Nations (and hence indirectly the United Nations). Rawls uses the term "peoples" instead of "nations" or "governments" to highlight the "moral character" of the participants in the federation and to emphasize that government is not "the author of all of its own powers" as he believes is implied by traditional notions of sovereignty. He aims to constrict government's powers so as to deny states "the traditional rights to war and to unrestricted internal autonomy."[1] In this way Rawls also seeks to accommodate recent changes in international law that tend in the same direction (*LP*, 25–27).

---

1. Kant similarly distinguishes between peoples and states in "Perpetual Peace" (2nd definitive article, 102–3). For a critique of recent attempts to erode the traditional understanding of sovereignty as a threat to self-government and the security of individual rights, see Jeremy Rabkin, *The Case for Sovereignty*. See also Stoner, *Common Law Liberty*, 159–63.

The "basic charter" of Rawls's Law of Peoples incorporates eight "familiar and traditional principles of justice among free and democratic peoples," including the observance of treaties; respect for the freedom and equality of all peoples and for human rights; the "duty of nonintervention" and a prohibition on war other than for self-defense; and the "duty to assist other peoples living under unfavorable conditions that prevent their having a just or decent political and social regime" (*LP*, 37). Rawls represents these principles as the outcome of a "second original position" among parties who choose under a veil of ignorance that prevents their knowing the size, population, or relative strength of the peoples whose interests they represent (*LP*, 32–33). Unlike the parties to the domestic original position, the representatives in the "second-level" position "are not given a menu of alternative principles and ideals from which to select," but "simply reflect on the advantages of these principles . . . and see no reason to depart from them or to propose alternatives." They debate only the many possible interpretations of the eight principles (*LP*, 41–42).[2] But since Rawls makes no effort to illustrate that debate or what the alternative interpretations would look like, the notion of an original position has no evident significance, other than to suggest the ostensible impartiality of his principles of international justice.

Rawls describes the Law of Peoples as a "realistically utopian" doctrine that will generate "stability for the right reasons," as distinguished from "stability as a balance of forces" (*LP*, 44).[3] In response to the "realist" view that international relations inevitably remain "an ongoing struggle for wealth and power," Rawls cites both the modern movement toward democratic reform and Montesquieu's argument that commerce tends to generate peace and such virtues as industry and probity (*LP*, 46). He attributes the persistence of the realist view to the failure to distinguish between "states," which pursue such goals as power, glory, wealth, and the advancement of their religion, without regard to justice, and "peoples," which need not do so: "What makes peace among liberal democratic peoples possible" is their "internal nature . . . as constitutional democracies" and the resultant change in citizens' "motives" (*LP*, 28–29). (For this reason, Rawls claims that the crucial distinction between peoples and states is that "just peoples are

---

2. Rawls does not explain his omission of a menu of alternatives to his principles, and the notion of being instructed simply to "reflect" on the value of the principles and then accept them hardly seems designed to foster deliberation. (Then again, as I have shown, Rawls's "original" original position leaves no room for genuine deliberation either.)

3. Note the parallel to the distinction between "overlapping consensus" and a mere "modus vivendi" in *PL*.

fully prepared to grant the very same proper respect and recognition to other peoples as equals" that they themselves demand [*PL*, 35], though he never explains how the wishes of peoples are to be distinguished in practice from those expressed by their respective states.) Additionally, however, a secure democratic peace presupposes that member nations assure to their own citizens equality of opportunity, "a decent distribution of income and wealth," "society as employer of last resort," "basic health care," and "public financing of elections" (*LP*, 50). Here Rawls's requirements for international legitimacy go far beyond Kant's; he does not explain the connection between these mandates and world peace. (At the same time, Rawls omits Kant's requirement that every member of a worldwide federation of nations be republican.)

While citing the absence of wars among constitutionally secure liberal states, Rawls attributes the tendency of "allegedly constitutional democratic regimes" like the United States to "intervene in weaker countries" and overthrow "democracies" such as Allende's Chile, Arbenz's Guatemala, Mossadegh's Iran, "and, some would add, the Sandanistas [*sic*] in Nicaragua" to "monopolistic and oligarchic interests" manipulating the government and its "handy appeal to national security" (*LP*, 53). (The only subentry under "United States" in the index to *LP* is "history of overturning weak democracies.")[4] In the world of liberal constitutional democracies that Rawls envisions, by contrast, peoples would no longer be "swayed by the passion for power and glory, or the intoxicating pride of ruling"; all being satisfied, they would have nothing fight about (*LP*, 47).[5]

---

4. Rawls is one of very few writers outside the former Soviet bloc who would call Jacob Arbenz's communist dictatorship in Guatemala a "democracy" or who would think of bestowing that title on the unlamented Sandinista regime. He supplies no source for these judgments. For a different view of Allende and the American role in Chile during his rise and fall, see Mark Falcoff, *Modern Chile, 1970–1989*, chaps. 7–8.

Rawls maintains that the national-security argument was irrelevant in the cases he cites, since each of these countries was too weak to threaten the United States (*LP*, 53). Soviet attempts to gain control over Iranian oil or a Central American beachhead in Guatemala or Nicaragua are not the sorts of problem that Rawls would deem threats to American security. But he is curiously one-sided in being hypersensitive to what he deems American governmental propaganda about the nation's security, and exceedingly credulous when it comes to the claims of assorted Marxist strongmen to have been "real" democrats.

5. Although Rawls cites Raymond Aron's *Peace and War* as the source of his term "satisfied peoples" (*LP*, 47n), his overall description of a "realistic utopia" recalls the Hegelian-Marxist thinker Alexandre Kojève's account of the "end of history," updated by Francis Fukuyama in *The End of History and the Last Man*. Rawls's account is free of any of Fukuyama's reservations about whether a wholly pacified world would be a truly human one, however (see chaps. 28, 31; Nietzsche, *Beyond Good and Evil*, sec. 201).

II.

The second part of what Rawls calls "ideal theory" regarding international relations governs relations between liberal and nonliberal peoples. It dictates recognizing nonliberal peoples as "equal participating members" of the Society of Peoples so long as they meet certain standards of decency (*LP*, 59–60). A "decent hierarchical people" must satisfy two criteria. First, it must renounce aggressive aims. Second, it must guarantee its members such rights as life, liberty, property, and formal equality before the law; impose "*bona fide* moral duties and obligations" on all citizens; and have laws that are "guided by a common good conception of justice" incorporating a "decent consultation hierarchy" and the right of political protest (*LP*, 64–66, 71–72).[6] Since Rawls believes that the doctrine of human rights doesn't depend on any comprehensive religious or philosophical view, he is confident that it will be acceptable to decent hierarchical peoples (although this seems tautological, since he has defined such peoples partly by their acceptance of such rights). Hence he infers that they will be willing to adopt the eight principles of international justice (*LP*, 68–69).

Rawls supplements the foregoing "ideal conception" of the Law of Peoples with a short treatment of "the questions arising from the highly nonideal conditions" of the world in which we actually live, "with its grave injustices and widespread social evils." The first part of nonideal theory concerns noncompliance with the rules of international justice (*LP*, 89).

Whereas forceful interference in the affairs of liberal and decent nonliberal societies is forbidden, "outlaw states," which violate the Law of Peoples, conduct wars for the mere sake of their "rational interests," and violate human rights, merit condemnation and "in grave cases" sanctions or even intervention. "Liberalism and decency" forbid us to "tolerate outlaw states" (*LP*, 80–81, 90). ("Outlaw states" include not only notoriously evil regimes such as Nazi Germany but also expansionist autocracies such as Spain, France, and the Hapsburg Empire in the early modern period [*LP*, 105–6].)

---

6. Additionally, Rawls holds that decent societies must guarantee their members the right "to the means of subsistence and security," since "the sensible and rational exercise of all liberties . . . always implies having general all-purpose economic means" (*LP*, 65). He means here not merely the right to have one's property secured against attack, as in the Declaration of Independence, but the right to be given such means if needed. The governments of the many impoverished countries that lack the resources to effectuate such a guarantee presumably fall under the category of "burdened societies," discussed below. But in intermixing the circumstantially dependent right to "all-purpose means" with the core liberal rights to security of life, liberty, and property, Rawls again threatens to weaken the latter rights by offering despots in less developed countries an excuse for denying them.

Only societies that honor human rights, that is, liberal and decent societies, along with "benevolent absolutisms" (which "honor most human rights" but are undemocratic), have the right to war in self-defense (*LP*, 63, 92). Even in fighting just, defensive wars, moreover, these societies are bound by principles regarding the conduct of war (corresponding to the *jus in bello* of traditional just-war theory), dictating that they distinguish carefully among the outlaw state's leaders, its soldiers, and its civilian population (who by definition, in an outlaw state, "cannot be those who organized and brought on the war").[7] Hence such attacks on the civilian population of outlaw states as the atomic bombing of Hiroshima and Nagasaki and the firebombings of Japanese cities earlier in 1945 were "very grave wrongs" (*LP*, 95).

While no decent person would deny Rawls's contention that even in wartime "well-ordered peoples must respect, so far as possible, the human rights of members of the other side" (*LP*, 94–96), it is doubtful that issues of military necessity can be so easily decided, especially in an era of fanatical and totalitarian ideologies, terrorism, and the threat of weapons of mass destruction, as he seems to believe.[8] To support his condemnation of the atomic bombings Rawls relies on a single article by the revisionist historian Barton Bernstein. Although Bernstein's argument is often tendentious (he suggests that the government may have used the bomb just to prevent the Manhattan Project from seeming "a gigantic waste"), even he acknowledges that the bomb spared many thousands of American lives (as well as Japanese ones) that would have been lost in an invasion.[9] Rawls asserts, however, that it was unnecessary to use the atomic bomb to secure victory since "the war was effectively over" by August 1945. He supplies no evidence that Japanese commanders would have surrendered without an invasion, a claim that even Bernstein falls short of endorsing.[10] In fact, that supposition has recently been decisively refuted through the release of previously classified transcripts of American intercepts of Japanese diplomatic and military radio communications during the weeks immediately preceding the use of the atomic bomb. The transcripts also provide evidence of a Japanese military buildup at the projected invasion site so great

---

7. Rawls omits the possibility that some states (e.g., Germany in 1914, Japan in 1941) may have launched aggressive wars with the widespread support of their populations.

8. Cf. Robert Kagan's observation of how contemporary Europeans' "Kantian" posture of rejecting power politics and the use of military force depends on America's own "willingness to use its military might to deter or defeat those around the world who still believe in power politics" (*Of Paradise and Power*, 73–76).

9. Bernstein, "The Atomic Bombings Reconsidered."

10. On the resistance of the Japanese chiefs of staff to surrender (and the attempted coup to prevent it) even after the Nagasaki bombing, see Richard Storry, *A History of Modern Japan*, 234–36; Arnold Brackman, *The Other Nuremburg*, 34–39.

that most American military leaders doubted the prudence of such an invasion at all.[11] But even had Rawls known these facts, he wouldn't have cared: whether it is correct to suppose that Japan would soon have surrendered without the bomb being used "makes no difference," he maintains, given the intrinsically evil character of the bombing. (How can Rawls know that the use of the bomb was inherently evil if an invasion would have cost many more military and civilian lives, including not only Americans and Japanese, but also an estimated 250,000 to 400,000 other Asians in countries subject to Japanese military rule, overwhelmingly noncombatants, who were dying each month the war continued?[12])

Additionally, continuing his posture of high moralism, Rawls observes "how foolish it sounds" to have regarded the Japanese as "barbarians" during the war; that description is applicable only to "the Nazis and Tojo militarists," not the many thousands who participated in their atrocities (*LP*, 100). Rawls's assertion that "the Holocaust might have happened anywhere" that "a powerful totalitarian and militaristic state . . . came to be" (*LP*, 100n) leaves aside the question of why the Nazis happened to come to power with widespread support in Germany rather than in some other country, and it seems to absolve the vast number who cooperated in Hitler's crimes from any responsibility for their deeds.

As in other instances, the question of the extent of a people's responsibility for actions committed by their country is an empirical rather than a definitional one. Arguments like Rawls's that deny the German and Japanese citizenry any culpability for their regimes' unprecedented crimes may feed the recent claim of some Germans that their country was "victimized" in World War II (sometimes blaming the Jews for their victimization) and the continued refusal of influential Japanese leaders to acknowledge their country's responsibility for aggression and war crimes.[13] (If the German people bore no responsibility for their country's crimes, wasn't it unjust for the West German government to tax its citizens to pay reparations to Holocaust survivors after the war?) Of course, such dispositions toward collective self-absolution are further buttressed by Rawls's denial in *JF* that America was any more democratic than Germany through the end of the Second World War, and his claim in an essay entitled "Fifty Years after Hiroshima" that America fought that war "with dirty hands" (*CP*, 566n).

Similar difficulties emerge in Rawls's prescriptions governing the immunity of civilians to military attack during an ongoing war. He holds

11. See Richard B. Frank, "Why Truman Dropped the Bomb."
12. Ibid., 24, citing the findings of the historian Robert Newman and others.
13. See Bartosz Jalowiecki, "Lies the Germans Tell Themselves."

(following Michael Walzer) that this immunity may legitimately be violated only during a "supreme emergency," such as may have been faced by Britain during the first years of World War II. It is a "duty of statesmanship" to prevent people's wartime passions from influencing the course of policy (just as, in *Theory*, Rawls argued that society's "long-range aim" must be fixed without regard to its present members' wishes). Rawls does not discuss what actions statesmen may need to undertake to mold people's passions sufficiently to sustain the war effort (as Lincoln did during the Civil War, for instance, or as Churchill did in 1940 and beyond). The effectiveness of America's armed forces during the Second World War would not have been affected, in Rawls's judgment, by abstaining from attacking civilians (*LP*, 98, 101–2). He does not address the issue of bombing factories used for military production. And in making this assertion, Rawls disregards a considerable scholarly literature to the contrary.[14]

It is regrettable that while Rawls pleads so strenuously for understanding the other side in America's military conflicts, he is so uninterested in considering works that challenge his own political predilections. Nor can we overlook the contrast between Rawls's criticism of the popular tendency to moralize military conflicts excessively and his own disposition, in his works on domestic justice, to suggest that most serious political controversies are so easily reducible to moral problems that it takes little effort to identify the good guys. (Even in *LP* Rawls renders the sweeping judgment that while "Washington and Lincoln were statesmen . . . Bismarck was not" [*LP*, 97], whereas most historians would render a more nuanced assessment of the latter's achievement.)

I have dwelt on Rawls's broad-brushed condemnations of Allied conduct during World War II to illustrate the dangers of imposing an abstract moral code to supplant or override the practical judgment of political and military officials who bear responsibility for defending constitutional regimes and promoting the cause of freedom. Certainly, democratic citi-

14. Two recent studies conclude that the bombing of German cities made an "essential" or "decisive" contribution to Allied military success, notably by diverting to air defense resources that would otherwise have strengthened Nazi armies (Williamson Murray and Allan R. Millett, *A War To Be Won*, 332–35; Richard Overy, *Why the Allies Won*, 127–33). See also Ian Kershaw, *Hitler, 1936–1945*, 587, 598 (the devastating effect of Allied air raids on German morale) and 732 (the competition between Germany's resources for air defense and air support on the Western Front). Earlier, Michael Walzer had made an impressively reasoned and nuanced case against the bombings of German cities, at least after 1940, as well as against the use of the atomic bomb against Japan, on which Rawls draws (*Just and Unjust Wars*, chap. 16). But while the use of military force against an enemy's civilian population centers is condemned by traditional just-war theory, it is arguable that nations that commit atrocities on the scale of the Nazis and Japanese with widespread popular participation constitute an exception to the rule.

zens must assess the wartime conduct of their governments, both during and after the fact, and stand in need of carefully articulated standards to help guide their judgment. But whereas scholars such as Walzer have undertaken this enterprise in a balanced and empirically based way, Rawls never engages in the sort of investigation and reflection needed to support his pronouncements.

The problematic character of Rawls's moral judgments on military conduct is of considerably more than historical interest today, amid the rise of "asymmetric warfare" on the part of terrorist organizations that acknowledge no moral boundaries to their methods, yet seek to manipulate Western opinion to make themselves seem like victims. (For instance, Hezbollah locates its missiles and other armaments in civilian neighborhoods of Lebanon so as to denounce the "atrocities" that result when Israel responds to its attacks on Israeli cities—encouraging transnational nongovernmental associations such as Amnesty International to accuse Israel rather than Hezbollah of committing war crimes, on the basis of abstract, purportedly impartial principles like Rawls's.)[15]

Just as international relations, by virtue of their lack of susceptibility to governance by law in the strict sense, are even less suited to the application of fixed universal principles than domestic affairs are (hence the broad latitude that Locke assigns to the executive's "federative," or foreign-policy, power),[16] rules of international law designed to regulate the relations of sovereign, law-governed nations have practically no relevance to dealing with terror organizations that recognize no law at all other than their own fiat. It is symptomatic of a certain lack of moral imagination on Rawls's part that the worst category he could think of for illegitimate regimes was "outlaw states," in which he included Louis XIV's France, the Hapsburg monarchy, and Bismarck's Prussia no less than Hitler's Germany, as if the difference between military aggression of a sort that had been practiced throughout human history (whether aimed at territorial aggrandizement or at preemptive defense, as in the Peloponnesian War launched by Sparta) and the attempt systematically to exterminate an entire people in gas ovens were only one of degree, not of kind. Such an approach can only tend to blunt rather than sharpen our moral sensibilities in an era of unspeakable terror

15. See, for instance, John Kifner, "Human Rights Group Accuses Israel of War Crimes in Lebanon." On the detrimental effects on American foreign policy of the cosmopolitan doctrine of "universal moral principles" advanced by the contemporary Western mass media, which can espouse "moral perfectionism" because they are unaccountable for the actual defense of justice and national well-being, see Robert D. Kaplan, *Warrior Politics,* 124–29.

16. Locke, *Two Treatises,* bk. 2, secs. 147–48.

and the spread of weapons of mass destruction to fanatical regimes like Iran's and Hitler-like despotisms like that of Kim Jong-il's North Korea.

III.

Beyond their duty to protect human rights against violation by outlaw states, well-ordered societies in Rawls's account are obliged to assist "burdened societies," which "lack the political and cultural traditions, the human capital and know-how, and, often, the material and technological resources needed to be well-ordered." "Merely dispensing funds will not suffice to rectify basic political and social injustices," Rawls observes, unless the burdened society's political culture is improved. In fact, since political culture is a greater determinant of a society's economic prosperity than its natural resources are, Rawls rejects Charles Beitz's argument mandating a global redistribution of resources (in accordance with the difference principle) from wealthier to poorer nations, on the ground that if applied "without end," it would unjustly punish some countries for having saved so as to industrialize (*LP,* 106, 108–9, 116–17).

While Rawls's response to Beitz is plausible, we cannot avoid noting how it highlights the deficiency of the difference principle in its domestic application, which I noted in chapter 7. Why is it any more just or beneficial to punish individuals for their thrift and hard work by redistributing their wealth to the less well-off (merely because they are less well-off) than to do so among nations?[17]

Rawls does not acknowledge his inconsistency. And when he proceeds to describe the Law of Peoples as indifferent about whether the situation of the worst-off individuals in two different nations is equalized (*LP,* 119–20), he seems to be expressing an arbitrary preference rather than offering a reasoned explanation of why this isn't a logical, or even necessary, extension of the difference principle. We are tempted to regard this as a failure of nerve: a sudden reluctance on Rawls's part to acknowledge the radical implications of his previous account of justice when it is extended to the global level, lest he seem *too* utopian.

While aiming at a worldwide just and well-ordered society of peoples all of whom abide by the Law of Peoples, Rawls does not favor world gov-

---

17. I do not mean to question the desirability of well-administered humanitarian aid to other countries, any more than to reject the need for carefully crafted programs of assistance to the truly needy domestically. My point is to challenge Rawls's claim that such programs are a mandate of justice rather than the consequence of magnanimity or compassion, which entails that their extent must be governed by prudence. See Cropsey, "The Right of Foreign Aid," in *Political Philosophy,* 189–206.

ernment, sensibly fearing (with Kant) that it would become a "global despotism" (*LP*, 36).[18] He does not consider the implications of the impossibility of decent world government for the question of whether there can be justice in other than a metaphorical or analogical sense in international relations.[19] Nor does he spell out the workings of a federation of peoples, beyond suggesting that it be composed of "regional associations . . . such as the European community," along with institutions such as the United Nations that are "capable of speaking for all the societies of the world" (*LP*, 70). He does not discuss the reasons the UN presently lacks this capability, elsewhere explaining that he is speaking of it as "ideally conceived" (*LP*, 38). Further reflection on the reasons for regarding a true world government as despotic, since it would be unaccountable, or on the presence in the actual United Nations of so many actual despotisms, might have tempered Rawls's hopes in this regard. Nor does Rawls take account of the fact that providing equal representation to all nations, as the UN General Assembly does (in accordance with the principle of sovereignty), means that the residents of tiny Nauru have a vote equal to that of the most populous countries: in what sense can such a system be said to "speak for" all peoples? And how can the UN speak for human rights when its Commission on Human Rights includes such notorious despotisms as Libya (which was made head of the commission in 2003) and Sudan (elected to the commission in the midst of its brutal military campaign against its own black and Sufi Muslim communities)?[20]

Rawls supplies no ground to support his belief that greater reliance on international institutions in place of America's independent action, joined with that of like-minded allies, will promote justice. In fact, as the European Union illustrates, subordinating national sovereignty to transnational institutions entails restricting democratic governance in favor of rule by unaccountable bureaucrats. (In their pursuit of uniformity, EU officials have imposed legally standardized sizes on everything from apples to condoms and have prohibited the broadcast of any program that is "offensive to religious or political beliefs." So much for the "priority" of

18. Cf. Kant, "Perpetual Peace," app. 1, 124–25.

19. Aristotle, for one, holds that distributive justice exists only for those who share in a regime (*NE* 1130b30–32, 1134b14–15). Hobbes, similarly, denies that there can be justice in the absence of law made and enforced by a known sovereign (*Leviathan*, chap. 13, 83; chap. 15, 94): without effectual guarantees of people's rights to life, liberty, and property, how can one draw meaningful limits to the actions a nation may legitimately take to defend itself, including pre-emptive attack?

20. On the incapacity of the UN as presently structured to serve as "the institutional embodiment" of Kant's or Rawls's visions of a just global community, see Thomas Cushman, "Introduction," *A Matter of Principle*, 19. On the EU, see Gerard Alexander, "Illiberal Europe."

liberty. Meanwhile, the UN has repeatedly demonstrated its impotence in such humanitarian crises as those in Rwanda, Sudan, North Korea, Saddam's Iraq, and Kosovo.)[21]

Contrary to Rawls, the doctrine of sovereignty, as understood in constitutional republics like the United States, never implied that government is "the author of its own powers": in the language of the Declaration of Independence, government derives its just powers from the consent of the governed. Our constitutional institutions limit the powers of government and ensure its accountability in a way that no transnational body could do. In fact, the endeavor in recent years by UN bureaucrats, activist judges, lawyers, and nongovernmental organizations to subsume sovereign constitutional institutions under a transnational moral code of their own devising, enforced by the new deference of American judges to a supposed international consensus on issues ranging from the death penalty to gay rights, constitutes a growing threat to the American people's right to govern themselves in matters of domestic as well as foreign policy.[22] (Of course such endeavors fully harmonize with the effort of American judges to read the same sort of code into the American Constitution in the name of Rawlsian "moral theory," as discussed in chapter 7.) Finally, with reference to Rawls's assumption that international bodies would promote justice more effectively than sovereign liberal republics, acting (when possible) in concert with like-minded allies, it is worth citing the judgment of the eminent historian Alonzo Hamby on the effects of "the concept of collective security embodied in an international organization enforcing international law and morality" in the 1930s, as Western democracies looked on passively while Nazi military power steadily increased: "Collective security required a widely shared sense of purpose and common interest which would have made an international body unnecessary . . . In practice, 'collective security' fostered the hope that somebody else would provide the security the collective needed."[23]

At the same time that he advocates some subsumption of domestic sovereignty under international institutions, Rawls defends the "qualified" right of countries to limit immigration to prevent their cultures from being overwhelmed by "global capitalism" (*LP,* 39n). (We note the tension between this

21. On the UN's historical inefficacy both in promoting human rights and in conflict resolution, see Bernard Lewis, "Iraq, India, Palestine," *Wall Street Journal,* May 12, 2004, A14. On the EU's elevation of irresponsible bureaucracy over self-government, see Rothstein, "Europe's Constitution."

22. See Andrew McCarthy, "International Law v. United States"; Rabkin, "Courting Abroad." For a book-length argument advocating the achievement of "global governance" by means of an international network of judges rather than elected officials, see Anne-Marie Slaughter, *A New World Order.*

23. Hamby, *For the Survival of Democracy,* 241.

concern and Rawls's reliance on Montesquieu's spirit of *doux commerce* to pacify international relations.) Although Rawls avoids spelling out how the right to control immigration may be qualified, we wonder (as with his response to Beitz) at his seemingly leaving it open to nations to protect their interests at the expense of what some would argue are moral obligations to afford refuge to victims of persecution abroad. Indeed, Rawls's subsequent remark that a nation "must take care that it does not overburden its lands and economy with a larger population than it can sustain" (*LP,* 108) is precisely the sort of argument made by opponents of America's accepting the large-scale immigration of Jews fleeing Hitler's persecution in the 1930s and by those who favor stringent measures to stem illegal immigration from Mexico today. While Rawls would undoubtedly have felt sympathetic toward the plight of such refugees, his sidestepping the issue exemplifies the difficulties obstructing his attempt to wall off his prescriptions for domestic justice from problems that arise when they are considered from a cosmopolitan perspective, and therefore again calls into question the "Archimedean" character of his doctrine.

Despite Rawls's occasional nods to a sort of realism, *LP* ends on a remarkably apocalyptic note. If a "reasonably just Society of Peoples" cannot be attained, Rawls asserts, "one might ask, with Kant, whether it is worthwhile for human beings to live on the earth" (*LP,* 128). This astounding remark (echoing a similar observation regarding domestic justice in the 1996 introduction to *PL* that I quoted in chapter 9) means that the very existence of the human race is of doubtful value unless we can find reasonable grounds for hoping that a hitherto unprecedented new world order can be brought about. As on other occasions we wonder whether Rawls considered the implications of his rhetoric with the seriousness that some readers he influences may do.[24]

Its conclusion aside, *LP* differs from Rawls's previous writings in its greater reliance on a few informed works (albeit sometimes tendentious ones) of political history and fact-based political theory, in place of the more abstract reasoning, often-uncritical borrowings from selected economic and psychological theorists, and dubious appeals to intuition that characterized *Theory* and *PL*. Unfortunately, Rawls's last treatise still exhibits his habit of issuing sweeping, ex cathedra judgments on debatable public policy issues, including, this time, not only military strategy in

---

24. Of course Socrates famously tells his judges that "the unexamined life is not worth living" (Plato *Apology of Socrates* 38a). But since Socrates is exhorting his audience to a life of thought, not action, and since self-examination can in principle be practiced by every individual, without regard to the circumstances of his society, Socrates' rhetoric does not entail the politically problematic consequences of Rawls's remarks.

World War II and U.S. foreign policy toward Latin America, but also unemployment benefits, without which he implausibly asserts "there would be massive starvation in every Western democracy" (*LP*, 109). (He doesn't pause to explain the absence of such starvation in Western democracies before the relatively recent institution of unemployment insurance.) In some respects Rawls's historical judgments in his last years remain frozen in the academic world of the 1970s: he condemns Hitler and Nazism but avoids mentioning Stalin or criticizing communism; he treats the former USSR as an actual republican "federation" or "commonwealth" akin to the European Community (*LP*, 70); and he goes so far as to attribute Hitler's demonic evil to the influence of Christianity (*LP*, 20–21), without of course mentioning his professed socialism. Nonetheless, Rawls's late move toward grounding justice more fully in the facts of political life rather than in personal intuitions was a promising one. The relative moderation that this sort of evidence induces might have had a salutary influence had Rawls applied it to the original formulation of his theory.

Still, Rawls's doctrine of international right hardly adds to what was already known about the conditions for a just world order. Most of the eight precepts of the Law of Peoples are familiar liberal homilies with which most American citizens and statesmen—in fact, most inhabitants of constitutional republics—would readily agree. What Rawls's list fails to address (much as Wilson's Fourteen Points failed to) is what to do when the precepts conflict (e.g., nonintervention vs. offering assistance to peoples suffering under oppressive regimes) or how to address problems that arise when (for instance) the sanctity of present geographic boundaries is challenged on the ground that they result from previous unjust aggression.[25]

Of course, these are difficult issues with which liberal statesmen are commonly confronted, and it is unlikely that they can be resolved by any sort of comprehensive, theoretical formula. Nonetheless, one might wish that Rawls had acknowledged their complexity, rather than encouraging the belief that there is a simple road to world peace and justice that merely requires us to "take the pledge." Nor, any more than in his previous writings, does Rawls ever comprehend the depth of the political passions that challenge his version of liberalism. Unlike such philosophers as Plato and Aristotle, he never attempts to address motives such as "the passion for power and glory, or the intoxicating pride of ruling" on their own ground or try to show how a just polity can offer a reasonable fulfillment of such

---

25. The failure to provide criteria regarding which of a variety of moral rules to follow in a given situation was the defect, it will be recalled, that Rawls attributed to intuitionism.

desires.[26] And what good does it do to denounce expansionist nations like eighteenth-century France as "outlaw states," let alone deny them the right to self-defense? What checked French ambitions for hegemony under Louis XIV and (a century later) Napoleon was not any appeal to international justice, but military coalitions led by statesman-generals such as Marlborough and Wellington, supported by the civic pride of the British people—a mantle of leadership that passed to the United States nearly a century ago. Just as Rawls underestimates the need for forceful sanctions to support domestic justice, his utopian account of a pacific world order encourages readers to overlook the dependence of freedom on preparedness to use force in its defense. How shortsighted this must appear to any sober-minded reader in the age of global terror.

Rawls has particular difficulty acknowledging the tension between his liberalism and his putative multiculturalism. We may doubt, for instance, that advocates of traditional but by historical standards "decent" Islamic rule (in those few places where it now exists) will find that Rawls's criteria of decency, such as the requirement that "any group representing women's fundamental interests must include a majority of women," allow "significant room" for popular "self-determination" (*LP*, 61, 110). More broadly, while Rawls urges, for the sake of "maintaining mutual respect between peoples," that we avoid insisting that all societies be required to become liberal, he then explains such respect for nonliberal peoples as simply "allowing them to find their own way" to honor liberal ideals, which hardly seems to leave them much of a choice (*LP*, 122). Rawls also overlooks the disanalogy between applying the principle of toleration as he conceives it within a nation (as in *PL*) and among nations: since (as he acknowledges in the case of war) we cannot assume that a government that is not constitutional-democratic truly speaks for all of its citizens— especially in nations that are divided by ethnic or religious strife—to "tolerate" a given government's practices may mean disregarding unjust discrimination against particular groups within that nation. (It is no solution to the dilemma, but only a tautology, for Rawls to deny that liberal peoples may accuse decent nonliberal ones of denying human rights, on the ground that by definition such peoples respect human rights. Then again, Rawls is arguing against a straw man when he opposes applying "politically enforced sanctions" against decent regimes merely because they are nonliberal [*LP*, 61]: aside from feminists who once organized

26. On Rawls's (and Nozick's) failure to address the central political passion of spiritedness, see Mansfield, *Spirit of Liberalism*, 104. On Plato's response to these passions, see Waller R. Newell, *Ruling Passion*.

boycotts of American states that had refused to ratify the equal rights amendment, no relevant examples come to mind.)

Beyond this, Rawls's denunciation of the supposed dangers of globalization—apparently reflecting his wish (as seen in *IPRR*) to show that his doctrine can accommodate the latest academic fads—understates the contribution that the growth of global trade makes to the prosperity of all nations, especially the poorest ones, as well as to moderating certain parochial "cultural" trends (still found, for instance, in most of the Middle East) that may constitute the greatest threat to justice and peace in the world today.[27] Finally, Rawls exhibits his own parochialism by showing no interest in comparing present-day doctrines of liberal internationalism with the serious alternatives to them to be found in the history of Western philosophy and theology.[28] (Hence the one-item "menu" presented for consideration in his second original position.) With respect to international justice no less than in his original theory, Rawls's doctrine embodies a considerable narrowing of the philosophical horizon—the opposite of the transcendence of particular biases that it was his professed aspiration to achieve.

27. On the benefits of globalization to the world's poor, see Tomas Larsson, *The Race to the Top*; Martin Wolf, *Why Globalization Works*; and Jagdish Bhagwati, *In Defense of Globalization*. As Larsson quotes UN secretary general Kofi Annan: "The main losers in today's very unequal world are not those who are too exposed to globalization, but those who have been left out" as a result of their governments' lacking the political strength "to confront those within their own countries who have come to rely on protectionist arrangements" (128).

28. For an excellent survey and critical analysis of historical doctrines of international justice, see Thomas Pangle and Peter Ahrensdorf, *Justice among Nations*.

───── Conclusion

I.

In the foregoing pages I have challenged the claim that John Rawls's work constitutes a contribution either to substantive political philosophy or to the reasoned pursuit of justice. I have denied that Rawls's work is genuinely philosophical. And I contend that his theory and the approach to political life that it embodies, far from offering meaningful guidance on how to fortify liberal institutions, threatens to worsen our situation in numerous respects:

—Contrary to his claims, Rawls does not provide a firm foundation for liberty. Instead, he endeavors to displace the Lockean natural-rights teaching on which America's constitutional institutions are founded with a purely artificial standard based on his "intuitions." And instead of addressing the real threats to liberty in the modern world, Rawls argues for his doctrine chiefly by comparing it to an abstract alternative, utilitarianism, that no actual government or significant political movement would take seriously as a guide to public policy. (When it comes to the substantive danger of a broadly utilitarian view of human life, represented by eugenics or cloning, Rawls has nothing to say.)

—Despite his ostensible prioritization of liberty, Rawls's "fair-value" doctrine invites the subordination of political liberty to the goal of economic equalization. Whereas the Declaration of Independence (which Rawls disparages for its "formalism") provides a clear and attainable standard for assessing the security of fundamental human rights throughout the world, the fair-value thesis (along with Rawls's deferring the priority of liberty until after citizens' "basic [material] needs" are met) offers an egregious alibi for despots who lack any regard for such rights.

—Unlike the American founders, Rawls thus shows little appreciation of the independent dignity of political freedom or self-government. In place of respecting the reasonable claims of actual human individuals, Rawls substitutes an abstract vision of the radically "autonomous" (but denatured) self that embodies the potentially most dangerous aspects of modern individualism. Such individualism is reinforced by Rawls's doctrine of primary goods, which represents such goals as wealth and power as "objectively" good, unlike the criteria of human excellence. The damage is not repaired by Rawls's subsequent denials that wealth maximization is a proper societal or individual goal, since these strictures were never incorporated into his principles. Additionally, Rawls seems unaware of the dangers that the Nietzschean doctrine of radical selfhood poses to liberal, constitutional government, because of his narrow view of the self and its possibilities. Hence he superimposes on his materialistic, individualistic view of the good an artificial ideal of "social union" that denies our real individuality: the homogeneity of the parties in the original position will be reflected in the boring sameness of lives devoted to the pursuit of trivial pleasures in Rawls's utopia.

—Through his disparagement of the constitutional-democratic process of political decision making (by frivolously encouraging civil disobedience, demanding severe restrictions on campaign donations, advocating the partial subsumption of American sovereignty under the irresponsible authority of assorted international bodies, asserting that political demands and moral convictions that challenge his program have "no value" and should be disregarded), Rawls further weakens respect for constitutional government. He also encourages the already corrosive tendency of an activist judiciary to disregard the constitutional text, citizen opinions, and the decisions of elected officeholders so as to impose judges' idiosyncratic "moral" convictions on us.

—Rawls's abstract conception of political philosophy, reflected in his determination to promote consensus by securing agreement on "simple" principles, obscures the tensions among the goals of the contemporary liberal state—for example, between protecting free "expression" and preserving the moral preconditions of freedom, and between assisting the genuinely needy and discouraging welfare dependency—while encouraging an unhealthy self-righteousness among professed liberals who attribute any disagreement with their preferred policies to lamentable ignorance or (more likely) narrow selfishness and outright vice. Rawls's endeavor to reduce complex policy questions to issues of moral "principle" threatens to heighten partisan tensions and erode America's broadly liberal consensus in a manner exemplified by the fervid rhetoric of anti-Bush partisans during the 2004 presidential campaign and beyond.[1]

—When it comes to real political crises involving issues of principle, such as the slavery controversy in 1860 or the fragility of the Weimar Republic in 1932, Rawls's pursuit of abstract agreement similarly offers no guidance: all he can do is throw up his hands and admit that philosophy in his sense has nothing to contribute, or else repeat tautological formulas (such as "overlapping consensus").

—Rawls's mechanistic account of the political process and his severance of justice from prudence (that is, considerations of "utility" broadly understood as the common good) further weaken appreciation of the deliberative character of lawmaking and the art of statesmanship, which the founders devised our institutions to promote. He disparages representative government by treating it as a process of responding to citizen "preferences" rather than serving what *The Federalist* calls the people's "deliberate sense,"

---

1. I have in mind partisans who employed terms such as "fascist" and "Nazi" to refer to the Bush administration—rhetoric essentially unheard of in America among the major political parties since the days of Senator Joseph McCarthy. (For samples one could look to the Moveon.Org Web site, or attend the meeting of the "progressive" Campaign for America's Future during the Democratic national convention, where the political *F-word* was employed by, among others, a scion of America's leading Democratic political family, while a former presidential contender accused the administration of favoring "book burning" [Byron York, "Their True Selves"].) By 2006, the rhetoric had descended in American and British media (including *The Guardian* and the Air America network) to calls for the president's assassination: see Jeff Jacoby, "A New Low in Bush-Hatred." But is that any worse, really, than Rawls's questioning whether *any* human beings deserve to exist if his vision of justice isn't achieved?

On Rawls's encouragement of "an unlovely tendency . . . to regard anybody who does not share the enthusiasm for an energetically redistributive liberalism as more than mistaken," such that "many opinions heard in public debate—on welfare reform, on abortion, on affirmative action—don't deserve a place at the table," see Berkowitz, "John Rawls and the Liberal Faith," 64–65. By "cloaking its political conclusions in the mantle of disinterested and universal reason," while labeling opposed convictions as inherently "unreasonable," Berkowitz observes, Rawls's teaching promotes "the illiberal conviction that left-wing progressives are separated from centrists and right-wing conservatives not just by opinions (over which reasonable people can disagree) but by a gulf akin to the one that separates civilized people from philistines and barbarians." For an analysis of the underlying psychology at work here, see Cohn, *Pursuit of the Millennium,* especially 69–72 and 182. On the resultant dangers to our political regime, see James Q. Wilson, "How Divided Are We?"

as articulated by their chosen representatives. Rawls shows no appreciation of the advantages of representative over plebiscitary democracy as seen by the founders, relying instead on irresponsible judges to override citizen wishes or the decisions of their representatives in the name of justice.

—At the same time, Rawls's difference principle, with its focus on assisting the arbitrarily defined "least advantaged" through economic redistribution, obscures the genuine, practical (moral and cultural) impediments to improving the lot of the underclass, making it appear that the advancement of the poor today depends chiefly on compelling their better-off peers to share more of their wealth, rather than on public policies and social arrangements (a strengthened family structure, a structurally improved educational system) that would encourage and assist the poor to better their own condition. While purporting to overcome envy, Rawls actually encourages this self-destructive vice.

—In the name of an ostensible impartiality among conceptions of the good, Rawls's first principle of justice (as he interprets it) would weaken the religious and moral supports that liberty and civic duty have traditionally enjoyed in America, as does his calling into question the moral legitimacy of the family on behalf of a far-fetched interpretation of equality of opportunity. His near agnosticism on the value of the family was first set forth at the very time that that institution began to come under attack from other debilitating social forces.

—By asking us to treat people's talents and their fruits as a "common asset," Rawls undermines the foundations of individual liberty as conceived in the Declaration, according to which individual rights (including the right to use one's capacities and lawfully acquired property to pursue happiness for oneself and one's family) are prior to, rather than derivative from, political authority. Rawls further weakens the dignity of the individual by insisting that our self-esteem is entirely dependent on how others regard us, and absurdly maintaining that justice prohibits society from valuing the greatest human achievements more than grass counting. By treating those who are economically least well-off at any given time as helpless victims, unable to advance themselves except by claiming their "share" of other people's earnings, Rawls denies them their humanity.[2]

—Rawls underestimates the vulnerability of free institutions to domestic as well as foreign threats (denying that democratic government may ever legitimately restrict the advocacy of subversive doctrines, encouraging civil disobedience, and questioning the need of criminal sanctions through "Hobbes's thesis"), while unjustly deprecating America's free

2. Cf. Lasch, *Revolt of the Elites*, 105–6.

institutions by calling our regime only allegedly democratic and our welfare state only a "so-called" one, etc.

—By demanding that political philosophy dispense with the very concept of truth, while proposing a scheme of "moral education" designed to induce everyone to accept his principles as the ultimate horizon for judging political and social arrangements, Rawls effectively endeavors to enclose us within the walls of Plato's cave, so that in his ideal world no one would even be capable of challenging his view of justice.

—Both in his gratuitous denunciation of people's "squalid" behavior and his questioning whether it is even worthwhile for human beings to live if they don't actualize his vision of justice, Rawls, however unintentionally, encourages a misanthropic and apocalyptic outlook that is downright frightening.

Despite my effort to document these criticisms (some of which have already been made by other scholars, including such prominent liberal critics as Schaar and Sandel), I recognize that some readers will still retain the feeling that Rawls's approach to justice and especially its most distinctive feature, the difference principle, somehow express a more "moral" outlook on life than that which is exhibited in the American Constitution and the way of life it has shaped. It is doubtless because of the belief that whatever the weaknesses of his argument, Rawls offered rhetorical support for "the right side" that so many readers have overlooked, tolerated, or even exaggerated his more outlandish assertions. This has been my experience on numerous professional panels, where Rawlsian partisans either poohpoohed his more outlandish remarks, such as his comparison of America to the Germany of 1870–1945 in its lack of "will" for democracy or his reservations about whether human existence would be "worthwhile" if his proposals were not actualized, or expressed unfamiliarity with them. (On the first American Political Science Association panel devoted to *Theory* back in 1973, one of Rawls's leading British admirers even supported Rawls's denunciations of America's unjust inequalities by citing as his example of a juster society the Stalinist dictatorship of Romania.)

Sometimes Rawls's defenders fudge the issues by softening his claims or raising them to such a level of generality as to amount to near triviality, asserting for instance that the difference principle dictates only that we endeavor "to arrange the starting points of American citizens in a way worthy of their claim to equality," without trying to "save them from their mistakes as grown-ups," or that we try "to set some limits on the power of luck to deform human lives." Others seem to agree with Schaar that despite its multiplicity of logical leaps and empirical errors, Rawls's theory might serve as a "civic religion" that would teach society's "winners . . . to show some care for the losers," as if present-day Americans failed to exhibit such concern.[3]

I can respond to those who applaud the difference principle on such grounds only by recapitulating the following points that I have already argued at length:

—Rawls himself never spells out any direct policy implications of the difference principle other than that it mandates either a (purely hypothetical) "liberal socialist" regime or a "property-owning democracy." The latter is distinguished from an (insufficiently just) "welfare state" only through inheritance laws that disperse the ownership of capital over time, "provisions for education and training," and "institutions that support the fair value of the political liberties" (*Theory*, xv).

—In fact, as I have shown, there is nothing inherent in the difference principle that would render illegitimate such economic inequalities as presently exist in the United States or other nations with largely free-enterprise economies. Likewise, nothing in Rawls's theory tells us how far, if at all, policies of redistributive inheritance taxation or antitrust enforcement would enhance or harm the long-range well-being of poorer people. How particular kinds and degrees of inequality, or policies that address them, affect the prospects of the less advantaged is an empirical question that Rawls's theory does nothing to resolve or clarify. Readers who draw a contrary conclusion are simply reading their own wishes (or Rawls's) into his theory, rather than attending to what the theory actually says. (Recall Rawls's acknowledgment that even a hereditary aristocracy, such as Burke and Hegel favored, is not necessarily incompatible with the difference principle.)

—Similarly, Rawls never demonstrates that the U.S. and other developed welfare states fail to provide the poor with adequate opportunities for "education and training" right now, while his "fair value" strictures not only fail to follow from his principles but promise to weaken the security of liberty.

—While morally decent people of all eras would agree that government and private individuals should try to alleviate the lot of those who are needy through no fault of their own—and even, in many cases, of those whose mistakes or vices may have contributed to their neediness—how this should be done (e.g., the proper balance between governmental and

3. The first quotation is from Yale law professor Bruce Ackerman, the second from Martha Nussbaum. (Both are in Matthew Miller, "Philosopher Rawls Taught Us to Be Thankful for Luck.") The third is from Schaar, "Reflections on Rawls' *Theory*," 162.

private assistance) and how far it is feasible to do so are similarly empirical issues with which statesmen, and in our time social scientists, continue to grapple. There is no reason to think that a theory like Rawls's will enhance those efforts. (Recall Rawls's criticism in *LP* of the assumption that a global redistribution of wealth would address the cultural causes of poverty, in unacknowledged contradiction to the domestic policies he advocates in the name of the difference principle.)

—If anything, far from benefiting the least advantaged, the ideology of libertarianism and nonjudgmentalism regarding alternative lifestyles that Rawls espouses would exacerbate the social pathologies that obstruct members of the underclass from rising to a condition of self-sufficiency and genuinely earned self-respect, befitting a nation of free human beings.[4]

—For the sake of theoretical simplicity, Rawls arbitrarily focuses on the needs of those who are materially least well-off, rather than addressing the problems of those who are, for instance, the victims of serious physical or mental disability. (Any attempt to encompass such problems in the difference principle would only further cloud its dictates, making more manifest how little value an abstract distributive principle can have for policymakers or citizens.)

—Despite the belief among Rawls's academic readership that becoming Rawlsians somehow makes them benefactors of the poor, there is thus no evidence to support that claim. If anything, by encouraging the belief that helping the poor is primarily the responsibility of government, Rawls's doctrine may promote a moral smugness that discourages actual works of charity.[5] Additionally, it offers academics an opportunity to lambaste the alleged moral failings of their fellow citizens—e.g., Martha Nussbaum's memorial tribute assailing Americans' "greed and partiality" and their "selfish passions that eclipse, so much of the time, the vision of the general good."[6] Those individuals, on the other hand, who favor Rawls's teaching

---

4. See Lasch, *Revolt of the Elites,* 105–7.

5. This sort of self-deception is illustrated by R. A. Musgrave's rationale for a "head tax on natural assets": it would compel "recluses, saints, and (nonconsulting) scholars who earn but little . . . to allocate more of their time to income earning activities in order to contribute more to redistribution" ("Maximin, Uncertainty, and the Leisure Trade-Off," 632). Musgrave evidently believed that the mere act of working as a consultant (as he did) constituted proof of one's greater social beneficence in comparison with other academics who pursued learning for its own sake, to say nothing of saints.

6. Nussbaum, "Making Philosophy Matter to Politics." Contrary to Nussbaum's diatribe, Americans, as I have noted, collectively display a substantially greater degree of charity, as well as volunteerism on behalf of their communities, than their peers in other developed nations.

out of a genuine instinct of charity, merit admiration more for their character than for the quality of their analysis.

—Above all, there is something terribly presumptuous, even a bit mad, about teaching human beings that we must not merely try to moderate the effects of ill fortune, but somehow overcome or "compensate for" the "arbitrariness" of the world itself. It is the latter goal, not merely the former, that Rawls calls for, and it is a recipe for bitterness and fanaticism rather than for justice or happiness.[7]

To be blunt, the difference principle, like Rawls's purported prioritization of liberty, is a red herring: a formal principle or expression of sentiment without substantive significance. Focusing on these abstractions diverts attention from the outright partisanship, ungrounded in any philosophic foundation, of Rawls's specific political pronouncements: his blanket denunciations of America's supposed injustices at home and abroad, his mandate of sexual liberation, his encouragement of civil disobedience, his proposals for restricting political campaigns, his demand that we equally esteem all ways of life, his exclusion of religiously grounded arguments from the public sphere, and his invitation to judicial activism on behalf of these goals and others (such as assisted suicide). If a serious case can be made for any of these positions, Rawls does not supply it. As a "moral theorist," he didn't think he needed to.

II.

In contrast to Rawls's combination of contentless abstraction and unsupported partisanship, I have argued that the original, Lockean liberalism of the American founders, particularly when developed and fortified by such interpreters as Lincoln and Tocqueville, provides the best available starting point for political reflection today. As I have observed, that older liberalism, unlike Rawls's, is far from doctrinaire and allows a polity founded on its tenets to incorporate significant insights from such

7. For the origins of the modern political project of mastering fortune, see Machiavelli, *The Prince*, chaps. 24–26. But the key to that Machiavellian project and its indirect offshoot, the American founding itself (see Hamilton, Madison, and Jay, *The Federalist*, No. 1, 1st par.) was a realism about what aspects of the world must be accepted or adapted to improve the human lot. (See Diamond, *As Far as Republican Principles Will Permit*, chaps. 12, 14.) By contrast, Rawls's project is reminiscent of the romantic-utopian "rationalism" of such late eighteenth- and early nineteenth-century dreamers and fanatics as Godwin, St. Simon, Babeuf, and (later) Marx, the political consequences of which (e.g., the French revolutionary terror and the Communist despotisms of the twentieth century) were far from salutary.

earlier writers as Aristotle. In addition, rather than push libertarian and egalitarian principles to an extreme, earlier American liberalism, as depicted by Tocqueville, harmonized the ethos of (depoliticized) religion and traditional, family-based morality with the spirit of liberty, fortifying our moral culture in a way that preserved people's capacity for self-government. While the founders' perspective became obscured over time by such theoretical developments as historicism and pragmatism, the particular deficiencies of the approach that Rawls would substitute for it reflect two more specific theoretical influences, both of which originated in the late eighteenth century: first, his "Kantianism"; and second, the British "analytic" tradition of philosophizing about morality.

At several points I have noted Rawls's questionable use of Kant's teaching: particularly, his implausible contention that in obeying the ostensible decision of the parties in his original position, we somehow achieve the transcendent freedom that Kant attributes to those who act out of respect for the moral law dictated by pure reason. But there is a key aspect of Rawls's doctrine that is indeed (in a broad sense) Kantian: his severance of morality from practical political judgment, with the former uncompromisingly elevated over the latter.

However we may admire individuals who strive to live dutifully in Kant's sense in their personal lives, the political legacy of Kantian idealism is not a promising one. While Kant himself favored a liberal state not greatly different from the American one, over time the political idealism he espoused became disjoined from liberal constitutionalism, as thinkers he influenced aimed at a radical world transformation of human life that would overcome man's "alienation" from the world, as well as the tension between morality and happiness.[8] The ultimate though indirect result was a series of romantic, utopian, and sometimes totalitarian movements ranging from the communism and Nazism of yesteryear to the radical environmentalism and even, in some measure, Islamic terrorism of today.[9] Political idealism became Western intellectuals' secular substitute for their lost religious

8. See Yack, *Longing for Total Revolution.* On the difficulties inherent in Kant's own endeavor to demonstrate how the historical process would culminate in the reconciliation of duty and happiness, see William Galston, *Kant and the Problem of History.* As the French Revolution makes evident, Kant's thought was far from the only source of modern political idealism, which is ultimately a radicalization of the original Machiavellian-Baconian project of conquering fortune, as discussed in the preceding note.

9. See Waller Newell, "Postmodern Jihad," regarding the link between today's Islamist terrorism and "European Marxist postmodernism." The connection between Islamist fanaticism and European idealism and antimodernism is also addressed by Ian Buruma and Avishai Margalit in *Occidentalism,* although they do not trace Western idealism to its Kantian roots or recognize the need perceived by Tocqueville to fortify the moral and spiritual foundations of liberal society in response to those who represent it as crassly materialistic and individualistic.

faith. It was fueled as well by the Nietzschean doctrine that since nature, understood through the lens of modern science, can no longer be seriously viewed as a guide or limit for human purposes, it is up to us to impose meaning on a meaningless universe through projects of self-imposed, collective commitment to a grand and demanding cause.

Rawls's remarks in *LP* and *PL* questioning whether human existence is worthwhile unless his vision of justice can be achieved exemplify the way in which certain theorists in the Kantian tradition, in contrast with the sobriety of the American founders, supplanted the longing for religious salvation with a less plausible or salutary hope or demand for paradise on earth.[10] The quasi-religious character of Rawls's enterprise is particularly manifest in *LP* when, after associating the Holocaust with the history of Christian anti-Semitism, he counsels us not to let such evils undermine our "reasonable hope" for the attainment of a just, worldwide "society of peoples" (*LP*, 22–23). Mere half-measures designed to promote justice and freedom in the world to the extent that we can would not satisfy Rawls's longings. Hence he remained blind to the fact that utopian ideological fanaticism has proved over the past century to be capable of generating evils at least as great as those inspired by perverted religious beliefs. And despite his professed liberalism, Rawls, like other intellectuals of his era, could never quite overcome the lure of socialism—albeit in an "ideal" form—given its supposed promise to actualize their vision of "social justice." (Indeed, in his last years, he became more overtly sympathetic to Marxism.) Rawls's two principles were a means to eat his liberal cake while having his socialist one as well—professing to uphold the priority of liberty, while subordinating the economy (and much of political liberty as well) to rules laid down by "philosophers" such as he believed himself to be.

The influence of the British analytic tradition is a more complicated affair, since it encompasses a considerable variety of thinkers. But the problem originates in part in the rejection by Bentham and his successors of the principle of natural rights, and for that matter of any notion of natural right (in the primary, premodern sense), and their quest to substitute for it some simple formula (such as Bentham's felicific calculus or J. S. Mill's "no-harm" principle) for resolving political disputes.

10. See, in this regard, Muravchik, *Heaven on Earth;* compare Cohn, *Pursuit of the Millennium,* 312. Again, see also Marini, "Theology, Metaphysics, and Positivism" on the transformation of religious faith in the nineteenth-century American academy under the influence of Comte's positivism and Hegelian historicism into a passion for "progressive" social change—fortunately of a far more moderate variety (thanks to the guiding hold of American constitutional institutions and our resultant political prosperity) than the utopian-totalitarian movements that attracted European intellectuals.

As I have acknowledged, some British ethical writers of the nineteenth and twentieth centuries, notably Mill in his topical essays, contributed important insights on the problems of liberal government in their time (and ours). But the belief of thinkers such as Bentham and (sometimes) Mill that fundamental ethical and political controversies should in principle be soluble by the adoption of a simple, universal formula distanced their doctrines from the classic liberalism of Locke, Montesquieu, and the American founders, which was grounded in an understanding of human nature and emphasized the structuring of political institutions to promote liberty, while appreciating the need for particular political issues to be resolved by a statesmanly prudence that took account of varying circumstances and popular opinions. In a way that parallels Kant's influence, Bentham and the two Mills opened a gap between ethical theorizing and political prudence that (as seen in Rawls's writing and that of his friendly antagonist Nozick) only widened as the analytic movement came to dominate American as well as British philosophy departments.[11] Otherwise put, in contrast to Aristotle's representation of ethics as part of political science, analytic ethical theorists supposed (in Isaiah Berlin's words) "that political theory is a branch of moral philosophy, which starts from the discovery, or application, of moral notions in the sphere of political relations."[12] Potentially, this constituted an open-ended invitation for ethical and jurisprudential theorists (following Kant's mandate) to lay down the law for politics, without having any well-grounded understanding of it.

Although British philosophical writers from the early nineteenth century on were often ardent advocates of "progressive" social reform, the academic environment they inhabited and the overall stability of their country's civic life generally deterred them from offering any radical challenge to the liberal consensus. In their ethical writings, those who purveyed theories like utilitarianism and intuitionism, such as Mill and Sidgwick, were debating the "foundation" of morality, without disagreeing significantly

11. Cf. John Gunnell's description of *Theory* and Nozick's *Anarchy, State, and Utopia* as exemplifying the transformation of political theory into an abstract, "contextless" enterprise that deceived academic writers into believing "that they were actually saying something about politics" (*The Descent of Political Theory,* 272–73).

12. Berlin, *Four Essays on Liberty,* 120; Aristotle *NE* 1.2. Weithman reports that Rawls was "deeply influenced" by Berlin during his studies at Oxford ("John Rawls: A Remembrance," 5). See, similarly, Nozick's claim that "[m]oral philosophy sets the background for, and boundaries of, political philosophy" (*Anarchy, State, and Utopia,* 6), and Hobhouse's 1922 assertion that "Politics must be subordinate to Ethics" (*Elements of Social Justice,* 4). Most revealing is Jeremy Waldron's praise of Rawls for insisting that "weasel-words like 'practicable' are to be defined in terms of 'a well-ordered society,' not the other way round," since "it is the task of a philosophical theory of justice to regulate . . . the background provisos of practicability" ("Plight of the Poor," 5).

about its content. Hence Nietzsche commented sardonically on the narrowness of perspective of his British counterparts, who while ostensibly uncovering the roots of morality actually endeavored only to justify a typically British view of happiness.[13] As recently as the mid-1960s, some analytic writers were lamenting the failure of their peers to propound serious alternatives to the political status quo.[14]

The increasingly abstract and apolitical character of British moral philosophy by the mid-twentieth century paralleled the rootlessness of American political liberalism in that period, as pragmatism and historicism eroded belief in, and distanced American theorists from endeavoring to understand, the natural-rights doctrine on which our country had been founded. In the postwar era, American political science came to be dominated by a wishy-washy liberalism that emphasized the pursuit of consensus or pluralistic accommodation without any concern for a deeper ground to our agreement on "the rules of the game."[15]

During the 1960s, this situation altered. Now, academic political theorists, inspired by the Continental model of the *engagé* intellectual, and eager to meet the new demand for "relevance," endeavored to show that their studies, far from supporting the existing regime, uncovered a need for more or less radical political change. It was in this context that *Theory* proved a godsend to Rawls's fellow academic "philosophers" and political theorists. Not merely a scholarly article addressing some relatively narrow issue or a book concerned with rival theories about the "ground" of ethics, here was instead a monumental tome with all the trappings of "technical" philosophy, yet issuing in a call for the broad transformation of liberal regimes. Kantian idealism was now united with the supposedly rigorous logical analysis characteristic of the British post-Humean philosophical tradition.

As applied to the American regime in particular, the ethical theorists' approach rested on a fundamental methodological or "category" error, one already foreseen by Aristotle and W. D. Ross, as I noted in chapter 1. In

13. Nietzsche, *Beyond Good and Evil*, sec. 228.

14. See, e.g., Barry's retrospective explanation of his aim in *Political Argument* to overcome the "cautious utilitarianism" of other recent British writers on political philosophy (Introduction to the revised edition, xxxvii–xxxviii).

15. The phrase last quoted comes from David Truman, *The Governmental Process*, a prototypical "pluralist" work that tried to reduce politics to a group "process" without addressing the underlying principles that made that process possible. As Herbert Storing once remarked, pluralist writers such as Truman lived in a birdcage created by James Madison: identifying the bars of their cage with the limits of political possibility, they never saw the peaceful pluralism of their environment as reflecting a constitutional choice among political alternatives, and as dependent on an institutional framework devised by the founders to support that choice.

effect, they tried to apply the analytic method of modern natural science, which breaks up substances into their smallest, most homogeneous components so as to reconstitute the substances in a way that serves human needs, to political phenomena. Because America is widely understood to be a liberal political regime, the theorists assumed it must be possible to reduce our polity to a set of simple, putatively liberal principles, in effect redoing the work of the American founders on a more "consistent" basis (as in Rawls's "four-stage sequence"), and then "logically" deriving from those principles (rather than from our actual Constitution) the institutional and policy consequences that Americans "ought" to enact to merit the liberal mantle. (And if it proved impossible in practice to persuade the citizenry to follow the theorists' directives, would it not be the proper role of judges to do the job for them, under the pretense of constitutional interpretation?)

In this light, one cannot avoid noticing that part of the reason for the popularity of Rawls's work in the contemporary academy is its appeal to the unacknowledged interest of liberal intellectuals. Historically, it has been widely recognized that a liberal political order presupposes a largely free economy. But despite the unfettered freedom of speech and writing that a liberal regime affords to intellectuals (to say nothing of the financial support offered by the modern university), it also frustrates their aspirations by elevating mere businessmen, entertainers, and professional politicians to stations of high influence and social status and allowing political as well as economic goods to be distributed in accordance with unguided popular tastes and preferences, rather than according to the intellectual's notion of a truly admirable or just social order. In this regard, Rawls's theory offered his academic audience a tempting claim to direct the uses to which the wealth generated by free economies could be put, as well as to alter other aspects of our constitutional system. Even while misleadingly purporting to uphold the "priority" of the sorts of liberty dear to intellectuals (roughly those described in the First Amendment), Rawls invited them—whether under a nominally free-enterprise system or a "liberal socialist" one it mattered not—to dictate the "just" distribution of economic goods (and indirectly, we have seen, political ones as well). Without having to work to earn ownership of large productive enterprises, to win elective office, or to acquire policy expertise through careers in government service, they were told that it was their right and duty to direct our polity in the pursuit of justice (most likely through the judicial process, but over the long run through their influence on their students). No wonder Rawls was agnostic on the issue of welfare-state "capitalism" versus socialism: under his scheme, left-liberal intellectuals come out on top either way (all the while convincing themselves that they are animated not by ambition, but by philanthropy toward an anonymous class labeled the "least advantaged"). Similarly, regarding international affairs, in *LP* Rawls identifies "the task of the student of philosophy" as "to articulate and express the permanent conditions of a well-ordered society," while the statesman, as his instrument, need only "discern these conditions and interests in practice" (*LP*, 97), as if merely studying philosophy qualified one to dictate the policies that a just polity must pursue. The rule of philosophy, represented by Plato as a practical impossibility, and a goal that great Enlightenment thinkers like Montesquieu aspired to achieve only through a complex project of "indirect government," is something Rawls takes for granted—and all one needs to earn such authority is a Ph.D. or law degree.[16] To ethical theorists and jurists convinced that their professional training and moral concern equip them far better to specify just policies than any business or government executive or politician, let alone the people at large, the temptation to claim the authoritative role Rawls offers them is almost irresistible, and not many have resisted it.

As I have shown, however, there is a fundamental disconnect between Rawls's "technical" inventions—the original position, the veil of ignorance, overlapping consensus, etc.—and the political consequences he purports to derive from them. Since those artificial devices were invented only to generate the consequences Rawls desired, they have no independent standing as a ground or criterion of justice. Nor, given their formalism, do Rawls's principles themselves yield any substantive policy guidance. As for Rawls's claim to vindicate these principles by showing that their consequences conformed to "our" considered judgments, he was increasingly compelled to acknowledge (notably in *PL* and *JF*) that the "we" whose judgments he expressed were not a cross-section of thoughtful human beings but only the subset of "progressive" intellectuals like himself. Rawls's account of his theory as "political not metaphysical" was another way of saying that it made no claim to objective truth, and therefore it shouldn't be liable to refutation by arguments that challenged its premises. This, I have argued, is the opposite of a philosophical procedure.

As citizens and beneficiaries of the most successful republican experiment in history, Americans have no need of a new "theory" to supplant the principles of natural right and the institutions of deliberative self-government already embodied in the Declaration of Independence and Constitution, respectively. Nor can any such theory eliminate our perpetual need for making principled, reasonable, and fact-based choices to

16. See Montesquieu, *Spirit of the Laws*, bk. 29, chap. 19, identifying lawgivers with such philosophers as Plato and Machiavelli.

address the welter of public policy dilemmas that will always confront us. Contrary to Rawls's denunciations of our institutions, the millions of immigrants who seek residence in this country attest to the fact that the American regime offers both unsurpassed opportunity for self-advancement and more compassionate treatment of its least advantaged inhabitants than practically any other nation on earth. Americans also display far more tolerance of divergent political opinions and religious views than practically any other people—in contrast to Rawls's putative liberalism, with its a priori strictures about "reasonable" policies and its dogmatic exclusion of religion from the public sphere (as well as its dismissal of contrary convictions as lacking "value").

The real constitutional cleavage in today's America, as I observed in chapter 2, is not between rich and poor, but between ordinary citizens, for whose reasonable ambitions and aspirations our constitutional order offers reasonable satisfactions, and ambitious intellectuals and jurists, whose longings entail imposing their self-generated ideals on a recalcitrant populace, often at the cost of weakening the mores on which a stable family structure and decent civic culture depend.[17] Our judges are encouraged by Rawls and his cohorts to contemn the supposed moral immaturity of their fellow citizens and to rewrite our Constitution in a way that undermines the people's right of self-government. Our intellectuals, like Rawls, too often promote a debilitating envy (and politicians who pander to it) instead of a manly spirit of democratic emulation, of the sort espoused by Jefferson and Lincoln, Booker T. Washington and Frederick Douglass. The steady expansion of federal and state bureaucracies, encouraged by writers like Rawls to regard the people as passive wards incapable of self-help, further threatens the constitutional bases for a genuine democratic pride.

As for the people themselves, while popular movements sometimes arise to challenge particularly bold acts of judicial usurpation (e.g., regarding abortion or gay marriage), there is no organized political movement dedicated to the cause of constitutional self-government as such. In this

17. On the cleavage in contemporary America between "the working and lower middle classes" who "favor limits on abortion, cling to the two-parent family as a source of stability in a turbulent world, resist experiments with 'alternative lifestyles,' and harbor deep reservations about affirmative action and other ventures in large-scale social engineering," on the one hand, and "upper-middle-class liberals" (Rawls's target audience), "cultured despisers of religion" who aspire "to keep religion out of public life," whose "overriding spiritual preoccupation" is "self-esteem," who seek "to extend the range of personal choice in matters where most people feel the need of solid moral guidelines," and who display an intolerant hatred or contempt "for those who stubbornly refuse to see the light" as they do, see Lasch, *Revolt of the Elites*, 15–16, 27–28.

respect, we are reminded of Tocqueville's fear that the passion of intellectuals for centralization and uniformity, combined with the individualism that diverts ordinary citizens from public to private concerns, will issue in a soft or "tutelary" despotism in which people forego active concern with self-government in return for having their material wants satisfied.[18]

The continuing acclaim for Rawls's work in the academy attests to the alienation of that world from the foundations of the American constitutional regime as well as from the great tradition of Western political philosophy. Having been trained in a narrowly technical version of "philosophy," Rawls never appreciated justice as a problem or questioned its susceptibility to being reduced to a theory. His sweeping prescriptions are striking not only for their lack of grounding in historical understanding or the actual operation of constitutional institutions, but for the thinness of his acquaintance with the writings of political philosophers before Hume and Kant (as well as with Nietzsche). Above all, Rawls's dismissal of the Lockean natural-rights teaching embodied in the Declaration exhibits a lamentable, but all-too-widespread, lack of understanding of the reasoning underlying that teaching. Buried under successive waves of historical scholarship like that of Laslett and Becker, which aimed more at situating Locke and the founders in their "context" than at reconstructing their reasoning, the original liberal teaching became a rote formula, presupposed by our institutions yet obscure to present-day scholars and their pupils.

Like Rawls, many influential contemporary professors of philosophy and political theory seem more interested in displaying their inventiveness than in learning from the wisest thinkers of the past.[19] Even scholars who offered probing criticisms of Rawls's arguments, such as Sandel and

---

18. Tocqueville, *Democracy in America*, vol. 2, pt. 4, chaps. 2–3, 6–7; Schaar, "Reflections on Rawls' *Theory*," 162.

19. Exemplary of this attitude is Barry's dismissal of studying "the classics" as unlikely "to advance the sum of human knowledge" (*Political Argument*, 290n). Like Rawls, Barry uncritically assumes that political philosophy is an inherently progressive enterprise rather than an ever-renewed endeavor to understand human nature and hence to assess the political institutions most likely to achieve the human good under varying circumstances—an endeavor in which it is quite likely the classic works have more to teach us than the latest theories. Previously, Peter Laslett, on the very page where he proclaimed political philosophy's demise, defined the British conception of that enterprise as one of "apply[ing] the methods *and the conclusions* of contemporary thought to . . . the contemporary social and political situation," similarly assuming that the thought of the past has nothing to teach us, and that there is no need to challenge "our" beliefs from a perspective transcending the present (*Philosophy, Politics, and Society*, vii [emphasis added]). Consider also Barry's wish to liberate political philosophy from the study of political facts, discussed in chapter 3.

Nozick, lauded his enterprise in glowing terms, not only out of partial agreement with his politics, but because they evidently shared his conception of political philosophy as an undertaking devoted to the construction of grand and "elegant" theories. When cut off from the substantive consideration of political issues and of pre-Kantian political philosophy, this endeavor reduces itself to a game in which novelty counts for more than depth or prudence. Contrary to Rawls and his peers, no genuine political philosophy can limit itself to laying out moral principles for human governance without regard to human nature and without consideration of their real-world consequences.

In the end, one cannot avoid being struck by the disparity between Rawls's theory and his own life and character. Admired for his humility and kindness, Rawls propounded a doctrine that is presumptuous, dogmatic, and sometimes misanthropic. The beneficiary of America's constitutional freedoms, as well as the resources of leading private universities derived from the contributions of wealthy donors, he denigrated our democracy and free-enterprise system and warned of the dangers of "meritocracy." A father of four, he disparaged the family and espoused a radical libertarianism and nonjudgmentalism with respect to sexual lifestyles. Representing himself as a democrat, he encouraged judges to resolve critical public policy issues without regard to citizens' beliefs and perceived interests. Having served his country honorably in the Pacific theater during the Second World War—and possibly having had his own life spared (along with hundreds of thousands, or millions, of others) when the atomic bombings made an invasion of Japan unnecessary—he denounced the immorality of the bombings. Despite or even because of the blessings he enjoyed, he doubted that human life can have worth or be "redeemable" except through the achievement of a "realistic utopia" such as he devoted himself to describing.[20] Professing to be a philosopher, Rawls recommended that philosophy dispense with the quest for truth in the name of justice and consensus.

Given his profession, it is remarkable how little Rawls learned from observing the times in which he lived. Having witnessed the rise and fall of communism and Nazism, he questioned whether a free-enterprise system could ever be as just as a socialist one, and he doubted that contemporary America was any more democratic than Nazi Germany. Having lived through the turbulence of the 1960s, he concluded that Americans were excessively inclined to obey the law rather than to challenge "the state." Amid the family breakdown of the last several decades, he thought that

20. See Pogge, "Brief Sketch," 14.

poverty could be cured if only government gave more money to the least advantaged while ensuring that women were "compensated" for child rearing. As domestic controversies arose over issues such as education, welfare reform, bioethics, immigration, abortion, and affirmative action, Rawls concluded that our politics chiefly suffered from an otherwise unnoticed impasse between Lockeans and Rousseaueans. As Brian Anderson remarks, Rawls's writings "do not speak to any recognizable political world and ignore almost completely the real dilemmas and tragedies of our time."[21] The narrowness of Rawls's focus on "technical" issues (despite his grandiose claims) exemplifies how philosophy, as Nietzsche lamented, has been reduced in our time from the queen of the sciences, the most comprehensive way of life, to an abstract, specialized discipline without real human meaning.[22]

Rawls reportedly was surprised by the popularity of *Theory*, and no wonder: the essays from which it evolved hardly contained the sort of substance that would interest anyone outside a small academic coterie. But in the meantime, Rawls had stuffed his work with the sorts of political program that would appeal to left-liberal intellectuals, who would happily overlook his jargon and convoluted prose, the inconsistencies in his arguments and his failure to provide any empirical support for his claims, in return for the "theoretical" support he offered to their demands. In sum, Rawls was both a political and philosophical *naïf*, insufficiently familiar with the philosophic tradition outside of British writings of the past two centuries along with Kant, and unappreciative of the difficulties of statesmanship, the fragility of constitutional government, and the complexity of political problems. Lacking well-thought-out political convictions of his own, or (it would appear) any great familiarity with life outside the academy, Rawls endeavored to satisfy his colleagues, being convinced that whatever views they found acceptable must reflect a consensus of enlightened and well-intentioned human beings, if not a universal truth. Rawls was not an original thinker, but a vessel who absorbed and purveyed to a wider audience some leading strands of "advanced" academic thinking about politics in his time, without recognizing their inconsistencies or their deleterious conse-

---

21. Anderson, "Antipolitical Philosophy," 40.
22. Nietzsche, *Beyond Good and Evil*, secs. 204, 211. Compare C. D. Broad's acknowledgment in the preface to his analysis of ethical theories that his own "range of experience, both practical and emotional, [was] rather exceptionally narrow even for a don," and that he found it "difficult to excite myself very much over right and wrong in practice" (*Five Types of Ethical Theory*, xxiv). Broad's awareness of the limitations of his academic environment at least helped spare him from issuing sweeping pronouncements on how to improve human beings or their political institutions.

quences for constitutional liberalism.[23] He suffered from a fantasy that an enterprise called "moral theory"—which required no deep study of politics, history, or economics, let alone the history of substantive political philosophy—could provide one with unique expertise on how to make our world more just. How could anyone with a serious grounding in the history of political philosophy ever have believed that merely asserting two principles that, reduced to their essence, "promote equal liberty" and "help the poor" (along with their supposed corollary, "advance world peace and justice") could entitle one to the status of a philosopher, let alone the authority to dictate the goals of statesmanship?

Such problems compel one to consider the psychological roots of Rawls's enterprise as described by some who knew him well. Despite the generally abstract character of Rawls's prose, and the apolitical orientation of his earliest essays, it is striking how far, judging from the testimony of close acquaintances, his lifework seems to have been designed to exorcise his own inner demons. According to Ben Rogers, friends described Rawls "as a complex and, in some sense, a troubled man, who, although not a believer, had retained an essentially religious outlook—he had a profound sense of 'there but for the grace of God go I.'" Rawls's student Thomas Pogge observes that Rawls's "religious upbringing" caused him to wonder "whether and to what extent human life is redeemable," since (he believed) "even the life of someone whose conduct and character are above reproach may seem to lack worth," given how much "time and energy are wasted on professional and personal projects that are ultimately pointless." Traumatized, moreover, by the death of two of his siblings in childhood from infections they had contracted from him, and deeply affected by his experiences in the Second World War, Rawls apparently believed that propounding a doctrine designed to benefit the least advantaged would help justify or compensate for his own ultimate good fortune (in accordance with the difference principle). As for his moral libertarianism, seemingly incompatible with the "moral earnestness" for which he was personally known, apparently that too reflected his sympathy for those he thought the victims of unjust discrimination, such as the aficionados of unconventional sexual

23. Although Ben Rogers claimed in his obituary that Rawls generally "kept his strongly held and radical political allegiances to himself" ("John Rawls"), the litany of orthodox left-liberal positions Rawls set forth in his books (as distinguished from his early essays) shows him to have been neither reticent about taking partisan political stands nor genuinely "radical," in the sense of challenging conventional wisdom and truly getting to the roots of things. (See Pogge, "Brief Sketch," 9–10, on Rawls's activism against the Vietnam War, which Rawls believed "from the very beginning . . . to be unjust," and the way in which *Theory,* composed in the 1960s, reflects his resultant political concerns.)

practices or devoted atheists who felt offended by public expressions of support for religion. (One can only wonder how Rawls could have believed that such libertarianism would make life more worthwhile or "redeemable.") As well, Rawls was deeply influenced by his mother's Democratic activism and feminism.[24]

While his outlook was very unlike the vengefulness expressed in Karl Marx's celebrated remark that he would make the capitalists someday pay for his carbuncles, Rawls's underappreciation of an existing constitutional order and free economy from which he derived so many benefits thus may have been no less rooted in personal motives. Despite the human virtues that won him so much affection, the abstract character of the "analytic" approach to philosophy that Rawls had been taught may have prevented him from fully acquiring the primary benefit of a genuinely philosophical education, a sufficient degree of self-knowledge to enable one to look critically at one's own assumptions and longings. Rawls's secularized but intemperate "piety" supports Irving Kristol's observation that it is the "death" of God that is the leading "political" event of our time, and the key to the disaffection of contemporary liberals with the original constitutional-liberal enterprise.[25]

While liberalism, in its original sense of guaranteeing the natural rights of individuals, necessarily constrains the means by which we pursue our good, it cannot deny the natural primacy of the good for each human being—including our quest for truth as well as our private and familial attachments. Hence liberal politics, to be just, cannot demand the suppression of our pursuit of the good in the name of an artificial vision of "community" like Rawls's. And philosophy, to be responsible, must not sever justice from prudence.[26] As the American constitutional republic offers academics a historically unparalleled freedom, they surely owe it in return an appreciation of its moral and practical achievement and (in the words of the Declaration) "a decent respect" for the opinions of their fellow citizens outside the academy.

If there is a remedy to the shallowness of much contemporary academic theorizing about politics and the indifference of many ordinary Americans to the judicial and bureaucratic usurpation of their right of self-

24. Rogers, "John Rawls"; Pogge, "Brief Sketch," 3–4, 14.

25. Kristol, "About Equality," 187. See also Gray, *Enlightenment's Wake*, 18, on the rise of "shallow optimistic creeds" among contemporary liberals "who have abandoned traditional faiths" while retaining "the need for consolation that traditional theodicy existed to satisfy"; Deneen, *Democratic Faith*, chap. 1. That Rawls conceived his work as a sort of theodicy is confirmed by Pogge, "Brief Sketch," 14.

26. Cf. Plato *Republic* 621c, where Socrates concludes his examination of justice by admonishing us to "practice justice with prudence," or prudently.

government, it lies above all in a restored civic and liberal education. Numerous surveys indicate the public's alarming ignorance of the Constitution as well as its apathy regarding public affairs. What is needed is not plebiscitary "deliberative polls" but a restoration at the elementary and secondary-school level of traditional education in political history and civics, designed to convey an awareness to students of all backgrounds of the good reasons for taking pride in our institutions and the common responsibility for helping them to endure. In our institutions of higher education, far more would be accomplished to prepare citizens for self-government by immersing students, as Wilson Carey McWilliams argued, in the study of great books that address political issues in comprehensive fashion, in place of half-baked contemporary theories. Such writers as Sophocles and Plato, Thucydides and Burke, Madison, Aristotle, and Shakespeare, McWilliams observes, "speak to the political animal in our souls," providing us with "the words and speech appropriate to a citizen."[27] Many of them, McWilliams notes, took an active part in political life. The political philosophers among them, such as Aristotle (who collected the constitutions of some 150 communities before writing his *Politics*) and Locke (who avidly perused the travel writings of contemporary explorers as well as classical histories) engaged in extensive comparative and historical studies before laying out their teachings. Above all, they remind us of the complexities of political life and refine our judgment of political and ethical problems, rather than subsuming such issues under simplistic formulas. Studying Tocqueville would be a good place to start.

As for the mixture of vast ambition and moral longing that impels today's alienated intellectuals in their quest to "redeem" the world, perhaps Aristotle was right in observing that there is no remedy except in (genuine) philosophy.[28]

---

27. McWilliams, "Toward Genuine Self-Government," 55. See, on how the study of classic works of American political thought can promote thoughtful citizenship, Diana J. Schaub, "Abraham Lincoln and the Pillars of Liberty." On the utility for liberal politics of an "older model of liberal education" based on the study of classic texts and aimed at "educating young people to deliberate well" in situations where "no precise solutions or rules for reaching such solutions exist," see Stephen Salkever, "'Lopp'd and Bound,'" 186–87). Salkever persuasively argues that the older conception, which aspires "not to *resolve* controversy [as Rawls aspires to do] but to encourage and educate it," provides a more adequate model for liberal theorizing than "the endless manufacture and refinement of theories of justice" directed at achieving "an unquestionable foundation" (193–95; Salkever's emphasis).

28. Aristotle *Politics*, 1267a10ff.

Bibliography

Books and Monographs

Ackerman, Bruce, and James Fishkin. *Deliberation Day.* New Haven: Yale University Press, 2004.

Amos, Sheldon. *Prohibition, Regulation, and Licensing of Vice in England and Europe.* London: Stevens and Sons, 1877.

Auletta, Ken. *The Underclass.* Rev. ed. Woodstock, NY: Overlook Press, 1999.

Barber, Benjamin. *The Conquest of Politics: Liberal Philosophy in Democratic Times.* Princeton: Princeton University Press, 1988.

Barber, Sotirios A. *Welfare and the Constitution.* Princeton: Princeton University Press, 2003.

Barry, Brian. *The Liberal Theory of Justice.* London: Oxford University Press, 1973.

———. *Political Argument.* Reissue, Berkeley: University of California Press, 1990.

Becker, Carl. *The Declaration of Independence: A Study in the History of Political Ideas.* 1922. Reprint, New York: Knopf, 1942.

Benhabib, Seyla. *The Rights of Others.* Cambridge: Cambridge University Press, 2004.

Bentham, Jeremy. *"Deontology," Together with "A Table of the Springs of Action" and "Article on Utilitarianism."* Edited by Amnon Goldworth. Oxford: Clarendon Press, 1983.

Berkowitz, Peter. *Virtue and the Making of Modern Liberalism.* Princeton: Princeton University Press, 1999.

Berlin, Isaiah. *Four Essays on Liberty.* Oxford: Oxford University Press, 1969.

Berns, Walter. *The First Amendment and the Future of American Democracy.* New York: Basic Books, 1976.

————. *Making Patriots.* Chicago: University of Chicago Press, 2001.

Bessette, Joseph M. *The Mild Voice of Reason: Deliberative Democracy and American National Government.* Chicago: University of Chicago Press, 1994.

Bethell, Tom. *The Noblest Triumph: Property and Prosperity through the Ages.* New York: St. Martin's Press, 1998.

Bhagwati, Jagdish. *In Defense of Globalization.* New York: Oxford University Press, 2004.

Blau, Francine D., and Lawrence M. Kahn. *Wage Inequality: International Comparisons of Its Sources.* Washington: AEI Press, 1996.

Blitz, Mark. *Duty Bound: Responsibility and American Public Life.* Lanham, MD: Rowman and Littlefield, 2005.

Bloom, Allan. *The Closing of the American Mind.* New York: Simon and Schuster, 1987.

————, ed. *Confronting the Constitution.* Washington: AEI Press, 1990.

————. *Giants and Dwarfs: Essays, 1960–1990.* New York: Simon and Schuster, 1990.

Bork, Robert H. *The Tempting of America: The Political Seduction of the Law.* New York: Free Press, 1990.

Brackman, Arnold. *The Other Nuremburg.* New York: William Morrow, 1987.

Broad, C. D. *Five Types of Ethical Theory.* London: Routledge and Kegan Paul, 1930.

Brooks, David. *Bobos in Paradise: The New Upper Class and How They Got There.* New York: Simon and Schuster, 2000.

Bullock, Alan. *Hitler: A Study in Tyranny.* 1953. Reprint, New York: Bantam Books, 1961.

Burke, Edmund. *Reflections on the Revolution in France.* Edited by J. G. A. Pocock. Indianapolis: Hackett, 1987.

Buruma, Ian, and Avishai Margalit. *Occidentalism: The West in the Eyes of Its Enemies.* New York: Penguin Press, 2004.

Calhoun, John. *Union and Liberty: The Political Philosophy of John Calhoun.* Edited by Ross Lence. Indianapolis: Liberty Fund, 1992.

Carrese, Paul O. *The Cloaking of Power: Montesquieu, Blackstone, and the Rise of Judicial Activism.* Chicago: University of Chicago Press, 2003.

Ceaser, James W. *Liberal Democracy and Political Science.* Baltimore: Johns Hopkins University Press, 1990.

———. *Nature and History in American Political Development: A Debate.* Cambridge: Harvard University Press, 2006.

Chavez, Linda. *Out of the Barrio: Toward a New Politics of Hispanic Assimilation.* New York: Basic Books, 1991.

Chinard, Gilbert, ed. *The Correspondence of Jefferson and Du Pont de Nemours.* Reprint, New York: Arno Press, 1979.

Clor, Harry M. *Obscenity and Public Morality.* Chicago: University of Chicago Press, 1969.

———. *Public Morality and Liberal Society.* Notre Dame: Notre Dame University Press, 1996.

Cohn, Norman. *The Pursuit of the Millennium: Revolutionary Messianism in Medieval and Reformation Europe and Its Bearing on Modern Totalitarian Movements.* 2nd ed. New York: Harper and Row, 1961.

Cox, Richard. *Locke on War and Peace.* Oxford: Clarendon Press, 1960.

Cronon, E. David, ed. *The Political Thought of Woodrow Wilson.* Indianapolis: Bobbs Merrill, 1965.

Cropsey, Joseph. *Political Philosophy and the Issues of Politics.* Chicago: University of Chicago Press, 1977.

Cushman, Thomas, ed. *A Matter of Principle: Humanitarian Arguments for War in Iraq.* Berkeley: University of California Press, 2005.

Dalrymple, Theodore. *Life at the Bottom: The Worldview That Makes the Underclass.* New York: Ivan R. Dee, 2001.

Daniels, Norman, ed. *Reading Rawls: Critical Studies on Rawls's "A Theory of Justice."* New York: Basic Books, 1975.

Das, Gurcharan. *India Unbound.* New York: Knopf, 2000.

De Jouvenel, Bernard. *The Ethics of Redistribution.* Cambridge: Cambridge University Press, 1951.

Deneen, Patrick. *Democratic Faith.* Princeton: Princeton University Press, 2005.

De Soto, Hernando. *The Other Path: The Invisible Revolution in the Third World.* New York: Harper and Row, 1989.

Dewey, John. *The Public and Its Problems.* 1927. Reprint, Denver: Swallow Press, 1954.

Diamond, Martin. *As Far as Republican Principles Will Permit.* Washington: AEI Press, 1992.

———. *The Founding of the Democratic Republic.* Itasca, IL: Peacock, 1981.

Dombrowski, Daniel A. *Rawls and Religion: The Case for Political Liberalism.* Albany: State University of New York Press, 2001.

Dworkin, Ronald. *Taking Rights Seriously.* Cambridge: Harvard University Press, 1977.

Easterbrook, Gregg. *The Progress Paradox: How Life Gets Better While People Feel Worse.* New York: Random House, 2003.

Eden, Robert. *Political Leadership and Nihilism: A Study of Weber and Nietzsche.* Gainesville: University of Florida Presses, 1983.

Edgeworth, Francis Ysidro. *Mathematical Psychics: An Essay on the Application of Mathematics to the Moral Sciences.* London: Kegan Paul, 1881.

Elshtain, Jean Bethke. *Democracy on Trial.* New York: Basic Books, 1995.

Epstein, David. *The Political Theory of "The Federalist."* Chicago: University of Chicago Press, 1984.

Falcoff, Mark. *Modern Chile, 1970–1989: A Critical History.* New Brunswick, NJ: Transaction Books, 1989.

Ferry, Luc, and Alain Renaut. *French Philosophy of the Sixties: An Essay on Antihumanism.* Translated by Mary Cattani. Amherst: University of Massachusetts Press, 1990.

Fleischacker, Samuel. *A Short History of Distributive Justice.* Cambridge: Harvard University Press, 2004.

Fleming, Macklin. *The Price of Perfect Justice.* New York: Basic Books, 1974.

Friedman, Milton. *Capitalism and Freedom.* Chicago: University of Chicago Press, 1962.

Fukuyama, Francis. *The End of History and the Last Man.* New York: Free Press, 1992.

———. *Our Posthuman Future: Consequences of the Biotechnology Revolution.* New York: Farrar, Straus, and Giroux, 2002.

Galston, William. *Kant and the Problem of History.* Chicago: University of Chicago Press, 1975.

———. *Liberal Pluralism.* New York: Cambridge University Press, 2002.

———. *Liberal Purposes: Goods, Virtues, and Diversity in the Liberal State.* New York: Cambridge University Press, 1991.

Gilder, George. *Wealth and Poverty.* New York: Basic Books, 1981.

Glendon, Mary Ann. *Abortion and Divorce in Western Law.* Cambridge: Harvard University Press, 1987.

———. *A Nation under Lawyers: How the Crisis in the Legal Profession Is Transforming American Society.* New York: Farrar, Straus, and Giroux, 1994.

———. *Rights Talk: The Impoverishment of Political Discourse.* New York: Free Press, 1991.

Gokhale, Jagadeesh, and Kent Smetters. *Fiscal and Generational Imbalances.* Washington: AEI Press, 2003.

Goldberg, Bernard. *Bias: A CBS Insider Exposes How the Media Distort the News.* Chicago: Regnery, 2001.

Goldwin, Robert A., ed. *Political Parties, U.S.A.* Chicago: Rand McNally, 1964.

———. *Why Blacks, Women, and Jews Are Not Mentioned in the Constitution, and Other Unorthodox Views.* Washington, DC: AEI Press, 1990.

Gottfried, Paul Edward. *After Liberalism: Mass Democracy in the Managerial State.* Princeton: Princeton University Press, 1999.

Gray, John. *Enlightenment's Wake: Politics and Culture at the Close of the Modern Age.* London: Routledge, 1995.

———. *The Two Faces of Liberalism.* New York: New Press, 2000.

Gunnell, John. *The Descent of Political Theory.* Chicago: University of Chicago Press, 1993.

Hamby, Alonzo L. *For the Survival of Democracy: Franklin Roosevelt and the World Crisis of the 1930s.* New York: Free Press, 2004.

Hamilton, Alexander, James Madison, and John Jay. *The Federalist Papers.* Edited by Clinton Rossiter, with new introduction and notes by Charles R. Kesler. New York: New American Library, 1999.

Harris, William F., II. *The Interpretable Constitution.* Baltimore: Johns Hopkins University Press, 1993.

Hayek, Friedrich A. *The Constitution of Liberty.* Chicago: University of Chicago Press, 1960.

———. *Law, Legislation, and Liberty.* 3 vols. Chicago: University of Chicago Press, 1973–1979.

Hegel, Georg W. F. *The Philosophy of History.* Translated by J. M. Sibree. New York: Dover, 1956.

Herrnstein, Richard, and Charles Murray. *The Bell Curve.* New York: Free Press, 1994.

Himmelfarb, Gertrude. *The Roads to Modernity: The British, French, and American Enlightenments.* New York: Knopf, 2004.

Hobbes, Thomas. *Leviathan.* Edited by E. M. Curley. Indianapolis: Hackett, 1994.

Hobhouse, L. T. *The Elements of Social Justice.* London: G. Allen and Unwin, 1922.

Howe, Mark DeWolfe, ed. *Holmes-Laski Letters.* Cambridge: Harvard University Press, 1953.

Humboldt, Wilhelm von. *The Limits of State Action.* Edited by J. W. Burrow. Indianapolis: Liberty Classics, 1993.

Hume, David. *An Enquiry Concerning the Principles of Morals.* 2nd ed. Edited by L. A. Selby-Bigge. Oxford: Clarendon Press, 1966.

———. *Essays Moral, Political, and Literary.* Edited by Eugene Miller. Indianapolis: Liberty Classics, 1985.

———. *A Treatise of Human Nature.* Edited by L. A. Selby-Bigge. Oxford: Clarendon Press, 1888.

Huntington, Samuel. *Who Are We? The Challenges to America's National Identity.* New York: Simon and Schuster, 2004.

Hutcheson, Frances. *Essay on the Nature and Conduct of the Affections and Passions.* Reprint, Menton, Yorkshire: Scolar Press, 1972.

Jacobsohn, Gary. *Pragmatism, Statesmanship, and the Supreme Court.* Ithaca: Cornell University Press, 1977.

Jaffa, Harry V. *Crisis of the House Divided: An Interpretation of the Issues in the Lincoln-Douglas Debates.* Garden City, NY: Doubleday, 1959.

———. *A New Birth of Freedom: Abraham Lincoln and the Coming of the Civil War.* Lanham, MD: Rowman and Littlefield, 2000.

Jefferson, Thomas. *The Life and Selected Writings of Thomas Jefferson.* Edited by Adrienne Koch and William Peden. New York: Modern Library, 1944.

Kagan, Robert. *Of Paradise and Power.* New York: Knopf, 2003.

Kant, Immanuel. *Critique of Practical Reason.* Translated by Lewis White Beck. Indianapolis: Bobbs-Merrill, 1956.

———. *Critique of Pure Reason.* Translated by Norman Kemp Smith. New York: St. Martin's Press, 1965.

———. *Education.* Translated by Annette Churton. Ann Arbor: University of Michigan Press, 1964.

———. *Foundations of the Metaphysics of Morals.* 2nd ed. Translated by Lewis White Beck. Upper Saddle River, NJ: Prentice Hall, 1997.

———. *Lectures on Ethics.* Translated by Louis Infield. Indianapolis: Hackett, 1980.

———. *The Metaphysical Elements of Justice.* Translated by John Ladd. Indianapolis: Bobbs-Merrill, 1965.

———. *The Metaphysical Principles of Virtue.* Translated by James Ellington. Indianapolis: Bobbs-Merrill, 1964.

———. *Political Writings.* 2nd ed. Edited by Hans Reiss. Translated by H. B. Nisbet. Cambridge: Cambridge University Press, 1991.

Kaplan, Robert D. *Warrior Politics: Why Leadership Demands a Pagan Ethos.* New York: Random House, 2002.

Kass, Leon. *Life, Liberty, and the Defense of Dignity.* San Francisco: Encounter Books, 2002.

Kekes, John. *A Case for Conservatism.* Ithaca: Cornell University Press, 1998.

Kershaw, Ian. *Hitler, 1936–1945: Nemesis.* New York: Norton, 2000.

Knight, Frank H. *The Ethics of Competition and Other Essays*. New York: Harper and Brothers, 1935.

Kosters, Marvin H. *Wage Levels and Inequality: Measuring and Interpreting the Trends*. Washington: AEI Press, 1998.

Krause, Sharon. *Liberalism with Honor*. Cambridge: Harvard University Press, 2002.

Kristol, Irving. *Two Cheers for Capitalism*. New York: Basic Books, 1978.

Kukathas, Chandran, and Philip Pettit. *Rawls: "A Theory of Justice" and Its Critics*. Stanford: Stanford University Press, 1990.

Landes, David. *The Wealth and Poverty of Nations*. New York: Norton, 1998.

Larsson, Tomas. *The Race to the Top: The Real Story of Globalization*. Washington: Cato Institute, 2001.

Lasch, Christopher. *The Revolt of the Elites*. New York: Norton, 1995.

Laslett, Peter, ed. *Philosophy, Politics, and Society*. New York: Macmillan, 1956.

———, and James Fishkin, eds. *Philosophy, Politics, and Society*. 5th ser. New Haven: Yale University Press, 1979.

Lebedoff, David. *The Uncivil War: How a New Elite is Destroying Our Democracy*. Lanham, MD: Taylor, 2004.

Levi, Edward H. *An Introduction to Legal Reasoning*. Chicago: University of Chicago Press, 1949.

Lewis, Bernard. *The Crisis of Islam: Holy War and Unholy Terror*. New York: Modern Library, 2003.

Lichter, S. Robert, Stanley Rothman, and Linda S. Lichter. *The Media Elite*. Bethesda, MD: Adler and Adler, 1986.

Lincoln, Abraham. *The Collected Works of Abraham Lincoln*. Edited by Roy P. Basler. 9 vols. New Brunswick, NJ: Rutgers University Press, 1953.

Locke, John. *An Essay Concerning Human Understanding*. Edited by Peter Nidditch. Oxford: Clarendon Press, 1975.

———. *A Letter Concerning Toleration*. Edited by Patrick Romanell. Indianapolis: Bobbs Merrill, 1955.

———. *Two Treatises of Government*. Student ed. Edited by Peter Laslett. Cambridge: Cambridge University Press, 1988.

Machiavelli, Niccolò. *The Prince*. Translated by Harvey C. Mansfield. Chicago: University of Chicago Press, 1985.

MacIntyre, Alasdair. *After Virtue*. 2nd ed. Notre Dame: University of Notre Dame Press, 1984.

Madison, James. *James Madison, Writings*. Edited by Jack Rakove. New York: Library of America, 1999.

Magnet, Myron. *The Dream and the Nightmare: The Sixties' Legacy to the Underclass*. New York: William Morrow, 1993.

Mahoney, Dennis. *Politics and Progress: The Emergence of American Political Science.* Lanham, MD: Lexington Books, 2004.

Malia, Martin. *The Soviet Tragedy: A History of Socialism in Russia, 1917–1991.* New York: Free Press, 1994.

Manent, Pierre. *A World Beyond Politics? A Defense of the Nation-State.* Translated by Marc LePain. Princeton: Princeton University Press, 2006.

Mansfield, Harvey C. *America's Constitutional Soul.* Baltimore: Johns Hopkins University Press, 1991.

———. *Manliness.* New Haven: Yale University Press, 2006.

———. *The Spirit of Liberalism.* Cambridge: Harvard University Press, 1978.

McGowan, William. *Coloring the News: How Crusading for Diversity Has Corrupted American Journalism.* San Francisco: Encounter Books, 2001.

McPherson, James. *What They Fought For, 1861–1865.* Baton Rouge: Louisiana State University Press, 1994.

McWhorter, John H. *Losing the Race: Self-Sabotage in Black America.* New York: Free Press, 2000.

Mead, Lawrence M. *The New Politics of Poverty: The Nonworking Poor in America.* New York: Basic Books, 1992.

Melzer, Arthur, Jerry Weinberger, and M. Richard Zinman, eds. *Multiculturalism and American Democracy.* Lawrence: University Press of Kansas, 1998.

Menand, Louis. *The Metaphysical Club.* New York: Farrar, Straus, and Giroux, 2001.

Mill, John Stuart. *Principles of Political Economy.* Edited by W. J. Ashley. London: Longmans Green, 1920.

———. *Utilitarianism, Liberty, and Representative Government.* New York: E. P. Dutton, 1950.

Montaigne, Michel de. *Essays.* Translated by Donald Frame. Stanford: Stanford University Press, 1957.

Montesquieu, Charles le Secondat, Baron de. *The Spirit of the Laws.* Translated by Anne Cohler, Basia Miller, and Harold Stone. Cambridge: Cambridge University Press, 1989.

Muller, Jerry Z. *Adam Smith in His Time and Ours: Designing the Decent Society.* New York: Free Press, 1993.

Muravchik, Joshua. *Heaven on Earth: The Rise and Fall of Socialism.* San Francisco: Encounter Books, 2002.

Murray, Williamson, and Allan R. Millett. *A War To Be Won: Fighting the Second World War.* Cambridge: Harvard University Press, 2000.

Myrdal, Gunnar. *The Political Element in the Development of Economic Theory.* Translated by Paul Streeten. London: Routledge, 1953.

Neely, Richard. *How Courts Govern America.* New Haven: Yale University Press, 1981.

Neuhaus, Richard John. *The Naked Public Square.* 2nd ed. Grand Rapids, MI: Eerdmans, 1986.

Newell, Waller R. *Ruling Passion: The Erotics of Statecraft in Platonic Political Philosophy.* Lanham, MD: Rowman and Littlefield, 2000.

Nichols, Mary P. *Citizens and Statesmen: A Study of Aristotle's "Politics."* Savage, MD: Rowman & Littlefield, 1992.

———. *Socrates and the Political Community: An Ancient Debate.* Albany: State University of New York Press, 1987.

Nietzsche, Friedrich. *The Portable Nietzsche.* Edited and translated by Walter Kaufmann. New York: Viking Press, 1954.

Nozick, Robert. *Anarchy, State, and Utopia.* New York: Basic Books, 1974.

Nussbaum, Martha. *Frontiers of Justice.* Cambridge: Harvard University Press, 2006.

Overy, Richard. *Why the Allies Won.* New York: Norton, 1995.

Pangle, Thomas. *Montesquieu's Philosophy of Liberalism.* Chicago: University of Chicago Press, 1973.

Pangle, Thomas, and Peter Ahrensdorf. *Justice among Nations.* Lawrence: University Press of Kansas, 1999.

Pangle, Thomas, and Lorraine Pangle. *The Learning of Liberty: The Educational Ideas of the American Founders.* Lawrence: University Press of Kansas, 1993.

Peffer, R.G. *Marxism, Morality, and Social Justice.* Princeton: Princeton University Press, 1990.

Phillips, Melanie. *Londonistan.* San Francisco: Encounter Books, 2006.

Pipes, Richard. *Property and Freedom.* New York: Random House, 1999.

Plato. *Republic.* Translated by Allan Bloom. New York: Basic Books, 1968.

Purcell, Edward. *The Crisis of Democratic Theory: Scientific Naturalism and the Problem of Value.* Lexington: University Press of Kentucky, 1973.

Rabkin, Jeremy. *The Case for Sovereignty.* Washington: AEI Press, 2004.

———. *Judicial Compulsions: How Public Law Distorts Public Policy.* New York: Basic Books, 1989.

Randall, John Herman. *Constitutional Problems Under Lincoln.* Urbana: University of Illinois Press, 1951.

Ravitch, Diane, and Joseph P. Viteriti, eds. *Kid Stuff: Marketing Sex and Violence to America's Children.* Baltimore: Johns Hopkins University Press, 2004.

Rhoads, Steven E. *The Economist's View of the World.* Cambridge: Cambridge University Press, 1985.

Richards, David A. J. *The Moral Criticism of Law.* Encino, CA: Dickerson Publishing, 1977.

Roosevelt, Franklin Delano. *Public Papers and Addresses.* Vol. 1. New York: Random House, 1938.

Rorty, Richard. *Contingency, Irony, and Solidarity.* Cambridge: Cambridge University Press, 1989.

———. *Objectivity, Relativism, and Truth.* New York: Cambridge University Press, 1991.

Rosenberg, Nathan, and L. E. Birdzell Jr. *How the West Grew Rich: The Economic Transformation of the Industrial World.* New York, Basic Books, 1986.

Ross, W. D. *The Right and the Good.* Oxford: Clarendon Press, 1930.

Rousseau, Jean-Jacques. *Emile, or, On Education.* Translated by Allan Bloom. New York: Basic Books, 1979.

———. *First and Second Discourses.* Edited by Roger Masters. Translated by Roger D. and Judith R. Masters. New York: St. Martin's Press, 1964.

———. *The Government of Poland.* Translated by Willmoore Kendall. Indianapolis: Bobbs Merrill, 1972.

———. *"On the Social Contract" with "Geneva Manuscript" and "Political Economy."* Edited by Roger R. Masters. Translated by Judith R. Masters. New York: St. Martin's Press, 1978.

Rudolph, Frederick, ed. *Essays on Education in the Early Republic.* Cambridge: Harvard University Press, 1965.

Salkever, Stephen. *Finding the Mean: Theory and Practice in Aristotelian Political Philosophy.* Princeton: Princeton University Press, 1990.

Sandel, Michael. *Democracy's Discontent: America in Search of a Public Philosophy.* Cambridge: Harvard University Press, 1996.

———. *Liberalism and the Limits of Justice.* Cambridge: Cambridge University Press, 1982.

Schaefer, David Lewis. *Justice or Tyranny? A Critique of John Rawls's "A Theory of Justice."* Port Washington, NY: Kennikat Press, 1979.

Schlesinger, Arthur M. *The Disuniting of America.* New York: Norton, 1992.

Schmitt, Carl. *The Crisis of Parliamentary Democracy.* 1923. Translated by Ellen Kennedy. Reprint, Cambridge: MIT Press, 1985.

Schwartz, Joel. *Fighting Poverty with Virtue.* Bloomington: Indiana University Press, 2000.

Schweizer, Peter. *Do as I Say (Not as I Do): Profiles in Liberal Hypocrisy.* New York: Doubleday, 2005.

Selby-Bigge, L. A., ed. *British Moralists.* Oxford: Clarendon Press, 1897.

Sidgwick, Henry. *The Methods of Ethics.* 7th ed. Indianapolis: Hackett Publishing, 1981.

———. *Outlines of the History of Ethics.* 5th ed. Indianapolis: Hackett, 1988.

Slaughter, Anne-Marie. *A New World Order.* Princeton: Princeton University Press, 2004.

Smith, Adam. *An Inquiry into the Nature and Courses of the Wealth of Nations.* Edited by W. B. Todd. Oxford: Oxford University Press, 1979.

———. *The Theory of Moral Sentiments.* Edited by D. D. Raphael and A. L. Macfie. Oxford: Oxford University Press, 1979.

Smith, Bradley A. *Unfree Speech: The Folly of Campaign Finance Reform.* Princeton: Princeton University Press, 2001.

Smith, Steven. *Reading Leo Strauss: Politics, Philosophy, and Judaism.* Chicago: University of Chicago Press, 2006.

Smith, T. Alexander, and Raymond Tatalovich. *Cultures at War: Moral Conflicts in Western Democracies.* Peterborough, Ont.: Broadview Press, 2003.

Sowell, Thomas. *Affirmative Action around the World: An Empirical Study.* New Haven: Yale University Press, 2004.

———. *The Economics and Politics of Race.* New York: Quill, 1983.

———. *Is Reality Optional? And Other Essays.* Stanford: Hoover Institution Press, 1993.

———. *The Quest for Cosmic Justice.* New York: Simon and Schuster, 1999.

Stauffer, Devin. *Plato's Introduction to the Question of Justice.* Albany: State University of New York Press, 2001.

Steele, Shelby. *The Content of Our Character: A New Vision of Race in America.* New York: St. Martin's Press, 1990.

———. *A Dream Deferred: The Second Betrayal of Black Freedom in America.* New York: HarperCollins, 1998.

Stoner, James. *Common Law and Liberal Theory: Coke, Hobbes, and the Origins of American Constitutionalism.* Lawrence: University Press of Kansas, 1992.

———. *Common Law Liberty: Rethinking American Constitutionalism.* Lawrence: University Press of Kansas, 2003.

Storing, Herbert J., ed. *The Antifederalist.* Chicago: University of Chicago Press, 1985.

———, ed. *Essays on the Scientific Study of Politics.* New York: Holt, Rinehart, and Winston, 1962.

———. *Toward a More Perfect Union.* Washington: AEI Press, 1995.

Storry, Richard. *A History of Modern Japan.* Baltimore: Penguin Books, 1960.

Strauss, Leo. *Natural Right and History.* Chicago: University of Chicago Press, 1953.

Tarcov, Nathan. *Locke's Education for Liberty.* Chicago: University of Chicago Press, 1984.

Teles, Steven M. *Whose Welfare? AFDC and Elite Politics.* Lawrence: University Press of Kansas, 1996.

Tessitore, Aristide, ed. *Aristotle and Modern Politics: The Persistence of Political Philosophy.* Notre Dame: Notre Dame University Press, 2002.

Thoreau, Henry David. *"Walden" and "Civil Disobedience."* New York: New American Library, 1960.

Thurow, Glen R. *Abraham Lincoln and American Political Religion.* Albany: State University of New York Press, 1976.

Tilly, Charles. *Contention and Democracy in Europe, 1650–2000.* Cambridge: Cambridge University Press, 2004.

Tocqueville, Alexis de. *Democracy in America.* Edited and translated by Harvey C. Mansfield and Delba Winthrop. Chicago: University of Chicago Press, 2000.

Trotsky, Leon. *The Revolution Betrayed.* Translated by Max Eastman. Garden City, NY: Doubleday, 1937.

Truman, David. *The Governmental Process.* New York: Knopf, 1951.

Tucker, Robert C., ed. *The Marx-Engels Reader.* 2nd ed. New York: W. W. Norton, 1978.

Walzer, Michael. *Just and Unjust Wars.* New York: Basic Books, 1977.

Warnock, Mary. *Ethics since 1900.* Oxford: Oxford University Press, 1960.

Washington, Booker T. *Up from Slavery.* New York: Doubleday, Page, 1901.

Washington, George. *George Washington: A Collection.* Compiled and edited by W. B. Allen. Indianapolis: Liberty Classics, 1988.

Welch, Finis, ed. *The Causes and Consequences of Increasing Inequality.* Chicago: University of Chicago Press, 2001.

Weldon, T. D. *The Vocabulary of Politics.* London: Pelican, 1953.

Westbrook, Robert B. *John Dewey and American Democracy.* Ithaca: Cornell University Press, 1991.

Wilson, Woodrow. *Congressional Government.* 1885. Reprint, New York: Meridian Books, 1956.

———. *Constitutional Government in the United States.* New York: Columbia University Press, 1908.

———. *The State.* Rev. ed. Boston: D. C. Heath, 1918.

Winch, Peter. *The Idea of a Social Science and Its Relation to Philosophy.* 2nd ed. London: Routledge and Kegan Paul, 1990.

Winter, Ralph. *Campaign Financing and Political Freedom.* Washington: AEI Press, 1973.

Wolf, Martin. *Why Globalization Works.* New Haven: Yale University Press, 2004.

Wolff, Robert Paul. *Understanding Rawls.* Princeton: Princeton University Press, 1977.

Yack, Bernard. *The Longing for Total Revolution.* Princeton: Princeton University Press, 1986.

———. *The Problems of a Political Animal: Community, Justice, and Conflict in Aristotelian Political Thought.* Berkeley: University of California Press, 1993.

York, Byron. *The Vast Left-Wing Conspiracy.* New York: Crown Forum/ Random House, 2005.

Young, James P. *Reconsidering American Liberalism.* Boulder, CO: Westview Press, 1996.

Zuckert, Catherine H. *Natural Right and the American Imagination: Political Philosophy in Novel Form.* Savage, MD: Rowman and Littlefield, 1990.

Zuckert, Michael. *Launching Liberalism: On Lockean Political Philosophy.* Lawrence: University Press of Kansas, 2002.

———. *The Natural Rights Republic: Studies in the Foundation of the American Political Tradition.* Notre Dame: Notre Dame University Press, 1996.

Articles, Essays, Addresses, and Book Reviews

Alexander, Gerard. "Illiberal Europe." *Weekly Standard,* April 10, 2006, 32–36.

"American Generosity." *Wall Street Journal,* editorial, May 13–14, 2006, A8.

Anderson, Brian. "The Antipolitical Philosophy of John Rawls." *The Public Interest* 151 (Spring 2003): 39–51.

Andrews, Edmund, and Robert Pear. "Entitlement Costs Are Expected to Soar." *New York Times,* March 19, 2004, A13.

Baier, Kurt M. "Justice and the Aims of Political Philosophy." *Ethics* 99, no. 4 (July 1989): 771–90.

Balcerowicz, Leszek. "The Wealth of Nations." *Wall Street Journal,* October 6, 2005, A14.

Banfield, Edward C. "In Defense of the American Party System." In Goldwin, ed., *Political Parties, U.S.A.,* 21–39.

Barber, Benjamin. "Justifying Justice: Problems of Psychology, Politics, and Measurement in Rawls." In Daniels, ed., *Reading Rawls,* 292–18.

Barry, Brian. "How Not to Defend Liberal Institutions." In *Liberalism and the Good,* edited by R. Bruce Douglass, Gerald M. Mara, and Henry S. Richardson, 44–58. New York: Routledge, 1990.

Bartlett, Bruce. "Class Struggle in America?" *Commentary* 120, no. 1 (July–August 2005), 33–38.

Baumann, Fred. "Affirmative Action: Human Rights at Home." In *Human Rights in Our Times: Essays in Memory of Victor Baras,* edited by Marc F. Plattner, 69–81. Boulder: Westview Press, 1984.

Beach, William W. "The Case for Repealing the Estate Tax." Backgrounder #1091. Washington: Heritage Foundation, 1996.

Beard, Charles. "Politics." In *Discipline and History: Political Science in the United States*, edited by James Farr and Raymond Seidelman, 113–27. Ann Arbor: University of Michigan Press, 1993. Original title of essay: "A Lecture Delivered at Columbia University in the Series on Science, Philosophy, and Art, February 12, 1908."

Berkowitz, Peter. "The Ambiguities of Rawls's Influence." *Perspectives on Politics* 4, no. 1 (March 2006): 121–27.

———. "John Rawls and the Liberal Faith." *Wilson Quarterly* 26 (Spring 2002): 60–69.

Bernstein, Barton J. "The Atomic Bombings Reconsidered." *Foreign Affairs* 74, no. 1 (January–February 1995): 135–52.

Besharov, Douglas. "Poor America." *Wall Street Journal*, March 24, 2006, A10.

Bloom, Allan. "Justice: John Rawls vs. the Tradition of Political Philosophy." *American Political Science Review* 69, no. 2 (June 1975), 648–62.

Buchanan, Patrick. Interview with Chris Matthews. *Hardball*, January 8, 2002.

Carrese, Paul O. "Judicial Statesmanship, the Jurisprudence of Individualism, and Tocqueville's Common Law Spirit." *Review of Politics* 60, no. 3 (Summer 1998): 465–95.

Carreyrou, John. "At French Utility, Union Wages War to Guard Its Perks." *Wall Street Journal*, May 10, 2005, A1.

Ceaser, James W. "Faith in Democracy: How the Debate over Religion in the West Distorts Our Understanding of Freedom in the Middle East." *Weekly Standard* 11, no. 8, November 11, 2005.

Center for American Progress. "Repeal/Reform of the Estate Tax." June 30, 2005. http://www.americanprogress.org.

Clinton, Bill. "Remarks at the Presentation of the National Medal of the Arts and the National Humanities Medal." September 29, 1999. http://clinton4.nara.gov/WH/New/html/19990929.html.

Cohen, Joshua. "Deliberation and Democratic Legitimacy." In *The Good Polity: Normative Analysis of the State*, edited by Alan Hamlin and Philip Pettit, 17–34. Oxford: Basil Blackwell, 1989.

———. "The Pursuit of Fairness." *Boston Globe*, December 1, 2002, D1.

Cohen, Marshall. Review of *A Theory of Justice*, by John Rawls. *New York Times Book Review*, July 16, 1972, 1, 18ff.

Cohen, Randy ("Ethicist"). "Uncharitable View." *New York Times Magazine*, June 20, 1999, 20.

Conway, Brendan. "Just Think About It." Review of *Deliberation Day,* by Bruce Ackerman and James Fishkin. *Wall Street Journal,* March 24, 2004, D12.

Cox, W. Michael. "It's Not a Wage Gap But an Age Gap." *New York Times,* op-ed, April 21, 1996, 15.

Craig, Leon. "*Contra* Contract: A Brief against John Rawls's *A Theory of Justice.*" *Canadian Journal of Political Science* 8, no. 1 (March 1975): 63–81.

———. "Traditional Political Philosophy and John Rawls's Theory of Justice." *University of Alberta, Department of Political Science, Occasional Papers* 3 (1976).

Daniels, Anthony. "Expensive Talk." *National Review* 52, no. 14 (August 8, 2005): 30–31.

Deere, Donald R. "Trends in Wage Inequality in the United States." In Welch, ed., *Causes and Consequences of Increasing Inequality,* 9–36.

Dolgov, Anna. "Belarus Vote Is Seen as Pivotal." *Boston Globe,* October 17, 2004, A6.

Easton, David. "The New Revolution in Political Science." *American Political Science Review* 63, no. 4 (December 1969): 1051–61.

Eberstadt, Nicholas. "The Mismeasurement of Poverty." *Policy Review* 138 (August/September 2006): 19–52.

Eckholm, Erick. "When Lies Kill." *New York Times,* June 16, 2001, sec. 4, 1, 4.

Eden, Robert. "The Rhetorical Presidency and the Eclipse of Executive Power: Woodrow Wilson's *Constitutional Government in the United States.*" *Polity* 18, no. 3 (Summer 1996): 357–78.

Edgeworth, Francis Ysidro. "The Pure Theory of Taxation." *Economic Journal* 7, no. 25 (March 1897): 46–70, and 8, no. 28 (December 1897): 550–71.

"The Entitlement Panic." *Wall Street Journal,* editorial, August 21, 2006.

Epstein, Richard A. "Rawls Remembered." *National Review Online,* November 27, 2002.

"Europe vs. America." *Wall Street Journal,* editorial, June 18, 2004, A10.

Faulkner, Robert. "The First Liberal Democrat: Locke's Popular Government." *Review of Politics* 63, no. 1 (Winter 2001): 5–39.

Fish, Stanley. "Our Faith in Letting It All Hang Out." *New York Times,* February 12, 2006, sec. 4, 15.

Frank, Richard B. "Why Truman Dropped the Bomb." *Weekly Standard* 10, no. 44 (August 8, 2005): 20–24.

"French Lessons." *Wall Street Journal,* editorial, November 11, 2005, A10.

Friedman, Thomas. "Arabs at the Crossroads." *New York Times,* July 3, 2002, A19.

Goldwin, Robert A. "Is There an American Right to Revolution?" In *Why Blacks, Women, and Jews Are Not Mentioned in the Constitution, and Other Unorthodox Views*, 46–56.

———. "Rights Versus Duties." In *Why Blacks, Women, and Jews Are Not Mentioned in the Constitution, and Other Unorthodox Views*.

Gourevitch, Victor. "Rawls on Justice." *Review of Metaphysics* 28, no. 3 (March 1975): 485–519.

Gray, John. "Can We Agree to Disagree?" Review of *Political Liberalism*, by John Rawls. *New York Times Book Review*, May 16, 1993.

Grenzke, Janet. "PACs and the Congressional Supermarket: The Currency Is Complex." *American Journal of Political Science* 33, no. 1 (February 1989): 1–24.

Gutmann, Amy. "The Central Role of Rawls's Theory." *Dissent* (Summer 1989): 16–20.

Habermas, Jürgen. "Révolutionnaires." *Le Monde*, May 3, 2003.

Hampshire, Stuart. "A New Philosophy of the Just Society." *New York Review of Books* 18, no. 3 (February 24, 1972): 37ff.

Hare, R. M. "Rawls' Theory of Justice." In Daniels, ed., *Reading Rawls*, 81–107.

Henninger, Daniel. "It Took 30 Years to Un-Learn Acts of Charity." *Wall Street Journal*, January 11, 2002, A10.

Holmes, Oliver Wendell. "Natural Law." In *Collected Legal Papers*, 310–16. New York: Harcourt, Brace, and Howe, 1921.

Jacoby, Jeff. "A New Low in Bush-Hatred." *Boston Globe*, September 10, 2006, D9.

Jaffa, Harry V. "The Nature and Origin of the American Party System." In Goldwin, ed., *Political Parties, U.S.A.*, 59–83.

———. "On the Nature of Civil and Religious Liberty." In *Equality and Liberty: Theory and Practice in American Politics*, 169–89. New York: Oxford University Press, 1965.

Jalowiecki, Bartosz. "Lies the Germans Tell Themselves." *Commentary* 117, no. 1 (January 2004): 43–46.

Johnson, Oliver A. "The Kantian Interpretation." *Ethics* 85, no. 1 (October 1974): 58–66.

Kessler, Sanford. "John Locke's Legacy of Religious Freedom." *Polity* 17, no. 3 (Spring 1985): 484–503.

Knippenberg, Joseph. "Moving Beyond Fear: Rousseau and Kant on Cosmopolitan Education." *Journal of Politics* 51, no. 4 (November 1989): 809–27.

Kotkin, Joel. "Our Immigrants, Their Immigrants." *Wall Street Journal*, November 8, 2005, A16.

Kraynak, Robert P. "John Locke: From Absolutism to Toleration." *American Political Science Review* 74, no. 1 (March, 1980): 53–69.

Krouse, Richard, and Michael McPherson. "Capitalism, 'Property-Owning Democracy,' and the Welfare State." In *Democracy and the Welfare State*, edited by Amy Gutmann, 79–105. Princeton: Princeton University Press, 1988.

Lewis, Bernard. "Iraq, India, Palestine." *Wall Street Journal,* May 12, 2004, A14.

Lyons, David. "Nature and Soundness of the Contract and Coherence Arguments." In Daniels, ed., *Reading Rawls,* 141–67.

MacFarquhar, Neil. "Pakistanis Find U.S. an Easier Fit than Britain," *New York Times,* August 21, 2006, A1, A13.

MacIntyre, Alasdair. Review of *Enlightenment's Wake,* by John Gray. *Review of Politics* 58, no. 4 (Fall 1996): 807–9.

Mansfield, Harvey C. "Good and Happy." *The New Republic* 235 (July 3, 2006): 30–33.

———. "On the Political Character of Property in Locke." In *Powers, Possessions, and Freedom: Essays in Honour of C. B. Macpherson,* edited by Alkis Kontos, 23–38. Toronto: University of Toronto Press, 1979.

———. "Party Government and the Settlement of 1688." *American Political Science Review* 58, no. 4 (December 1964): 933–46.

———. "Self-Interest Rightly Understood." *Political Theory* 23, no. 1 (February 1995): 48–66.

Mardiros, Anthony. "A Circular Procedure in Ethics." *Philosophical Review* 61 (1952): 223–25.

Marini, John. "Theology, Metaphysics, and Positivism: The Origins of the Social Sciences and the Transformation of the American University." In *Challenges to the Founding: Slavery, Historicism, and Progressivism in the Nineteenth Century,* edited by Ronald J. Pestritto and Thomas G. West, 163–94. Lanham, MD: Rowman and Littlefield, 2005.

McCaffery, Edward J. "The Uneasy Case for Wealth Transfer Taxation." *Yale Law Journal* 104 (November 1994): 283–365.

McCarthy, Andrew. "Free Speech for Terrorists?" *Commentary* 119, no. 3 (March 2005): 27–36.

———. "International Law v. United States." *Commentary* 121, no. 2 (February 2006): 41–48.

McWilliams, Wilson Carey. "Toward Genuine Self-Government." *Academic Questions* 15, no. 1 (Winter 2001–2002): 50–55.

Melloan, George. "'Tis the Season to Be Generous, Thoughtfully." *Wall Street Journal,* December 21, 2004, A19.

Michelman, Frank. "Rawls on Constitutionalism and Constitutional Law." In *The Cambridge Companion to Rawls,* edited by Samuel Freeman, 394–425. Cambridge: Cambridge University Press, 2003.

Mill, John Stuart. "Remarks on Bentham's Philosophy." In *John Stuart Mill on Politics and Society,* edited by Geraint Williams, 97–115. Glasgow: Fontana/Collins, 1976.

Miller, Matthew. "Philosopher Rawls Taught Us to Be Thankful for Luck." *Boston Globe,* November 30, 2002, A10.

Moore, Stephen. "The Wages of Prosperity." *Wall Street Journal,* August 29, 2005, A9.

Muirhead, Russell, and Nancy L. Rosenblum. "Liberalism vs. 'The Great Game of Politics': The Politics of Political Liberalism." *Perspectives on Politics* 4, no. 1 (March 2006): 99–108.

Munoz, Vincent Phillip. "George Washington on Religious Liberty." *Review of Politics* 65, no. 1 (Winter 2003): 11–33.

Murphy, Kevin M., and Finis Welch. "Wage Differentials in the 1990s: Is the Glass Half-Full or Half-Empty?" In Welch, ed., *Causes and Consequences of Increasing Inequality,* 341–64.

Murray, Charles. "The British Underclass: Ten Years Later." *The Public Interest* 145 (Fall 2001): 25–37.

———. "The Hallmark of the Underclass." *Wall Street Journal,* September 29, 2005, A18.

Musgrave, R. A. "Maximin, Uncertainty, and the Leisure Trade-Off." *Quarterly Journal of Economics* 88, no. 4 (November 1974): 625–32.

Nagel, Robert F. "Is 'Rationality Review' Rational?" *The Public Interest* 116 (Summer 1994): 75–87.

Nagel, Thomas. "Rawls on Justice." In Daniels, ed., *Reading Rawls,* 1–16.

Newell, Waller. "Postmodern Jihad." *Weekly Standard* 7, no. 1 (November 26, 2001): 26–28.

Nisbet, Robert. "The Pursuit of Equality." *The Public Interest* 35 (Spring 1974): 103–20.

Nussbaum, Martha Craven. "Aristotelian Social Democracy." In Tessitore, ed., *Aristotle and Modern Politics,* 47–104.

———. "The Enduring Significance of John Rawls." *Chronicle of Higher Education* 47, no. 45 (July 20, 2001): B7ff.

———. "Making Philosophy Matter to Politics." *New York Times,* December 2, 2002, A25.

O'Grady, Mary Anastasia. "Cuba's Jailed Librarians Get No Succor from the ALA." *Wall Street Journal,* June 30, 2003, A9.

Okin, Susan. Review of *Political Liberalism,* by John Rawls. *American Political Science Review* 87, no. 3 (December 1993): 1010–11.

Oren, Michael. "A Soldier's Story." *Wall Street Journal*, August 23, 2005, A10.

Orwin, Clifford, and James Stoner Jr. "Neoconstitutionalism? Rawls, Dworkin, and Nozick." In Bloom, ed., *Confronting the Constitution*, 437–70.

Owen, J. Judd. "The Task of Liberal Theory after September 11." *Political Science and Politics* 2, no. 2 (Summer 2004): 325–30.

Pangle, Thomas. "Rediscovering Rights." *Public Interest* no. 50 (Winter, 1978): 157–60.

Parekh, B. "Reflections on Rawls' *Theory of Justice.*" *Political Studies* 20 (December 1972): 478–83.

Parker, Emily. "China's 'Netizens.'" *Wall Street Journal*, July 16, 2004, A12.

Parker, Richard B. "The Jurisprudential Uses of John Rawls." In *Nomos XX: Constitutionalism*, edited by J. R. Pennock and J. W. Chapman, 269–95. New York: New York University Press, 1979.

Persson, Ingmar. "A Basis for (Interspecies) Equality." In *The Great Ape Project: Equality Beyond Humanity*, edited by Paola Cavalieri and Peter Singer. New York: St. Martin's Press, 1993.

Phillips, Melanie. "What about the Overclass?" *The Public Interest* 145 (Fall 2001): 38–43.

Plattner, Marc. "Capitalism." In Bloom, ed., *Confronting the Constitution*, 314–33.

Pogge, Thomas. "A Brief Sketch of Rawls's Life." In *Developments and Main Outlines of Rawls's Theory of Justice*, edited by Henry S. Richardson, 1–15. New York: Garland Publishing, 1999.

Ponnuru, Ramesh. "Investor Class, Investor Nation." *National Review* 66, no. 2 (February 9, 2004): 28ff.

Postrel, Virginia. "Why Bush Stiffed Enron." *Wall Street Journal*, January 25, 2002, A18.

Rabkin, Jeremy. "Courting Abroad: The Use and Abuse of Foreign Law by the U.S. Supreme Court." *Weekly Standard*, April 10, 2006, 29–32.

Rector, Robert E., and Kirk A. Johnson. "Understanding Poverty in America." Backgrounder #1713. Washington: Heritage Foundation, January 5, 2004.

Robbins, Gary. "Estate Taxes: An Historical Perspective." Backgrounder #1719. Washington: Heritage Foundation, 2004.

Rogers, Ben. "John Rawls." *The Guardian*, obituary, November 27, 2002.
———. "Portrait: John Rawls." *Prospect* 42 (June 1999): 50–55.

Rorty, Richard. "The Priority of Democracy to Philosophy." In *Objectivity, Relativism, and Truth*, 175–96.

Rosenblum, Nancy. "Replacing Foundations with Staging: 'Second-Story' Concepts and American Political Development." In Ceaser, *Nature and History in American Political Development*, 113–40.

Rothstein, Edward. "Europe's Constitution: All Hail the Bureaucracy." *New York Times*, July 5, 2003, A17.

Rotunda, Ronald. "The 'Liberal Label': Roosevelt's Capture of a Symbol." *Public Policy* 17 (1968): 377–408.

Rutenberg, Jim. "TV Shows Take on Bush, and Pull Few Punches." *New York Times*, April 2, 2004, A1.

Ryan, Alan. "How Liberalism, Politics Come to Terms." *Washington Times*, May 16, 1993, B8.

Salkever, Stephen. "The Deliberative Model of Democracy and Aristotle's Ethics of Natural Questions." In Tessitore, ed., *Aristotle and Modern Politics*, 342–74.

———. "'Lopp'd and Bound': How Liberal Theory Obscures the Goods of Liberal Practices." In Douglass, Mara, and Richardson, eds., *Liberalism and the Good*, 167–202.

Sandel, Michael. "A Just Man." *The New Republic* 227, no. 25 (December 16, 2002): 42.

Sawhill, Isabel. "The Behavioral Aspects of Poverty." *The Public Interest* 153 (Fall 2003): 79–93.

Schaar, John. "Equality of Opportunity, and Beyond." In *Nomos IX: Equality*, edited by J. Roland Pennock and John W. Chapman, 228–49. New York: Atherton, 1967.

———. "Reflections on Rawls' *A Theory of Justice*." In *Legitimacy in the Modern State*. New Brunswick, NJ: Transaction Books, 1981.

Schaefer, David Lewis. "Libertarianism and Political Philosophy: A Critique of Robert Nozick's *Anarchy, State, and Utopia*." *Interpretation* 12, nos. 2–3 (May–September 1984): 301–34.

———. "The State Department as Cultural Critic." *American Enterprise Online*, February 6, 2006. www.taemag.com/issues/articleID.18996/article_detail.asp.

Schambra, William. "The Roots of the American Public Philosophy." *The Public Interest* 67 (Spring 1982): 36–48.

Schaub, Diana J. "Abraham Lincoln and the Pillars of Liberty." *Academic Questions* 16, no. 1 (Winter 2002/2003): 23–31.

Schlesinger, Steven R. "Civil Disobedience: The Problem of Selective Obedience to Law." *Hastings Constitutional Law Quarterly* 3, no. 4 (Fall 1976): 947–59.

Schneewind, J. B. Review of *Justice As Fairness*, by John Rawls. *New York Times Book Review*, June 24, 2001, 21.

Schrock, Thomas. "The Liberal Court, the Conservative Court, and Constitutional Jurisprudence." In *Left, Right, and Center: Essays on Liberalism and Conservatism in the United States,* edited by Robert A. Goldwin, 87–120. Chicago: Rand McNally, 1967.

Schwartz, Joel. "Growing Pains: Can Economic Progress Coexist with Moral Decline?" *Weekly Standard* 11, no. 46 (August 14, 2006): 38–39.

Shapiro, Samantha M. "The Dean Swarm." *New York Times Magazine,* December 7, 2003, 56ff.

Shell, Susan Meld. "'Kantianism' and Constitutional Rights." In *Old Rights and New,* edited by Robert A. Licht, 148–63. Washington: AEI Press, 1993.

Smart, J. J. C. "An Outline of a System of Utilitarian Ethics." In *Utilitarianism: For and Against,* by J. J. C. Smart and Bernard Williams, 3–74. Cambridge: Cambridge University Press, 1973.

Smith, Craig S. "French Premier Considers Easing Job Law." *New York Times,* March 22, 2006, A8.

———. "French Strike against Cuts in Pensions Jams Traffic." *New York Times,* June 11, 2003, A10.

Smith, James P. "Why Is Wealth Inequality Rising?" In Welch, ed., *Causes and Consequences of Increasing Inequality,* 83–115.

Smith, Thomas W. "Aristotle on the Conditions for and Limits of the Common Good." *American Political Science Review* 93, no. 3 (September 1999): 625–36.

"The Soros Agenda." *Wall Street Journal,* editorial, December 30, 2003, A10.

Stephens, Alexander H. "Cornerstone Speech." In *Alexander H. Stephens in Public and Private,* edited by Henry Cleveland, 717–29. Philadelphia: National Publishing, 1866.

Stephens, Bret. "Coming to America." *Wall Street Journal,* January 2, 2002, A18.

Strauss, Leo. "An Epilogue." In Storing, ed., *Essays on the Scientific Study of Politics,* 305–27.

———. "Relativism." In *Relativism and the Study of Man,* edited by Helmut Schoeck and J. W. Wiggins, 135–57. Princeton: Van Nostrand, 1961.

Students for a Democratic Society. "The Port Huron Statement." In *American Radical Thought: The Libertarian Tradition,* edited by Henry J. Silverman, 357–79. Lexington, MA: D. C. Heath, 1970.

"Taxing Words." *Wall Street Journal,* editorial, November 1, 2005, A10.

Taylor, Stuart. "The Court's Gone Too Far in Purging Religion from the Square." *National Journal* 35, no. 35 (August 30, 2003): 2603–4.

Tyler, Patrick E., and Don Van Natta Jr. "Militants in Europe Openly Call for Jihad and the Rule of Islam." *New York Times,* April 26, 2004, A1, A10.

United States Bureau of the Census. "The Effects of Government Taxes and Transfers on Income and Poverty: 2004." www.census/gov/hhes/www/poverty/effect2004/effect2004.html.

Van den Haag, Ernest. "Is Liberalism Just?" *The Public Interest* 113 (Fall 1993): 122–27.

Waldron, Jeremy. "The Plight of the Poor in the Midst of Plenty." *London Review of Books* 21, no. 14 (July 1999): 3, 5–6.

Walker, Marcus, and John Carreyrou. "French Labor Model Fuels Riots." *Wall Street Journal*, November 9, 2005, A14–15.

Walzer, Michael. "Flight from Philosophy." Review of *The Conquest of Politics*, by Benjamin Barber. *New York Review of Books*, February 2, 1989, 42–44.

"Wealth." *The American Enterprise* 15, no. 1 (January–February, 2004): 61.

Weber, Max. "Politics as a Vocation." In *From Max Weber: Essays in Sociology*, edited by Hans Gerth and C. Wright Mills, 77–128. New York: Oxford University Press, 1958.

Weicher, John C. "Increasing Inequality of Wealth?" *The Public Interest* 126 (Winter 1997): 15–25.

Weigel, George. "Europe's Two Culture Wars." *Commentary* 122, no. 5 (May 2006): 29–36.

Weithman, Paul. "John Rawls: A Remembrance." *Review of Politics* 65, no. 1 (Winter 2003): 5–10.

West, Diana. "All That Trash." *The Public Interest* 156 (Summer 2004): 131–35.

Wiggins, David. "Neo-Aristotelian Reflections on Justice." *Mind* 113, no. 451 (July 2004): 477–512.

Will, George. "'Fixing' Education." *Boston Globe*, January 7, 2002, A15.

Williams, Bernard. "The Idea of Equality." In *Philosophy, Politics, and Society*, 2nd ser., edited by Peter Laslett and W. G. Runciman, 110–31. Oxford: Basil Blackwell, 1962.

Wills, Garry. "Ethical Problems." *New York Times Book Review*, June 25, 1978, 13.

Wilson, James Q. "Capitalism and Morality." *The Public Interest* 121 (Fall 1995): 42–60.

———. "How Divided Are We?" *Commentary* 121, no. 2 (February 2006): 15–21.

Winthrop, Delba. "Aristotle and Theories of Justice." *American Political Science Review* 72, no. 4 (December 1978): 1201–16.

Winthrop, John. "Christian Charity: A Model Thereof." In *Puritan Political Ideas, 1558–1794*, edited by Edmund S. Morgan, 76–93. Indianapolis: Bobbs-Merrill, 1965.

Wolfson, Adam. "Biodemocracy in America." *The Public Interest* 146 (Winter 2002): 23–37.

Wolfson, Dorothea Israel. "Tocqueville on Liberalism's Liberation of Women." *Perspectives on Political Science* 25, no. 4 (Fall 1996): 203–7.

"The World Is Flat." *Wall Street Journal,* editorial, October 7, 2005, A16.

York, Byron. "Their True Selves." *National Review* 56, no. 16 (August 23, 2004): 18–20.

Zuckert, Michael. "Justice Deserted: A Critique of Rawls's *A Theory of Justice.*" *Polity* 13, no. 3 (Spring 1981): 466–83.